First published in 2018 by Barrallier Books Pty Ltd,
trading as Echo Books

Registered Office: 35-37 Gordon Avenue, West Geelong, Victoria 3220, Australia.

www.echobooks.com.au

Copyright ©Adam Lunney

National Library of Australia Cataloguing-in-Publication entry.

Creator: Lunney, Adam, author.

Title: Ready to Strike: the Spitfires and Australians of 453 (RAAF) Squadron over Normandy

ISBN: 9780648355229 (softcover)

A catalogue record for this book is available from the National Library of Australia

Book and cover design by Peter Gamble, Canberra.
Set in Garamond Premier Pro Regular, 13/17, Trajam Pro 3 and MinervaModern.

www.echobooks.com.au

Front cover images: main image, *Spitfire Mk IX FU-N in Normandy* (Olver family);
Pilots left to right, *Don Smith* (AWM UK1333), *Vern Lancaster* (Cowpe family),
Pat McDade (Cowpe family), *Jack Olver* (Olver family).

Back cover: *Spitfire Mk IX P-FX (TD314) over Kent in 2015* (Author).

READY TO STRIKE

The Spitfires and Australians
of 453 (RAAF) Squadron
over Normandy

ADAM LUNNEY

Contents

Foreword	vii
French town pronunciation guide	ix
Introduction	xi
Formation and defeat in the Pacific	1
The Plane	21
Scotland to Normandy	73
Normandy	163
April 1944	185
May 1944	201
June 1944	223
July 1944	275
August 1944	343
Leaving and returning to Normandy: A journey	383
Epilogue: A matter of pride	389
Glossary	395
Bibliography	397
Acknowledgements	405

Foreword

I have enjoyed reading *Ready to Strike: The Spitfires and Australians of 453 (RAAF) Squadron over Normandy*. It is not often that you get a chance to read about an Australian Squadron at war, let alone an Australian Spitfire Squadron engaged in the most intense operation of the war—Operation Overlord.

Adam has brought 453 Squadron to life. His research of the war journals and personnel accounts from those involved, not many of whom are left with us, provides a rare insight into what life in 453 would have been like during those days leading up to, during and after the operation. Many might have visions of squadron aircraft launching on missions and always engaging with the enemy, however the facts are somewhat different. Minutes of sheer terror separated by hours or days of boring patrols.

As Patron of the Spitfire Association Australia, I want to thank Adam for capturing the history of an Australian Spitfire Squadron in World War II and reminding us of those who served and those who paid the ultimate sacrifice.

AVM (Retd) Mark Skidmore AM

French Town Pronunciation Guide

Many an English speaker has mangled the French language, not necessarily deliberately, but often through ignorance. Some years ago I was waiting in line in a car rental office in Paris when I heard a person at the front of the line try and tell the salesperson in an increasingly loud voice that they wanted to go to 'Cain, CAIN'. They meant, of course, Caen, but looking at a map is not enough when trying to determine how to pronounce the name of a foreign town. So, with many thanks to the very patient Frederique Verbeke, a native of Normandy, here is a guide to pronouncing many of the towns that appear in this book.

Town	Phonetic Pronunciation
Alençon	Al-on-sonn
Abbeville	Ab-vill (with or without pronouncing the middle 'e' is acceptable)
Argentan	Arr-zhon-tonn
Arromanches	Ar-o-monch
Bayeux	Bar-yoo
Cabourg	Car-boorch (the 'ch' is that throaty sound non-Europeans find difficult)
Caen	Conn (with the 'co' sounding like the 'co' in coffee)

Camembert	Camm-on-bear
Carpiquet	Car-pee-kay
Coutances	Coo-tonce (the coo being like the start of cook)
Crisbecq	Kriss-beck
Domfront	Door-fron
Evreux	E-vroo (rolling the r)
Falaise	Far-laiz-e
Flers	Flair
L'Aigle	Leg-le
Le Havre	Ler-arvre
Lingèvres	La-zhe-vre
Lisieux	Lizzie-err
Livarot	Lee-var-ro (rolling the last r)
Longues-sur-Mer	Longe-sir-mair (rolling both r's)
Mezidon	Mezzy-donn
Ouistreham	Wiss-tre-am (rolling the r in 'tre')
Orne (river)	Or-ner
Pont L'Eveque	Pon-le-veck
Rouen	Roo-o (with last 'o' like the 'o' in 'on')
St Marcouf	Sarn-Mar-coof (rolling the 'r' at the end of 'mar')
Thury-Harcourt	Too-ree Arr-corr
Villers-Bocage	Vee-lair Bor-car-zhe
Vimoutiers	Vee-moo-tee-air
Vire	Veer (rolling the r)
Yvetot	Eva-toe

INTRODUCTION

I've been interested in military history for as long as I can remember. I don't know where this interest came from, but it was there, the same way some people are drawn to musical instruments or cars. I grew up watching *The Longest Day*, *The Battle of Britain* and *A Bridge Too Far*. Factual inaccuracies aside, I still enjoy these films today. Movies led to books, and a number of military magazines that were popular in the 1980s.

My maternal grandfather, Bruce Gordon Cobban, fought in New Guinea in the Second World War, and as is so often the case, when I was old enough to want to learn about what he did, I didn't know what to ask him or how to ask it. Teenagers tend not to be good at those things. Read enough dedications in history books—especially those of personal accounts written by a relative after a person has passed away—and you'll often find the same sentiment. If I'd known then what I know now, maybe I would have been able to find out a lot more about his wartime experience.

I've been fortunate enough to combine my interest in military history with my love of travel, and have visited many of the places that I had read about for so long, including the beaches of Normandy. The tourism industry in Normandy is, in my experience, largely linked to two events: the Norman invasion of England in 1066; and Operation Overlord, the Allied landings on 6 June 1944. In many shops you can buy something related to the landings. There are museums scattered all over the region, some the size of a small house; some larger than an aircraft hangar. There are companies that run battlefield tours—some based locally, some based as far away as the United States. There are many squares, streets and laneways in Normandy named for the troops that fought there, and the biggest events of each anniversary of the landings, especially in recent times, are the parachute landings. These are carried out by serving British, American, French and even German paratroopers. Sometimes a veteran can be found in a tandem jump setup amongst all the modern troops and planes. Sometimes civilian parachuting groups participate. It's very easy to see the effect of such events on the crowds gathered, and to appreciate what the soldiers did when you can walk through the towns and fields where they fought.

But what about those who didn't fight on land? How can we understand what contribution they made?

On a visit to the Hartenstein Hotel museum in Oosterbeek, in the Netherlands, some time ago, I spoke with a group of veterans and learned that one of them was in the Royal Navy. He said that he toured with army veterans because he could see what they did. The who, what, where, when and why of their contribution can be grasped much more easily than what he did in the navy. He couldn't take someone into the middle of the North Atlantic and explain a convoy escort to them. It just isn't done, but he could walk the grounds of the hotel in Oosterbeek and appreciate the experiences of the soldiers as they explained what they went through. He raised an important issue that the monuments to the soldiers tend to mask. Just as you can't put a memorial in the middle of the ocean for sailors, you can't put a memorial five, ten or thirty thousand feet in the air for the pilots. How can you mark the efforts of those who contributed so much to the result achieved by the soldiers whose unit marker you can find on the side of the first house in the village? At that time I didn't have an answer.

In 2014 I returned to Normandy for the 70th anniversary of the landings. Prior to leaving home, I searched for activities to do there, and found a 17 km hike advertised for the area around Longues-sur-Mer. I thought it would be good to see the terrain and farms surrounding the gun battery and perhaps learn more about the area. What I thought was an educational battlefield walk turned out to simply be a local French hiking group's day out that happened to have been scheduled for the week leading up to the anniversary of the landings. I was the only tourist in the group and, as we assembled at the meeting point at Commes, I wondered what I had signed up for—my French being quite poor, to say the least. But I was welcomed by the group and introduced to a few English speakers.

As we arrived at the gun battery, I asked the group leader if I could give a short talk at the B.11 Advanced Landing Ground memorial about the Australians in Normandy so that they might better understand why an Australian might visit, since most of the English-speaking visitors to the area are British, American and Canadian. She said that it was a good idea and asked that my talk not be too long or too technical, and said that someone would translate for the group.

At the memorial, the group gathered, including the guide for the gun battery. I placed a small Australian flag in the ground on each side of the memorial and told the group about the Empire Air Training Scheme, the mixing of different nationalities in the Commonwealth squadrons—and even within individual aircraft, such as the Lancaster bomber. I told them that the Australian pilots flew the famous Spitfire, pointed out the plane and squadron number on the memorial and said: 'The Australians were here too'.

At the end of my talk, which lasted only a few minutes, the group expressed their thanks for the Australians who went to France to fight for the liberty of the French people. They asked if I would like to commemorate the pilots with a minute's silence. It was a very moving experience and I felt rather embarrassed and very humbled by the group's response. I certainly didn't warrant the thanks—I didn't serve in Normandy, nor did any of my relatives. I had often witnessed the French people's sincere gratitude for Allied assistance during the war, but I had never been the recipient of it. All this from a group of people I had known for less than two hours. No-one in the group had heard any of what I told them before. It was all new to them. Seventy years after the landings in Normandy, there were still discoveries to be made, stories to be told, experiences to be related.

Each anniversary, the spotlight of the events of 6 June 1944 falls squarely on the army units, especially the paratroops. The purpose of this book is to take just a sliver of that spotlight and shine it on some Australians. 453 Squadron flew Spitfires on sorties across the English Channel in the months leading up to the landings, attacking targets far and wide in an effort to make the ground assault more likely to succeed. They looked for the Luftwaffe, spoiling for a fight, so that, when the troops landed, they would have one less thing to worry about. When the troops finally did land, the Australians continued to provide support—initially from England and later from Normandy itself. Rising out of the dusty airfield at Longues-sur-Mer to ensure that the air superiority they had fought for was maintained, and that Germans could not reinforce their positions as the Allied pushed inland from the beaches.

The monument at Longues-sur-Mer, near where the B.11 airstrip once operated, is one of hundreds located across Normandy that are dedicated to those who helped liberate Normandy, then France, then Europe from the Nazis. The memorial is there for a reason. So who were these Australians flying Spitfires over Normandy? What was it like for the members of 453 Squadron (RAAF), mixed in with the British, Canadians and the French, flying out of B.11, not far from the cliffs at Longues-sur-Mer, back in June 1944? What difference could one squadron make?

The word 'hero' is perhaps used too frequently these days. I am not going to use it, but consider this: when someone is called a 'hero' or, even

The author at the B.11 memorial in Longues-sur-Mer, Normandy, June 2014.

more dramatically, a 'national hero' for playing sport well, compare that to what the men of 453 did. These men did not 'win' their medals, they were not competing in a race or game; war is neither of those things. They weren't in it for money or glory. I have met some of my heroes and they are not the attention-seeking types. If anything, they'll put you in your place for using the 'H' word and quickly remind you that, to them, the true heroes are the ones who didn't come back. Nevertheless, these people stood up and went forward, knowing that someone would be doing their best to make sure they didn't see home again. But they didn't just do it once: they did it over and over again, for days, weeks, months and even years. Some are still doing it now.

My research has uncovered some sources where the pilots described what happened to them, and how they felt about it, in their own words. Their descriptions about what they saw, did and felt are important. The extracts from the Personal Combat Reports submitted by the pilots are stories in themselves and have been only slightly edited for ease of reading.

Allied air superiority in Normandy was total—so much so that some books on Operation Overlord simply say just that. They bypass the experiences of many thousands who played a part in the operation, perhaps because they feel it wasn't enough of a competition to make for a good story. This book seeks to rectify that in the case of one squadron: the pilots, ground crew and support staff of 453 Squadron who were—not all, but mostly—Australian.

Spare these men a sliver of the spotlight because they were there, too.

Formation and Defeat in the Pacific

When Britain declared war on Germany on 3 September 1939, Australia's response was clear, and a similar declaration was made on the same day.[1] What Australia would actually do beyond this declaration was, however, less apparent. In this, the hand of Prime Minister Robert Menzies was somewhat forced by New Zealand's promise of an expeditionary force, something that Menzies was still considering[2] as he was greatly concerned about home defence. It took almost a week for the Menzies Government to promise a division for overseas service,[3] and this first division of the Second Australian Imperial Force (2nd AIF)—the 6th Division—formed slowly and, in accordance with policy made at the time, would be filled only by volunteers.[4] Promoting the recruitment into this new formation was not a priority for the government, since the defence of Australia was the primary concern. Moreover, the Menzies Government held only a slim majority and could not afford to simply push through decisions in Parliament as it wished. Bold or radical decision-making was not an available strategy.[5]

With this relatively slow start, there was not a rush for further action by the other services. It was not until 7 November 1939 that an order was signed for the Royal Australian Navy (RAN) to serve under the Royal Navy, that is, British control.[6] This was more than two months after the declaration of war and a less swift agreement than was made in 1914.[7] Conditions were placed on the use of RAN ships, the most strict being that all units would be recalled if Australia or New Zealand were attacked.[8] As inadequate as it was, the majority of the Royal Australian Air Force (RAAF) was offered to Britain around the same time.[9] However, many staff and aircraft were actually retained in Australia to fulfil obligations under the Empire Air Training Scheme (EATS).[10] This was a scheme for training aircrew to be supplied to the Royal Air Force (RAF) and had been in development for some years, though it was not formally signed off until 17 December 1939.[11] By the end of that year, there were as many Australians serving in the RAF as there were in the RAAF.[12]

But on 6 May 1941, a signal was sent to the Commander-in-Chief Far East asking if an EATS squadron should be sent to the Far East and, if so, then that squadron should be counted towards the eighteen that were to be formed under the scheme. The New Zealanders would also be contributing a fighter squadron (488 (RNZAF) Squadron) under the scheme.[13] The Allies, especially Australia, anticipated war with Japan, and had done so for some time. Prime Minister Robert Menzies was very concerned by Japanese activity in Asia and was reluctant to send assets—be they men, ships or planes—away from Australia to aid Britain when war was declared against Germany.

The fear of an expansionist Japan was long-held in Australia, predating Federation.[14] The British were well aware of these concerns and when they assured Japanese control of German-held Pacific islands north of the equator during the First World War, Australia was not informed.[15] This act, freeing up the Royal Navy for deployment closer to home, was an example of Britain's habitual practice of leading the way for their own benefit. After all, it was their Empire, and Australia was but a member. Australia's geographic isolation had long been a concern of the federal government, and even before the RAAF was formed in 1921, there was a realisation that Australia had to be self-sustaining in time of war. In the late 1920s, it was admitted that

Australia could not build a plane from scratch, nor an engine for a motor car,[16] so exactly how was Australia's self-sustenance to be achieved? By 1939, it had not.

Following the end of the First World War, the Singapore Strategy was developed in response to potential Japanese aggression. A naval base at Singapore was to be built to house a large Royal Navy fleet should British interests in Asia—including Australia and New Zealand—be threatened.[17] Australia held doubts about the effectiveness of this strategy from the outset, and these persisted over time, though these were often quelled by the promise of support from Britain.[18] This lack of faith in the Singapore Strategy, with the associated belief that, should Australia require assistance, Britain could not—or would not—come to its aid, emphasised one salient point of Imperial Defence: that each nation should be responsible for its own defence.[19] At this time, Australia was reliant on Britain for advice as well as strategic intelligence and had no ability to influence British strategic decision-making.[20] With this in mind, Menzies had to remind the British that their 'Far East' was Australia's 'Near North'.[21] Australia was unsatisfied with Britain's responses to Australia's repeated requests for definite answers on British Far East policy.[22] Menzies was well aware that Australia was not a full partner in the Empire, and was wary of the British and their reassurances and promises.[23]

Despite supplying forces from all three services, the Australian Government had reservations about how those forces would be deployed, and the extent of their independence. The Australian attitude to EATS was also influenced by experience during the First World War,[24] and there was no intention to surrender the resources of Australian aircrew to the RAF. Overall, this scheme was detrimental to Australian interests, and left Australia with fewer aircrew than desired to man the rather ill-equipped RAAF of the time.[25] In fact, Australia was expected to provide 40% of total EATS pupils while possessing just 35% of the combined population of the three contributing nations, being Australia, Canada and New Zealand.[26] With almost no influence over the deployment of these aircrew or the European-based RAAF squadrons they supposedly manned, Australia's EATS pilots had indeed been 'surrendered' to the British, as Menzies rightly pointed out.[27] So, despite concerns about Australian security, Imperial Defence came first.

However, among the more favourable conditions of EATS, Dominion squadrons would be labelled for their origin, for example: 453 (RAAF) Squadron and 485 (RNZAF) Squadron. Under Article XV of the scheme, Canadians, Australians and New Zealanders were to serve in squadrons of their own nationality, and RAAF EATS squadrons were to be commanded by RAAF staff 'to the fullest extent possible'.[28] On 20 September 1939, the Australian Government approved the deployment of six RAAF squadrons to the UK for service there by the end of the year. But, with EATS obligations, this was impractical.[29] While it was planned that 18 Australian squadrons would be created under the scheme, it was envisaged that most would see service in Great Britain, so the plan would be fulfilled in any case. These new and only-for-the-war squadrons were also known as Article XV squadrons, the Article being an element of the EATS agreement which stated:

> The United Kingdom Government undertakes that pupils trained in accordance with this agreement shall, after training is completed, be identified with Australia either by the method of organising Australian units or formations, or in some other way, such methods to be agreed upon by the two Governments.[30]

To some, retaining Australian identity would be an important element of service during the war, but it was often not a practical consideration—for individuals or the war effort overall. Many Australians serving in the UK were much more interested in being posted to an operational unit rather than waiting for a vacancy at an Australian one, and they were also quite happy to be posted out of an Australian unit if it meant being promoted.[31] Closer to home, keeping Australians together was not an issue, but the regular (pre-war RAAF) squadrons were expected to serve near Australia and the EATS squadrons elsewhere, though this was not always the case. For example, a pre-war squadron, 10 Squadron, flew Sunderlands from the UK from the first days of the war, and 3 Squadron served in the Middle East. EATS squadron numbers were allocated to keep them separate from RAF squadrons so they were allocated the 400-series of numbers, the Canadians using 400 onwards, the Australians taking over at 450 and the New Zealanders utilising 480 onwards.

The Australian Government also reminded the Royal Navy that, should Australia be attacked, they expected RAN vessels to be released and recalled to Australia.[32] Clearly, despite providing forces from all three services in accordance with the principles of Imperial Defence—all of which was to aid Britain—strong reservations were held in Australia, and no provision of troops was unconditional. Menzies was loyal to Britain and true to his obligations, but he (and his staff and military commanders) were not blind to Australia's needs.

Despite this, by the end of 1939, Australia had British officers serving as the head of all three services,[33] and the Australian Government frequently sought advice from Great Britain on matters where it was felt that they lacked sufficient expertise to make independent decisions. This effectively subordinated the entire Australian military to British command, though each service commander did not necessarily hold the official Imperial outlook above Australian interests.[34] By this time, Poland had been defeated and divided between Germany and the USSR, and there was, as yet, no further fighting on land in Europe. Despite being at war, the (temporary) end of land fighting meant that no great sense of urgency prevailed in Australia and, while the 6th Division was forming in February 1940, five months after the commencement of hostilities, it was announced that another division (the 7th) would be formed for overseas service.[35]

Menzies fought against the prevailing attitude of apparent complacency, and worked hard to instil a sense of urgency for mobilisation.[36]

This apparent complacency during the 'Phoney War'—the period covered from the end of the invasion of Poland to the start of the invasion of France and the Low countries, was swiftly overturned with the invasion of the Low Countries and France on 10 May 1940. The end of the Phoney War caused great concern, but it was not until 21 May that Menzies made his famous declaration of an 'all in' effort from Australia.[37] Following the disastrous turn of events in Europe, the formation of the 8th Division of the 2nd AIF was announced, and additional RAAF and RAN resources were promised in May and June of 1940.[38] Enlistment in the new AIF units accelerated as the threat of a British defeat loomed larger on the horizon.

With the fall of France and the Netherlands in Europe, Britain's ability to protect their colonial possessions in the Pacific was greatly weakened, and it was feared that the Japanese would take advantage of the situation and attack. This increased Australian concerns about the need to preserve forces for home defence. By 13 June 1940, Britain admitted that no fleet could be sent to the Far East and, finally, the Singapore Strategy, which had been strongly promoted by the British for so long, was proven to be a false hope.[39] At this time the British asked for a division to be sent to Malaya but, as Australia had already promised the three new 2nd AIF divisions to the Middle East,[40] this request was declined with the statement that no more troops would be provided for operations outside Australia until sufficient forces had been assembled and trained for home defence.[41] Along these lines of self-preservation was the declaration that Australia would use its growing munitions-producing capacity to serve its own needs, and only once those needs had been met would exports be considered—Australia would look after itself.[42] However, the Far Eastern defence conference held in the latter half of 1940 highlighted the danger to British possessions in Asia now that her position in Europe was greatly weakened. Following the conference, and, despite the previous refusals of support, the Australian Government relented and sent a brigade of troops to aid in the defence of

Malaya, which the British admitted was at a 'gravely inadequate' standing.[43] Once again, Australia was providing forces for overseas deployment—albeit reluctantly—and was dutifully carrying out its role in Imperial Defence, despite strong reservations about the adequacy of home defence.

On 29 December 1940 the Australian Government was informed[44] that the official Allied strategy for the conduct of the Second World War was to be 'Germany First', a decision that had been drafted in October that year, but was not to be signed until March 1941.[45] Of course, the Japanese threat to western interests was at that time allegedly only theoretical, the Japanese and Chinese being fully engaged in China. The defence of the Pacific (and therefore Australia), was now, unofficially, a secondary concern, and prior suspicions about the honesty of British assurances were shown to be well-founded. But, as far as the defence of Australia went, almost no discussion took place in relation to the need for fighters, and one bold suggestion was put forward that Australia should place an order of aircraft with Japan of all places. Consideration had been given to what type of attacks might be launched against Australia, and the conclusion was reached that 'no strong case could be made on purely military grounds for the provision of fighter squadrons'.[46] So the question must be asked, if Australia was going to be attacked from the air, what would defend it from those aircraft? Had everyone missed that particular event in Europe called the Battle of Britain? Would an invading army not arrive under the cover of air support?

The signals announcing the formation of 453 (RAAF) Squadron were sent in May 1941 and by the end of the month most staff had reported for duty at Bankstown in New South Wales.[47] Trouble started early, with some members of the squadron posted back to their original formations, the ground crew musterings (skill classifications such as mechanic or fitter) being required to remain in Australia. However, these postings were made after these members had finalised their affairs, including selling their house and furniture. Staff made it known that, unless those members remained with the squadron, they would inform the press and politicians. In light of this, the men were given the option of remaining with the squadron and the matter was resolved. From there, they were sent to Singapore on 29 July, embarking on the ships SS Katoomba and SS Marella. Two stowaways were found upon arrival and a message was sent recommending that they be posted to 453 Squadron until such time as disciplinary action could be taken.[48] The squadron established themselves at RAF Station Sembawang, on the north side of Singapore and received nine Brewster Buffalo aircraft on 6 August, with another nine scheduled to follow later. But by 27 August, the squadron records registered complaints that there were still no electrical fitters, wireless electrical mechanics or wireless/telephone (W/T) operators posted or attached to the squadron.[49] During this time a signal was received stating that 'Air Ministry advise that extensive enquiries fail to find suitable Australian officer to command 453 Squadron'. The British would be sending one of their own.[50]

The Brewster Buffalo was no Spitfire, or Hurricane for that matter. To show exactly how underestimated the Japanese were, the Buffalo was described as 'eminently satisfactory'.[51] In reality it was a short, fat and heavy fighter, and ground crew described it as:

> Second-rated to anything else. We tried everything to get a [sic] extra bit out of them, we reduced the fuel so they wouldn't be able to stay up as long, the weight. They altered the magnetos on them to try and alter the timing a bit to get more speed but they couldn't get up to the height of the Zero or they couldn't manoeuvre as well as the Zeros.[52]

There were no Hurricanes or Spitfires on their way to the Far East at this time, the British could not produce enough for home defence and the Middle East as it was—planes had to be sourced from the United States, which was not yet at war with anyone.[53] Furthermore, it was US policy at the time to sell aircraft overseas only once a superior model was in service with its own forces.[54] In other words, the United States was prepared to sell the Buffalo because they now had something better. Squadron Leader

(S/Ldr) Allshorn documented his complaints about the Buffalo, saying that the undercarriage often stuck in the down position and that the four .50 calibre machine guns were affected by corrosion and rusting in the electrical system and therefore could not be guaranteed to fire when needed. Proper facilities in the Pacific were almost impossible to find. The two and a half mile walk the squadron had to make just to get their meals didn't help either.[55]

Aircraft being landed by inexperienced pilots without their undercarriage down did not assist in matters. The squadron was not yet operational and still had a lot of work to do before being declared ready, though when the Buffalo fighters later took to the air against the Japanese Zero, 'ready' was not a word that would describe the pilots of 453, nor any other Allied squadron in the Pacific for that matter. Some pilots who had been instructed on Avro Ansons (which was certainly not a single engine fighter in the style of the Brewster Buffalo) required a conversion course on Wirraways before advancing (perhaps a generous term) to the Buffalo. Others had to do dual time in Wirraways, accumulating flying experience in a plane similar to the Buffalo, before being allowed to fly one,[56] all of which had shipped direct from the United States.[57] Meanwhile, Australian ground crew practised getting their aircraft ready and into the air, flights competing against each other to promote performance in anticipation of the fight to come. This period was when the ground crew really started to get to know the pilots, and Ed Parker, a ground crew Corporal with B Flight also planned on how to get out of Sembawang if they had to—in a Buffalo with a pilot to do the flying. They didn't actually ever take off with two of them in the single-seat fighter, but they practised on the ground to test the viability of the plan.[58]

On 12 September it was recorded that S/Ldr W.J. Harper (RAF) would be arriving to take command of the squadron, which was typical of both RAF and RAAF decision-making of the time. S/Ldr Allshorn, the RAAF Officer in charge, was to be moved to another squadron. Australians were not highly regarded by the RAF and, to put it bluntly, were not trusted to command squadrons, the RAF being much more experienced—having fought in France, during the Battle of Britain, and in North Africa. While Australian pilots also fought in these battles, they were generally not given command positions, and therefore gained little or no experience in such matters, which meant they could not be promoted. By the end of September 1941 the squadron was still not ready and, while all pilots had been cleared to fly the Buffalo, lack of parts and ground crew kept airtime to a minimum.[59]

Harper arrived on 2 October and officially assumed command a week later[60] with S/Ldr Allshorn posted to 21 Squadron (RAAF). Harper was not well thought of by some members of the squadron, especially once the Japanese attacked, as they viewed that he took the easy options: flights described as 'milk runs', as opposed to those where there was a chance of combat.[61] On the 25th, an army co-operation exercise was held, in which 453 acted together with 243 (RAF) Squadron and it was deemed a success. One aspect of the exercise was for aircraft to provide close support to a parachute landing, something the Japanese would themselves undertake early in 1942. Orders for the exercise under the section heading of 'Degree of Realism' provided that: 'Defending fighter aircraft will not be represented', and the paratroopers did not actually jump from aircraft, instead they were transported to the landing zones prior to the commencement of their part in the exercise.[62]

453 Squadron was declared operational on 19 November at the completion of an inspection by the Air Officer Commanding, Air Headquarters, Far East, Air Vice-Marshal (AVM) Pulford.[63] Despite this declaration, 453 was described as an unhappy squadron and that 'some of the personnel were not entirely suitable for a fighter squadron.'[64] Flying hours had improved dramatically with the posting of RAF ground crew to fill positions and reached just over 543 hours in October (compared to a little over 260 hours in September). Operational declaration or not, they were still short of equipment. Readiness levels were stepped up in the first

week of December[65] while, on the 7th, the Japanese attacked Pearl Harbor and made their big move in the Pacific and South East Asia.

On 8 December 1941, the Japanese bombed part of Singapore Island and the first air raid siren went off at 0400. Two Buffaloes were written off in crashes on the 9th and, on the 10th Royal Navy battleships HMS Prince of Wales and Repulse were sunk by Japanese air attack. 453 Squadron was supposed to protect them, but they were only scrambled once the ships were under attack—and they were 165 miles away. In fairness to 453 Squadron, AVM Pulford had expressed great doubts to the navy when he was asked if 453 could provide the necessary air cover, and later confirmed that they could not, but the naval force nevertheless proceeded with the operation.[66] On the 12th the squadron was ordered to move to Ipoh, about 170 km north of Kuala Lumpur, to assist 21 Squadron. On 13 December, the first three aircraft took off and ran into a storm, force-landing in Sumatra. Two pilots were killed and another survived, uninjured. The remaining thirteen aircraft took off at staggered intervals and landed safely at Ipoh. Upon arrival, three were scrambled and attacked Japanese bombers attacking Penang. Two bombers, described as Type 97s (Ki-27 Sally) were shot down by F/Lt Vanderfield (who would later fly Spitfires, though not with 453 Squadron)[67] and Sgts Read and Collyer reported shooting down three Junkers Ju-87s, or at least a type of Japanese plane that looked like them. Sgts Read and Collyer then landed, rearmed and refuelled and carried out strafing attacks on Japanese transports and infantry. In these actions, F/Lt Vigors was shot at by a Japanese aircraft as he descended in his parachute, his Buffalo having exploded.[68] This was not the last time a pilot from the squadron would be targeted whilst vulnerable in their parachute.[69]

After landing and refuelling at Ipoh, a number of aircraft proceeded to Butterworth and, upon arrival, were ordered to take off again as a raid warning was received. One pilot was killed, one shot down a Japanese fighter and escaped into cloud, and the remainder were shot down or crash landed. By 15 December, only three serviceable aircraft remained at Ipoh, as no ground crew had been sent with them—their stay had only been expected to last 24 hours. The pilots were less effective as a result and, in one interception of bombers by 453 Squadron Buffaloes, only four machine guns fired, the equivalent of a single serviceable aircraft. More ground crew were sent to Ipoh to keep up the serviceability but, due to lack of aircraft, the best the airfield could manage was dispersal or a standing patrol. It was decided to make a standing patrol to keep the planes together, though it was hard on the pilots and aircraft, and no doubt the ground crew also. Sgt Haines of the ground crew was singled out for praise by the pilots in getting their guns working again.[70] The airfield was attacked twice by bombers on the 18th, and there was suggestion that a fifth column was operating, as the bombers disappeared when the scrambled aircraft took off, but reappeared when they landed, though no damage was sustained.

On 19 December, instructions were passed down the chain of command that any airworthy, but not operationally capable, aircraft should be withdrawn to Singapore, and six aircraft were withdrawn. This left a total of seven Buffaloes and, in the morning, there was a raid warning, but again the bombers did not appear when the fighters took off. When three of the Buffaloes came down to refuel, they found the tenders had remained in their concealed positions and did not return to the airfield, so refuelling proceeded by petrol can and funnel. When the final two top cover Buffaloes came in to land, the bombers returned and these two Buffaloes were destroyed. Instructions then came to withdraw all serviceable aircraft to Kuala Lumpur and the last five Buffaloes flew there in the afternoon. As soon as they landed they were camouflaged as best as could be achieved and serviced to get them ready for action.[71]

On 21 December, two Buffaloes, piloted by Sgts Petersen and Leys, took off for airfield defence and ran into 14 dive-bombers and 15 Zeroes. Both engaged the attackers and Leys was quickly shot down. He survived this—and six more attempts on his life—as he drifted down in his parachute. Petersen managed to shoot down one dive-bomber, claimed another as a probable and damaged a third before landing safely, despite the massive odds against him. A number of other sorties were flown and, in one large engagement the following day, two pilots were killed, including Sgt Read, who either collided with or rammed a Japanese plane. A number of pilots were injured and, again, one was shot at while descending in his parachute after bailing out. Five planes were lost and the remainder were damaged. Three Japanese planes were claimed as destroyed though, based on later information, up to eight may have been shot down.[72]

On 23 December, 21 and 453 Squadrons were withdrawn, managing to get seven serviceable aircraft into the air and to Sembawang while the ground crew moved by truck or train. The two squadrons were merged as 21/453 Squadron on 24 December 1941. A number of improvements for the Buffalo were attempted around this time. These included removing the radio mast, rear vision mirrors, flattening the gun cowlings and reducing the size of the gun ports, all to reduce wind resistance and make the plane smoother, as each protrusion increased resistance and slowed the plane down. The two .50 calibre machine guns in the wings were replaced with .303 calibre machine guns and the fuel capacity was also reduced. This reduced the weight of the aircraft by around 1,000 lbs. Tests on these modified Buffaloes showed them to be faster and they could even loop (a fighter that can't loop is asking to be shot down).[73]

Reconnaissance was the main role of the combined squadron for the next month, and a number of convoy escorts were flown, including a convoy escort to Singapore, with some of the 16 replacement aircraft.[74] Numerous bombing raids took place on various targets in and around Singapore but the Buffaloes could never gain enough height to make a successful interception, and sometimes they could not even catch the bombers. Despite the modifications, the Buffalo was still too slow. On the rare occasion the Buffaloes did have a height advantage over the Japanese bombers, they were only able to make one diving attack before the bombers got away.[75] If they ever engaged in combat, it was against the Mitsubishi Zero, and the Japanese were so superior that it was never an even fight by any means, though the Buffalo pilots fought as best they could with what they had. Around this time Hurricanes arrived, morale soared and they began to take on the Zero, but even they were no match. Jack Kinninmont, a pilot with 21 Squadron, wrote:

> The Zero was just about the nippiest, most highly manoeuvrable fighter in the world. They buzzed around the Hurricanes like vicious bees.[76]

Despite these troubles two bombers were shot down on 15 January 1942. Around this time, the Japanese broadcast propaganda messages via radio encouraging Australian troops to go home, stating they had been let down by the British. The propaganda messages promised that if the Australians did so, they would be left alone and Australia could resume trade with Japan.[77] On the following day, 21/453 Squadron strafed a large Japanese road column causing many casualties and only suffering minor damage in return. They also performed a number of escorts to Hudsons, Glen Martins, Vildebeestes and Albacores flown by British, Australian and Dutch pilots. Sembawang was bombed on the 17th, resulting in the loss of three more Buffaloes. Two opposing raids clashed on 19 January, both sides losing fighters and bombers, with 453 claiming three Japanese fighters shot down. Sembawang was bombed again the following day and, while 453 suffered no losses, other squadrons did. On the 25th 453 combined with 488 (RNZAF) Squadron for a strafing sortie near Batu Pahat. While 453 carried out the strafing, 488 provided top cover and lost some planes to Zeroes.

On 26 January, the Japanese made a large landing at Endau, and aircraft from a number of Allied squadrons were sent to the area to bomb and strafe the ships and troops. 453 sent four Buffaloes to meet up with two more from 21 Squadron as an escort for Hudsons of 1 and 8

Squadrons (RAAF). The Allied force was engaged by 50 Japanese fighters. The Allied aircraft got in one attack before the Japanese fighters got to them and, while a number of the Buffaloes and Hudsons were damaged, none were shot down (one Hudson later crashed just before landing), with claims of four Zeroes destroyed by the 21/453 combination. Sembawang was bombed again on the 27th but no personnel or aircraft were lost.[78] This day also saw 453 split from 21 Squadron, taking all the Buffaloes with them. 21 Squadron was moved to Sumatra, minus a few pilots posted to 453.[79]

On 3 February, Sembawang was shelled and, two days later, with the shelling continuing, the squadrons were withdrawn to Tengah. Some planes were lost to shelling prior to this move, and more were lost at Tengah. The Buffaloes landed amongst an artillery barrage, leading to a move to Kallang which resulted in more losses, the very few remaining Buffaloes being flown to Palembang, escorted by a Hudson for navigation.[80] By 6 February, 453 was the only squadron on the island, the others going to Sumatra, Java, Australia or disbanding. On 10 February, the squadron was withdrawn to Batavia where they were quartered in a RAF transit camp at Buitenzorg. The officers of the camp were addressed by AVM Maltby on issues of service pride, discipline and morale, with the officers of 453 being called aside afterwards and given a second talking-to. When AVM Maltby addressed the squadron on matters of discipline, rather than motivating them, his talk had the opposite effect, leaving the men feeling that their efforts had not been appreciated. When one officer spoke up asking to address the claims of cowardice levelled by the RAF, his request was denied.[81] At this time, 453 Squadron had two operational aircraft, and they were later told they would have to prepare to defend the island with the army units available. Browning machine guns were removed from aircraft and mounted on makeshift tripods, and a British Army Captain was posted to the unit to assist in their defensive preparations.

With the end of the operations at Singapore, 453 Squadron was evacuated to Colombo on the SS Orcades, which carried mainly Australian personnel. However, the behaviour of some officers and airmen was called into question, as evidenced by a message from Air Ministry (Whitehall), in the UK, stating 'Regret conduct of Squadron during last period Far East unsatisfactory'.[82]

While airfields and bases were being shelled, though other squadrons and personnel had stood by to perform their duties, the messages alleged that: 'a number of ranks of 453 Squadron abandoned station when being shelled. Shelling not heavy'. It was planned that eleven airmen and two officers who were found some five miles from their station would be court martialled, though having to evacuate Singapore prevented this from happening, and alleged obstruction from within the squadron prevented some of the people involved being identified. It was felt that the squadron held an unjustified belief that they were entitled to be withdrawn to Australia, though the intention was to rearm them with Hurricanes. Though other squadrons were in the same position—and some were entirely without aircraft—they had accepted their position, yet it seemed 453 had not. The report into the matters of discipline concluded with the words:

Recommend consideration be given to break up and distributing personnel amongst other unit their return to Australia appearance inadvisable in view their insubordinate attitude regarding this point.[83]

On 25 March 1942 a British Air Ministry message was received containing two important sentences:

Air Ministry do not repeat not wish 453 Squadron to retain its identity. Question of forming another squadron to be known as 453 will be considered at a later date.[84]

The question about the continuation of 453 Squadron had been raised just ten days earlier. And so 453 Squadron ceased to exist, for a time, at least. When the Squadron re-formed, it would not be flying Buffaloes, but Spitfires.

Notes

1. Jeffrey Grey, *A Military History of Australia*, Cambridge University Press, Melbourne, 1990, (2008), p. 144.
2. Craig Stockings, 'Others People's Wars', in Craig Stockings (ed), *Anzac's Dirty Dozen*, Newsouth, Sydney, 2012, p. 83.
3. Gavin Long, *The Six Years War, Australia in the 1939- 45 War*, Australian War Memorial, Canberra, 1973, p. 15.
4. Long, *The Six Years War*, p. 21.
5. Long, *The Six Years War*, p. 28.
6. Long, *The Six Years War*, p. 17.
7. Long, *The Six Years War*, p. 17.
8. James Goldrick, '*Australian naval policy 1939-45*' in David Stevens (ed), *The Royal Australian Navy in World War II*, Allen & Unwin, St Leonards, 1996, p. 7.
9. David Horner, *High Command, Australia and Allied Strategy 1939–1945*, Australian War Memorial, Canberra, 1983, p. 24.
10. Long, *The Six Years War*, p. 19.
11. Peter Dennis, Jeffrey Grey, Ewan Morris, Robin Prior, Jean Bou (eds), *The Oxford Companion to Australian Military History, 1995*, (2008), Oxford University Press, South Melbourne, p. 197.
12. Gillison, *Australia in the War of 1939-1945*, Series Three: Air Volume I: Royal Australian Air Force 1939-1942, p. 82.
13. NAA: A1196, 36/501/192
14. Horner, *High Command*, p. 23.

15 Stuart Macintyre, *A Concise History of Australia*, Cambridge University Press, Melbourne, 1999, (2009), p. 158.
16 Douglas Gillison, *Australia in the War of 1939-1945*, Series Three: Air Volume I: Royal Australian Air Force 1939-1942, Australian War Memorial, Canberra, 1962, pp 2-3, 16, 34-35.
17 Horner, *High Command*, p. 1. and Peter Dennis et al, (eds), T*he Oxford Companion to Australian Military History*, p. 495.
18 Horner, *High Command*, p. 3.
19 Long, *The Six Years War*, p. 1.
20 Horner, *High Command*, p. 13.
21 Horner, *High Command*, p. 14.
22 Horner, *High Command*, p. 14.
23 Stockings, '*Others People's Wars*', p. 85.
24 Peter Dennis et al (eds), *The Oxford Companion to Australian Military History*, p. 198.
25 Grey, *A Military History of Australia*, pp. 150-151.
26 Gillison, *Australia in the War of 1939-1945*, Series Three: Air Volume I: Royal Australian Air Force 1939-1942, p. 83.
27 Peter Dennis et al (eds), *The Oxford Companion to Australian Military History*, p. 198.
28 Gillison, *Australia in the War of 1939-1945*, Series Three: Air Volume I: Royal Australian Air Force 1939-1942, pp. 85, 87, 116.
29 John Herington, *Australia in the War of 1939-1945*, Series Three: Air, Volume III: *Air War Against Germany & Italy 1939-1943*, Australian War Memorial, Canberra, 1954, pp 1-3.
30 Herington, *Air War Against Germany & Italy 1939-1943*, p. 4.
31 Herington, *Air War Against Germany & Italy 1939-1943*, p. 128.
32 Goldrick, *Australian naval policy 1939-45*, p. 7.
33 Long, *The Six Years War*, p. 23.
34 Grey, *A Military History of Australia*, p. 133.
35 Long, *The Six Years War*, p. 25.
36 Peter Dennis et al (eds), *The Oxford Companion to Australian Military History*, p. 357.
37 Long, *The Six Years War*, p. 29.
38 Long, *The Six Years War*, p. 30.
39 Long, *The Six Years War*, p. 33.
40 Carl Bridge, 'Appeasement and After: Towards a Re-assessment of the Lyons and Menzies Governments' Defence and Foreign Policies, 1931-1941', *Australian Journal of Politics and History*, Volume. 51, No. 3, 2005, pp. 372-379, p. 378.

41 Long, *The Six Years War*, p. 33.
42 Long, *The Six Years War*, p. 39.
43 Long, *The Six Years War*, p. 39.
44 Horner, *High Command*, p. 53.
45 Mark A. Stoler, *Allies in War: Britain and America against the Axis Powers 1940–1945*, Hodder Arnold, London, 2005, (2007), pp. 20-22.
46 Gillison, *Australia in the War of 1939-1945*, Series Three: Air Volume I: Royal Australian Air Force 1939-1942, pp. 139, 145, 157.
47 ORB–453 Sqn
48 OAFH: 529_453 file M254
49 ORB–453 Sqn–27-8-41.
50 NAA:A1196,36/501/192
51 Gillison, *Australia in the War of 1939-1945*, Series Three: Air Volume I: Royal Australian Air Force 1939-1942, p. 158.
52 AWFA: Edward Parker
53 Gillison, *Australia in the War of 1939-1945*, Series Three: Air Volume I: Royal Australian Air Force 1939-1942, p. 158, 167.
54 Gillison, *Australia in the War of 1939-1945*, Series Three: Air Volume I: Royal Australian Air Force 1939-1942, p. 176.
55 Gillison, *Australia in the War of 1939-1945*, Series Three: Air Volume I: Royal Australian Air Force 1939-1942, p. 196.
56 ORB–453
57 NAA:A2217, 22/36/ORG
58 AWFA: Edward Parker
59 ORB–453
60 ORB–453
61 AWFA: Edward Parker
62 OAFH: 552_453: S/59/13/AIR
63 Gillison, *Australia in the War of 1939-1945*, Series Three: Air Volume I: Royal Australian Air Force 1939-1942, pp. 159, 167.
64 Gillison, *Australia in the War of 1939-1945*, Series Three: Air Volume I: Royal Australian Air Force 1939-1942, p. 197.
65 ORB–453
66 Gillison, *Australia in the War of 1939-1945*, Series Three: Air Volume I: Royal Australian Air Force 1939-1942, pp. 250-253.
67 Andrew Thomas, *Osprey Aircraft of the Aces*: Volume 87, *Spitfire Aces of Burma and the Pacific*, Osprey, Oxford, 2009, p. 73.

68. Gillison, *Australia in the War of 1939-1945*, Series Three: Air Volume I: Royal Australian Air Force 1939-1942, pp. 197, 257.
69. Gillison, *Australia in the War of 1939-1945*, Series Three: Air Volume I: Royal Australian Air Force 1939-1942, pp. 279, 280.
70. Gillison, *Australia in the War of 1939-1945*, Series Three: Air Volume I: Royal Australian Air Force 1939-1942, p. 258.
71. OAFH: 550-453
72. ORB–453
73. Gillison, *Australia in the War of 1939-1945*, Series Three: Air Volume I: Royal Australian Air Force 1939-1942, p. 281.
74. Gillison, *Australia in the War of 1939-1945*, Series Three: Air Volume I: Royal Australian Air Force 1939-1942, p. 324.
75. Gillison, *Australia in the War of 1939-1945*, Series Three: Air Volume I: Royal Australian Air Force 1939-1942, pp. 329, 335.
76. Gillison, *Australia in the War of 1939-1945*, Series Three: Air Volume I: Royal Australian Air Force 1939-1942, p. 340.
77. ORB–453
78. ORB–453
79. Gillison, *Australia in the War of 1939-1945*, Series Three: Air Volume I: Royal Australian Air Force 1939-1942, p. 348.
80. OAFH: 550-453 and ORB–453 Sqn.
81. Gillison, *Australia in the War of 1939-1945*, Series Three: Air Volume I: Royal Australian Air Force 1939-1942, pp. 437-438.
82. OAFH: 526_453 Signal AX 684
83. OAFH: 526_453 Signal AX 684
84. NAA:A2217,22/36/ORG

The Plane

At an air show, the sound of a Spitfire can silence a crowd of thousands and bring grown men to tears. Cameras are at the ready. The silence is broken by a low hum and a speck appears on the horizon. Everyone knows the familiar sound of the famous Merlin engine.

The Spitfire passes low across the fields of Duxford in Cambridgeshire, roaring by the adoring crowd and they applaud loudly, those not applauding taking photos as fast as their expensive cameras will allow. The Spitfire banks to the left and circles around the back of the crowd, temporarily out of sight while everyone tells the person next to them how wonderful those few seconds of sight and sound were.

As the Spitfire approaches again from the west it makes a sweeping banked turn, faster this time, howling in, showing off the elliptical wings that are just one of its trademarks and the cameras chatter away. Someone in the crowd nearby can't resist the urge to say, 'Takka, takka, takka, takka, takka.' Perhaps they've seen the movie *The Battle of Britain* one too many times. The Spitfire sweeps along the grass airstrip fifty feet above the ground, roaring across the full frontage of the many thousands gathered before it, and pulls up into a curving starboard climb as the crowd applaud.

Spitfire. That word is enough to bring forth images and powerful emotions to people around the world. But how did this assembly of wood, metal, glass and plastics come to have this effect so long after the first one was built? Let's go back in time a little ...

Reginald Joseph Mitchell was born on 20 May 1895 at 115 Congleton Road, Butt Lane, Stoke-on-Trent.[1] He would not live to see the full extent of his influence upon the world, nor to hear the praise of the thousands who flew his Spitfire and the millions more who wished they could. As a child, he had an interest in planes and, in 1911, at the age of 16, he left school and started working at the locomotion engineering firm of Kerr, Stuart and Co.[2] After workshop training, he moved into the drawing office. He then took up a job at Supermarine as personal assistant to the owner, Hubert Scott-Paine and in 1918, at the end of his first year with the company, was promoted to assistant works manager which was followed by a promotion to the technical directorship in 1927.

During this time, Mitchell had designed a number of aircraft and Britain had started entering international Schneider seaplane races—the Schneider Trophy, the first of which was held in 1913.[3] These races were established by Frenchman Jacques Schneider in 1912, to promote aviation development, especially in the realm of seaplanes.[4] They were not held during the First World War, but resumed in 1920 with victory going to the Italians, and they were victorious again in 1921, both races being held in Venice.[5] This Italian dominance was a great concern to other competitors as competition rules stated that any nation who won the race three times in succession was to keep the trophy in perpetuity. In 1922 the race was held in Naples and entries from Italy, France and Britain took part. The British won with a seaplane called the Sea Lion II, a Supermarine entry. In 1923, the race was held at Cowes, the winner of the previous race naturally hosting the next year's event. At Cowes, the British, French and Americans competed and the race was won by the Americans. However, in 1924 only the Americans had a plane ready to race and, very sportingly, they postponed the race until the following year.[6]

In 1925, the famous Australian pilot Bert Hinkler flew for Gloster, the company later famous for the Gladiator biplane and Meteor jet. Supermarine's entry was the S.4, the first monoplane to race for the Schneider Trophy, and which was built in just five months. Unfortunately, the S.4 crashed the day before the race was held. The race was won by an American pilot, Lieutenant James Doolittle, who, having shared the skies with Australian Bert Hinkler in 1925, would share them again with Australians over the Normandy beaches in June 1944, in his P-38 Lightning. Doolittle won in a Curtis R3C-2 at an average speed of 232.57 mph. Shortly after the race, Doolittle set a new world speed record in the same plane.[7]

For the 1927 race, the Royal Air Force formed a High Speed Flight. Supermarine secured government funding to support an entry, and they produced the S.5 which was successfully flown against the Italians in Venice (no other countries entered that year) and won with an average speed of 281.66 mph.[8] The Schneider races were a genuine focus for aircraft testing and development and not a plaything for millionaires to throw their money at. As can be seen by comparing the increase in average speeds of victorious aircraft in just these few years, the race really was an aviation development showcase. Not only did the Mitchell-designed S.5 win the race but, in accordance with his contract, 1927 was the year that Mitchell was made a director of Supermarine.

In 1928, the Vickers company took over the much smaller Supermarine and, as part of the deal, Mitchell was obliged to stay on. This talented man was not going to be allowed to leave. At the time of the takeover, a certain Barnes Wallis (later of the dambusting bouncing-bomb fame) was working for Vickers, and though an attempt was made to get Mitchell to work with him, their differing styles and philosophies made this impractical.[9] One can only speculate at what the two might have conjured up together. This was also the year that the Schneider Trophy rules were changed to modify it from an annual event to one held every two years, giving the developers more time to design, test and prepare their entries.[10] In his designs, Mitchell was influenced by the Curtis-designed planes raced by the American teams.[11] The next race in the series was held in 1929 for which Mitchell designed the S.6, which was to be paired with a Rolls-Royce R-series engine, the Napier engine of previous entries having been judged to have reached its maximum potential.[12]

In 1929, only Britain and Italy competed, and the British won with the S.6 managing an average speed of 328.63 mph. While a number of Schneider race competitors later came to prominence during the Second World War, it is notable that one person associated with the British team had already made his name in the First. The Secretary to the Wing Commander in charge of the 1929 Schneider team for the British was none other than a Mr Lawrence, formerly of Arabia.[13] With victory in 1929 sealing a partnership between Supermarine and Rolls-Royce that would last more than 20 years, Mitchell was presented with a Rolls-Royce car in appreciation for his contribution to the British victory and he never had to buy a car again.[14]

The British national budget had been very tight for several years and, in 1931, the British Government could not afford to support an entry in the Schneider Trophy race. Fortunately, a private donation was made by Lady Lucy Houston which enabled the British to compete.[15] However, little time remained before the race when this saving donation was made, certainly not enough to design and test an S.7, so an S.6B was developed from the S.6. Longevity was not a dominant factor in the design process and the planes really only had to be able to fly for the duration of the race in addition to the pre-race testing, leading to some design traits that had one pilot describe the S.6B as a *flying radiator*.[16] America did not enter in 1931 and the French and Italians asked for the race to be postponed, but the British were not as sporting as the Americans had been in 1924 and refused, resulting in no genuine competition. On race day, 13 September 1931, the S.6B flew the course with a new record average speed of 340.08 mph. The third victory secured the British hold on the Schneider Trophy and it became theirs in perpetuity. On New Year's Day 1932 Mitchell was awarded a CBE (Commander of the Most Excellent Order of the British Empire).[17]

While the Schneider Trophy seaplane races were taking place, development was going ahead in the realm of land-based fighters. In 1930 the British Government issued a request for designs for a day/night fighter in specification F.7/30.[18] One RAF Officer responsible for the issuing of these specifications, from 1930 to 1936 was a certain Hugh Dowding—later AM Hugh Dowding, commander of RAF Fighter Command, who, under his leadership, was victorious in the Battle of Britain.[19] Mitchell's submission, known as the Type 224, was not selected, the Gloster Gladiator was. It was to be the last biplane purchased by the RAF.[20] Mitchell had submitted a single seat monoplane fighter which did not perform to expectations. Disappointed but not discouraged, Supermarine and Rolls-Royce designed a new fighter and, in response to this (instead of the other way around), the Air Ministry issued specification F.37/34.[21] This plane was known as the Type 300, and was fitted with a better engine than the Type 224. The engine was a PV-12 by Rolls-Royce, the PV standing for Private Venture, 12 representing the number of cylinders. While in development, the requirement for four machine guns was increased to eight, and this was incorporated by Mitchell into what became the Spitfire, and by Sidney Camm, into his design put forward by Hawker, the Hurricane.[22]

However, the need for eight machine guns meant that, in the thin wing of the Spitfire, they had to be spaced out, leaving no room for additional fuel in the wings.[23] This lack of fuel reduced the range of the Spitfire and was forever its weakness. Don Andrews, who led 453 Squadron on many cross-Channel sorties in his favourite Spitfire marked FU-?, described operations as both taxing and worrying but, regardless of the type of sortie flown, he was always worried about fuel.²⁴ This range limitation was even more prominent when later marks of the Spitfire were compared to their contemporaries, such as the P-51 Mustang, which could fly much further and provided much-needed escort to the US 8th Air Force daylight bombing raids. That the Spitfire was a defensive fighter never designed for this type of work escapes some and, while the Spitfire and Mustang were both fighters, they were designed and developed for different tasks. Some pilots, such as Lysle Roberts (of 457 (RAAF) Squadron), who flew the Spitfire, Kittyhawk and Mustang in RAAF service, argued that to make a comparison between the Spitfire and Mustang is unreasonable. While the Mustang was a little faster and had more modern aerodynamics, in his opinion, for climb and manoeuvrability, compared to the Mustang, 'the Spitfire ate it, absolutely ate it'.²⁵

Director of Vickers, Sir Robert McLean, named the Supermarine design the Spitfire. This was in reference to his daughter Ann, whom he considered a *little spitfire*. It was a good choice, though Mitchell wasn't impressed, he thought it silly.²⁶ The name was officially approved on 10 June 1936.²⁷ At this time and for some years after, the rule of alliteration generally applied, thus the Gloster Gladiator, the Hawker Hurricane, the Fairey Fulmar and the Supermarine Spitfire.

The Air Ministry allocated serial number K5054 to the Type 300. The first test flight of K5054, painted a pale blue, was on 5 March 1936 at Eastleigh and Captain J. Summers, the chief Vickers test pilot had the honour.²⁸ The flight lasted just eight minutes.²⁹ The test pilots' often quoted: 'Don't touch a thing' was really more an instruction to leave the controls alone than a request to not change the design.³⁰ However, the *Summary of Flying Qualities for the Handling Trial of K-5054* starts with the sentence: 'The aeroplane is simple and easy to fly and has no vices'.³¹ Mitchell had his fighter. The flights and demonstrations were so successful that an order for 310 Spitfires was placed on 3 June 1936. However, Supermarine was a relatively small company, and had to subcontract the construction of the planes.³² While it is generally well known that, during the Battle of Britain, Hurricanes outnumbered Spitfires in service by more than two to one, the initial order for Hurricanes also outnumbered the initial order for Spitfires by more than two to one.³³

During this whole process, Mitchell had been battling bowel cancer, having first had surgery for it in August 1933, resulting in a colostomy. Sir Henry Royce also had a colostomy as a result of surgery due to cancer of the intestine sometime around 1912,³⁴ so Mitchell shared both the highs and lows of life's fortunes with his partner in racing and design. Not only did he have this to contend with, but the Type 224 and 300 were not the only projects he was working on. He also designed what became the Walrus amphibian, a seaplane that had its first sale to Australia, and one which would serve in the Second World War, rescuing many pilots from the Channel, including, of course, many who flew Spitfires.³⁵ He also starting flying lessons in December 1933, and obtained his pilot's licence in July 1934.³⁶ As development on various aviation projects proceeded, so did treatment for Mitchell's bowel cancer. In April 1937 he flew to Vienna as a last resort for medical treatment but it was not successful and he returned to Britain to see out his final days. He passed away on 11 June 1937, just 42 years old, never to know the greatness of his achievement.³⁷

On 15 May 1938 the first flight of a production Spitfire (K9789) took place and it was delivered to 19 Squadron at Duxford on 4 August that same year. Joe Smith took over the position of Chief Designer at Supermarine after Mitchell's death, and he saw to it that the Spitfire evolved as the Second World War progressed.³⁸ On 1 September 1939, Germany invaded Poland and, on 3 September, Britain and much of the Commonwealth, including Australia and New Zealand, declared war on Germany. On this day, 2,160 Spitfires were on order and 306 had actually been delivered, of which 187 were operational in ten squadrons.³⁹

By July 1940 there were 19 squadrons of Spitfires.[40] There was a lot of catching up to do. On 4 September K5054 was destroyed in a crash landing, killing pilot Flight Lieutenant (F/Lt) White.[41]

The Spitfire evolution mainly involved changes to the propeller and engine. The first propeller was a fixed pitch two-bladed wooden version paired with a 1030 hp Merlin II engine providing a top speed of 347 mph, one of the last combinations being a five bladed propeller matched with a 2035 hp Griffon 65 engine giving a top speed of 439 mph. Rolls Royce produced about 60 % of all British aircraft engines during the First World War,[42] however, it was the American Curtiss 12 cylinder engine (though not a V-12) which was sent to Rolls-Royce for evaluation that really put them on a path to success. After examining the American engine, they produced the Kestrel, all Rolls-Royce engines being named after birds of prey. The Kestrel ultimately evolved into the famous Merlin. The Merlin was seen as such an excellent engine (one for a Spitfire or Hurricane, four for a Lancaster) that, during the war, plans for it were sent to the United States for safekeeping.[43]

The Merlin was later produced in the United States, under the name Packard-Merlin and, once fitted to the average-performing P-51 Mustang, that plane really started to show promise.[44] Without focusing on the brilliance of the Merlin too much, one Spitfire pilot with experience on a number of fighters has said: 'A Mustang with an Allison was an absolute dog of a machine'.[45] Towards the end of the war the Merlin was replaced by the Griffon and this took some getting used to for the pilots. While the Griffon was more powerful than the Merlin, it also rotated in the opposite direction, the Merlin had swung to the left and the Griffon to the right, so the settings pilots applied to counter the Merlin for a smooth take-off had to be reversed.[46] Perhaps more than one old-hand Spitfire pilot in his newly delivered Griffon-powered plane found himself in a little trouble on the airstrip while everyone else ran for cover.

Due to the location of the wheels, the Spitfire had quite a narrow track when taxiing and, when flying, the wheels folded outwards into the wings. To stop the wheels spinning and rattling away in the wing cavities after take-off, the pilot had to give the brakes a gentle tap.[47] By comparison, the Hurricane had wheels that retracted inwards, which necessitated them being placed further apart and provided a wider and more stable wheelbase. Early mark Spitfires also had a hand-pump undercarriage, later replaced by a lever which retracted them automatically. The hand pump required quite a bit of effort to get the wheels up, and less experienced pilots would find themselves porpoising along in an undulating flight path as they pumped away.[48] This narrow track and the high nose position when sitting on the ground caused by the low and small tail wheel made for a zigzag taxiing route so that the pilot could see where he was going. Sometimes in North Africa, the Mediterranean and the Pacific, a member of the ground crew would sit on a wing and guide the pilot around until they were in the position for take-off.

Landing was also not as straightforward as might be expected, and the Spitfire was usually landed from a sweeping approach to assist the pilots in seeing where they were going instead of straight-on.[49] The Spitfire also had a tendency to bounce when landing, usually taking a few landings of decreasing bounces for it to stay down, whereas the Hurricane sat down quickly when coming in and stayed down.[50]

Building the Spitfire was not an easy task, however—certainly not as easy as building a Hurricane.[51] Every Spitfire was tested by a pilot at the factory, first at Southampton, then, when that was bombed in September 1940,[52] Castle Bromwich.

Spitfire Marks progressed in Roman numerals up to XX and from that point onwards Arabic numbers were used. Unlike many other aircraft, the letter following the mark designation referred to the type of wing armament fitted. Thus while the P-51D was the D model of the P-51, the Spitfire Mk IXE was the Spitfire, Mark nine, fitted with the E-wing armament.

However, according to Fred Cowpe, who flew with 453 Squadron in the UK and Normandy: 'You can't take notice of the numbers ... the Mark VIII was a more modern aircraft than the XVI'.[53] The wing designations were as follows:[54]

A-Wing	Eight machine guns (.303). The Mk IA had 300 rounds per gun, later marks had 350 rpg.
B-Wing	Two 20 mm cannon (60 rpg in Mk IB and 120 rpg in later marks) plus four machine guns (.303) with 350 rpg.
C-Wing	Universal type wing able to be fitted with A or B combinations, or four 20 mm cannon. C-Wings can be distinguished from others by having the outboard cannon mounts plugged.
E-Wing	Two 20 mm cannon with 120 rpg plus two machine guns (.50 calibre) with 250 rpg.

These wing armaments were combined with a gunsight which also evolved as the war progressed. The success of a pilot in combat, in addition to the often-wished-for 'luck', also relied on their skill in the art of deflection shooting.[55] In very simple terms, deflection shooting involves firing not directly at a target, but at the location in space where the target will be, so that when the bullets and cannon shells arrive there, so too will the enemy aircraft. Early gunsights consisted of an illuminated fixed ring, and pilots would aim off a certain amount of 'rings', leading to comments in Personal Combat Reports such as 'I gave him three rings of deflection'. Later gyroscopic gunsights were estimated to have doubled gunnery effectiveness. As the aircraft turned after a target, the gyroscope also tilted the mirror and therefore the projected image of the illuminated ring, which could also be set for the wingspan of particular aircraft.[56] This combination of factors was then expected to enable the pilot to get their rounds on target with greater consistency and remove some of the human error naturally occurring in the heat of combat. While the gunsights were not popular with the aces, because they obstructed the view forwards, aces do not win wars by themselves. Therefore the increase in effectiveness of the average pilot was what really mattered.[57] The gunsight could have its effectiveness brought undone rather easily though, and pilots were advised to not use the sight as a support when entering the cockpit, as the frame could be easily bent, throwing off the whole accuracy of the device. A memo was sent round 83 Group in February 1944 pointing this out after a pilot had to return early from an operation as their guns were out of alignment with harmonisation (the point in space at which the firepower of the guns converge).[58]

Some pilots had a natural skill for deflection shooting, as explained by Arthur (Nat) Gould, who flew Spitfires in the UK and Hurricanes in the Soviet Union before returning to Australia to fly Kittyhawks and (later) Spitfires:

> If you see an aircraft, say you're firing your guns at him, you've got to fire well ahead, because by the time your rounds get there he's done that ... So you finish up in a steep turn. If you can get right behind him, right up his backside, there's no deflection, you've got a dead aim shot ... Three famous blokes told us how they did it. [One] was a Canadian. He was just a mathematician. He shot down a lot of aeroplanes. He could tell you of your gun sight ... about deflection shooting. You could say to him, 'Messerschmitt 109 doing 220 knots, 30 degrees off.' He'd say, '2 1/4 rads.' He mathematically told you where to aim to get it. The second bloke who was good is a famous bloke called Sailor Malan. 'That's all bloody nonsense,' he said, 'You wanna shoot the aircraft down, get on his tail, get both hands on the stick and fly up until his tail wheel from your cockpit sight you can't miss.' Why with both hands? He said, 'Because you're right in the bloody slip stream you fool.' The third one, who I loved dearly, Bluey Truscott, quite a famous bloke, he didn't go for any of this nonsense at all. Bluey was a duck shooter. He was just one of these fellows who knew exactly where to aim your sight. The boffins, the mathematicians worked out, that if a JU88, which was a fairly big aircraft, if he came across at nearly 90 degrees and you had 8 guns firing ... the most you could put in him was 11 rounds,

> which meant it was impossible almost at 90 degrees. Bluey was leading the whole wing across the Channel on a sweep and he had about 24 aircraft behind him. A 109, which is much smaller than the JU88, came at it from 90 degrees and doing not 280 knots, doing 220 ... Bluey just pulled the stick back, boom, it fell out of the sky. He just knew exactly. He just had a feel for it. Like clay shooting.[59]

Bluey Truscott was indeed a marksman of the air, scoring 15 kills before his death in a flying accident in 1943.[60]

The first squadrons to be equipped with the Type 300 Spitfire Mk I were 19 and 66 Squadrons, RAF, in 1938. 19 Squadron was based at Duxford, later home to a branch of the Imperial War Museum and very fittingly, home to the Battle of Britain Memorial Air Show (amongst others). A total of 1,566 of the Mk I and variants were made, and it was in this first Mark that one of the identifying traits of the Spitfire was introduced: the bubble canopy, which replaced the previous flush canopy which had blended more smoothly with the fuselage, but cramped the taller pilots.[61] These early Spitfires had a two bladed fixed-pitch wooden propeller and this was later replaced with three bladed constant speed propellers, providing the Spitfire with a higher speed above 20,000 ft, a higher service ceiling and a shorter take off, all just in time for the Battle of Britain,[62] which commenced on 10 July 1940.

It has been claimed that Spitfires won the Battle of Britain. While this may continue to be debated for years to come, the beginning of the Spitfire's role as a fighter in operational service was not so highly praised. The first aircraft shot down by Spitfires in air to air combat were two fighters on 6 September 1939, just days after war was declared, but unfortunately it cost the RAF two Hurricanes.[63] It was more than a month later that Spitfires had their first encounter with the Luftwaffe, with two bombers being shot down on 16 October.[64] While the Hurricane was the more numerous of the two fighters during the Battle of Britain, the Spitfire could sometimes reach the Me-109s flying above 28,000 ft during the later stages of the campaign when the 109s were used as fighter bombers on hit and run raids. The Hurricane could not reach these altitudes, and was therefore less effective during these later operations. The Spitfire was also twice as likely to survive contact with the enemy due to an overall superior performance and smaller silhouette.[65] However, one major drawback at this early stage of development was that the Merlin would cut out when inverted, whereas the fuel injected engine of the 109 did not, enabling to German fighters to dive away without much fear of effective pursuit.[66]

The armament of the Mk IB was upgraded to two 20 mm cannon but the aircraft trialled by 19 Squadron suffered frequent stoppages. This was caused in part by the mounting of the cannon on their sides as the Spitfires had a thinner wing than that of the Hurricane,[67] a later mark of which was fitted with four cannon, though not in time for the Battle of Britain. After complaints about these cannon-armed Spitfires, 19 Squadron got their Mk IAs back. Turning was one of the main tactics of the Spitfire in dogfights throughout its service, and early model Spitfires had a shudder that would give warning of the coming stall.[68] This stall would result in the aircraft falling from the sky, a move that was virtually impossible to follow, the near-vertical wing position of the aircraft removing all lift properties of the aircraft. Spin recovery was then necessary to get back into combat or withdraw.[69] Of the Spitfire, Dick Peters (453 Squadron) said: 'If you treated them kindly and gently they were a delight to fly', and Norm Swift (453 Squadron) described them as 'Very smooth and manoeuvrable'.[70] Russell 'Rusty' Leith (also of 453 Squadron) was even more complimentary describing it as 'probably the most wonderful aircraft produced in World War Two' also stating that 'it's a very intimate aircraft that wraps itself around you'.[71]

In fact the British tested a captured Me-109E loaned to them by the French in May 1940 (they didn't get it back) against a Spitfire Mk I and the Germans tested a captured Spitfire Mk I against a Me-109. Both air forces found that their own aircraft was superior to the captured model, which certainly implies a degree of home side bias on everyone's part.[72]

The Type 329 Spitfire Mk II was fitted with a Merlin XII engine producing 1175 hp. 750 Mk IIAs and 170 Mk IIBs were built. These were fitted with a three-bladed propeller, as were later production Mk Is.[73] In June 1940 the Nuffield factory at Castle Bromwich began to mass produce the Mk II, the first of these being delivered to 611 Squadron in August 1940, with three more squadrons equipped by September.[74] After the Battle of Britain, in November 1940, metal ailerons were fitted, replacing the fabric ones which were found to balloon at high speeds, thus increasing high-speed handling.[75] The LR (Long Range) Mk II, with a fixed fuel tank under the port wing, was introduced in an attempt to alleviate the limited range of the Spitfire highlighted during the operations covering the evacuation from Dunkirk. At the time, the RAF did not use drop tanks. However, the development was not popular and the aircraft handled poorly in comparison with the non-LR Marks. Upon his first inspection of a LR Mk II and, being told that the external tank could not be jettisoned, one pilot replied in horror, 'My God!' To take off, the pilot had to apply full right rudder with full right stick and only take off into the wind.[76] The modification was not brought in during the Battle of Britain, though some were deployed in 1941 as bomber escorts.[77] The first Spitfires issued to EATS Squadrons were delivered in April 1941, going to 452 (RAAF) Squadron and 485 (RNZAF) Squadron, the Canadians of 403 (RCAF) Squadron would follow a month later.[78] Nat Gould, an Australian EATS pilot who would go on to fly more types of aircraft than some people could name, arrived in the UK in December 1940. While the Battle of Britain had wound down by that time, there were still raids, and his reaction to seeing Spitfires take off for the first time is telling:

> I remember we were there [Uxbridge] and I saw my first Spitfires take off. Oh, boy. That was absolutely wonderful. Saw them going off on an intercept...[79]

While many young fighter pilots like Nat lusted after the Spitfire, he was first posted to a Hurricane squadron. In comparing the two he said:

> The Hurricane was a pretty heavy type of aeroplane. I flew the Spitfire much later on and for pure flying the Spitfire was delightful. The Hurricane ... could take more punishment than the Spitfire. It could be shot up quite a bit more. It was a bit slower than a Spit. It was one of the nice things about it, it was a more robust aeroplane to land. In those days we didn't have runways, we landed on grass airfields and so on. A Spitfire was easily bent. The wheels were a little bit fragile compared to a Hurricane. So that was always in our favour when you were coming back and you were probably a little bit tired and a bit frightened and all you wanted to do was go out and have a beer or something and your landing wasn't as good as it should be, a Hurricane was more reliable.[80]

Once he was posted to 134 Squadron in Northern Ireland, Nat had his first flight in a Spitfire:

> I loved them too. It's hard to describe what it was like to fly one. It was absolutely beautiful. I describe it rather like a ballerina. It was delightful to fly ... It had no vices except it was very fragile. Couldn't take much punishment either on air or land. It had a little dainty undercarriage that would collapse. Just for pure flying it was delightful. It really was lovely.[81]

The Type 349 Spitfire Mk V was a real improvement, and was the first to feature another identifying Spitfire feature, the clipped wing. While the large elliptical wings were a signature of the Spitfire from the beginning, the clipped wing was just as distinctive, and was introduced to improve performance at low levels. The clipped wing Mk Vs were often referred to as 'clipped, cropped and clapped'. Clipped for the wings, cropped for the modified supercharger, and clapped meaning clapped out, as they were often fitted with overhauled engines rather than brand new ones. While they were designed for low-level work, they were still used for escorting bombers across the Channel on Circuses and other sorties. Their performance at the altitudes required on these sorties was sub-standard and, generally, pilots were glad to see them go. Engine life for a Spitfire was generally about 240 hours, (about nine months' flying time) assuming they survived that long. After this, they were sent to a maintenance unit where they would be refurbished and sent on to another unit, who had no doubt hoped to be equipped with brand new Spitfires, not those already worn in (and out).[82]

The first time Sid Handsaker flew a Spitfire was in a Mk V, and, compared to the planes he'd flown in training, the acceleration was what really struck him.[83] According to Sid, before you knew it you'd taken off and were away. He loved the Spitfire:

> When you get in that plane, no other plane is like it. And whatever you do, whatever you think you might do, the bloody plane will do it for you ... I used to think to myself when I was in England, 'Oh, I wish my family could see me here!' I'd be doing slow rolls and everything and flying the best plane in the bloody world and here I am, coming from nothing into that ... what I used to love to do was bring it up almost to the stall and then let it fall and then go down with it and then give it a bloody burst and then come up, do a loop and roll off the top, come out that way ... That's living.[84]

Models of the Mk V designed for use outside Europe, such as in the Mediterranean or North Africa, featured an engine intake dust filter under the nose, which also appeared on the Mk VIII used in the Pacific. There were two versions of the filter, the larger, prominent and pouting Vokes filter for the Mk VC and the smaller 'Aboukir' filter fitted to a smaller number of Mk VCs and the Mk VIII. By May 1941 eight squadrons were equipped with Mk Vs[85] and 6,693 of the Mk V (though some sources quote a figure of 6,787) were produced, including unarmed photoreconnaissance models.[86] The Spitfire Mk V claimed a number of firsts, including the first Spitfire to be fitted with a bomb, the first with a drop tank (also called 'slipper' or 'jet' tanks) and the first to operate in the desert.[87] The 30 gallon tanks gave an extra 30 minutes flight time but reduced speed by 10 mph. Considering that the tanks were dropped as soon as the fuel was used or prior to combat, this speed reduction was not a great disadvantage, assuming that the tanks did in fact jettison correctly.[88]

Some Spitfire Distinguishing Features Illustrated

Early Spitfire engine exhausts

Mk V and Early Mk IX tail section

Mk IX engine exhausts

Late Mk IX tail section

Early Spitfire radiator and oil cooler combination

Late Spitfire twin fairing combination

Pre-Mk VII Spitfires can also be identified from underneath or from the front by the radiator underneath the starboard wing in a rectangular fairing and the tubular oil cooler under the port wing, whereas Spitfires from the Mk VII onwards had rectangular fairings under both wings.[89] The starboard fairing held the radiator while the other contained the intercooler and oil cooler. While giving a more symmetrical view of the Spitfire, the twin rectangular fairings were also found to balance the Spitfire when diving, reducing the yaw experienced in earlier Marks.[90] It is also noteworthy that Spitfire marks did not always progress in numerical order as some developments were long-term plans and others (such as the Mk IX) were pushed through, while some features, such as the broad chord rudder were applied to later productions runs of the same aircraft. Thus, early versions of the Mk IX can be distinguished from the later ones. The early batches of Mk IXs were in fact modified Mk V airframes, and retained the rounded rudder of the Mk V, the later Mk IXs having the broader and more pointed rudder common to later Spitfires. The Mk V was also the first Spitfire to be fitted with a 50-series Merlin, those having the negative-g carburettor which ensured that the engine did not cut out if the aircraft flew upside down for a few seconds or nosed over into a dive, referred to as 'bunting'.[91]

Outside the UK, the greatest need for the Spitfire was on Malta, but it was not until 7 March 1942 that the first Spitfires, all Mk VBs, arrived after launching from the aircraft carrier HMS Eagle.[92] This first batch of 16 Spitfires was steadily reinforced until there were five squadrons on the island by the end of May. Only in June 1942 did the first Spitfire squadron (601) transfer from Malta to North Africa, and even then only because the situation in North Africa was so desperate at the time, with the loss of Tobruk and the Afrika Korps on the advance again.[93] Two squadrons of Mk Vs had arrived in Egypt in April 1942, and even 42 of the 48 Spitfires destined for Australia were diverted to North Africa in an attempt to save the situation.[94] The Australian Government was upset by this decision, having asked for planes back in March 1942,[95] and quite angry messages were sent to the UK by Prime Minister Curtin. The Australian Government eventually subordinated their needs to those of the Middle East after some strongly worded telegrams from Stanley Bruce, the former Australian Prime Minister who was now Australia's High Commissioner in London.[96] Mr Bruce stated there were perceptions by some that Australia was acting in an 'entirely selfish' manner and was 'over-playing her hand in her special needs'.

This was followed by a message from Churchill in which he attempted to reassure Australia that the supply of Spitfires was not a forgotten or broken promise and there would be a delay of only one month, and he referenced the American success at the Battle of Midway as reducing the perceived threat to Australia.[97] In Churchill's mind, the threat to Australia was only that, and he believed that Australia was not in danger of a serious attack. Churchill wrote to Bruce on 3 April:

> You use the expression 'if Australia is in deadly peril', whereas what I said and mean is 'if Australia is being heavily invaded'. You use the expression 'a major threat to Australia'. I have never said anything about diverting troops to meet 'threats' …[98]

Australia certainly did not want to have to wait until they were 'heavily invaded' before they would be sent assistance. According to Churchill, 'heavily invaded' was defined as an invasion by ten or more Japanese divisions,[99] yet Australia did not have ten of her own to defend herself with. Through all this the Australian Government had been making perhaps too much noise, having been informed in April 1942 that the Japanese did not intend to invade,[100] but perhaps being the squeaky wheel is what it took to get the planes they wanted. Though Australia was not in the Japanese invasion plans, this did not mean Australia would not be bombed or attacked. The fighting in New Guinea and the Solomon Islands did threaten to cut Australia off from the United States, and the northern port of Darwin was bombed 64 times in twenty months from February 1942.[101] While the Japanese weren't going to invade, the raids could not be allowed to happen without resistance, just as the British would not let the Germans have free reign over their territory though the threat of invasion was well past. Being invaded and being cut off from the rest of the world are different, but both have frightening consequences for the victims.

In June 1942 three Spitfire squadrons were allocated to the defence of Australia: two RAAF EATS squadrons: Nos 452 and 457, and one RAF squadron: No. 54. Two more RAF Spitfire squadrons were formed in Australia in November 1943, numbered 548 and 549, with the ground crew provided by the RAAF. Two more Australian squadrons were later formed: Nos 79 and 85, and a great deal of correspondence passed between Prime Minister Curtin in Australia and Dr Evatt and Mr Bruce, the Australian representatives in London, about whether it was prudent to ask for even more Spitfires due to the need to cover spares and wastage (losses due to crashes, combat etc.). This was particularly important since the fourth squadron formed (79 Squadron) was created with the Spitfires that at the time were in excess of the wastage and prior to the promise of the two additional RAF squadrons. The decision to form a fourth squadron was not disclosed to Prime Minister Curtin. As wastage varied, the ability to keep this fourth squadron operational was in doubt, and the question about whether to ask for even more Spitfires arose, especially with the loss of fifteen (only five in combat) on 2 May 1943.[102] The first three squadrons (452, 457 and 54) were formed into RAAF No 1 (Churchill) Wing[103] and did not make their first combat deployment to airfields in and around Darwin until January 1943, and did not see combat until February 1943.[104] Their purpose was 'defeating the Zeros at maximum height, thereby enabling our striking force to operate with maximum effectiveness'.[105] Of course this was all secret and so all references to Spitfires were replaced with the word Capstan, a brand of cigarettes, in an effort to maintain secrecy until the Japanese had been surprised in the air, the public announcement being made by Prime Minister Curtin on 4 March 1943.[106]

In November 1942, two 'Capstan' Mk VC Spitfires were tested against P-40E Kittyhawks at altitudes between ground level and 20,000 ft while based at Richmond, in New South Wales. The engines of these particular Spitfires cut out when negative G was encountered, something that had since been overcome by an engine modification but otherwise the test results were mixed. The results showed that the Spitfire was more manoeuvrable and climbed faster at all altitudes, the rate of climb increasing further above 13,000 ft. However, in level flight, the Kittyhawk was faster by 5–25 mph depending on altitude, it had a better acceleration than the Spitfire—both when diving and in level flight. The Kittyhawk was also considerably faster in a dive and the subsequent 'zoom' climbing out to gain altitude afterwards. In mock combat lasting five to seven minutes it was pretty much even, after which the Kittyhawks were able to decline combat and dive away to safety, doing so with enough of a speed differential to prevent being fired on. It was therefore determined that the Kittyhawk had the advantage in combat, as it could apply the hit and run tactics they were already using against the Japanese, and then decline combat altogether if the situation became unfavourable.[107]

Yet the Spitfire did not lose out totally, being assessed as easier to fly, with less manipulation of controls at differing speeds, automatic mixture and boost controls and a shorter takeoff. It was at this point of the assessment that the Vokes filter came in for criticism, the estimated loss of 20–30 mph (up to 8%) putting the Spitfire at a disadvantage and it was 'considered that this loss of speed is very serious.'[108] It was suggested that the filter be removed because airstrips in the top end of Australia were sealed, and therefore dust was less of a problem than elsewhere, such as North Africa. However the airstrips in the north of Australia were not all sealed so the matter was not so easily resolved. The original, pouty, Vokes filter and cowling, was meant to prolong the life of the engine, which had been found to be just 50 hours, about the same as the fuselage itself under operational conditions. The figures supplied in the comparison tests carried out at Richmond were questioned because figures supplied by the RAF (in relation to speed lost after modification) were in the realm of just 8 mph at 370 mph (or 2%) for the Mk VC and similar percentages for other aircraft such as the Beaufighter. It was suggested that the proposed replacement filter was such an easy fit it could be switched daily if necessary, depending on operational requirements.

A specific report then followed on Spitfires fitted with the new cowling in place of the Vokes model. It was submitted by a pilot with about 500 hours on Spitfires of various marks, who assessed that the benefit of replacing the Vokes filter with a new cowling was not sufficient to offset the likely damage done to the engines without the protection of a filter. This report was supported by a squadron engineering officer. In the end, more testing was called for, but no change was made and the aircraft were deployed with their Vokes filters.[109]

Though not yet formed, surely the RAF had plans for what was to become 453 (RAAF) Squadron at the time 452 and 457 were withdrawn from their combat zones. All three could then have been sent home to Australia, but to do this would have amounted to a 'recall' of Australian units and there was enough political animosity between Australia and Great Britain at the time based on the recall of the army units from the Middle East to defend against the Japanese attack. The matter had to be handled carefully and correspondence specifically states:

> Doctor Evatt and Mr Churchill have emphasised that this does not in any way involve the recall of our sqdns to Australia but is a special contribution made by the United Kingdom Government to the air defence of Australia at this critical period in the Australian situation.

54 Squadron was included 'to keep the flag flying'—the British flag that is, and the record of correspondence on the matter of Spitfires for Australia went on to describe Spitfires as 'the best fighters in the world'.[110] 453 would, however, serve as a source of pilots, as the Australian Government did not want pilots direct from Operational Training Units (OTUs).[111] The offer made by Churchill was not always seen in the light in which it was intended,

one War Conference Minute extract including the note that the Australian Government 'appeared to accept the R.A.A.F. squadrons as a favour and a concession whereas ... they and more should be forthcoming as a right.'[112]

Despite the need for the Spitfires to engage the Zeros, basing them at Darwin (usually south of Darwin, not actually within the harbour area), their role was to intercept Japanese bombers attacking the shipping and facilities in Darwin, in a miniature 'Battle of Britain' style engagement. However, basing them south of Darwin greatly reduced their ability to make effective interceptions and this was further hampered by their need to climb to heights of at least 20,000 ft to reach the bomber formations. Furthermore, the radius of action for the Mk VCs delivered was estimated to be only 130 miles when fuel consumption for combat and climbing was taken into account,[113] which would only enable them to reach out to sea a short distance north of Melville Island, for those based at Strauss. However, the Americans showed no enthusiasm for the Spitfire in the Pacific and suggested that they be based at Perth, which was rightly described by the RAAF as 'absurd'.[114] During this time the P-38 Lightning entered US service and was the newest fighter available to the Pacific. While its longer range may have served Australian squadrons well in the defence of Darwin, there was no way they would be provided to non-US squadrons, as Kittyhawks and Airacobras still equipped more than half of all US fighter squadrons until July 1943.[115]

At the time of Operation Husky, the invasion of Sicily in July 1943, more than two-thirds of Spitfire squadrons in the Mediterranean and North Africa were still operating Mk Vs.[116] From the Mk V also came the Seafire, and though its narrow undercarriage was a disadvantage when landing on aircraft carriers, its performance in the air was what mattered most, initially at least. The Seafires first saw action during Operation Torch on 8 November 1942 during the invasion of North Africa.[117] While five squadrons supported Operation Torch, 106 flew from five aircraft carriers on the first day of the Allied landings at Salerno in Italy on 9 September 1943.

Within two days, 42 had been lost to landing accidents.[118] It was usually the case that more Seafires were lost due to damage during landings than enemy action and, especially at the end of the war, the British Pacific Fleet fared much better with the heavier and sturdier F4U Corsair. The first unit to be equipped with Seafires was 807 Squadron Fleet Air Arm, and while it was a relatively popular plane, it just did not have the flight time endurance required of fleet planes and so failed to shake off one of the most common criticisms of the Spitfire.[119] The first real Seafire was built in April 1943, all previous Seafires being Spitfire conversions. In total 25 Fleet Air Arm Squadrons were equipped with Seafires from 1942–1950.[120]

The Mk VII was a purpose-built high altitude version of the Spitfire, designed to take on the high-altitude Luftwaffe reconnaissance/bombers harassing the British at home and in North Africa (they carried only one bomb and never ventured over in squadron strength). It was built with a pressurised cockpit and wingtip extensions, giving them a distinct point at the tips.[121] In addition, the Mk VII featured a retractable tail wheel (for better aerodynamics) and an additional internal fuel tank, with consumption being higher in the climb to altitudes over 40,000 ft. A few Mk VIs (from which the Mk VII was developed) were sent to Egypt but they were too heavy for the task so a number of Mk Vs were modified and stripped down of everything except the essentials. After first operating singly, they modified their tactics and eventually operated in pairs—one serving as 'Marker' (who was in radio contact with ground control), and the other as 'Striker' (waiting higher and off to one side away from the target).[122] About 100 Mk VIs were built between April and October 1942. While only 140 Mk VII were built, the last being delivered in May 1944, its thunder was stolen by a modified Mk IX (no Mk VIIs were operationally ready at the time) which took credit for the highest aerial combat of the war. On 12 September 1942 F/O Emanuel Galitzine engaged a Ju-86R at 43,500 ft in the lightened Mk IX, and had one of his cannon not jammed, he may well have shot it down. But, despite some damage, it returned safely to base in France.[123] This engagement proved that these high-altitude flights were no longer risk-free for the Luftwaffe. The Mk VII was withdrawn from service in January 1945.[124] Perhaps the worst feature of the Mk VI and VII was that, to ensure the cockpit maintained its cabin pressure, the canopy had to be bolted on when the pilot got in.[125] There'd be no bailing out.

The Type 360 Mk VIII was equipped with either a Merlin 61 (1565 hp) or 63 (1710 hp) engine and was paired with a four-bladed propeller.[126] It was essentially a Mk VII but with regular wings and cockpit. The first of 1,652[127] was built in November 1942 and, due to their longer range, were all sent to squadrons operating outside the UK.[128] They were modified for tropical use and these replaced the earlier Mk VCs in service with Australian and British squadrons operating against the Japanese from Darwin, 245 of which (plus a single Mk VB) had been delivered to Australia from August 1942 onwards. The Mk VIII was a welcome replacement in Australia. According to Spitfire pilot Lysle Roberts, who flew both the Mk V and VIII in Northern Australia, to compare the two was:

> ... chalk and cheese. The V was a lovely little aircraft but it struggled at 25,000ft, whereas the VIII hurtled through 25,000 ft and didn't start to slow down until 40[thousand]. So you knew you had a lot more power there plus you had ... the twin turbo. It was a little heavier, in fact I thought a lot more stable.

More stable as a gun platform certainly and, comparing the Spitfire to other planes that he flew during the war:

> A Spitfire always wanted to leave the ground and didn't want to come back. A Mustang was better behaved. It would leave the ground and if you so cared would come back. A Kittyhawk never wanted to leave the bloody ground and was so quick at wanting to come back.[129]

For Lysle Roberts, the Spitfire was it, but as for flying them according to training:

> You do your training in the Tiger Moth, you do your training in the Wirraway and everything has to be perfect ... Everything must be beautiful. You get into a fighter, forget the lot. Never, ever fly straight and level ... all of that goes out the back door ... the aim of the game, to get on his bum. Doesn't matter how you do it, get there![130]

Like Lysle Roberts, Nat Gould also flew Kittyhawks, and didn't see the argument all onesided. He'd first flown the Hurricane, then the Spitfire and was sent back to Australia and posted to a unit to fly Kittyhawks:

> Our first impression of Kittyhawks was not very good ... we described it as a bulldozer. It was a great big heavy aeroplane ... hefty and strong. Could take a real belting. Thank goodness it could, 'cause after we'd fought up there [New Guinea] a little while we got sent up to Milne Bay ... Milne Bay was bloody awful. Never stopped raining ... The strip was just mud with steel planking on it. When you landed ... mud would fly up. Spitfires wouldn't have lasted ... First of all they were too fragile for the conditions we had. Not only that, they didn't have the range and endurance as an up and down interceptor. Whereas the Kittyhawks we had were far more versatile. We had a lot longer range. We could go out a lot further. So this was very useful.[131]

The limited range of the Spitfire was its eternal handicap.

However, Nat had an unsettling experience with a Mk VIII when they started to replace the Mk Vs in the Darwin area:

> I was one of the senior pilots in the squadron, so I got in an aeroplane to see how fast this thing can go. I went up to about 30,000 feet, rolled it on over the top and dived to see how fast I could go. After I don't know what speed, the aeroplane went mad. It went all over the damned sky. I couldn't control it, I lost control completely. So I finally got it back somehow, came in and landed and told the engineer officer about it. He said 'I think we've got a rogue.' ... Every now and then you get an aeroplane that doesn't conform to what it should do. So they measured every aerodynamic measurement they could think of and couldn't find anything wrong with it. They said it was just a rogue. So I don't know what they did with it, but I didn't fly it any more.

It was only years later that he realised what had really happened:

> In a Spitfire, which was not a particularly good aeroplane aerodynamically... I was hitting this sonic barrier. Obviously the aeroplane was going all over the sky. So there was nothing wrong with the aeroplane, in those days we'd never heard of the speed of sound.[132]

New Zealand pilot Alan Peart, who flew against the Japanese in Burma, was also complimentary about the Mk VIII:

> The Mk VIII Spitfire was a really beautiful machine. It had a retractable tail wheel, clean lines and a pointed tail. The Stromberg carburettor permitted negative 'G' without engine cutting, and it had a two-stage supercharger which gave us considerable additional power flying above 18,000 ft.[133]

One Spitfire in 155 Squadron fighting in Burma had some modifications applied to improve its performance even further. It had the rear vision mirror, the two outer machine guns, armoured backplate for the pilot and ballast in the tail removed, resulting in 'quite a boy racer!'[134] It was all unofficial, of course. In the UK, specific instructions in relation to the consequences of removing the outer machine gun on each wing had been issued in July 1943 and these were later reinforced, so the idea had obviously done the rounds and became known at very high levels of command. The removal of the two Brownings was said to reduce the weight of firepower by one pound of metal per second, while providing a negligible increase in speed and height, especially since the Mk IX (to which the memo primarily referred) had a higher ceiling than the FW-190 in any case. Likewise the benefit to the rate of roll and climb was assessed as negligible. The memo closed with the statement that 'it would be unprofitable to remove any of the armament of the Spitfire'.[135] When a Mk VIII and Mk IX (both fitted with Merlin 63 engines to minimise obvious performance issues) were tested against each other in July 1943, the difference was found to be largely negligible, though the Mk VIII performed slightly better at higher altitudes and the Mk IX had a better roll, as the Mk VIII wing had shorter ailerons.[136]

Australian pilot Ron Cundy complained in his account as a pilot in the Second World War, *A Gremlin on my shoulder*, that his squadron (260 Squadron, RAF) was still equipped with P-40 Kittyhawks at the Battle of El Alamein in October 1942. This was some two years after the Battle of Britain had concluded. In his opinion, they could—or should—have been equipped with Spitfires.[137] Likewise, a New Zealander fighting with the RAF in India, F/Lt Lawrence Weggery, wanted a Spitfire but was told that the temperatures in which they were operating were too high for the Spitfire to cope with. The Hurricanes his squadron was equipped with blew air through the radiator to help keep the glycol temperature down, whereas the Spitfire did not do likewise as the radiator for the Mk V then available was under the starboard wing and received no such benefit.[138]

Two views of Mk VIII Spitfire serial number A58-758 at Temora NSW in 2015.
(Author)

The Temora Spitfire was the last one delivered to Australia and is flown regularly at the museum's flying days. It has a 'C' wing, as shown by the inboard position of the cannon adjacent to the blank stubs and, in the first photo is showing off the twin rectangular fairings that differentiate it and others from earlier marks. Also, note that the tail wheel has been retracted, a feature not available in earlier marks. According to Lysle Roberts, 'When I'm at Temora and the guys are putting on a good show it can bring tears to my eyes. The sound of that Merlin can bring back a lot of memories.'[139]

The capture of a Focke-Wulf FW-190A belonging to JG26 on 23 June 1942[140] led to the production of the Type 361 Mk IX Spitfire. This had a strengthened airframe, a four-bladed propeller and a 60-series Merlin engine. A number of variants were produced, including a low-level clipped wing version and a high-level version with extended wingtips.[141] The 60-series Merlin necessitated a slightly longer nose, but this was not an issue[142] and the improved engine more than made up for any other concerns. These 60-series Merlins also had a two-speed, two-stage supercharger for increased performance and there were more settings and tailoring options.[143] The plane could also carry an additional ten gallons of fuel, increasing the range a little more[144] and 5,665 of them were built. While early Spitfires used A and B to differentiate between the wing armaments, for the Mk IX, A and B referred to the installation of different models of Merlin.[145] Don Andrews described the Mk IXA and B as 'both glorious aircraft to fly', and overall the Spitfire 'was a magnificent aircraft, you felt so much in command of it'.[146]

The first operational squadron equipped with Mk IXs was 64 Squadron in July 1942.[147] Fortunately for those flying the Mk IX, it replaced the Mk V which was being outperformed by the Focke-Wulfs in the cross-Channel fighter sweeps both sides were conducting. This led to the Luftwaffe being surprised on a number of occasions, expecting Mk V performance but being on the receiving end of a Mk IX, there being very little to distinguish the two until well within firing range. Thus, the German pilots had to make a decision, to warily treat all Spitfires as Mk IXs or risk a beating by assuming that they were up against the inferior Mk Vs and only learn the truth when it was too late. The Allies, on the other hand, had no such issues, as a FW-190 and Me-109 were quite different in appearance and combat could be declined if the Allied pilots were in an inferior position.[148]

In that same month, a Mk IX with a 61-series Merlin was flown against the captured FW-190A. The test found that at varying altitudes, the speed difference was not more than 10 mph and the Spitfire was usually superior, but only by a small margin. In a climb, the FW-190A was slightly better due to its superior acceleration, but not remarkably so, while in a dive the FW-190A was better, especially in the early stages. The roll of the FW-190A was far superior to that of the Mk IX, and the overall manoeuvrability was superior, except in the case of turning circles, where the Mk IX could get inside the FW-190A for the all-important killing shot. However, the ability of the Spitfire to turn was one of its most well-known traits, and experienced Luftwaffe pilots would likely have avoided this at all costs in any case. One noticeable advantage of the FW-190A was its ability to get away from a Spitfire by doing a flick-roll in the opposite direction to the angle of attack and then diving away, so Allied pilots were warned to expect this move.[149] An instruction was issued to all Spitfire pilots in August 1942 giving advice on dealing with the new threat from the cockpit of a Spitfire. Paragraph two of the document included the instruction: 'To defeat this aircraft and to avoid casualties on our side, our aircraft must fly as fast as possible whenever they are in the combat zone'. The document recognised that pilots had previously been instructed to economise and save fuel '... but it is essential, as soon as they are liable to be detected, that they open up to maximum power for duration flying.' Pilots were reminded that the Spitfire's acceleration is relatively poor, and they should avoid cruising when there was a possibility of engagement. The instruction continued with safety tips, concluding with: '... when in the vicinity of Huns, fly maximum everything and in good time'.[150] A notice distributed to Spitfire Mk V pilots in the Middle East titled 'Who's Afraid of the Little Focke Wulf' echoed these instructions and emphasised the turning ability of the Spitfire against the Focke-Wulf: 'The Spitfire V's only tactical advantage over the F.W. 190 in the air is its ability to turn in a smaller circle, but that's a lot'.[151]

During the Normandy campaign any Luftwaffe pilot trying this manoeuvre was followed down to ground level and maximum effort was put into shooting them down rather than allowing them to get away due to the temporary advantage of speed gained in the dive. It was the aim of 2TAF (2nd Tactical Air Force—the primary formation and source of British air support for the Normandy landings) to wipe out the Luftwaffe, and it was found that Allied pilots were superior at low altitudes[152] as many of the Luftwaffe pilots were being pushed into combat with fewer flying hours under their belt. The first Mk IXs were delivered to squadrons based in the Mediterranean and Middle East in January 1943.[153] Often in the role of a fighter-bomber, the Mk IX had the capacity to carry bombs but it was not permitted to do so in combination with a centreline bomb or the 90 gallon 'jet' or 'slipper' tank. In September 1944 this restriction was removed, provided that the Mk IX was upgraded with Mk VIII wheels and tyres and with take-off at a maximum weight of 8,700 lbs from a smooth surface only. The instruction also reminded pilots that flight with the drop tank remained 'limited to straight and level' and that the drop tank should be jettisoned before attempting dive-bombing.[154]

No doubt somewhat related to the shortage of rubber in the UK during the war, instructions were also issued about the proper care of tyres on Mk IXs. Pilots were advised to handle the aircraft properly while taxiing, to avoid harsh use of brakes, (including NOT locking on one brake and sharply turning the plane with the power of the engine!) and manhandling the aircraft into position at dispersal rather than turning them as described above. They were also warned to not take off with any more boost than necessary, as the torque generated by the boost had a negative impact on the wheels and therefore, the tyres.[155] One late-war piece of footage of Australian Spitfire pilots shows ground crew helping them comply with this instruction by hanging onto the leading edge of one wing and dragging or digging their heels in, acting as an anchor so the plane could make a tight turn.[156] That's teamwork for you.

Joe Barrington of 451 Squadron coming in to land in a Mk V in North Africa.
(Courtesy of the Barrington family)

A pilot of 453 Sqn coming in to land during their move from Wales to Scotland in late 1943. The markings of this Mk V had not yet been painted over to reflect the new owners. Note the way the pilot leans forward in both photos. (Courtesy of the Olver family)

The Mk IX seems to be regarded by many pilots as the peak of Spitfire development. AVM 'Johnnie' Johnson was quoted as saying 'fighter pilots of every nationality thought the Spitfire Mk IX was the best close-in fighter of them all'.[157] Another pilot, in correspondence with AVM Johnson was quoted as saying: 'I flew most of the various marks of Spitfires, but I felt sort of invincible in the Spitfire Mk IXB. It was a beautiful aeroplane and I was very happy to fly and fight with her.'[158]

Joe Barrington flew with 451 (RAAF) Squadron from Corsica supporting operations in Italy and later the landings in the south of France for Operation Dragoon. He'd learned on old Mk I and V Spitfires at Abu Sueir in Egypt, but was introduced to the Mk IX on Corsica—his logbook recording his first flight in one on 11 July 1944 with the note 'Very Nice.'[159] Of the Spitfire (generally) he would later say:

> It was such a manoeuvrable aircraft, you could do anything with it but you're not worth a stamp as a fighter when you're carrying bombs ... the greatest pleasure was to go up when there was a blue sky, full of towering cumulus clouds which looked like mountains and valleys to fly around, and for sheer pleasure was to fly around for pleasure, not for war.

However for war:

> [T]hey taught me in OTU, if somebody got on your tail, the best way to avoid it, if you could, was you go into a tight turn, you try and turn out of his range and if you go into a very tight turn where you've got no real support to the aircraft, it stalls. It's called a high-speed stall, and one wing drops down and you're spinning off. Now if somebody's trying to get you in his sights, this is something he never expects and you're out of trouble, instantly.

Fortunately he never had to use it.[160]

Likewise, William Bennett, who joined 453 Squadron in 1944, upgraded to the Mk IX after flying Hurricanes and Mk Vs on previous squadrons and said of the change: 'After the old clipped, cropped and clapped VBs, the nines sounded like the answer to a fighter pilot's dream.'[161]

The Type 366 Mk XII was fitted with a Griffon II or IV engine of 1720 hp and most were clipped-wing models. The higher speeds and performance of the clipped wing at low levels made them very effective at intercepting the V-1 buzz-bombs, also known as Doodlebugs or Divers, launched at London from Europe.[162] Though this was their role from 1944 onwards, they were initially ordered as a counter to the tip-and-run campaign[163] waged by the Luftwaffe against coastal towns from March 1942 to June 1943.[164] The Mk XII entered service in early 1943, though the first came off the production lines in August 1942.[165] Griffon-engined Spitfires can be differentiated from those powered by Merlins by the additional fairing above the six exhausts on each side of the fuselage. The first batch delivered to 41 Squadron were quite troublesome, being converted Mk Vs and there were many engine and fuel problems, the squadron being given six weeks to acclimatise themselves and become operational before moving to the south-east of England, where most of the action was. Later Mk XIIs were actually converted from Mk VIII airframes and this was a much more agreeable state of affairs. It was a good plane to fly, and had a slightly better forward view than Merlin-equipped Spitfires. While operating in the south-east against the tip and run raids they did have run-ins with Typhoons, apparently anything with a square-cut wingtip was automatically identified as a Me-109 or FW-190.[166] Unfortunately for the RAF, one pilot was shot down and captured in mid-1943 whilst in possession of the manufacturer's handling notes for a Griffon II engine, and a series of memos were distributed reinforcing the requirement that no such documents be taken on flights which may result in a pilot being captured. Indeed, all pilots were reminded to empty their pockets of all unnecessary documents prior to flight.[167]

The Type 373 Mk XIV was based on the Mk VIII and had a Griffon 65 engine of 2035 hp with a five-bladed propeller and a larger fin and rudder. Early production models had the regular Spitfire bubble canopy, while later models had a teardrop canopy that gave better all-round vision, similar to the Hawker Tempest and P-51D Mustang.[168] They were first operational with 610 Squadron in January 1944, but were not operational in the Far East until August 1945 and saw no action there.[169] In early 1944 the Air Fighting Development Unit at Duxford tested a new Mk XIV against a Mk IX, Me-109G and FW-190A. Against the Mk IX it was judged to be an overall improvement and 30–35 mph faster at all heights. The even longer nose hindered the forward view and turns to port were noticeably better than those to starboard. Against the FW-190A it was judged to be better, and estimated to be equal to the FW-190D, with a speed advantage of 20–60 mph depending on altitude. In typical Spitfire fashion it was able to out-turn the FW-190A, but had to be wary of the flick-roll and dive getaway tactic that the FW-190A's superior roll gave it. Against the Me-190G it was 10–40 mph faster depending on altitude and could out-turn, out-climb and out-roll this ageing rival.[170] Though not identified by Mark number, the arrival of the Mk XIV in RAF service was announced in Australia in the *Sydney Morning Herald* on 9 March 1944 with the article 'Powerful Spitfire'. The Griffon was described as having a cylinder size 23% greater than that of the Merlin but the horsepower was not divulged and was described as 'still a secret', the new Spitfire being described as 'the most powerful of all Spitfires'.[171]

The Type 361 Mk XVI was the last of the Merlin-powered Spitfires and consisted of a US-built Packard-Merlin 266 (equivalent to a Merlin 66) and the airframe of a Mk IX. 1,054 were built in two different models, a XVIC, with a clipped wing, standard canopy and rounded, early IX style fin and the XVIE with a regular wing, teardrop canopy and late Mk IX pointed fin.[172] Sid Handsaker, a Spitfire pilot with 451 Squadron, first went solo on a Mk VB in January 1945 at No 53 OTU in Kirton-in-Lindsay. These were old training aircraft and when he arrived at 451 Squadron in April they were equipped with Mk XVIs. After his third flight in one he recorded in his pilot's logbook: 'Much heavier a/c than Mk V. Lovely to fly'.[173] The Mk XVI was first delivered to squadrons in October 1944, 453 and 602 being two of the first, and they were used primarily to dive-bomb V2 sites.[174] These Spitfires were also fitted with a special Two-Way Automatic Bomb Distributor. This switch had two settings. In the 'up' position, marked 'Single & Salvo', all bombs were released simultaneously. In the 'down' position, marked Port and Starboard, the port and centreline bombs were released 0.3 seconds before the bomb on the starboard rack. This produced a greater spread, the spread increasing in proportion to the speed of the aircraft,[175] and hopefully increasing the chance of an effective hit, especially on the railway lines that led to a number of the V-2 sites.

The Packard-Merlin 266 in these MK XVIs had sparkplug trouble though, which caused rough running of the engine. An instruction was issued that they should be changed during the 20 hour inspections instead of every 40 hours. To reduce the possibility of sparkplug trouble, the whole set were to be changed on each occasion. To prevent the engine fouling that had caused issues with the Mk XVIs, pilots were instructed to run the engines up to 2350 rpm with +9 lbs boost and, during flight when practical, to clear the engines every 15 minutes by opening up to a minimum of 2650 rpm with +7 lbs boost.[176] This resulted in a stream of black muck being thrown out of the exhausts and formations opened up when this procedure took place so as not to soil the windscreen of nearby aircraft, or have the engines of fellow pilots ingest what had just been thrown out of the plane in front.[177]

While not operated by 453 Squadron, there were a number of photographic reconnaissance (PR) variants of the Spitfire built, many of which were unarmed. Early PR Spitfires were converted Mk Is and the Spitfire PR Mk IV was built with extra fuel capacity and no armament whatsoever.[178] An Australian, Wing Commander (W/Cdr) Sidney Cotton, paved the way for Spitfire PR operations, having done much of his own freelance work, essentially spying on the Luftwaffe before the war started.[179] The unit he commanded went by a number of titles, such as No. 2 Camouflage Unit, which were designed to distract from their true role. They eventually became designated as Photographic Reconnaissance Units (PRU) and it was in these units that the white, pink and blue Spitfires originated. An early, armed Spitfire could barely reach Paris from England but, by comparison, an unarmed Spitfire with 90 additional gallons of fuel could reach Sweden, Berlin or Italy. Though not equipped with Spitfires from the outset, once they were the mainstay of the unit, Cotton noted that it was easier to train a pilot to fly a Spitfire than to get a Spitfire pilot with the 'wrong' attitude to do PRU work well.[180] Later Marks of PR Spitfires carried some armament, but fuel was one of the most important considerations, as reconnaissance had to cover as much of Europe as possible.

Australian PRU Spitfire pilot Keith Campbell volunteered when a RAF Officer came by the Personnel Dispatch and Reception Centre at Bournemouth looking for 'some volunteers for our unit. The best airplanes that we've got, lots of action, who wants to be in it? So I put up my hand and bingo that was it.'[181] Within a few days he was out of Bournemouth (some waited months to get a posting) and went to navigation school then to an OTU with blue Spitfires. The blue was great camouflage against those observing from the ground, they were very hard to spot but, from above, they stood out clearly against the ground, so PRU pilots had to make sure an enemy fighter never got above them. The first thing he noticed was the lack of armament. 'What about this? Where are the guns?' he asked, and was told they didn't have any since, if they were given armament, they'd be tempted to fight it out rather than head for home.[182] The PRU Spitfire had to make it back to base to be of any value. If a Mk V or IX was shot down after it had dropped its bomb on a bridge, that was totally different—the bridge might be destroyed and the sortie was done but, until the film was developed from the PRU Spitfire that made it home, nothing had been achieved.

In this unit, Keith learned how to fly a Spitfire and do aerial photography, though the Spitfire was not ideal for the task because of the angle the plane had to be banked at to achieve a good series of photos. But, like so many others, he rated it 'an easy plane to fly'.[183] Flying PRU sorties also included finding the contrail layer—that point of altitude where a plane leaves a trail behind it, which a PRU aircraft could not afford to do—then dropping down another thousand feet to provide a buffer zone. Mirrors on PRU Spitfires weren't for looking out for other aircraft, they were for spotting your contrail. When the unit received Mosquitos later on, they were rated as much better for the task, but that was not for some time, so in Spitfires Keith went

> ...way past Berlin, whether you could get back again was another matter. It was quite crazy, but after a while, the Luftwaffe used to object to this violently and they used to shoot at you occasionally. It was a job, I volunteered.

Did he know what he was getting himself into? 'I didn't have the faintest clue'. As far as the fuel situation went, the PRU Spitfires had the range to do the job, but that was it—any extra boost, especially pushing it through the gate to get away from a pursuing Messerschmitt or Focke-Wulf would soon see the plane run out of fuel, and they'd have to come down, even if the Germans hadn't fired a shot.[184] Photo-reconnaissance work was dangerous, straight and level was the order of the day, and it was a PR Spitfire that took the photos of the dams breached by the Lancasters of 617 Squadron in May of 1943.[185] The Spitfire PR Mk XIX was developed from the Mk XIV and had fuel tanks in the wings.[186]

The Type 509 Trainer Mk IX was actually built after the war ended, and had a second seating position behind and slightly higher than the normal pilot's position. The timing of the arrival of this Mark is important and gives an indication of the difficulty of flying a Spitfire for the first time. Despite all the ground training, cockpit familiarisation and taxiing practice, the first time a pilot flew a Spitfire they were on their own! Spitfire modifications and Marks progressed throughout and beyond the Second World War, but they became less Spitfire-like. The final three Marks of Spitfire, of which the Mk 21 was the first, were all armed with four 20 mm cannon, two in each wing, but less than 500 were made of all three Marks.[187] A Mk 24 was judged to be too heavy and unbalanced compared to previous Marks and, while it flew well enough, it had perhaps progressed too far for some.[188] Likewise, a Mk 21 flown by Sir Brian Inglis (who joined 453 Squadron just before Normandy) was judged to be not as good as earlier Marks, though with a Griffon engine he stated it was possible to take off without full throttle, something he hadn't done previously.[189]

Of all the Spitfires built, some 22,789 of all Marks and their variants,[190] it is estimated that 1,500 were paid for by people or organisations. To 'buy' a Spitfire, an organisation or group had to raise £5,000, compared to the actual cost of manufacturing one at the time of about £7,500.[191] Once bought, the Spitfire 'presented' by the purchaser was delivered to a squadron with the name of the presenter painted on the side near the cockpit. One example of these Spitfires is memorialised in London at the *Spitfire Mk Vb W3311 Gate* at the Old Spitalfields Market. The Market's fruit and vegetable traders pooled their funds and bought the Spitfire in 1941, naming it 'Fruitation'.[192] Its service was short, lasting barely a month, with pilot Sgt Smith of 611 Squadron shot down and captured while escorting bombers on 6 July 1941.[193] The feasibility of a similar 'presentation' scheme was raised in Australia in mid-1941 but was rejected on the grounds that 'any such funds would really amount to contributions to the British Treasury, and they could not be authorised'.[194]

In February 1948, the last Spitfire built was delivered to the RAF and the Royal Navy Fleet Air Arm (FAA) took delivery of the last Seafire in January 1949.[195] These aircraft would continue to serve for a number of years, but the jet age had arrived and, eventually, most would be scrapped. Writing in 1992, Fred McCann, who flew Spitfires with 452 (RAAF) and 453 (RAAF) Squadrons, expressed himself in emotional terms:

For what it's worth, I loved the Spitfire—I never once stepped into one without thinking how lucky I was to 'own' one. To me they were the most beautiful a/c in the sky and I still think so. I flew them from early 1941 until March 1946 when I had the horrible job of guiding them to their final resting place with the ones that arrived in October 1945—as I walked away I felt like Cecil Lewis when he wrote 'fool—the best is over!' I was O.C. Test Flight at Oakey and I flew the new Mustangs as they were assembled—they were good but somehow could not replace the Spitfire in my affection.

Ah Well!—they are gone too—only a few ghosts remain, flying carefully around lest they fracture. Goodbye Spitty, you were all Mitchell designed you for.[196]

Spitfire Gate, Spitalfields Markets, London, 2015. (Author)

Selected Spitfire Marks: Statistics and features[197]

Mark	Engine fitted	Statistics	Design note
Mk IA	1030 hp RR Merlin II, III	Wingspan: 36 ft 10 in Length: 29 ft 11 in Ceiling: 34,500 ft Max speed: 362 mph at 18,500 ft	8 x .303 machine guns (A Wing)
Mk IB	1030 hp RR Merlin III		Initially equipped with 2 x 20 mm but then upgraded to 2 x 20 mm and 4 x .303 (B Wing)
Mk IIA	1175 hp RR Merlin XII		Produced at Castle Bromwich
Mk IIA (LR)	1175 hp RR Merlin XII		30 gallon fuel tank fixed under port wing. Not a popular decision with pilots.
Mk IIB	1175 hp RR Merlin XII		B wing version of Mk II
F. Mk VB	1470 hp RR Merlin 45 1415 hp RR Merlin 46	Wingspan: 36 ft 10 in Length: 29 ft 11 in Ceiling: 37,500 ft Max speed: 371 mph at 20,000 ft	Merlin 46 for higher altitudes
LF Mk VB	1585 hp RR Merlin 45M		Merlin 45M for lower altitudes. Some LFs were 'clipped'
F. Mk VC	1470 hp RR Merlin 45, 50, 50A, 55, 56		Universal Wing (C Wing). 84 gallons of fuel carried internally
Mk VI	1415 hp RR Merlin 47		Pressurised cabin
Mk VII	1710 hp RR Merlin 64		Pressurised cabin and 2 speed, 2 stage Merlin

F. Mk VIII	1565 hp RR Merlin 61 1650 hp RR Merlin 63 1710 hp RR Merlin 63A 1720 hp RR Merlin 66		120–123 gallons of fuel of which 26–27 were in wing tanks (figures vary)
F. Mk IX	1565 hp RR Merlin 61 1650 hp RR Merlin 63 1710 hp RR Merlin 63A	Wingspan: 36 ft 10 in Length: 31 ft 4 in Ceiling: 43,000 ft Max speed: 408 mph at 25,000 ft	
F. Mk IXE	1565 hp RR Merlin 61 1650 hp RR Merlin 63 1710 hp RR Merlin 63A		2 x 20 mm cannon and 2 x .50cal machine guns (E Wing)
Mk XII	1735 hp RR Griffon III, IV	Max speed: 393 mph at 18,000 ft	Griffon rotated in opposite direction to Merlin
Mk XIVC	2035 hp RR Griffon 65	Wingspan: 36 ft 10 in Length: 32 ft 8 in Ceiling: 43,000 ft Max speed: 439 mph at 24,500 ft	C Wing
FR Mk XIVE	2035 hp RR Griffon 65	Max speed 448 mph at 25,400 ft	Teardrop canopy in the style of Typhoons and Tempests. Armed reconnaissance version fitted with camera.
LF Mk XVIE	1580 hp Packard Merlin 266		Packard-Merlins were manufactured in the USA.
Mk 21	2035 hp RR Griffon 61		
PR (Photo Recon) Type A	1030 hp RR Merlin III		
PR Type B	1030 hp RR Merlin III		Extra 30 gallons of fuel behind pilot

PR Type C	1030 hp RR Merlin III		Additional fuselage fuel as in Type B plus port wing tank as in Mk IIA (LR)
PR Mk X	1475 hp RR Merlin 77		Pressurised cabin and 2 speed, 2 stage Merlin
Seafire Mk IB	1470 hp RR Merlin 45 1415 hp RR Merlin 46		Conversions from Mk VB
Seafire Mk F.III	1470 hp RR Merlin 55		Folding C Wing

Notes

1. Mitchell, Gordon, *R.J. Mitchell: Schooldays to Spitfire*, The History Press, Stroud, (1986), 2009, p.27.
2. Mitchell, *R.J. Mitchell: Schooldays to Spitfire*, pp. 29–31.
3. Mitchell, *R.J. Mitchell: Schooldays to Spitfire*, p. 42.
4. Stewart Wilson, Spitfire, Aerospace Publications, Fyshwick, 1999, p. 12.
5. Mitchell, *R.J. Mitchell: Schooldays to Spitfire*, p. 44.
6. Mitchell, *R.J. Mitchell: Schooldays to Spitfire*, pp. 62-63.
7. Mitchell, *R.J. Mitchell: Schooldays to Spitfire*, pp. 64-68.
8. Mitchell, *R.J. Mitchell: Schooldays to Spitfire*, pp. 79–82.
9. Mitchell, *R.J. Mitchell: Schooldays to Spitfire*, p. 98.
10. Mitchell, *R.J. Mitchell: Schooldays to Spitfire*, p. 101.
11. David Curnock, *Little Book of Spitfire*, G2 Entertainment Limited, United Kingdom, 2011, pp. 16–18.
12. Mitchell, *R.J. Mitchell: Schooldays to Spitfire*, p. 102.
13. Mitchell, *R.J. Mitchell: Schooldays to Spitfire*, pp.104–109.
14. Mitchell, *R.J. Mitchell: Schooldays to Spitfire*, p. 109.
15. Mitchell, *R.J. Mitchell: Schooldays to Spitfire*, p. 113.
16. Mitchell, *R.J. Mitchell: Schooldays to Spitfire*, Appendix 8, p. 339.
17. Mitchell, *R.J. Mitchell: Schooldays to Spitfire*, p. 127.
18. Mitchell, *R.J. Mitchell: Schooldays to Spitfire*, p. 141.
19. Mitchell, *R.J. Mitchell: Schooldays to Spitfire*, p. 141.
20. Wilson, *Spitfire*, p. 12.
21. Mitchell, *R.J. Mitchell: Schooldays to Spitfire*, pp. 142–143.

22 Mitchell, *R.J. Mitchell: Schooldays to Spitfire*, pp. 142–145 and Appendix 3, p. 314.
23 Jonathan Glancey, *Spitfire: The Biography*, Atlantic Books, London, 2007, p. 39.
24 Temora Interview–Don Andrews.
25 Interview with Author–Roberts
26 Curnock, *Little Book of Spitfire*, pp. 20–29.
27 Wilson, Spitfire, p. 56.
28 Mitchell, *R.J. Mitchell: Schooldays to Spitfire*, pp. 149–150.
29 Glancey, *Spitfire: The Biography*, pp. 42–43.
30 Curnock, *Little Book of Spitfire*, pp. 32–33.
31 Martin Robson, *The Spitfire Pocket Manual*, Conway, London, 2010, p. 44.
32 Mitchell, *R.J. Mitchell: Schooldays to Spitfire*, p. 153.
33 Mitchell, *R.J. Mitchell: Schooldays to Spitfire*, Appendix 6, p. 323.
34 Mitchell, *R.J. Mitchell: Schooldays to Spitfire*, p. 236.
35 Mitchell, *R.J. Mitchell: Schooldays to Spitfire*, pp. 135–136 and 142.
36 Glancey, *Spitfire: The Biography*, p. 36.
37 Mitchell, *R.J. Mitchell: Schooldays to Spitfire*, pp. 191–195.
38 Mitchell, *R.J. Mitchell: Schooldays to Spitfire*, pp. 204 and 213.
39 Wilson, Spitfire, p 65.
40 Glancey, *Spitfire: The Biography*, p. 48.
41 Wilson, Spitfire, p. 65.
42 Curnock, *Little Book of Spitfire*, p. 50.
43 Curnock, *Little Book of Spitfire*, pp. 50–58.
44 Curnock, *Little Book of Spitfire*, p. 58.
45 Interview with Author–Roberts
46 Curnock, *Little Book of Spitfire*, pp. 61–62.
47 Wg Cdr T.F.Neil, *From the Cockpit: Spitfire*, Ian Allan Ltd, Shepperton, 1980, p. 12.
48 Neil, *From the Cockpit: Spitfire*, p. 46.
49 Curnock, *Little Book of Spitfire*, p. 71.
50 Thomas, *Spitfire Aces of Burma and the Pacific*, p. 28.
51 Martin Robson, *The Spitfire Pocket Manual*, Conway, London, 2010, p. 8.
52 Wilson, *Spitfire*, p. 15.
53 Temora Interview–Fred Cowpe.
54 Wilson, *Spitfire*, p. 15.
55 Dr Alfred Price, *Osprey Aircraft of the Aces*: Volume 5, Late Mark Spitfire Aces 1942–45, Cadmus Communications, USA, (1995), 2010, p 70.
56 Mitchell, *R.J. Mitchell: Schooldays to Spitfire*, p. 71.
57 Mitchell, *R.J. Mitchell: Schooldays to Spitfire*, p. 71.

58 File A11335 Z2-453 Crew Order Book
59 AWFA: Nat Gould
60 Dennis Newton, *Australian Air Aces*, Aerospace Publications, Fyshwick, 1996, p. 113.
61 Curnock, *Little Book of Spitfire*, p. 39.
62 Dr Alfred Price, *Aircraft of the Aces: Men & Legends, Volume 1: The Legendary Spitfire Mk I/II 1939-1941*, Del Prado, Madrid, (1996), 1999, p. 18.
63 Price, *The Legendary Spitfire Mk I/II 1939-1941*, pp. 7-8.
64 Price, *The Legendary Spitfire Mk I/II 1939-1941*, p. 10.
65 Dr Alfred Price and Tony Holmes, *Aircraft of the Aces: Men & Legends, Volume 17: RAF Aces of the Battle of Britain*, Del Prado, Madrid, (1995), 2000, pp. 45-47
66 Price and Holmes, *RAF Aces of the Battle of Britain*, p. 19.
67 Price and Holmes, *RAF Aces of the Battle of Britain*, pp. 50-52.
68 Price and Holmes, *RAF Aces of the Battle of Britain*, p. 55.
69 Interview-Joe Barrington.
70 Temora Interviews-Dick Peters and Temora Interview-Norm Swift.
71 Temora Interview-Colin Leith.
72 Price, *The Legendary Spitfire Mk I/II 1939-1941*, p. 61.
73 Curnock, *Little Book of Spitfire*, p. 40.
74 Price, *The Legendary Spitfire Mk I/II 1939-1941*, p. 21.
75 Price, *The Legendary Spitfire Mk I/II 1939-1941*, p. 46.
76 Richard C. Smith, *Hornchurch Eagles: The Life Stories of Eight of the Airfield's Distinguished WWII Fighter Pilots*, Grub Street, London, 2002, p. 145.
77 Price, *The Legendary Spitfire Mk I/II 1939-1941*, p. 46.
78 Wilson, *Spitfire*, pp. 76-77.
79 AWFA: Nat Gould
80 AWFA: Nat Gould
81 AWFA: Nat Gould
82 Neil, *From the Cockpit: Spitfire*, pp. 35-36.
83 Interview with Author-Handsaker
84 Interview with Author-Handsaker
85 Price, *The Legendary Spitfire Mk I/II 1939-1941*, p. 49.
86 Glancey, *Spitfire: The Biography*, p. 96.
87 Wilson, *Spitfire*, p. 17.
88 Neil, *From the Cockpit: Spitfire*, p. 40.
89 Curnock, *Little Book of Spitfire*, pp. 40-42.
90 Robson, *The Spitfire Pocket Manual*, p. 116.
91 Wilson, *Spitfire*, p. 16 and 80.

92 Price, Dr Alfred, Tomasz Drecki, Robert Gretzyngier and Wojtek Matusiak, *Aircraft of the Aces: Men & Legends, Volume 13: Spitfires Over the Mediterranean & North Africa*, Del Prado, Madrid, 2000, p. 9.
93 Price, et al, *Spitfires Over the Mediterranean & North Africa*, pp. 16–17.
94 Price, et al, *Spitfires Over the Mediterranean & North Africa*, pp. 24 and 37 and NAA: A5954, 23111.
95 Graham Freudenberg, *Churchill and Australia*, Pan Macmillan, Sydney, 2008, pp. 407–408.
96 Museum of Australian Democracy http://static.moadoph.gov.au/ophgovau/media/images/apmc/docs/08-Bruce-Web.pdf
97 NAA:A5954, 23111 and Freudenberg, *Churchill and Australia*, pp. 426–427.
98 Freudenberg, *Churchill and Australia*, p. 410.
99 Freudenberg, *Churchill and Australia*, p. 410.
100 Stanley, Peter, 'He's (not) Coming South' The Invasion that wasn't, in Steven Bullard and Tamura Keiko (eds.) *From a hostile shore: Australia and Japan at war in New Guinea*, viewed 1 May 2014,<http://ajrp.awm.gov.au/ajrp/ajrp2.nsf/WebI/Chapters/$file/Chapter2.pdf?OpenElement> p. 52.
101 Thomas, *Spitfire Aces of Burma and the Pacific*, pp. 6–7.
102 NAA: A1196, 1/501/474 and Thomas, *Spitfire Aces of Burma and the Pacific*, pp. 13–15.
103 Wilson, *Spitfire*, p. 92
104 Wilson, *Spitfire*, pp. 98, 128.
105 NAA: A1196, 1/501/474
106 NAA: A5954, 23111
107 NAA: A1196, 1/501/478
108 NAA: A1196, 1/501/478
109 NAA: A1196, 1/501/478
110 NAA: A5954, 23111
111 NAA: A1196, 1/501/474
112 NAA: A5954, 23111
113 NAA: A1196, 1/501/474
114 NAA: A5954, 23111 Ref CAS.34/1942 3 Sept 1942.
115 Gillison, *Australia in the War of 1939–1945, Series Three: Air Volume I: Royal Australian Air Force 1939–1942*, p. 653.
116 Price, et al, *Spitfires Over the Mediterranean & North Africa*, p. 45.
117 Glancey, *Spitfire: The Biography*, p. 108.
118 Wilson, *Spitfire*, p. 102.

119 Mitchell, *R.J. Mitchell: Schooldays to Spitfire*, Appendix 11, pp. 363–364.
120 Wilson, *Spitfire*, p. 23.
121 Dr Alfred Price, *Osprey Aircraft of the Aces*: Volume 5, Late Mark Spitfire Aces 1942–45, Cadmus Communications, USA, (1995), 2010, p. 9.
122 Price, et al, *Spitfires Over the Mediterranean & North Africa*, pp 37–39.
123 Price, *Late Mark Spitfire Aces 1942–45*, p. 13.
124 Price, *Late Mark Spitfire Aces 1942–45*, p. 20.
125 Douglas McRoberts, *Lions Rampant: The Story of 602 Spitfire Squadron*, William Kimber, London, 1985, p. 190.
126 Curnock, *Little Book of Spitfire*, p. 42.
127 Wilson, Spitfire, p.20.
128 Price, Late Mark Spitfire Aces 1942–45, p. 20.
129 Interview with Author–Roberts
130 Interview with Author–Roberts
131 AWFA: Nat Gould
132 AWFA: Nat Gould
133 Thomas, *Spitfire Aces of Burma and the Pacific*, pp. 29–30.
134 Thomas, *Spitfire Aces of Burma and the Pacific*, p. 63.
135 NAA: A11335 Z2-453 Crew Order Book
136 NAA: A11093 452/A58 Part 1
137 Cundy, Ron, A Gremlin on my shoulder, Australian Military History Publications, Loftus, 2001, (2003), p. 87.
138 Malcolm Laird, and Steve Mackenzie, Spitfire-The ANZACS, Ventura Publications, Wellington, 1997, p. 40.
139 Interview with Author – Roberts
140 Breffort, Dominique, German Fighters Volume II: Bf 110–Me 210–Me 410–Fw 190–Me 262–Me 163–He 162, Histoire & Collections, Paris, 2014, p. 10.
141 Curnock, *Little Book of Spitfire*, p. 43.
142 Robson, *The Spitfire Pocket Manual*, p. 114.
143 Wilson, Spitfire, p. 18.
144 Robson, *The Spitfire Pocket Manual*, p. 114.
145 Price, Late Mark Spitfire Aces 1942–45, p. 14.
146 Temora Interview–Don Andrews.
147 Price, Late Mark Spitfire Aces 1942–45, p. 9.
148 Mitchell, *R.J. Mitchell: Schooldays to Spitfire*, p. 214.
149 Price, Late Mark Spitfire Aces 1942–45, p. 87.
150 NAA: A11093 452/A58 Part 1

151 NAA: A11093 452/A58 Part 1
152 Robson, *The Spitfire Pocket Manual*, p. 129.
153 Price, et al, *Spitfires Over the Mediterranean & North Africa*, p. 41.
154 NAA: A11335 Z2-453 Crew Order Book.
155 NAA: A11335 Z2-453 Crew Order Book.
156 AWM Film F02557.
157 Mitchell, *R.J. Mitchell: Schooldays to Spitfire*, Appendix 9, p. 349.
158 Mitchell, *R.J. Mitchell: Schooldays to Spitfire*, Appendix 9, p. 348.
159 Logbook–Barrington
160 Interview–Barrington.
161 AWM: MSS 1952 (Bennett)
162 Curnock, *Little Book of Spitfire*, p. 44.
163 Price, Late Mark Spitfire Aces 1942–45, pp. 28–29.
164 Chris Goss with Peter Cornwell and Bernd Rauchbach, *Luftwaffe Fighter-Bombers Over Britain: The Tip and Run Campaign*, 1942–43, Stackpole Books, Mechanicsburg, 2010, pp. 15–16.
165 Glancey, *Spitfire: The Biography*, p. 111 and Wilson, Spitfire, p. 21.
166 Neil, *From the Cockpit: Spitfire*, pp 64–68.
167 NAA: A11335 Z2-453 Crew Order Book.
168 Curnock, *Little Book of Spitfire*, p. 44.
169 Price, Late Mark Spitfire Aces 1942–45, pp. 32–33.
170 Price, Late Mark Spitfire Aces 1942–45, p. 88.
171 NLA: Trove–'Powerful Spitfire' SMH 9 March 1944.
172 Wilson, Spitfire, p. 20.
173 Logbook–Handsaker.
174 Wilson, Spitfire, p. 113.
175 NAA: A11335 Z2-453 Crew Order Book.
176 NAA: A11335 Z2-453 Crew Order Book.
177 Interview with Author–Handsaker.
178 Wilson, Spitfire, p. 16.
179 Wilson, Spitfire, p. 67.
180 Herington, *Air War Against Germany & Italy 1939–1943*, pp. 31–32.
181 AWFA: Keith Campbell
182 AWFA: Keith Campbell
183 AWFA: Keith Campbell
184 AWFA: Keith Campbell
185 Wilson, Spitfire, p. 99

186 Wilson, Spitfire, p. 22.
187 Wilson, Spitfire, pp. 22–23.
188 Mitchell, *R.J. Mitchell: Schooldays to Spitfire*, Appendix 2, p. 300.
189 Temora Interviews–Sir Brian Inglis.
190 Mitchell, *R.J. Mitchell: Schooldays to Spitfire*, p. 203.
191 Mitchell, *R.J. Mitchell: Schooldays to Spitfire*, pp. 225–227.
192 http://www.oldspitalfieldsmarket.com/the-market/the-history-of-the-market and Author photo.
193 http://www.airhistory.org.uk/spitfire/p012.html
194 NAA: A2676, 1115.
195 Wilson, *Spitfire*, pp. 123–124.
196 Fred McCann letter to Mike Kerr dated 17-2-1992.
197 Robson, *The Spitfire Pocket Manual*, pp. 12–15, Glancey, *Spitfire: The Biography* pp. 221–230, NAA: A11093 452/A58 Part 1 and Wilson, *Spitfire*, pp. 21–22.

Scotland to Normandy

453 (RAAF) Squadron was reformed in Scotland, at RAF Station Drem, on 18 June 1942. The airfield was located approximately 16 miles east of Edinburgh in a relatively quiet sector of the coast. Drem was first opened in 1916 under the name of West Fenton and was expanded during the First World War before being closed in 1919. The airfield was reopened as Drem in 1939 and hosted a Flying Training School. The first operational squadron based at Drem in the Second World War was 602 Squadron in their Spitfire Mk Is, commencing operations there in October 1939.[1] 602 and 453 Squadrons would have much more in common by the war's end.

The officer appointed to lead this new Australian Spitfire squadron was S/Ldr Francis Morello. After the first eight Mk VB Spitfires were delivered on 23 June and checked out by the ground crew, flying commenced on 26 June. Six of the aircraft were new, so hours were brought up on the aircraft at an uneven rate so that they would not all require major services at the same time. When the weather was poor the squadron had lectures or practised on the Link trainer, an enclosed and very basic flight simulator.[2] Hours spent on the Link trainer still went into a pilot's log book and were sometimes listed separately in the back so as not to be mistakenly counted towards actual flying hours.[3] Drem was an easy enough start for any squadron, located as it was away from the action of the southeast of England, but the landscape was terrible, with the landing approach obstructed by a hill, resulting in many accidents especially for those squadrons with new and inexperienced pilots.[4]

Pilots from Australia, Canada and Rhodesia arrived in the UK fully trained for flying but, without special instruction on specific types of aircraft flown in their new squadrons, the high accident rate of newly-arrived pilots necessitated a refresher course to be carried out before further advancement in pilot training. From early on, pilots had to spend a few weeks back in Tiger Moths to get them in the right mindset and practising their flying skills, which had dropped off somewhat on the sometimes very long voyages from their previous training locations, especially Australia.[5]

The first pilots and other officers allocated to the squadron were:

Nationality	Names
British	S/Ldr F.V.Morello, F/Lt Campbell-Colquhoun P/O J.A. Abbott (Adjutant), P/O Carey-Browton (Engineer officer), F/O W.E. Chapman (Medical Officer).
Polish	F/O O. Sobiecki, F/O G. Schmidt, P/O T Jankowski
Canadian	F/Lt G.U. Hill
Australian	F/Lt J.R. Cock DFC (enlisted in the RAF), P/O J.Barrien, P/O A.G.B Blumer, P/O R.J. Darcey, P/O R.H.S. Ewins, P/O D.M Fowler, P/O D.J. Reid, P/O C.G Riley, P/O T.A. Swift, P/O F.T Thornley F/Sgt A.E. Batchelor, F/Sgt Clemesha, F/Sgt M.H.I de Cosier, F/Sgt J.H. Ferguson, F/Sgt R.C Ford, F/Sgt J.R. Furlong, F/Sgt F.K Halcombe, F/Sgt L.J. Hansell, F/Sgt C.R. Leith, F/Sgt B.T. Nossiter, F/Sgt H.M. Parker, F/Sgt G.J. Stansfield, F/Sgt D.H. Steele, F/Sgt W.W. Waldron, F/Sgt W.J White, F/Sgt G.J. Whiteford

There were no Australian ground crew in the squadron at the time[6]—all were RAF, many posted in from 154 Squadron[7].

All the officers were experienced and ready to teach their new Australian pilots how things were done. It was common practice to post experienced RAF pilots to new squadrons in order to build the team up for operations, as had been done with 452 and 457 Squadrons in 1941.[8] When those two squadrons were sent to Australia, 453 was the only Australian fighter squadron in the UK and they could not absorb all the Australian fighter pilots being trained. Therefore these additional pilots were posted to whichever squadron needed pilots. In 1942 alone, 240 Australians served various lengths of time with 51 different fighter squadrons in the UK.[9]

When Colin Russell 'Rusty' Leith (Service no. 411790) finished his OTU, he only flew training flights before being posted to 453. He'd passed his EFTS in Australia and Service Flying Training School (SFTS) in Canada, and now he was in an operational fighter squadron.[10] He rated the presentation of his wings in Canada as the greatest moment in his life. Unfortunately that day also saw the burial of two pilots before they were granted theirs. It would not be the last military funeral Rusty would have to attend.[11] There was training, and now there was the reality of life on a squadron, and it was the experienced pilots—such as the Poles—who would be teaching him and the others how to survive in the air. He'd accumulated 250 flying hours in a year of training and now things were really developing:

> We did more training there, more flying, more formation, more air to air, more air to ground and generally, gradually worked ourselves up to be operational condition.[12]

As there were not enough Australian fighter squadrons in the UK to take on all the Australian pilots being trained, Rusty was lucky to be posted to 453 and wrote home about it:

> I don't know whether I told you or not that I am on an Australian squadron. You can imagine how pleased I was when I heard the news at OTU. There are a few 'foreigners' in the squadron, who are more or less teaching us.[13]

Bonding took place fairly quickly, the new pilots had similar levels of experience and, apart from flying together, they played sports and took trips to Edinburgh in small groups. They met some of the local Scots, and even went out shooting grouse on the moors with some of the more well-to-do members of society. They didn't always hit their targets but they had the concept of deflection shooting down pat, so it was just a matter of practice. The Poles were tough and didn't get too close to the new pilots—presumably they'd seen enough of others being shot down in quick time and weren't going to try and develop bonds only to have them broken.[14] They weren't being unkind, it was just a method of preserving their feelings to prevent them being worn down too quickly.

Rusty got his nickname from boarding school. His given name was Colin, but since that was his father's name, his middle name, Russell, was most often used to avoid confusion. However, Russell was a bit of a tongue twister for the youngsters starting out at school, and so it was converted into Rusty.[15] He was born to Australian parents on 5 May 1922 in Fiji, where his father worked as an estate manager for CSR. Though his first school was in Fiji, much of his later schooling was in Australia. Rusty signed up for the RAAF in 1940 but, like so many others, was told to come back later: there were simply too many volunteers and the system could not cope. To get into academic shape for his training, he attended one of the many schools set up to run pre-enlistment courses in morse code and other military-related subjects.[16] When he returned in 1941, Rusty was posted to 8 EFTS at Narrandera and, after graduating, was sent to Camp Borden, Ontario, Canada.[17] After training on Yales he was sent across the Atlantic, arriving in Scotland on 29 March 1942 and receiving a posting to an Advanced Flying Unit (AFU) at Tern Hill.[18]

F/Lt Cock had flown Hurricanes in the Battle for France and later the Battle of Britain and was awarded his DFC in October 1940. He had shot down seven German planes and had to bail out three times.[19]

Colin Russell 'Rusty' Leith, one of the first pilots to be posted to the reformed 453 Squadron. (Courtesy of the Leith family)

Most of the pilots in 453 Squadron were transferred direct from OTUs, but the story of Flight Sergeant (F/Sgt) Ron Ford deserves attention. It has often been said that anyone who refuses to admit they're scared when participating in combat operations is a liar, but admitting you're scared was more than just frowned upon at the time. Prior to being posted to 453 Squadron, Ford had served with 457 (RAAF) Squadron. He was one of many from the banking industry who found themselves flying Spitfires, and had served some time with the Sydney University Regiment prior to enlisting in the RAAF. His posting to this new squadron came about in a very interesting way. On 18 May 1942, when holding the rank of Sergeant, he wrote a letter to a friend in which he recounted an escort sortie during which his squadron were jumped by FW-190s. Unfortunately, in the letter, Ford revealed that the squadron was based at Redhill, and gave details of the sortie. He also admitted that he was scared. This letter was intercepted and brought to the attention of the Station Commander. Ford was immediately interviewed in the presence of his Squadron Leader and was temporarily removed from the Squadron and posted to Shoreham airfield as Duty Pilot. A report was called for from his Commanding Officer (CO) and the squadron Medical Officer.[20]

A file was created, and an investigation commenced which dragged on for several months. The Australians saw it as a case of mishandling by the RAF, though did place some blame for the matter at the feet of Ford for breaking the rules regarding censorship. However, on numerous occasions, the file stressed that the circumstances were not those which should lead to Ford being regarded as a 'waverer'. Perhaps this was a formal term for coward, or perhaps just someone not suited to combat operations, but at no time did Ford lose the confidence of his CO. As mentioned above, it saw him posted to 453 Squadron shortly after its reformation in Scotland. There he was assessed by the then CO, S/Ldr Morello, who was obliged to report on

Sergeant Ron Ford during his time with 457 (RAAF) Squadron.
(AWM SUK10031)

the matter and responded that Ford possessed 'marked capabilities' but that he also 'showed a lack of enthusiasm'. Morello also stated in another file that Ford had 'improved beyond all recognition'.[21]

Not satisfied with this report, Fighter Command deemed these comments to be contradictory, and the file notes that S/Ldr Morello was perceived to be a poor judge of his pilots. When S/Ldr Jack Ratten took over 453 in November 1942 Ford was reassessed and found to be not classified as a 'W'.[22] Ratten wrote that, while Ford presented as a nervous person, it should really have been attributed to his shyness. His file records favourable comments by Ratten, but the Group Captain recorded that Ford was 'rather reserved' and needed to be 'brought out' a little. The dreaded 'W' was superseded by the even more dreaded LMF (Lack of Moral Fibre, otherwise known as cowardice) and the file recorded that he was grounded for this specific reason and would not be reconsidered for promotion until he had proven that he had gotten over his fear.[23]

Ford was passed over for consideration for commission, but did attain the rank of Warrant Officer on 27 July 1942. On 15 April 1943 Ford was recommended for a Commission by S/Ldr Ratten, which was supported by the AVM Commanding No 11 Group (RAF). He received his promotion to Pilot Officer in June 1943 (backdated to 15 April) but on a probationary term, and was confirmed at the rank of Flying Officer on 15 October that year. In his written statement at the very beginning of the matter, Ford stated that he thought it had all come about because he was honest enough to admit that he was scared. He also stated that, given time and experience he would get over this and be the best he could be.[24] Surely these are entirely sensible feelings for a combat pilot during wartime, but keeping it to yourself and getting on with the job was the preferred method of dealing with it. Talking about your feelings was not encouraged and, while many others may have felt the same way, he was indeed punished for his honesty.

Operations carried out by the RAF during the post-Battle of Britain period went by a number of codenames such as Circus, Rhubarb, Ramrod, Roadstead and Rodeo. When the V-1 threat materialised, operations against these sites were codenamed Noball. 453 Squadron participated in all these types of operations during the war.

Circus: An operation by bombers or fighter-bombers escorted by fighters and designed to bait the Luftwaffe into combat.

Rhubarb: Small scale fighter attacks on ground targets, such as trains.

Ramrod: An operation smaller than a Circus but with the intention of destroying a ground target. Cannon-armed fighters (such as Westland Whirlwinds) could be substituted for bombers.

Roadstead: An operation to escort bombers on attacks against shipping.

Rodeo: A fighter sweep without bombers.[25]

While popular with some in providing the opportunity for engaging with the enemy, and somewhat necessary to provide pilots with operational experience, these operations launched across the Channel were frequently criticised, both at the time and after the war, for being wasteful. W/Cdr Tom Neil, who led some of these operations and flew Spitfires, said: 'ridiculous forays resulted in the deaths of countless gallant and experienced pilots who were sacrificed with very little to show for their efforts'.[26] However, they also provided ongoing reconnaissance over enemy territory, minimised the opportunity for enemy reconnaissance and provided inexperienced pilots with practice in mass formation flying.[27]

Much time during the first weeks at Drem were spent on sports and training, the relatively new pilots practising formation flying and air-to-air firing using a drogue towed by a Lysander. Once the correct equipment arrived, a Spitfire was also used to tow the drogue. Ink was used to colour the rounds fired so they could be counted on the drogue, and each drogue could be targeted by three pilots in a training sequence.[28] Dogfighting tactics and cine-gun training was also carried out, and slowly all the pilots began to increase their confidence and hours flown. As the squadron developed, experienced officers were posted in to take command of the Flights, but they did not always stay long, as in the case of F/Lt Cock DFC who requested a transfer to night fighters. It is interesting to note that three of these initial experienced officers were Polish.[29]

From 10 July 1942 onwards, the squadron provided readiness sections, aircraft ready to take off at a moment's notice to intercept any target they were directed to. They shared this task with 242 Squadron, but on a ratio of 1:3 owing to their level of (in)experience, though the work was shared evenly from 21 July. Navigation in the UK was much more difficult for those trained in Australia than those trained in the UK and this was something pilots had to become accustomed to very quickly. Back in Australia, flying schools were generally in country areas, with few roads and railway lines, in fact there might only be one. This allowed a pilot to navigate with these few landmarks, as they were quite distinct and maps were of a much larger scale. However, in the UK, there were a lot more terrain features, roads, railway lines and villages with the maps at a much smaller scale.[30] Without the luxury of a training area free of the enemy and the ability to cruise around the skies, a pilot had to be on the ball from the moment they took off. Sid Handsaker (451 Squadron) recalled that, in England:

> ... everything is compacted and all the towns were all together, you don't know where you are, and by the time you look down and make up your mind you're in it, you're out of it. They used to do what they called the 'iron compass', the main railway lines were picked out. So you would find planes going to the left of the railway line and planes going to the left of the railway line coming the other way, so they each kept to the left so we didn't prang one another.[31]

Norman Francis Swift (Service no. 411404) arrived at the end of July, yet another inexperienced Australian, but with over 70 hours on Spitfires in his logbook.³² Before enlisting in April 1941 Norm was a clerk in Sydney. By late June he was at 10 EFTS (Temora) and on 10 July he went solo after 12 hours and 15 minutes on the DH-82 Tiger Moth. He passed out of 10 EFTS with a 'Just Average' comment in his logbook then went overseas to continue training in Canada, his posting being 14 SFTS at Aylmer, Ontario.³³ There he flew Harvards from October 1941 to February 1942 before being shipped to the UK, commencing training at 17 AFU Watton, Norfolk in May on the Master II. Next stop was 53 OTU at Llandow in South Wales where he first flew a Spitfire, (an older Mk I) on 26 May 1942.

The squadron's first loss occurred on 1 August 1942 when Flying

Norm Swift in a photo taken in late 1944.
(AWM UK2041)

Officer (F/O) Charles Riley crashed in a Mk VB (EN774) while on a flight to practise aerobatics above cloud. He was seen to spin through cloud from 15,000 ft and crash into a farmhouse at Cairns Place farm near Ansruther, near the town of Crail. A formal investigation took place but no reason for the crash could be found. Evidence was called from a number of Engineering Officers, squadron pilots and ground crew. S/Ldr Morello stated in his evidence that he had been 'more than satisfied' with the quality of workmanship of the maintenance of aircraft by the ground crew. He also stated that while some things had been carried out slowly, this was due to a lack of parts and not a lack of ability. Evidence was also provided stating that pilots had regular discussions in relation to aircraft handling etc., and therefore no accusation of lack of education or awareness could be levelled. This evidence was provided by Campbell-Colquhoun, Darcey and Leith (Darcey and Leith being two pilots chosen at random from those available). Sgt Steele, who had been partnered with Riley, had returned early when his canopy had blown off. This was assessed as a material defect, not due to poor maintenance. One witness near the farm stated that the Spitfire appeared to be in a spin and that the engine had cut out, the noise heard at the time implying that the pilot was attempting to restart it. The investigation concluded that the pilot had gone into a spin, and then entered a flat spin. To get out of this, the pilot attempted to enter a regular spin which all pilots are well trained in escaping, but the height was not sufficient to achieve this and, due to inexperience, the crash followed. A later re-investigation came to the same conclusion: pilot error.[34] Riley's remains (and some extra material to make up the weight of a body for the coffin, not uncommon) were buried at Leuchars on 4 August and the funeral was attended by a piper and many members of the squadron. Reality hit the squadron hard, life as a pilot wasn't just about telling all the girls you met that you flew a Spitfire.[35]

F/Lt J.R. Ratten (Service no. 405111) took over 'A' Flight on 4 August and the first Australian ground crew, led by Sgt Woods, arrived the following day. John Richard Ratten was born in Tasmania in 1912 and joined the RAAF in Hobart on 31 January 1941, aged 28 and armed with a qualification as a mining engineer. He was posted to 1 Initial Training School (ITS) at Somers and learned to fly at 7 EFTS Western Junction before moving on to 2 SFTS at Wagga Wagga. He departed Sydney for the UK on 16 October 1941 and flew Spitfires with 72 Squadron at Biggin Hill from February to August 1942 before being posted to 453 Squadron. Like many of his generation, Item 12 on his Personal Record of Service Form (Nationality) was stamped 'BRITISH'.[36]

Air Chief Marshal Sir Sholto Douglas arrived on 8 August for an inspection, but the poor weather prevented any showing off in the air. The second casualty for the squadron—though not a fatal one—occurred on 11 August when F/Sgt Gerald Whiteford crash landed his Mk VB Spitfire (BL941) in a field after losing oil pressure over the sea. He was in a section of three practising attacks on another section of three when the emergency occurred. Luckily, he made landfall, but could not reach the airfield. Fearing being trapped and burned upon landing, Whiteford jettisoned his hood, took off his flying helmet, undid his harness and was ejected when the Spitfire crashed into a stone wall and he 'landed on his head on a heap of stones'. He had a slight concussion and fortunately required only two stitches for a scalp injury.[37] Investigation of the wreckage showed that the aircraft had suffered a crankshaft bearing failure, which had resulted in significant vibration in the engine and a drop in oil pressure. However, it was not determined if there had been engine failure, or if the pilot had simply used excessive boost and revs in flight. Whiteford returned to the squadron after a week in hospital.[38]

On 12 August 1942, two sections were scrambled in the afternoon after two enemy aircraft. This was the first operational flight for the reformed 453. Ron Ford in BL445 had to turn back due to radio/telephone (R/T) trouble and a number of pilots watched what they thought was a Beaufighter follow him down. It was, however, a Ju-88 which dropped eight bombs on the airfield—fortunately causing no damage. The following day saw the departure of the very experienced F/Lt Hill and on 14 August was the first visit by the press, resulting in a number of newspaper articles.[39] Because the weather was good, the squadron was able to put on a flying display and the reporters stayed for dinner in the mess and talked to many of the pilots, though some were reluctant to be interviewed. An article announcing the formation of two new Australian squadrons in Scotland (one fighter and one torpedo-bomber) appeared in the *Brisbane Courier-Mail* on 19 August, S/Ldr Morello quoted as saying the Australians were 'particularly promising'. While the squadron number was not disclosed, it was described as the third Australian Spitfire squadron to be formed.[40] Proud of their local contribution, the *Newcastle Morning Herald and Miners' Advocate* singled out 21-year-old James Humphrey Ferguson, son of a local bank manager, for praise at his posting to the new fighter squadron.[41]

Having been operational for only a very short time and with so many inexperienced pilots, 453 Squadron was left out of operations covering the Dieppe raid, but their aircraft were loaned to 222 Squadron for a number of days. On their return, all aircraft were given a full service, and flying and training resumed.

On 28 August, there was another squadron fatality when David Steele dived vertically into the ground near the town of Garbald while on a dogfighting exercise with Rusty Leith. There was no apparent attempt to pull out.[42] Steele had been flying with Riley earlier in the month when Riley crashed, and this time was flying Spitfire VB – 'D' (BM647) in company with Rusty Leith in 'J'. The aircraft had been fully checked out and all documents accounted for. A number of ground crew gave statements as to the airworthiness of the aircraft including the checking and replacement of the oxygen system which was three-quarters to seven-eighths full and that the supply was turned on at the bottle, the pilot having been advised of this. Evidence was also taken from a pilot who had used the aircraft in the days beforehand. Again, Rusty Leith was called to give evidence and stated that they climbed to 20,000 ft, at which time he performed a number of turns, in order to keep the airfield in sight. During these manoeuvres Steele slowly dropped back and Leith lost sight of him and assumed that he had taken up a line astern formation. Leith climbed to 30,000 ft and once at that altitude he performed a number of turns. After a few minutes he called up Steele on the R/T but there was no response. Having advised Steele he was going to dive, Leith did so and levelled out at 12,000 ft and performed a number of turns but Steele was not to be seen. He could not be raised by the ground controller either. Leith hadn't seen him in difficulties nor had he heard him on the R/T making any complaints, so he didn't suspect anything at the time. Leith landed and the investigation commenced. Examination at the crash site showed wreckage spread out over a 200m radius from the impact, the engine having exploded on impact with the ground.[43] Considering the event later on, Rusty Leith came to the conclusion that it was possible Steele had forgotten to turn his oxygen on (at the mask), and had slowly been starved of oxygen as the aircraft climbed their way towards 30,000 ft.[44]

During the month, the squadron scrambled a few times to intercept incoming aircraft and carried out convoy patrols usually of 60–90 minutes duration. On 5 September, S/Ldr Morello was married in London and only one of the Polish pilots attended to represent the squadron, as the distance to travel was too great—due to wartime restrictions—for more to attend.

Pilot Officer (P/O) John William Yarra, DFM (Service no. 402823) joined the squadron on 10 September, greatly adding to its level of experience.[45] 'Slim' Yarra was born in Stanthorpe, Queensland on 21 August 1921 and was a cadet printer and journalist in Armidale (where Rusty Leith went to school) when he signed up in October 1940. He completed his SFTS in Canada before being sent to the UK and was posted to 232 Squadron in October 1941. He later flew with 64 Squadron from Malta in February 1942, then 185 Squadron on Hurricanes before they converted to Spitfires. He also flew with 249 and 126 Squadrons on Spitfire Vs and became an ace while defending the beleaguered island. He was then posted back to the UK and to 453 Squadron. His citation for this Distinguished Flying Medal read:

> Has shot down four enemy aircraft (in) air battles. One occasion when protecting rescue launch in face [of] numerous enemy aircraft shot down one Messerschmitt probably destroyed another. When ammunition exhausted made feint attacks and kept enemy at bay three quarters [of an] hour.[46]

On 16 September, Jack Ratten returned to the squadron after a month-long gunnery course and promptly shredded a number of drogues, humbling a few pilots who, until then, thought they'd been doing quite well. On 21 September, the squadron was advised that they would be moved to Gravesend, but this was changed to Hornchurch (located east of London and north of the Thames) on the 22nd. Of course a party was held in the mess and money was laid down for drinking bets. The squadron diary records that Alexander Blumer 'failed miserably' in his attempt to drink a gallon of beer during the evening, but Russ Ewins won his bet of drinking half a gallon in half an hour and he 'cleaned up nicely'. All aircraft and crew arrived at Hornchurch by 26 September, and they gratefully exchanged their Mk VBs for IXs, taking over those of 64 Squadron.[47]

The squadron was then ordered to move to Southend for Operation 'Aflame' on 2 October, which involved attacks by a number of bomber squadrons covered by mass fighter sweeps. They put up eleven aircraft, led by Jack Ratten in BL516, and patrolled the area from Ostend to Ypres, then Dunkirk at 28,000 ft as high cover. While they saw a number of enemy aircraft and dogfights, they were not involved in any. They returned safely, and on 6 October carried out a shipping sweep at just 500 ft on the route Boulogne to Dieppe then Cap Gris Nez but returned without having engaged any enemy.[48] The squadron returned to Hornchurch on 9 October and performed a number of convoy patrols.

The proximity of the squadron to London made it easy for the pilots and ground crew to visit by train, and Rusty Leith and Bob Clemesha went a number of times, to visit the Boomerang Club (where they were almost guaranteed to meet someone they knew), go shopping, see movies, and attend dances.[49] Australians were considered a little exotic by many of the English, despite otherwise obviously close ties. One conversation between Jim Ferguson and a young boy at the movies was recounted by Rusty Leith in a letter home:

Boy:	You're Australians aren't you?
Jim:	Yes.
Boy:	There are both friendly and unfriendly natives in Australia, aren't there?
Jim:	Yes.
Boy:	But you're the friendly kind aren't you?
Jim:	Yes.
	A little later on I [Leith] said to him: 'What language do you think they talk in Australia?'
Boy:	I don't know. Do they talk the same as the English?
Jim:	What the hell do you think we are talking?[50]

On the afternoon of 11 October 1942, the squadron was returning from a fighter sweep and noticed they were being tailed by six FW-190s. All the aircraft were weaving in an effort to present a difficult target to any surprise attackers and to keep the best view possible to either side and behind them when F/Sgt Alan Menzies in AB792 and P/O Bennet Nossiter in AD298 collided. Menzies' Spitfire cut Nossiter's in half just behind the cockpit and tore off his own wing. Nossiter's Spitfire was not seen again, but Menzies went into a flat spin and took some time to hit the ocean, about five miles off Deal. No parachutes were seen and it was thought that both may have been knocked unconscious by the collision. Menzies had perhaps one month more operational experience than Nossiter,[51] but, with both of them weaving and looking for the enemy perhaps more than each other, it was an added danger to that presented by the FW-190s. The bodies of the two pilots were never recovered, but they could not be immediately declared deceased—they first had to be listed as 'Missing presumed killed'. Only when a letter was received by the Air Force from the family, stating that they 'have received no further news (of your son) since the date when he became missing'[52] could they be declared deceased. The final declaration of Menzies' and Nossiters' presumed deaths was not made until May 1943. An investigation into the incident determined that such violent weaving was unnecessary unless the aircraft were actually under attack. Jack Ratten was informed of this finding so it could be passed on to the rest of the squadron, lest it happen again.[53]

So, in four months of flying, the squadron had lost four pilots, all to accidents. One pilot was also scrambled to intercept an enemy aircraft that turned out to be a Spitfire and, as the aircraft was approaching head-on, recognition was difficult at the very high closing speeds. Fearing that he was being engaged by an enemy pilot in a head-on attack, the Australian pilot fired, but did not down the Spitfire. It would not be the last encounter 453 Squadron had with what is very misleadingly called 'friendly fire'. On 12 October the squadron acted as escort to Whirlwind fighter-bombers (sometimes called Whirlibombers) but the E-boat targets were not sighted and all returned safely.[54] Patrols were uneventful for the next week or so, though on 22 October, three FW-190s that had just dropped bombs on Deal were spotted by a patrol but could not be caught in time.

The Luftwaffe had commenced its hit and run campaign (much like the RAF Rhubarbs) in March 1942, starting with modified Me-109s and converting to FW-190s in mid-June. The raids would come across the Channel at low level to avoid radar, much like the RAF did travelling in the opposite direction. Spitfire Vs and Allison-engined Mustangs were no match for the Focke-Wulfs and so five Typhoon squadrons were sent to the southern sectors where the raids were occurring in an attempt to counter them, the Typhoons being more suited to low-level work in any case. These Typhoons also had black and white identification markings on the nose and underneath the wings, so there would be less chance of being attacked by other RAF aircraft. Spitfire Mk XIIs were also sent as they became operational, their Griffon engines giving them an edge over the Merlin-equipped Mk Vs. The Luftwaffe raids targeted a whole range of locations, but had a primary goal of terrorising the British population, and so included targets ranging from gas facilities, hotels and strangely enough, herds of sheep. Some were described as reprisal raids for attacks by Bomber Command but the two could hardly be compared. By the end of June 1943, the Luftwaffe units were withdrawn from France and moved to Italy where they were needed most.[55] The period saw a number of RAF memos issued in relation to these operations. One memo, dated 31 July 1943, warned pilots of returning over the coast at heights less than 1,000 ft, this being the free-fire zone for anti-aircraft guns. As the high closing rate of aircraft approaching at low heights over the coast gave gunners little time to accurately identify their targets, anything flying at less than 1,000 ft was fair game. Indeed, anything below 500 ft approaching from seaward could be fired on prior to any identification.[56]

On 27 October 1942, the squadron took advantage of low cloud and launched a two-plane Rhubarb. Jack Yarra and Lionel Hansell headed across the Channel to Ostend with the intention of doing some strafing in Bruges. When they reached the Belgian coast the weather was clear and, with no clouds to escape into or launch a surprise attack from, they instead did a coastal sweep but no shipping was noted.

The last day of the month saw a number of coastal patrols and the loss of James Furlong. Rusty Leith in EN914 and Furlong in BL923 took off at 1455 for a convoy patrol as Yellow Section, 1 and 2 respectively. About 1525 Furlong called up with engine trouble. He was asked if he needed an escort and replied that he could make Manston. Leith flew S-turns to keep pace with Furlong but after one turn straightened out to see Furlong dive straight down into the Channel from 500 ft with white smoke pouring from the plane. There was no radio message or call for help. Leith immediately called mayday and launches set off from the convoy and went to the crash site but found only two small pieces of wreckage, no plane, no pilot. It was thought that perhaps the plane had stalled, being unable to maintain a glide back to land, or that Furlong had been overcome by glycol fumes and had passed out.[57]

That afternoon, the squadron engaged a large number of enemy aircraft sent across the Channel to attack Canterbury. The raid was made up of fighters and fighter-bombers from several Luftwaffe units including ZG 2, JG 2 and JG 26, though some records make no mention of the Ju-88 bombers also present.[58] 453 Squadron was operating in sections of two, with a relief taking place just as a call came over the R/T: 'There are hundreds of the bastards coming. For Christ's sake send somebody out'. All pilots from 453 engaged the enemy with enthusiasm and perhaps more than a little desperation. Green Section (Swift and Blumer) engaged some FW-190s and Ju-88s near Deal and broke up the formation, that being about all they could do, though they fired into the mass of bombers. Norm Swift had two FW-190s on his tail so into the clouds he went, the sky being too full of the Luftwaffe to simply try to outfly them. He had fired on a Ju-88 going through the formation and, though he didn't see it go down, he claimed it as damaged, being very proud to have made the first combat claim by 453— even more so because he was a Sergeant Pilot, and not an officer.[59] Norm recorded in his logbook:

> Spotted 40+ (JU88s + FW190s) crossing at Deal heading towards Canterbury. Lost green 1 + attacked JU88. Had 30 (JU88s + FW190s) to myself. Broke off attack on JU88's was jumped by 190's claim 1—JU88's damaged. Jeff Galway shot down but bailed out OK. Jim Furlong bought it same day. Engine failure and dived into channel.[60]

Black Section (Ewins and de Cosier) engaged two FW-190s that were headed back across the Channel and, though they fired on them, the range was too great and they couldn't make any claims.

Red Section (Galwey and Barrien) attacked a formation (one of three sections of FW-190s totalling about 40 aircraft between them) despite that group having a height advantage and Geoffrey Galwey was shot down, leaving John Barrien alone and hopelessly outnumbered, so he wisely returned to base. Once he realised that he couldn't control his aircraft any longer, Galwey prepared to bail out and felt a sudden jolt, which he thought was the plane hitting the water. He recovered from this and though very low, bailed out. He deployed his parachute just a few seconds before hitting the water and was somehow uninjured. He had trouble with his parachute and dinghy and found his knife useful in cutting himself free.[61] Spitfire pilots (and presumably others) were advised to carry a knife as sometimes the CO_2 bottle that was used to inflate the dinghy could go off and, to put it mildly, that could really upset a pilot in flight! Sid Handsaker of 451 Squadron had a knife sent to him by one of his brothers back in Australia and carried it with him on every sortie.[62]

Galwey made it into his dinghy and paddled for hours, trying to make his way back to shore but lost one paddle and found that his torch worked for only a few minutes. The sea was rough and he became seasick and didn't eat any of the survival pack, though wished for some water, even just to wash his mouth out with. During the night there was a crash nearby but he didn't investigate. He was seasick, cold and thirsty and not equipped to rescue someone else. He saw a light whilst paddling and steered for the buoy but missed it and later found another. This time he was successful and tied his dinghy to it at about 0500. He tried to keep warm by jumping up and down, and found that he quickly became bored, so instead danced the Charleston, though he was interrupted from time to time by the foghorn on the buoy. At daylight he was rescued by an Air-Sea Rescue (ASR) launch and taken to RAF Hawkinge to dry out. By 10am he was on the phone asking to be picked up.[63]

S/Ldr Morello had been ill with bronchitis[64] for some time and was not expected to return to a flying position so, on 1 November 1942, Jack Ratten was promoted to Acting S/Ldr to take his place. This was the first time that squadron's flying staff had been entirely made up of Australians.[65] His regular plane was 'F', the higher ranks in the squadron usually having their 'own' plane, while the lower ranks shared. His Spitfire had the name *Shangri-La* on it along with the stick figure drawing of 'The Saint' from detective stories of the time and, underneath that, the name *Tikkie*, his wife's nickname.[66]

In the first few days of November, the weather was generally poor. A convoy patrol was carried out, though a Rhubarb had to be abandoned when fair weather was encountered on the far side of the Channel. A sweep to St Omer on 6 November proved unprofitable and another to Felixstowe, Dunkirk and Gravelines on the 8th produced the same result. During this first week F/Lt Kelvin Barclay, was posted in to be flight commander of 'A' Flight. For the next few days the weather continued to be poor, and time was spent on the Link trainer and watching instructional films, though the squadron diary noted that 'London is only ¾ hour away and the bar here is open from time to time'.

During this time, the squadron lost two pilots to other squadrons: Whiteford was swapped to 129 Squadron, and Waldon to 131 Squadron. However, two men were gained in exchange, one of whom was P/O E.A.R Esau (Service no. 405473). Ernest Arthur Roy Esau was a business manager when he enlisted on 31 March 1941. He passed his EFTS in Australia and moved on to Camp Borden, Canada to complete his SFTS. He passed through 57 OTU at Eshott before being posted to 129 Squadron in July 1942 where he remained until his posting to 453.[67]

Once the weather improved, there were convoy patrols and night flying, though one crash at night was blamed on the duty pilot magically 'winding down' the airfield, causing P/O Reid to think that at 30 feet above ground he had landed. He was fine, not so the plane.

On 17 November, the experience of the squadron was boosted with the arrival of P/O Fred McCann (Service no. 402129), formerly a clerk in Hobart[68] but most importantly, formerly of 452 Squadron. He had flown with 452 Squadron for 7 months from May to December 1941, in the company of such pilots as Keith 'Bluey' Truscott and 'Paddy' Finucane. Finucane had actually saved McCann's life on 27 August 1941. On that day, the sortie to St Omer had included a rendezvous with bombers but it was not made, and the squadron proceeded to St Omer without them. When he spotted Me-109s diving on them from behind as the squadron was near Dunkirk, McCann tried to call a warning but his R/T was out of action and a dogfight developed with what he estimated to be about one hundred Me-109s. He was nearly shot down by one of the first bursts but, after relying on the Spitfire's tight turn to get him out of trouble, saw that somehow the sky seemed to be empty. Looking around, he saw a formation heading to England and went down to join them but they turned out to be Me-109s and they turned and attacked him. He dove from 28,000 ft down to 10,000 ft, turning into attacks to cut them off when he saw them coming and straightening out when he could to maintain his speed, but even though a Spitfire could out-turn an Me-109, it could not out-dive one, and he couldn't shake them. He continued down past 10,000 ft and found himself at almost sea level and, as he turned to avoid another attack, he looked over his shoulder to see the 109 unable to make the turn, as expected. What he didn't expect was to see the 109's cockpit shattered under cannon fire. Down into the Channel it went, and Paddy Finucane and Ray Thorold-Smith went flashing by. McCann turned after them and, still behind, continued to dodge 109s as they chased him back to the White Cliffs of Dover. He made it, too low over the Channel to even bother measuring in feet, and landed safely—if shakily—at Kenley.[69] A few days before that sortie, on 9 August, Fred's had been one of many aircraft carrying out searches for a dingy thought to contain Douglas Bader, the famous ace who had actually been shot down over land, but on the wrong side of the Channel. Some years after the war, Bader visited Hobart and met Fred, signing his logbook on the page containing the entry for his dingy search. As if this wasn't enough, while carrying out duties as a flying instructor at RAF College SFTS Fred had instructed none other than Pierre Clostermann,[70] who, as a pilot in 602 Squadron, later flew with 453 Squadron over Normandy. After the war Clostermann wrote a number of books, the most famous being *Le Grand Cirque* (The Big Show).

Fred McCann (directly under nose cone in mae-west), in his days with 452 Squadron in Great Britain. 'Paddy' Finucane is fourth from left and 'Bluey' Truscott is second from right, both with mae-wests. (AWM SUK15118)

Over the next few days there were shipping patrols and an aborted Rhubarb followed by bad weather and, on 24 November 1942, the squadron moved to Martlesham for an air firing course. Lack of action (and flying hours, for that matter) were blamed on the poor weather and, apart from the commissioning of a number of the Flight Sergeants, nothing of interest occurred for the rest of the month.[71] Alex Blumer perhaps found these early few months with 453 not as exciting as he had hoped and, in November 1942, applied for a transfer to the Middle East. After passing through various personnel camps, he found his place in 601 (County of London)

Squadron, again flying Spitfires. He participated in a number of operations and was slightly injured when shot down on 24 January 1944 over the Allied beachhead at Anzio. He was later posted home to Australia where he joined 452 (RAAF) Squadron in the Pacific at Morotai. Interestingly, during his time in the Middle East and Mediterranean theatres he accrued over an hour flying experience in an Italian Macchi 202.[72]

Until 6 December 1942, the squadron continued at the air firing course and recorded the highest average score ever achieved. Norm Swift, then just a Flight Sergeant, broke the record for the highest individual score, shooting the entire drogue away on two occasions and scoring 130 hits on another.[73] While they were away, the squadron was moved and so flew to Southend where they reunited with their ground crew and the first patrol was flown three days later. However there was one other thing to resolve before anyone took off: who nearby had a rugby team they could play against?[74] The men of 453 made a favourable impression at Hornchurch during their stay, W/Cdr Kilmartin (RAF), a veteran of the fighting in France and the Battle of Britain stating 'The Australian pilots were excellent, they were very game ...'[75]

The squadron participated in a sweep across the Channel with 122 Squadron, who had the benefit of being equipped with Spitfire IXs. As 453 carried out the sweep, 122 stayed up-sun in order to bounce any German fighters that attacked 453, but no engagement took place.[76]

On 10 December, a large patrol took off at 1100 for a shipping patrol. Coming in right at sea level, the patrol sighted a small convoy of merchant ships and a single flak ship of 700 – 1,000 tons proceeding in line astern about 10 miles off Flushing. The Spitfires crossed the coast, split into pairs and made an attack from the landward side, this being the side from which the ships should have had the least expectation of attack. The Spitfires came in low, cannon and machine guns blazing and made a single pass over the ships.[77] Both Jack Yarra in 'U' (EN824) and

Matthew de Cosier in 'W' (BL899) were shot down by flak. de Cosier was too low to bail out and was unable to get enough height to do so. His plane stalled and went into the Channel, taking him with it. Yarra was able to bail out but collided with the tail section of his plane in the process, and tumbled into the water, his parachute streaming behind him. Neither pilot survived. One merchantman was left burning and all had their decks raked by cannon and machine gun fire, killing and wounding numerous crew.[78] The remaining Spitfires broadcast a mayday and circled for some time but had to leave when enemy aircraft were reported in the area.[79] They didn't have enough fuel left for a dogfight. Bailing out of aircraft was never an easy undertaking and a number of memos were circulated during the war in relation to correct procedures and advice on how to avoid accidents. One such message included advice on trimming the aircraft into a nose-heavy attitude before rolling the aircraft over onto its back. This was designed to keep the tail high and reduce the likelihood that the pilot would strike it when falling from the aircraft.[80]

For the next few days little flying was done, and bad weather allowed the ground crew to work on the planes—the squadron's VBs now becoming a bit old and tired, so the two new aircraft delivered that week were gratefully received.

The squadron flew as a diversion squadron for Circus 244 on 20 December in the area of Abbeville, St Omer and Cap Gris Nez but didn't engage the enemy. To illustrate how large these operations were, and to put the operations of 453 Squadron into perspective, consider the number of participating units and aircraft for Circus 244:[81]

    1st Diversion: 131 and 165 Squadrons (Fighters)

    2nd Diversion: 350, 453, 302, 308 Squadrons (Fighters)

    3rd Diversion: 334, 335 and 336 Squadrons (US Fighters)

    4th Diversion: 303 and 316 Squadrons (Fighters)

MAIN ATTACK:

Bombers: 80 Flying Fortresses and 20 Liberators (US Army Air Corps)

Fighters: 1st Fighter Cover: 122, 306 and 315 Squadrons

2nd Fighter Cover: 401, 402, 340 and 611 Squadrons

1st Rear Support: 412, 616, 131 and 165 Squadrons

2nd Rear Support: 310, 312, 313, 302 and 308 Squadrons

Early Circuses had smaller numbers of bombers (usually about six), but the principle remained the same. An escort would get the bombers to their target, where that escort would be joined by additional fighter squadrons tasked as 'target cover', in anticipation of an engagement with the Luftwaffe. Should none appear, this target cover group were then able to make ground attacks if appropriate and the return leg would be taken over by another escort, who, having just arrived, would have more fuel available should they need it for engagements.[82]

20 December 1942 also saw the arrival of F/Lt Donald George Andrews (Service no. 404795). He was born on 5 September 1921 and enlisted on 8 November 1940—just 19 years old. The former bank clerk was posted to 8 EFTS in Narrandera where his pilot's log book had a comment that it was 'disgraceful'[83] as his ability to complete it in a neat and tidy manner according to regulations was called into question. By the time his course was completed in March 1941, Andrews was rated as an above average pilot and his papers were stamped 'Recommended for fighter pilot'. His next stop was 1 SFTS at Camp Borden in Canada where he flew a mix of Harvard and Yale trainers. By the end of his course had maintained his above average piloting rating and had earned an exceptional rating in navigation. He graduated fourth in his class, with a remark on his record stating that he 'Has made rapid progress throughout the course to finish an Above Average Pupil' and he was recommended for a commission.[84] Patrick McDade, who would also go on to fly Spitfires with 453 Squadron, was on the same course, graduating

23rd.[85] Andrews was probably lucky not to be posted to Coastal Command with a navigation rating so high, and his assessment actually recommended him for bombers but, in August 1941 he was at 53 OTU in Llandow in Wales, flying Miles Masters, his first flight in a Spitfire coming on 3 September 1941. There he maintained his above average rating and, at the end of his course, was asked to stay back and act as an instructor, with the promise that at the end of the next course he could have a posting of his choosing.[86] The RAF kept their word and, surprisingly, the now F/O Andrews chose Hurricanes and was posted to 615 Squadron. He started there in November 1941 flying Hurricane IIBs, IICs and Long Range IIBs. In December 1941 he was posted to 245 Squadron at Middle Wallop, still on Hurricanes and in the following March, survived a crash when his engine cut out as he was coming in to land, wrecking the plane but leaving him unhurt.[87] Andrews was posted to 175 Squadron in July 1942, still on Hurricanes and now at Warmwell. The squadron moved to the coast for the Dieppe operations in August and, while 453 were loaning out their Spitfires, he flew two sorties on the 19th in support of the operation. In September, Andrews was posted to 536 Squadron for just a week before returning to 175, and was credited with a 'probable' sinking of an E-boat during a shipping attack in October.[88] After all that time on Hurricanes, he was posted to a Spitfire squadron, 453, in December 1942.

The BBC attended the airfield on 22 December and recorded a short program that included an address by the Station Commander, S/Ldr Gadney, including the line, 'We're very proud to have a Dominion Squadron here, at this station'. Jack Ratten replied to the toast stating: 'We're fast becoming a strong team and I would like to say here that I'm very honoured and proud to lead the squadron'. Geoffrey Galwey also gave an account of his bail out over the Channel and his night on the buoy:

> I had the usual reaction, I didn't think of my past or anything like that—I felt like swearing... I thought I'd have a go at it so I pulled the hood release, the hood didn't come away so I bashed the

> cover with my fist ... luckily at that stage the aircraft was upside-down and I fell out! And as I was leaving the aircraft I thought it was the moment of impact and I was hitting the water. ... I pulled the ripcord and there was a sudden jerk and I found myself floating a few feet off the water ... I 'Charlestoned' for about an hour and then I climbed up on to the light ... and held myself over the light hoping that someone would see the light wasn't working. It was very dangerous and most uncomfortable and I got very cold so I climbed down again and 'Charlestoned' again until daylight.

The broadcast was concluded with Tom Swift singing, 'It's worth fighting for.'[89]

Christmas dinner at Southend was a less austere event than one might expect, given wartime rationing. The offerings increased with rank, but the menu of the Sergeant's Mess gives an idea of the evening's feast. First up was crème of tomato soup, followed by fried fillet of fish, roast turkey, ham stuffing and forcemeat (perhaps somewhere between sausage meat and spam). For vegetables, there were Brussels sprouts, boiled and roast potato, runner beans, bridge rolls and onion gravy. For sweets, Christmas pudding with brandy sauce and mince pies were available, followed by a dessert of apples, biscuits and cheese, coffee, beer and cigarettes.[90] The Christmas meal was much appreciated and, while the weather was not terribly good, a number of patrols were flown in the last week of the month. There was a shortage of ground crew, ensuring that the rest were both overworked and doing work they were not necessarily qualified to do, but the squadron made do and pleaded their case for more staff as often as possible to little or no effect. Tiger Moths were handy little odd-job planes as well as training aircraft: on 29 December Norm Swift and Fred Halcombe took one to Gatwick 'to pick up F/Lt D. Andrews' dog'. How well the dog coped in the Tiger Moth on the return journey is not recorded.[91] Fred McCann had been transferred to the Aeroplane and Armament Experimental Establishment at Boscombe Downs on 13 December and paid a visit to the squadron on the 30th to show off the Mk XII he was testing. They were suitably impressed by his flying demonstration.[92]

New Year's Day 1943 brought poor weather, so recovery from the previous evening was not interrupted by flying. On 2 January the squadron flew with the other two squadrons of the Wing—350 and 122—on a diversionary sweep across the Channel. The squadron crossed the English coast at Hastings at 1,000 ft and by the time they hit the French coast at Cayeux had reached 22,000 ft. The squadrons were stepped up, with 350 low in front, 453 in the middle on the starboard side and 122 on top on the port side. No flak or enemy aircraft were met and all returned safely. The rest of the first two weeks of the year was taken up with convoy patrols when weather permitted. On 4 January, Don Andrews, who had been flying 'R' regularly as Flight Commander, decided to have the individual identification letter changed from 'R' to '?', noting this in his logbook: 'Changed 'R' to '?' II'. His favourite Hurricane that he flew in 175 Squadron in 1942 had carried this same marking.[93] On 13 January, Andrews' plane was hit by flak on a sweep over the French coast carried out with 350 Squadron and the aircraft was put out of action for a while, though he landed safely and uninjured. He was sufficiently annoyed by this for it to be recorded in the squadron diary, and he didn't fly '?' again until February.

Jack Ratten was sent on a course in mid-January and the squadron was temporarily taken over by RAF W/Cdr Slater, AFC. There were a number of alerts to scramble during day and night hours but due to the weather or the targets turning before they could be engaged, no contact was made and the squadron was still to make a claim of an enemy aircraft destroyed. Many of the pilots and ground crew—especially the Australians, who were unused to English winters—were hospitalised during the middle of the month due to suffering from feverish colds. At one time there were 13 pilots in hospital. A number of convoy patrols were flown but there were no engagements.

During January, Sir Courtauld Thompson allowed his house at Burnham to be used as a rest house for the squadron and this was much appreciated by them, being so far from home with few or no relatives or non-service friends to spend time with.[94]

A photo of FU-? sent home by F/Lt Andrews. The message on the back reads 'The mighty query'. The '?' marking can be seen underneath the nosecone of this Mk VB, possibly AD383. (Courtesy of the Andrews family)

A photo of the same Mk VB with the Gremlin (painted behind the rearmost exhaust) which would adorn many Spitfires flown by Don Andrews throughout the war. It holds a sign saying, 'You have been warned'. (Courtesy of the Andrews family)

A morning Circus was flown on 3 February, 453 contributing twelve Spitfires led by W/Cdr Slater to escort Venturas to Cambrai. Jack Ratten returned to the squadron and joined the second sortie in the afternoon, escorting Venturas to Abbeville. Three days later, Fred Thornley played football for the RAAF against the NZ Combined Services and despite a good showing the New Zealanders won 8–5.⁹⁵ Tom Swift gave a running commentary in the match which was recorded for later broadcast to Australia.

F/Sgt Jack Olver (Service no. 408503) arrived on 8 February. John Frederick Olver was born on 9 October 1920 and was a bank clerk and member of the militia, from which he received a discharge so that he could he enlist in the RAAF on 26 April 1941. Within a short time he was at 1 ITS Somers, signing a will leaving all his property to his mother. Training was a dangerous business, and many would-be fighter pilots, and sometimes their instructors, never made it out of Australia, instead being buried near their training fields. He had completed both his EFTS and SFTS in Rhodesia, arriving in the UK on 19 September 1942. He only had to wait a few weeks before he was posted to 17 (P)AFU for further instruction, this time on the Miles Master, followed by his first solo in an old Mk I Spitfire on 15 December 1942 at 52 OTU. By the time he was ready to join an operational squadron, Olver was rated as 'Above Average'.⁹⁶ 453 Squadron was his first posting.⁹⁷

The weather was typically poor and no action took place until 9 February when F/Sgt Wood was strafed by a Do-217 while riding his bicycle on the perimeter track. The plane then headed to Romford and dropped its bombs before disappearing. Despite having a section on aerodrome defence, the first they heard of the incoming plane was when it crossed the perimeter track, it had apparently come in below radar. By then it was too late and it got away. A 'Special Shipping Recce' took place that day, with Don Andrews and Ernie Esau looking for an unnamed ship in Ostend, Flushing and West

Capelle. They were fired at by flak guns defending the harbours and chased by some FW-190s which they evaded by going into cloud. Their report concluded with the words 'F/Lt Andrews certain that the ship for which Recce was made was not in any harbour or part of harbour seen.'[98]

There was a Circus to Dunkirk on 15 February, followed by a Rodeo fighter sweep of the same area the next day with no engagements taking place. Having come back to the squadron in mid-January and participated in operations, Fred McCann thought that he would apply some of his test-piloting experience and dive a Spitfire in an air test on the 16th and happily recorded '450 mph OK' in his logbook.[99] Handy to know! Two more Circuses were cancelled due to bad weather that week, which also grounded the squadron for the five days following that.

26 February 1943 sought to make up for the inactivity of the previous weeks with three Circuses in one day. All were part of Circus 274 parts one, two and three—each of which consisted of a large number of fighter squadrons and twelve Ventura medium bombers. The aim was to attack a merchant ship in Dunkirk harbour, and 453 and 350 Squadrons were to provide the close escort. The first took off at 0945 but didn't bomb due to cloud cover over the target area and 122 Squadron in their Spitfire Mk IXs, had an engagement with some FW-190s after the bombing took place.[100] The second took off at 1400 with some bombs seen to land in the target area. The third and final part left at 1635 and the bombers made their attack, but the results were not observed. The ship targeted was referred to as the 'Dunkirk Raider' and it was this 5,000 ton ship that Andrews and Esau had been looking for earlier in the month. For more than two weeks it had been hunted and the British thought it was the Germans' intention to get it from the Baltic to a French Atlantic port so it could commence operations. The numerous attacks upon it had evidently caused sufficient damage for major repairs as, on 28 February, it was seen entering the mouth of the Elbe escorted by a number of minesweepers.[101]

A final Circus for the month was flown on 27 February, again escorting 350 heavy bombers to the Dunkirk area. They observed a number of red marker flak shells bursting to gauge height before the anti-aircraft barrage commenced.[102]

From 1 to 13 March 1943, the squadron participated in Exercise 'Spartan' and were assigned to the 'defending 'army.[103] They played the role of the Luftwaffe defending against an Allied force attempting to take back post-landing lost ground. Each side of the exercise had the same number of aircraft available—bombers, fighters, army co-operation and reconnaissance. As the 'enemy', white stripes were painted from the propeller to the mid-point of the cockpit on each side of the fuselage to distinguish them from the other aircraft involved. The mobile system for the landings in France was tried and tested, as were all aspects of RAF logistics to support operations, including the use of advanced landing grounds.[104] Sorties were flown daily from the 5th to the 11th, attacking 'enemy' ground forces and escorting reconnaissance Mustangs on other sorties. The diary noted that on numerous occasions 'enemy' troops simply looked up at the planes as they attacked, or sat and ate their rations rather than run for cover. Perhaps the most exciting event was a scramble and dogfight with 'enemy' Spitfires who attacked the aerodrome. A second dogfight with 'enemy' aircraft took place when the squadron was bounced while carrying out strafing attacks on trucks. At the conclusion of the operation, the squadron returned to routine patrols, readiness, Ramrods and Rodeos, including the escort of Whirlibombers, Westland Whirlwind fighter-bombers equipped with bombs.

14 March saw a successful dive-bombing of Abbeville airfield by Whirlibombers of 137 Squadron[105] with 453 providing the close escort. An attempt to repeat that success on the 24th was thwarted by the weather, as noted in Andrews' logbook: 'Weather U/S, bombs not dropped over France, S/F/A Doing.'[106]

On 25 March, 453 flew close escort to 137 Squadron again, this time attacking the marshalling yards at Abbeville[107] and, on the following day, a successful Rhubarb (the first by 453)[108] was flown by Rusty Leith in 'C' and Morath in 'E'. They were

> ... bored stiff sitting around doing nothing so we decided to do this. We went to CO and he said, 'No we can't do this. We are moving tomorrow to another station. All the aircraft are getting ready to do this.' So anyway we persisted and finally we got approval from higher up so we took off the two of us just with machine guns and we went across from the Thames estuary at water level or at zero feet as the expression is and so we got to the Belgium, Dutch coast and we just pulled up and went over the hills on the other side.[109]

Leith and Morath patrolled the area around Knocke and Dixmude in Belgium and returned with claims of one barge and two trains damaged.[110] The trains were both goods trains and were travelling in opposite directions. One came to a complete stop belching clouds of steam. Leith and Morath were waved at by school children and farmers as they headed back to the coast and England.[111] While attacks on passenger trains during daylight were against operational instructions, those carrying goods were fair game.[112]

On 27 March, the squadron moved from Southend to Hornchurch and took over Spitfire IXs left by a previous squadron. Andrews described them as 'beautiful'.[113] After local flying on the 28th to get to know the local landmarks and test out the IXs, patrols were resumed on the 29th and continued to the end of the month.[114] Unfortunately, on 29 March Norm Swift in Mk IX FU-S was vectored to Boulogne and kept up at 25,000 ft for too long and ran out of fuel on the return flight, crashing just off Southend. He was hospitalised with a broken leg and didn't return to flying until February 1944 but not to 453. After a short posting to 80 Squadron he converted to Typhoons and flew with 137 Squadron (often in SF-T or SF-X) and was based at B.78 Eindhoven in the Netherlands from 28 September 1944. His squadron flew ground support sorties around the German-Dutch border, attacking trucks, tanks, trains and barges with rockets and cannon. They also were sent to attack the headquarters of General Kurt Student on 12 October, but weren't successful in the attempt to remove the famed General from the battlefield. On 27 December, in support of American operations during what came to be called the Battle of the Bulge, Norm's engine packed it in for no apparent reason while behind enemy lines and he crash landed south of St Vith in Belgium. He was immediately captured and spent the rest of the war as a prisoner.[115]

Towards the end of March, Sergeant Ross Currie (Service no. 413108) arrived. Born on 5 August 1922, Currie had been employed on the railways with the unflattering job title of 'Junior Useful' when he enlisted on 16 August 1941. His flying training took place at 6 EFTS and 7 SFTS in Australia before being sent to the UK. Like many aircrew, he was bored while awaiting a posting so spoke up and asked to be sent to a squadron. In 1942, three hotels in Bournemouth were taken over by the Australians for use as a Personnel Dispatch and Reception Centre. As much as staying in a hotel might seem like a nice way to spend some time, these men had joined the RAAF to fight, and the processing delays were not appreciated. Despite being poorly organised early on, eventually a syllabus was designed to keep the Australians busy and entertained, including subjects such as navigation, radio use and dinghy drill, with a specified number of hours to be spent on each topic. However, this did not satisfy everyone and one particularly sarcastic and militant group proposed a 'Bournemouth Long Service Medal' for a stay of three months, and a 'bar' (an additional award of the same medal) for further 'meritorious delay'.

During the earliest time of the setup, 100 aircrew signed a petition to be returned to Australia to fight the Japanese, they were so bored and frustrated by the slowly turning cogs of the system to which they had signed up for the duration plus 12 months.[116] Unfortunately, they would have done no better in Australia in any case, had they been sent back—there was not enough aircraft for them, and certainly no Sunderlands, Spitfires or Hurricanes. Had they taken to the skies in Australian-built Wirraways, they would have all been shot down. Ross Currie got what he asked for, but not necessarily what he wanted—time as a ferry pilot at Gibraltar. After he settled in with 453, he named 'his' plane 'Ruth' after his girlfriend back in Australia. They'd met in high school and corresponded during the war. After he returned home at the conclusion of the war they struck up a stronger relationship and married in 1946.[117]

It was at Southend that the squadron was asked to send a volunteer to return to Australia. It wasn't a popular option, the squadron was in the UK to fight the Germans, to do their bit for Australia and the Allies in Europe. While the idea of going home to Australia did have an appeal, Rusty Leith summed up their feelings well:

> The reasons for our wanting to stay are numerous. From what we hear the Yanks have a monopoly on all the first line fighters (and bombers too) in Australia and surrounding areas.

It was certainly true, American industrial policy dictated that.

> Another point is that I wouldn't like to fly any fighter other than a Spitfire. We are all unanimous in the belief that it is the best fighter plane in the world. It is better than anything the Yanks have turned out and still better than the enemy's latest effort. Still another point is that now I am over here I would like to be in for the kill or the big push if and when it comes.[118]

While 453 wanted to stay in Europe, 451 (RAAF) Squadron had voted to return to Australia earlier in the war when the Japanese had made their extensive gains in the Pacific. They were told that they were required to remain in the Desert/Mediterranean theatre and they did so, as ordered, they could hardly do otherwise. Some members of 451 though, in what can only be described as pitifully uninformed actions on the senders' behalf, received white feathers in the mail,[119] a traditional form of accusing someone of cowardice. This shows the extent of the feeling, by at least some of the Australian population, that their forces should have been entirely withdrawn from all other theatres of war to meet the Japanese threat. Indeed, when Spitfire pilot Nat Gould returned to Australia in 1942 and transitioned to Kittyhawks, he and the others who had come back from the UK encountered a great deal of hostility. The pilots who had been fighting in New Guinea accused him and others of having an easy time of it in the UK: flying in the morning, going to the pub for dinner and having a warm bed at night. These Australian pilots were entirely ignorant of the stresses of having the Luftwaffe just a couple of minutes away across the Channel. According to them,

> ... the PNG blokes had a rough time, squalid camp, lived in bloody tents and so on and they accused the Spitfire blokes of living in the lap of luxury and beautiful messes over in England and the pub down the corner with pretty girls and not real dangerous.

That animosity lasted until they were back in action against the Japanese in New Guinea.[120]

In March 1944 Rusty Leith made mention of white feathers in a letter home:

> In todays papers there is a report that members of the RAAF over here are receiving white feathers from certain people in Australia and letters accusing them of dodging the war by staying in England. I haven't met or heard of anyone who has received one but I suppose these things come from the ignorant lower types.[121]

The first weeks of April 1943 consisted of relatively good weather with Rodeos and Ramrods across the Channel, including a sortie on the 3rd as the first flown in Mk IXs,[122] and despite some enemy aircraft being seen, none were engaged until the Circus of 8 April. The Wing was led by Jack Ratten in his usual 'F', 453 and the other escorts crossing the French coast at Cayeux, arriving at a height of 25,000 ft, having left Hastings at 1,000 ft. They turned to port towards Abbeville and Drucat and had a number of warnings of enemy aircraft, but it was not until a number of FW-190s were seen below them heading northeast near the forêt de Crécy that Jack Ratten took them down on a diving attack from out of the sun. He, Don Andrews and P/Os Rickard and Swift all claimed one FW-190 damaged but nothing further, and the squadron used their speed from the dive to regain height and turned for the coast and home. It was in this action that Rusty Leith fired his first shots at a German plane, just a one second burst at a fleeting target as it crossed in front of him, much too fast to even make a claim of any sort.[123] On the 10th the Under Secretary for Air, Lord Sherwood, accompanied by Lord Wimborne, attended the airfield and visited the squadrons. This was followed by a visit the next day by AVM Coles and W/Cdr Ryland (RAAF). A Ramrod with Whirlibombers was held on 13 April and a number of censor approved photos were taken for publication in Australia.[124]

A Ramrod to Bruges was carried out on 14 April, repeating the previous days' performance, and was followed by an escort to Bombphoons (Typhoons carrying bombs) making an attack in the Le Havre area. There was another Circus on the 17th but crowding with all the Spitfire squadrons involved (there were ten squadrons participating)[125] meant that some got in each other's way and prevented the interception of some FW-190s.

18 April consisted of a Rodeo to Flushing followed by a Ramrod to Nieuport with no engagements taking place. A Circus followed by a Ramrod took place on the 20th and another VIP visit completed the day.

On the 23rd a Gunnery Flight was formed by the Wing to give regular and consistent training to pilots in cine-gun and air-to-air firing, with the overall aim to improve the gunnery of all pilots within the Wing.

A large operation was planned for the 27th and, when this was cancelled, all aircrew were available for the visit of AVM Wrigley of RAAF Overseas Headquarters who was most interested to see the last remaining Australian Spitfire Squadron in the UK. The squadron failed to rendezvous with Whirlibombers on the 29th and made their way to France independently for a fighter sweep but returned empty handed.[126]

Rusty Leith and Jack Olver spent a week's leave together in April, hosted by a Mr and Mrs Butler of Beedon Manor, Newbury, who were participants in the Lady Frances Ryder hospitality scheme. The family lived on a thousand-acre farm with many outbuildings, crops, a pond and some cows. While hosted by the family, the two went into Oxford for some sightseeing, Rusty describing it as 'a funny old place and we weren't very impressed at all'. There were some luxuries to be had while on the farm, including horse riding, ice cream, meringues and real cream, made right there on the farm. A show in London finished off the leave, and they returned to the squadron, much rested, Rusty describing it as 'perhaps the best I have had in my twelve months over here'.[127]

May 1943 started with a Circus, this time led by W/Cdr Kilmartin (RAF), and no engagement took place. Jack Ratten went on leave on the 2nd and Kel Barclay took over in his absence. Disaster struck on 3 May when the squadron was to escort Venturas of 487 (RNZAF) Squadron to Amsterdam. Eight squadrons of Spitfires were detailed for the various escort tasks but German radar was alerted when two of the squadrons arrived too early and too high over the Dutch coast. Not only did this alert the Luftwaffe, but additional fighters happened to be in the area that day due to a VIP visit.[128] 453 received a recall three quarters of the way there—30 miles off the Dutch coast (Zandvoort)[129]—but apparently the Venturas didn't receive the message, and ten of the eleven were shot down, only one making it to the target and overshooting with its bomb load. S/Ldr Trent (RNZAF), pilot of this aircraft, turned back to the coast but didn't make it and was shot down, though he and a number of crew from other Venturas survived and were taken prisoner. After the war, when the full story of the sortie became known, he was awarded the Victoria Cross.[130]

On 5 May, 453 Squadron was given a lecture on Army co-operation and the situation in North Africa and the Mediterranean by Major Egerton-

Smith, and Don Andrews was sent on a gunnery course. He returned to the squadron on 2 June, having scored top of the class.

On 6 May, Sergeant Robert Ernest Yarra, brother of Jack (who had been killed the previous December) was posted in. Robert Yarra (Service no. 413707) was a Junior Clerk with Grafton City Council prior to enlisting on 12 September 1941, aged 18. He was posted to 6 EFTS Tamworth then 8 EFTS Narrandera, but completed his SFTS in Canada, arriving in the UK in November 1942. 453 Squadron was his first operational posting.[131]

On 10 May, a lecture was given by Sgt Wareling, who had escaped from a German P.O.W. camp. This type of practical advice would come in handy for a number of the pilots before the war was over.

On the 11th, Jack Ratten was posted as Wing Commander of the Hornchurch Wing. He was the first Australian to be given command of a Wing within Fighter Command. His promotion was celebrated in Australia in the *Examiner* newspaper of Tasmania and *The Daily News* newspaper of Perth, on 5 June.[132] Even Ratten's celebratory dinner held at the Watling Chophouse in London rated a mention.[133] F/Lt Barclay was promoted to Squadron Leader and was a popular choice, as was the concept of keeping the promotion 'in house'. Ernie Esau was promoted to Flight Lieutenant to take his place.

On 13 May, AVM Saunders, Commander of 11 Group, visited the squadron with a number of Australian politicians, followed by Lord Trenchard the following day.

Flying on 13 May consisted of a Circus, a Ramrod and a 'Secret Mission'. The diary records that four Spitfires of the Squadron, Ernie Esau in 'L', Bill Morath in 'F', Russ Ewins in 'S' and Jack Stansfield in 'U' took off from Hornchurch at 1855 and landed at Manston at 1905. After refuelling, they took off at 1935 to escort two Lancasters 'out to sea' and returned to base at 2020. The month also saw the first operational flights for a number of new pilots and the screening of instructional and educational films including 'Sex Hygiene' which was described as 'very unpleasant but highly educational'!

A number of uneventful Rodeos and Circuses were flown towards the end of the month, primarily with United States Army Air Force (USAAF) Flying Fortresses. The Wing was usually led by the newly promoted W/Cdr Ratten (though once by S/Ldr Barclay in his absence) and some of these operations included up to 22 squadrons of fighters.[134] No engagements took place, though two pilots fired at FW-190s on 29 May for no apparent result and no claims were made. No planes or pilots were lost to enemy action and, with each flight lasting about 90 minutes, all pilots were building up their flying hours, though that elusive first kill was yet to be claimed. A number of staff participated in 'Wings for Victory' parades and a number were also interviewed for potential commissions.[135] The Wings for Victory parades were a fundraising effort encouraging the civilian population to donate money for the purchasing of aircraft, particularly Spitfires and Lancasters.[136] May also saw Fred Halcombe posted out of 453 and, by July, he was flying with 126 Squadron from Malta.[137]

On 1 June, the squadron engaged in a Rodeo and Ramrod. The Rodeo was led by Kel Barclay and resulted in an engagement with a number of FW-190s. Bill Morath had to force-land after take-off and was admitted to hospital with head injuries. It was later learned that Morath would probably lose the sight in one eye and never return to flying duties.

The Luftwaffe knew that these sorties were performed by masses of Spitfires and so simply dived away if they found themselves at too great a disadvantage. No claims were made, and this was borne out by review of the gun footage. When the squadron landed, they were met by Air Marshal Sir Trafford Leigh-Mallory who was visiting the station. It was announced that Jack Ratten was to be awarded a DFC on this date for his leadership, skill and praiseworthy example.[138]

Another Rodeo operation took place on 4 June, the Wing crossing the French coast at Berck and, later, being directed towards Abbeville where they spotted some FW-190s. 453 dived after them with 222 Squadron acting as top cover. At the same time more FW-190s dove into the action from the south and the battle was joined. This time Kel Barclay claimed a FW-190 damaged, Don Andrews claimed one damaged, Jack Ratten claimed a FW-190 destroyed and was ably protected by his No 2, Rusty Leith. Rusty wrote in his logbook: 'Saw W/C Ratten hit a FW-190 which burst into flames and crashed'.[139] Andrews described the action as 'bags of fun'.[140] The squadron reformed intact and returned to base. A party was held in town to celebrate Ratten's DFC and the day's claim.

Two journalists, Mr Lloyd-Dumas of the *Adelaide Advertiser* and Mr Kennedy of the *Sydney Sun*, arrived at the squadron on 5 June and gave the men an update on events in Australia in addition to getting stories of their own.[141]

On 9 June, Fred McCann received his orders for a posting home to Australia.[142] He left with a recommendation that he would make a good Flight Commander, as he had acted as such on a number of sorties and was rated as an above average pilot. He would later fly with his old 452 Squadron at Darwin and went on to become a flying instructor and test pilot.[143] Upon arriving home in Australia, he gave an interview to *The Mercury* newspaper in Hobart, which printed an article recounting some of his experiences. It included a comment about his time as a flying instructor and the attitude of the Poles. He said that they made great fighter pilots and 'If they can't shoot them down they ram them'.[144]

12 June saw a late Ramrod take-off at 1855, crossing the French coast at Dieppe, patrolling inland and failing to entice the Luftwaffe. On the following day, the squadron was visited by S/Ldr Payne who had just arrived from Australia and wanted to collect some 'gen'. An uneventful Ramrod was flown on the 15th but the squadron saw action on the second sortie flown on the 17th. Not only were six of the squadron granted their commissions but Don Andrews, in his favourite '?', made a claim of one FW-190 probably destroyed. The Wing swept the Ghent, Antwerp and Flushing area and

were warned of enemy aircraft to the south. 453 Squadron, with the Wing Commander leading, went to investigate, leaving 222 Squadron as top cover. They met between fifteen and twenty FW-190s who broke formation as 453 came down, and they would likely have all gotten away had some not climbed. Surely even the Luftwaffe was tired of diving away anytime they saw a squadron of Spitfires and, naturally enough, some wanted to fight. After a combat involving a number of pilots firing at long range (as well as the closer engagement—close enough for pieces shot off the other plane to hit Don Andrews' own)[145] the squadron was ordered to reform and head for home. The FW-190s finally dived away inland, knowing that the limited range of the Spitfire would see them in trouble if they attempted to follow. Andrews marked the success with a swastika in his logbook.[146]

On 18 June, the squadron held a party to celebrate its first anniversary. A sports day was held on the 20th, with the airfield's squadrons competing in a number of events and 453 came away with a few awards and prizes.

There was a Ramrod on 22 June which took off at 0930, the role of the Wing being to escort Flying Fortresses home from a raid in Germany. They intercepted a number of FW-190s approaching the bomber formation in fours and S/Ldr Barclay claimed a FW-190 damaged but the squadron lost F/O Edward Gray, who was last seen spinning down and away from the formation. However, the squadron did their job and broke up the attacks on the bombers. For some time, Gray was listed as 'Missing presumed killed' but he survived the crash and was taken prisoner (the formal report of this reached the Allies in August). In his later report on the matter, Gray stated that he'd been attacked by a FW-190 and had taken cannon hits on the port wing and engine. The engine stopped and his Spitfire went into a spin but, due to the port aileron being damaged, he couldn't get out of it and so bailed out at about 15,000 ft, waiting until about 4,000 ft before opening his parachute. He thought he'd landed on one of the Dutch islands and was thankfully uninjured, landing about 50 yards from his plane. Within two minutes, he was a prisoner of war. Cliché or not, for him the war was over. His first camp was Dulag Luft in Frankfurt until July 1943, after which he was at Stalag Luft III (Sagan)—the location which became famous for The Great Escape. He was there until January 1945 and was moved as the war in the east closed in on Germany. He was liberated at the end of the war and, in his post-release interview, Gray said that rations were 'fair' until June 1944 and then things went downhill. At Sagan they had hot showers twice a week in a shower house built by the prisoners and, at the final camp, when things were much worse, had one hot shower every three weeks outside the camp.[147]

Three Ramrods took place on 24 June, followed by another as escort cover two days later.[148] No claims were made nor losses sustained. 27 June was more profitable, with Jim Ferguson in 'U' flying as Blue 2 to S/Ldr Barclay in 'A' as Blue 1 claiming a Me-109 destroyed and Kel Barclay damaging another. Both 109s were last seen in vertical dives.[149] Jack Olver regularly flew as No. 2 to Don Andrews and Jack recorded in his logbook: 'Chased Huns. We were split up and Don Andrews + I did our own private sweep. Jim Ferguson got a 109. Good on him!'[150] Rusty Leith was separated from the squadron during the engagement and joined with the Kenley Wing, which had been led by W/Cdr Johnson (who shot down a FW-190 in the engagement), for the return journey.[151]

On 28 June, the squadron bade farewell to Hornchurch and moved to Ibsley, just north of Bournemouth in 10 Group, away from the main action.[152] Ground crew stayed behind, as did the aircraft—only the pilots and immediate administrative staff made the move, going by rail.[153]

1 July saw the arrival of two US pilots, 1st Lts Weast and Riggins, but they made only a few operational flights. They were followed by an Australian, P/O Patrick McDade (Service no. 403000) on 2 July. Patrick Vincent McDade was working as a survey assistant for the Department of Main Roads in NSW when he enlisted on 11 November 1940. He started his flight training at 5 EFTS Narromine before continuing training at Camp

Borden in Canada. He had previously served with 167 and 322 Squadrons before arriving at 453. His posting record from (P)AFU to OTU contains the comment that he was: 'A young officer of unusual keenness.'[154]

4 July included an early evening Roadstead escort sortie to rocket-firing Hurricane IVs on a shipping patrol around the Channel Islands but they didn't find any targets and thankfully the flak was inaccurate. Another pilot was posted in on the 5th to fly Mk IXs but, as the squadron had reverted to VBs and VCs after the move[155] to Ibsley, he was reposted almost immediately.

The squadron carried out regular convoy patrols including another escort to rocket-equipped Hurricane IVs from 164 Squadron[156] on 9 July, and Don Andrews took over the squadron while Kel Barclay went on leave. 10 July saw Ibsley host a number of Wings on their way to participate in a Ramrod—453's role being to escort the Flying Fortresses on their return from bombing Le Mans and the now-Wing Commander Jack Ratten visited his old squadron. For the operation, Don Andrews was deputy Wing Commander.

12 July saw a squadron-sized armed shipping recce return after 20 minutes. Two official reasons are given for this in the squadron records, one being 'a terrific shriek on the R/T', another being 'jamming'. The third and less diplomatic was recorded in the logbook of Don Andrews: 'Some clot left his pipsqueak on.'[157] Pipsqueak was the slang term for the broadcasting system used by fighters for the purpose of being tracked and identified by friendly radar. It seems that no one admitted to the mistake, and the squadron flew a circuit afterwards to check that the 'jamming' didn't take place again and everything was clear. But this clearly illustrates that one simple mistake can ruin a whole sortie.

The next week involved operations based out of Predannack in Wales and Redhill near London but the weather generally didn't cooperate. A Ramrod on 14 July saw the squadron escort bombers back to the UK from a sortie to France. One bomber was seen to slowly lose height and Blue

Section, led by Don Andrews, flew escort for it, throttling back to give it the protection it required. The plane made it to about 25 miles off the English coast and there it ditched, the crew evacuating the aircraft and its position was reported by 453.

On 17 July, while 'beating up' an Army unit, the flight controls for '?' locked up and Andrews had to bail out. He landed safely and was very disappointed in himself, losing '?' and recording in his logbook: 'Hit something (wires?) Had to bale [sic] out. Very poor show'.[158]

More bad weather followed and the Group Public Relations Officer came by to take photos of the pilots. On 24 July, the squadron went to Bradwell Bay to take part in a number of operations and also flew from Tangmere and Martlesham before the end of the month. On this date, Jack Olver was commissioned as a Pilot Officer, with the comment on his file added by Don Andrews describing him as 'An above average pilot very keen and of good character'.[159]

25 July saw a Ramrod escorting Mitchell bombers to the north of Ghent where there was an oil installation. The formation was engaged by FW-190s operating singly and in pairs. Russ Ewins and Jim Ferguson each claimed one damaged. The next day saw another Ramrod escorting Mitchells to bomb the airfield at St Omer.

On 27 July, the squadron put up eleven Spitfires, led by Don Andrews in a new '?' and Esau in 'L'. They participated in an 11 Group Ramrod targeting the coke ovens at Zeebrugge, followed by a 12 Group Ramrod targeting Schiphol aerodrome[160] and, though the Luftwaffe was seen, they weren't engaged by 453. A total of 12 squadrons of Spitfires were involved in the second Ramrod, far too many to be managed on the single radio frequency allocated and the squadrons equipped with Mk Vs had a hard time trying to keep up with the Mitchell bombers in a climb.[161] Another 12 Group Ramrod was flown on the 28th, this time as escort cover to the Fokker Works near Amsterdam,[162] followed by other Ramrods on the last two days of the month.¹⁶³ The first escort flown by Rusty Leith on 30 July resulted in an interesting entry in his logbook:

> Close escort for 23 Marauders to Woensdrecht aerodrome. Bombers flew all over Europe and lost one, but shot down one Me 109 which I saw. Saw a Spit go down in flames—pilot ok. Yanks claimed about 8 destroyed—as usual!!¹⁶⁴

1 August saw two Americans, Captain Swenning and 1st Lt Louden, posted to the squadron to replace the previous two, again for operational experience. Thanks to a heavier rate of operations and more favourable weather they managed about twice the number of flying hours as those attached in July. This date also saw a new record set for a scramble, with Francis McDermott and Jack Olver getting airborne in 70 seconds—five seconds faster than the previous best, set on 31 July by P/Os Ford and McAuliffe. An exercise was carried out with bombers on 2 August, with the Spitfires of 453 practising their attacks and the bombers practising their defensive tactics. The following day saw an escort of Whirlibombers from 263 Squadron¹⁶⁵ to the Channel Islands on a shipping recce and F/O Long in 'E' was hit by flak in the fin but made it back without too much trouble. The late afternoon operation was a Circus to a Luftwaffe airfield near Brest where Whirlibombers made a successful attack.

4 August saw a Ramrod to the docks at Le Trait, 15 squadrons of Spitfires escorting 36 USAAF Marauders.¹⁶⁶ 453 was based for the day at Tangmere and was engaged during the sortie by German fighters who dived through the squadron, Jack Olver recording in his logbook: 'Saw Paris clearly. 2 190's tried to bounce but missed badly.'¹⁶⁷ Yellow section went after them, but the Germans got away by rolling onto their backs and diving to the deck.

On 5 August, AVM Wrigley (RAAF) and General Smart (Australian Chief of Staff) visited the squadron and spoke to the pilots and ground crew to get an impression of operations and their views on events as they affected 453. The ground crews especially appreciated having their views heard by the brass.

On the next two days, the bi-monthly aircraft recognition tests were held, the results of which were no cause for alarm, with some pilots scoring an 'excellent' grade. Flying also consisted of uneventful scrambles and convoy patrols.

F/O Norman Baker (Service no. 410205) was posted in to 453 Squadron on 13 August. Previously an audit clerk in Victoria, and with two years militia service before joining the RAAF, Baker started his flying in April 1940 at 1 EFTS, Parafield, South Australia and progressed to 7 SFTS at Deniliquin in New South Wales where he flew the dreaded Wirraway, surviving its faults. In January 1943 he went to the UK by ship where he passed through his additional fighter training, 453 Squadron being his first operational posting. Though hardly top of the line, by this stage of the war the change from old OTU Mk II Spitfires to a Mk VB was surely a welcome change.[168]

14 August saw another 'Army beat up' led by Don Andrews in '?'[169] and everyone returned safely. The next day was far more dramatic, and Andrews nearly had to hit the silk again. The squadron provided twelve Spitfires as part of the escort to Mitchells bombing an airfield in the Netherlands. The rendezvous was fair, the bombers having arrived early, and 453 didn't catch up with them until they were near Walcheren. While they could have engaged the boost to catch up faster, this would not have left them with enough fuel to carry out the sortie, so it had to be done economically. S/Ldr Barclay had asked for the sortie to be recalled as he didn't consider the weather suitable for bombing, but this was not done. Near Tholen the squadron was bounced by a squadron of FW-190s. S/Ldr Barclay radioed for the squadron to stick to the bombers and conduct a withdrawal and, almost immediately, Don Andrews was seen diving vertically away, his section being the last in the formation and taking the most fire from the FW-190s. He seemed to take most of the Germans with him, and the squadron returned with F/O Fred Thornley reported missing. He must have gone down in that first attack as well. Thornley was one of the few pilots who were married, having tied the knot with his wife, Heather, in Australia in January 1941, two months before

he enlisted.[170] Andrews in his '?' must have seemed to be a goner, but he fought back, ducking and weaving and using the turn of the Spitfire and all his fighting skills to dodge the fire aimed at him.

From the Personal Combat Report submitted and signed by Don Andrews:

> I was leading Blue Section when Yellow 4 reported aircraft at 6 o'clock. As I had been left behind in a turn and was flying rear man in the Squadron I turned right to have a look at these aircraft.
>
> There were 5 plus in the first bunch approaching dead astern and diving out of the sun at 16,000 ft. Recognising them as F.W. 190s I warned the Squadron of an impending bounce and broke violently. I noticed one Spitfire beside me break too and presume this was F/O Thornley.
>
> More enemy aircraft then came out of sun, but instead of attacking the Squadron they pulled up and began to attack me. During one of these breaks I noticed an aircraft which I took to be a Spitfire, flying straight and level with two F.W. 190s behind. The leading machine then went straight down without sign of smoke and I presume this was F/O Thornley.
>
> I called for help but my message was evidently jammed. From then on I was attacked by approximately 12 F.W 190s and during one 90° deflection attack my R/T failed. Several times during these attacks I noticed their fire was missing me and going very close to their compatriots.
>
> During this time all E/A were circling me and making head on and 90° to line astern attacks on me with telling results on my morale. As I could make no headway I lost height to 0 feet about two miles N.W. of Walcheren. During my descent the ground defences opened up on me adding insult to injury. By this time my aircraft had been hit in several places and I felt the impact of bullets. Gradually the number of F.W. 190s decreased until I was left with only four making attacks on me. What with continuous breaking I was only making short progress towards home.
>
> In one particular attack from dead astern which I could not

evade until the last moment the F.W. 190 used machine gun only which incidentally I could hear. Up to this time I had no opportunity to press the tit or use my guns.

Two of the remaining four E/A then left me and the others continued to attack. By using full boost and revs now I could make several miles towards home before breaking to the next attack. Having now got out to ten miles west of Walcheren at 0 feet I had several opportunities to fire my guns. On my third burst I made a 20° head on attack on a F.W.190 allowing it to run through my fire. Just before breaking from an attack made by the other E/A I saw an explosion ahead of the cockpit and after evading the attack of others I saw a tremendous splash in the sea where the first aircraft had gone in. I consider this was a lucky shot as from where it hit the other aircraft I estimate it went through and killed the pilot.

I claim this F.W. 190 destroyed.

After the E/A had crashed into the sea the other hurried away at full speed and I did the same, but in the opposite direction, landing at Manston without brakes.

All the E/A seemed to concentrate on 90° fly through deflection shots.[171]

Amongst other comments in his logbook, Andrews records that he was 'Very shaken', and one more swastika went in the logbook.[172]

16 August saw an escort to a Sunderland carrying a VIP and an escort to bombers in the morning, including Don Andrews, though in 'W' this time. He could have taken a day off or asked to be rested for a few days, but he was a leader and he knew where his place was. In the years to come many people— even the children of pilots who had flown with Don Andrews—would speak of the love and respect everyone had for him. This leadership shown so soon after cheating death at the odds of 12:1 was just one reason why.

18 August brought news of another long-term move, this time to Perranporth in Wales, about 45 miles west of Plymouth, and preparations began, the actual packing taking well over 12 hours. A scramble by Hansell and Swift on the same day set a new record: 60 seconds. No interception

took place but a 'Well Done' was passed down from Group.

21 August 1943 was the day of the actual move, and more new pilots arrived including Flight Sergeants Daff and Kinross, just in time to catch the train with everyone else. Accommodation at Perranporth consisted of a hotel taken over by the RAF which sat atop a 200 ft cliff overlooking a sandy beach and the Atlantic Ocean.

Keith Frederick Daff (Service no. 409090) was born on 24 June 1920 and was working as a florist when he enlisted on 19 July 1941, though he had once been fined for carrying a gun without a permit. He had served in the 37/39th Militia Battalion before joining the RAAF[173] and, considering how tough a time the 39th had it in New Guinea, fighting in the mud against the Japanese up and down the Kokoda Track, there's no doubt he preferred to be flying a Spitfire. But would a gun-toting Methodist florist make a good Spitfire pilot?

Kenneth Charles Kinross (Service no. 409147), of Essendon Victoria, was born on 25 September 1921 and was working as a clerk when he enlisted on 19 July 1941. After his initial training in the ways of the RAAF, which included plenty of marching and saluting, he was shipped off to Rhodesia via South Africa, where he completed his EFTS and SFTS. In November 1942 he embarked for the UK and arrived there in December 1942. 453 was his first posting.[174]

The squadron was flying again by 23 August, and Kel Barclay took Ernie Esau and Ron Ford to Portreath to get acquainted with the staff there. They also got a look at the captured FW-190 on the airfield. It was around this time that Rusty Leith was taught to drive, despite having been a pilot for more than a year. The Americans attached to the squadron instructed him in their jeep, most other pilots having cars of their own at the time.[175] The squadron was advised that they'd be receiving seven new pilots for training, though in fact for the month the squadron received two officers and sixteen NCO pilots. These postings included best mates Flight Sergeants Fred

Cowpe and Roderick Lyall as well as two other Flight Sergeants by the name of Scott and another two with the name of Wilson. It was getting a little crowded.

Roderick 'Froggy' Lyall (Service no. 409160) was born on 2 April 1922 and was a student at the time of enlistment on 19 July 1941. His initial RAAF training was at 1 ITS, Somers, Victoria and he completed his EFTS and SFTS in Rhodesia, soloing on a Tiger Moth after just over 10 hours instruction. He progressed to the Harvard and after a few months on the type he was rated as of average ability and progressed to more frequent solo flights, accumulating over 87 hours on the type. He arrived in the UK in December 1942 where, after the mandatory Tiger Moth reassessment, he completed his (P)AFU on the Miles Master, finally achieving his first Spitfire flight in a Mk IA on 30 May 1943 at 61 OTU before being posted to 453 Squadron with 54.20 hours on the Spitfire.[176]

One of the Scotts—Joshua William Scott (Service no. 405939)—was born on 26 December 1919 and was working as a farmer in Queensland when he enlisted on 22 June 1941. He completed his EFTS at Archerfield and his SFTS at Uranquinty, skipping the need for further training in Canada, and arrived in the UK in March 1943. 453 Squadron was his first operational posting.[177]

Fred Cowpe (Service no. 412491), born on 18 September 1919, was an apprentice boilermaker[178] when he joined the RAAF in 1941 to fly:

> That's the reason I joined the Air Force, nothing else, I was going to be no hero, I wasn't going to fight for me country, I just wanted to fly a Spitfire.[179]

After basic RAAF training in Australia, Fred was one of many Australian aircrew who went to train in Rhodesia, including a number of pilots who would fly with 453, including 'Froggy' Lyall, Jack Olver and John Barrien. From Tiger Moths in Australia, he went to Tiger Moths in Africa. After about 80 hours on them it was time for the Harvard, and a great many more hours as the training exercises became more complicated, and he arrived in the UK rated as an average pilot.[180] Various marks of the Miles Master were flown at (P)AFUs and OTUs prior to moving on to the Spitfire and he described them as: 'One of the easiest aircraft I have ever flown'. At the end of his training, he was given the choice of a number of aircraft to fly and had to list three in order of preference. He wrote Spitfire, Spitfire, Spitfire. Of this he later wrote: 'I was a fairly confident bloke in those days'.[181] 28 May 1943 was a big day for Fred, he was signed off on the cockpit drill, written test and familiarity with other systems on the Spitfire, and he had his first flight in one two days later—one hour up and around the blue but cloudy skies of England. Training could be as uncertain as operations as his entry for 12 July showed: 'Nearly 'had it' this morning, motor cut out when 12 miles out to sea off Birkenhead, but picked up enough to force land at Sealand'. Despite this incident, Spitfires and Fred got along just fine and after just over 50 hours on type, and rated as a good average, he was posted to B Flight, 453, which was being led by Russ Ewins.[182]

Don Andrews and Ross Currie carried out an escort of the captured FW-190 to Colerne, no doubt getting a very good look at it, since most glimpses of those in combat were rather too fleeting, though Don did have more experience with them than the rest of the squadron. Two successful Air Sea Rescues (ASR) were also carried out with overlapping patrols flown to keep an eye on the dinghies, but the squadron was disgusted on 31 August when a dinghy and pilot they had located and been circling using overlapping patrols just 15–20 miles from the French coast did not have a launch or ASR plane sent out. It didn't fill them with confidence.[183]

September began with poor weather and the squadron sending planes to a number of airfields where they flew patrols and waited for big shows that didn't happen. On September 3 and 4, aircraft were deployed to Portreath for the day on convoy patrols, and cover for friendly Motor Gun Boats (MGBs) returning from operations off the French coast. Conditions

Keith Daff (centre) and Fred Cowpe with pipe (second from right) in Cape Town October 1942. (Courtesy of the Cowpe family)

at Perranporth were so bad that to take off on the 4th, planes for the 1010 sortie had to taxi with men sitting on the tails and wings to keep them stable. On the following day, packing commenced for a move to Kenley. Two pilots were sent ahead to ensure things were set for their arrival, and the remainder practised interception of enemy aircraft, using a Wellington and Beaufighter as their targets, and discussing tactics after completing the exercise. Ground crew moved by plane or rail to Kenley on 6 September, and the rest of pilots moved on the 7th.

On 8 September, the squadron flew two Ramrods from Kenley. The first was as escort cover[184] for 72 Marauders bombing an airfield near Lille, and the second was a coastal patrol as medium cover [185] between Cap Gris Nez and Boulogne while the bombers proceeded inland to their target.

That evening there was a briefing for the next day's Operation 'Starkey'. The original plan was to threaten a landing on the French coast and then, if circumstances permitted, actually carry one out with the troops on board. However, this was wound back to a deception-only plan, and no landing troops were to be risked. It would, however, serve as a large scale exercise for the landings planned (at that time) for May 1944. The Luftwaffe would be baited into attacking this 'invasion force' and be shot down by the dozens.[186]

453 Squadron flew two patrols on the morning of 9 September over the convoy as it sailed towards the French coast, and Bostons laid smoke screens to mask the approach and retreat of the mock assault force, described by Andrews as 'all sorts of ships',[187] which had no intention of landing in France. The naval departure was the final stage of the operation, but the Germans refused to be baited, especially since 39 squadrons of Spitfires were involved, in addition to numerous other squadrons of other types.[188] Coastal batteries and gun positions were bombarded from the air in numerous attacks, as were thirteen airfields in the area. But, at day's end, only two Luftwaffe aircraft were claimed shot down.[189] Total claims for the 2,000 sorties flown on this single day were 12 enemy aircraft destroyed, so some must have been destroyed on the ground during the numerous airfield raids that took place. Some aircraft bore black and white stripes to aid identification, (though in a slightly different style to those applied for Normandy) and the success of these for this operation led to the large-scale adoption for Operation Overlord in June 1944.[190]

A Ramrod was launched at 1359 on the afternoon of 9 September, the squadron flying escort cover to Mitchells attacking an airfield near Brias, about 20 miles north west of Arras. This was due to be followed by another, but it was cancelled due to the weather. That was the end of the temporary move and the award of the DFC to Don Andrews was made on 10 September, the citation making mention of his recent Focke-Wulf encounter.

The squadron could not make it back to Perranporth in one flight due to weather and stopped at Exeter for the night. Upon arriving at Perranporth the next day, they were put on readiness as soon as the aircraft had been checked over, and were twice scrambled that afternoon.[191]

Convoy patrols were flown on 12 September, and the four-seasons-in-one-day weather continued to play havoc with operations. After cine-gun practice on the following day, Mervyn Nolan overshot his landing and,

Studio photo of Don Andrews with his newly-awarded DFC ribbon. (Courtesy of the Andrews family)

when halfway down the airfield, put on power to do another circuit and try again, but left his landing gear down. These caught on telegraph wires at the end of the airfield and slowed the plane so much that he stalled and crashed his Spitfire VC (EE727)[192] into houses, killing himself, a resident and injuring two others. The investigation found that he should have retracted his undercarriage and failure to do so caused the crash. Kel Barclay enclosed a set of his wings in the letter sent to the family. The letter included the following paragraph:

> I had been his commanding officer for only two months but in that time I quickly realised he was of the brand of men we needed. His air of quiet confidence and perpetual good nature soon made him a friend to all and we miss him very much.[193]

The weather continued to be variable and a number of uneventful scrambles and convoy patrols were made over the next few days. On 18 September, eight aircraft led by Kel Barclay and Don Andrews were detailed on a 'secret Naval Liaison job'.[194] After lunch, the squadron forward deployed to Bolt Head for an operation which was later cancelled, and they returned, to be released for the first time since they'd been at Ibsley. They could all relax—in the wind and rain of course.

19 September saw the announcement of the commission of Jack Olver to Pilot Officer, backdated to July, though he was on a three week fighter course and did not return to the squadron until 22 September. The 21st saw Don Andrews made a member of the Caterpillar Club for his successful bail out back in July.

The squadron was sent to Bolt Head again on 22 September and, this time, the Ramrod went ahead, with Mitchells bombing an airfield at Guipavas on the outskirts of Brest. Another Ramrod was carried out on the following day, and the squadron was based at Tangmere for the day.

The first Ramrod on 24 September was the first operational sortie for Norman Baker, flying 'G'. All other flights were uneventful scrambles, practice flights or convoy escorts. This time Baker was taking the fight to the Germans and later recorded that he was 'scared stiff'.[195] Near Brest, the target for the day, the lead fighter escorts were charged head-on by Me-110s. 453 dived down to join in, but the Luftwaffe did their usual dive away and so the Australians took up a position to the starboard side of the bombers, but not before both sides suffered losses and flaming wrecks dramatically fell from the sky into the ocean below.

After the bombing took place, FW-190s dived down and attacked a straggling Mitchell bomber which was under escort, and 453 were told to stay out of it and keep an eye out for any others that might come down out of the sun. Staring too much in that direction and not keeping an eye on his section, Baker found himself out of position by half a mile or more, and looked down at the throttle: there was a wire across the final section. This was 'the gate', which blocked throttle progress since giving the engine all it was worth was to be done only in an emergency, and a broken wire would let the ground crew know how a pilot had been treating the engine. On his first operational flight in the face of the enemy, being alone and out of formation was sufficient justification for Baker to deem it an emergency and he pushed the throttle through the gate and, with a powerful surge from the Merlin, he made his way back to the squadron. While he made it back to them safely enough, everyone gave him a hard time about it later on, in the way young men do.

Baker participated in the next Ramrod that afternoon and was a little more relaxed, with the Luftwaffe not making an appearance.[196] Fear was rarely mentioned but ever-present. While many years later such events and the emotions of those who lived through them are often glossed over by those who heap praise on the dashing and brave fighter pilots, these experiences of Norm Baker and Ron Ford illustrate the brutal reality of the situation. Young men were flying planes built for the purpose of shooting down other planes piloted by other young men who were in the air for the exact same purpose. Despite the notions of beauty and glory associated with the Spitfire, it was a killing machine and, if you were flying one, someone else would be trying to kill you. Bravery is not necessarily the lack of fear, but it is being able to do what is necessary even when you are scared, as Baker, Ford and all those who fought in the war knew.

On 28 September, Kel Barclay went on rest and was posted to 10 Group. Don Andrews was promoted to Squadron Leader and was a very popular choice; the squadron had been able to achieve promotions from within on the last few occasions positions had been vacated and they were quite happy to have it that way. At the end of the month the weather had taken its toll, and quite a few pilots were out of action with colds.[197]

October started with convoy patrols on the 2nd, and on the 3rd things got busy. The Perranporth Wing, of which 453 was a part, flew to Bradwell Bay, northeast of London, with S/Ldr Loftus of 66 Squadron acting as Wing Commander. From there they escorted Marauders on a Ramrod to the Netherlands. After returning from this operation, they moved to

West Malling in Kent and acted as close escort in the next Ramrod, with Marauders bombing the airfield at Beauvais, about 45 miles east of Rouen. On the return journey some FW-190s jumped 66 Squadron but they broke and the FW-190s dived away, their advantage lost when Don Andrews called a warning. Dick Darcey, flying in 'X' as Blue 1, saw some FW-190s approaching the rear of the bomber formation and turned his section after them, only to find a FW-190 on his tail. He avoided it successfully and Blue 2 and 3, Jack Olver in 'U' and Lionel Hansell in 'R' both took shots at the FW-190s behind the bombers but made no claims. They landed at Kenley at the end of this sortie and spent the night there, returning to Perranporth the next day after stopping at Exeter along the way.[198]

The next few days were restricted by poor weather but offensive patrols were flown on 7–8 October. The seven-plane patrol on the 8th was led by Don Andrews in '?' and took off at 0735 for an anti-Me-110 patrol. These patrols were sent out to look for the long-range Me-110 twin-engine fighters that were in turn hunting RAF Coastal Command Sunderlands.[199]

Don Andrews (right) farewells Kel Barclay, October 1943.
(Courtesy of the Andrews family)

The action and reaction sequence went as follows:

> The convoys were sent to the UK from Canada and the USA.
>
> The U-boats were sent to sink to convoys.
>
> The Sunderlands were sent to sink the U-boats.
>
> The Me-110s were sent to shoot down the Sunderlands.
>
> The Spitfires were sent to shoot down the Me-110s.

In the Bay of Biscay, the RAF fought another, similar war, out of the range of Spitfire protection:[200]

> Sunderlands were sent to sink U-boats who were based there.
>
> The U-boats were trying to get to the Atlantic to sink the convoys.
>
> Ju-88s and Me-110s were sent to shoot down the Sunderlands.
>
> Beaufighters and Mosquitos were sent to shoot down the Ju-88s and Me-110s.
>
> FW-190s were sent to shoot down the Beaufighters and Mosquitos

From these examples it can be seen how long a chain reaction of planning and operations can be, and how many units can become involved. Both 10 and 461 Squadrons operated in these areas and modified their Sunderlands by fitting extra machine guns to help cope with the threat.[201] These two Australian squadrons performed this valuable—but rather monotonous, and rarely exciting—task throughout the war. In the case of 10 Squadron, they had been in the UK since war was declared. On the third leg of the patrol, at 0833, Don Andrews spotted eight aircraft travelling towards the northwest and, upon closer inspection, they were discovered to be two vics of four Me-110s at just 200 ft, just what they were looking for. Andrews led the patrol down in a diving attack and the Me-110s made a slow turn to port, too much drastic action at that height liable to lose them what little height they had, or put them into the sea altogether. When the Spitfires were about 500 yards away from the Me-110s, the Germans broke and a wild melee followed as the Australians tore into them. Rusty Leith was, quite rightly, always very conscious that 'flying is a three dimensional thing ... you can make a lot of mistakes',[202] so trying to force these on your opponent is one of the goals of air to air combat. He was after one particular Me-110 who always turned into him as he opened fire, trying to force a sharp angle on the attack that could not be maintained, thereby forcing the attacker to miss, while the Me-110s rear gunner also fired at the Spitfire. As the German pilot made these turns he was losing height, so Rusty pulled up to gain some height of his own and make a diving attack. After a few of these the Me-110 turned one too many times, too low, and put its left wing into the water '... there was a huge splash and that was the end of him'.[203] Though Andrews' cannons both jammed,[204] by the end of the combat two Me-110s had gone down in flames, one was steadily losing height with its wheels down but nowhere to land, and a fourth was making for France with smoke coming from both engines.

During the combat, F/O Parker in 'J' was seen to dive down at a steep angle and crash into the ocean. Russ Ewins called up on the R/T with engine trouble after the combat, and once his plane had been assessed by Ross Currie and deemed to be incapable of getting him back to shore, he rolled it over and bailed out while the plane was upside down, letting gravity do some of the work, and with perhaps less chance of hitting the tail as so many fighter pilots did during the war. On the way down in his parachute, Russ inflated his 'mae west' and, upon hitting the water, went under for just a second before inflating his dingy and climbing in. Don Andrews stayed low and kept track of Russ as he got into the dinghy and put the sail up, while others climbed for altitude and broadcast his location so that he could be picked up. He gave them a wave to indicate that he was okay and, when fuel became critical, the Spitfires headed for home. He tried some chewing gum but was soon seasick, much to the delight of some seagulls.

After Andrews and the rest returned to base, they were replaced by some others but apparently they did not see him, and he tried to fire some distress rockets, but they failed to fire, except the one which backfired and made a hole in the bottom of the dingy which he had to plug. He was circled by some Hurricanes while he sat with the sail out, and they were later replaced by a Mosquito but no one could stay for long, and it was probably for the best as eight Me-110s also passed overhead, headed south from a patrol of their own. He also watched an engagement between two Spitfires and eight Me-110s and had the satisfaction of seeing one of the 110s go down. Shortly afterwards, after 1400, two destroyers approached and he was rescued by the navy and taken to Mount Batten.[205] After reviewing the combat and comparing notes, final claims were: two for McDade, two for Leith and one for Ewins.[206] The victory was celebrated in a number of newspaper articles back in Australia, with Rusty Leith getting a mention in the 13 October edition of *The Armidale Express and New England General Advertiser*, with reference to his time at The Armidale School.[207] Both he and Pat McDade received a mention in the *Queensland Times* of 11 October which credited them as being 'Two pilots from an Australian Spitfire Squadron'.[208]

Don Andrews and his German Shepherd 'Sprog'. 'Sprog' was slang for a new pilot. The message on the back of the photograph reads: 'This is Sprog the day after I bought him. Pretty BA of myself. Had a party the night before'.
(Courtesy of the Andrews family)

'Sprog' some time later with a member of ground crew. Don Andrews loved his dog and sent many photos of him home to Australia.
(Courtesy of the Andrews family)

Don Andrews, 'Sprog' and a Mk V with slipper tank. October 1943.
(Courtesy of the Andrews family)

9 October saw the squadron move to Bolt Head from where they escorted Mitchells on a bombing sortie to an airfield in France, and Russ Ewins returned to the squadron, having stayed the night at Mount Batten. News of another move came through on the following day, and three pilots, Galwey, Darcey and Greaves, were sent home to Australia on the 11th. The final news of the move came through on the 13th, the destination being Skeabrae up in the Orkney Islands, almost as close to Norway as you could get and still be in Great Britain. The squadron had its send-off drinks at their regular drinking hole, The Stork, and souvenired the sign board on the way home.

The train journey was close to 1,000 miles with 16 transfers (including a motorcycle, of course, and a final boat journey which caused some seasickness). This was the longest move of an RAAF Squadron in the UK during the war. The logistics of the move were simplified by leaving all the ground crew except Sergeant McKinnon at Perranporth. While Sergeant McKinnon was held in high regard, and they would have preferred everyone to go together, but it was not to be. The popularity of the move dipped even lower when it was made known that their replacements, a Free French Squadron, had originally been directed to the Orkneys but they had complained so much that 453 were sent in their place. That a Polish squadron had avoided the posting by the same method gave the squadron the distinct impression that being from a 'Dominion' put them at a disadvantage, and they didn't like it. This disappointment was balanced by the expectation that there would be more eggs available, though how the logic of this came about is not known. Most sadly of all, 'Sprog', the German Shepherd belonging to Don Andrews, had to be left behind.

The squadron inherited clipped-wing Mk VBs from the Free French and those flying them took a number of days to get to the new airfield, the weather being less than agreeable on the trip. The group's first question on arrival was: 'What's the food like?' 'Satisfactory' was the answer. Better than bad at least. The officers of the squadron were met with the gift of two dozen fresh eggs by the station Intelligence Officer, which they gladly accepted. The Nissen huts had almost rusted through in the two years they had been there, and all water had to be boiled. The station Medical Officer was not allowed to inspect the water filtration system—it belonged to the Royal Navy, and he did not.[209] The weather was terrible, with a 60 mph wind described as a 'mild breeze' and 100 mph wind as 'normal'. Fred Cowpe described it as: 'one of the most desolate places on earth'.[210] A number of squadrons would rotate through the area during and after the war. In May 1945, when 451 (RAAF) Squadron were moved up there, Sid Handsaker recorded in his pilot's logbook: 'Good trip to Orkneys. What a dump!'[211]

Whilst in the Orkneys, the squadron was to be known as 'S' Squadron in an attempt to confuse the Germans. Almost every day 'Weather Willie', a Ju-86 based in Norway on weather recce sorties, flew over the North Sea and paid them a visit. Another regular Luftwaffe visitor was a photo-reconnaissance sortie flown by 'Recce Reggie'. By 18 October, everyone had arrived, those flying the Mk Vs crediting the 'wizard navigation' of Don Andrews getting them there safely. They were immediately tasked to perform readiness duties.[212] On the 20th, one Flight was detached to Sumburgh in the Shetlands, about 100 miles away from Skeabrae and almost as far north as Oslo. The move of this Flight took more than a day and the squadron was effectively cut in two, this being the standard deployment for squadrons based at Skeabrae.[213] For the rest of the month, both Flights conducted local patrols and exercises when the weather permitted. The pilots really had to entertain themselves, as Rusty Leith described in a letter home:

> You may be surprised to know that I have had an attempt at growing a 'mo'. When we landed in the Shetlands we all decided to grow moustaches. After many days a few straggly bits of stuff appeared, and after a couple of weeks something reasonable was visible to the naked eye. However, it came early in November and I was to go off on leave, so I shaved 'it' off, much to the disgust of the lads who said I was letting the side down. It was quite good fun and was the topic for some most uncomplimentary remarks to hurl at each other.[214]

The first week of November 'up north' saw little flying, an exercise was cancelled due to the weather, and a number of pilots went on leave. A unique feature of this deployment was the attachment of Spitfire Mk VIIs, the high-level interceptors based in the area and passed from squadron to squadron as they rotated through. Some pilots, including Don Andrews, Jack Olver and Fred Cowpe took flights in these Spitfires (one of which was coded Z and another Y) to test their capabilities.[215] These were scrambled on 7 November, but no interception was made, though they made it to 37,000 ft on this particular flight. The squadron also traded visits with the Royal Navy, some pilots having a look at a submarine and showing some sailors around their Spitfires in return. A number of exercises were carried out under the name of 'Driver' with aircraft attacking and defending shipping to familiarise themselves with tactics and best approaches. The weather was highly variable and some patrols were flown but, overall, it was a cold and dreary November. Despite this, they had some fun with an airfield defence exercise during which John Barrien and Ron Ford attacked the airfield, taking the AA defences by surprise even though they knew the Spitfires were coming.

A number of pilots were posted in and out of the squadron, diluting the level of experience.[216] One of those to leave was Rusty Leith, posted for a rest to 57 OTU at Eshott as a gunnery instructor. While it wasn't a welcome posting (pilots were sometimes reluctant to leave their squadron mates, even though they might be well above the maximum flying hours nominated before mandatory rest periods), and the inexperienced pilots caused him some concern (as new pilots are prone to do), Leith made the most of the position and spent as much time as he could playing rugby.[217] He wanted to be back with his squadron as soon as his time was up.[218] While he was gone, he was not forgotten, and Don Andrews and the squadron sent him a cable wishing him a happy Christmas, and he was lucky enough to chat with them on the phone also.[219]

Action soon followed, when the third scramble of 2 December brought Ernie Esau and Leo McAuliffe in contact with a Ju-88 which they both engaged. It was flying at 1,500 ft about 35 miles south-southeast of Sumburgh and when they opened fire on it, it went into a dive and the rear gunner opened up. To get under his fire, the Spitfires took a steeper dive and both attacked from underneath, using all their ammunition and leaving it slow and smoking trying to cross the North Sea.[220] They claimed a probable, though the next day it was upgraded to a destroyed when German radio messages were intercepted confirming their success.

The squadron held a party at Skeabrae on 6 December, though not everyone from the Shetlands was able to attend. Jack Ratten made a welcome appearance and those left at Sumburgh went to an Entertainments National Service Association (ENSA) show on the following day as a mild form of compensation. Jim Ferguson was posted to 57 OTU as a flying instructor, and would not return to the squadron until late July 1944.[221]

December 10 and 11 saw the Sumburgh detachment engaging with Royal Navy FAA Barracudas and Seafires on interception exercises, Ernie Esau visiting the commander of the Seafires in person to hand out some advice when he thought that the whole formation could have been wiped out had 453 been a Luftwaffe squadron. The next few days saw more exercises, defending against an amphibious landing and another against a fighter raid.

On 12 December, things got a little out of hand when, after a few drinks, some of the squadron decided to write a letter to the recently posted Jim Ferguson. Members generally wrote a few sentences or a paragraph before passing it on to someone else. It is very enlightening, especially for anyone who may be under the impression that, during the Second World War, swearing was limited to descriptions of events or people being 'frightful', or maybe even 'terribly frightful'. Even by modern standards, this letter has required some censorship to enable it to be presented here:

Dear Fergie,

Thanks very much for your letter which arrived two days ago. We've had wizard weather since you left us and have done bags of flying. I have shown your letter around all the boys. They all of course thought it was a wizard letter. It brought its fair share of laughs. I was surprised to hear that you were welcomed by a beer.

Am pretty disgusted with myself being a teetotaller myself you know. Well Fergie you old bastard you're a lucky man to be at a real OTU. I reckon as how you must be one of the bestest little instructors ever. This is just a clapped out second hand EFTS up here now with me as chief black putter upper—Hope to go solo soon. In case you don't know who this is—Well folks call me Joe around here.

Fergie, this is the old Rog, still got the finger wedged. Is W/C Gough still CFO? All the best—my own personal letter following in exactly two days time, Roger.

Thank God he's gone. Well hello again. Had better piss off myself. See you Foosdy, Fergie old son. Was bloody sorry to hear you'd gone and the old gang has gone for a burton properly now.

Rog again—remember me to Win/Co Gough—he put me up for Commis. All the best and keep the finger out.

P/S Len & Rog Bush have taken over the letter. You may have Jack Olver soon. At the moment he is organising some more grog. We had a wizzo party to celebrate the JU88 destroyed by Ernie MacAuliffe. One of the boys came down from Sumburgh, 25 of us devoured 260 pints of beer and 8 bottles of whiskey. We finished up with our ties as belts doing Volga Boatman acts all around the place. Judging by the state of my shirt the next day I must have lain on the beer swamped floor at some stage or other. During a mock fight I changed the colour of Roger Bush's eye. Winco Ratten was here also. I should mention that as this is Sunday night we have just had quarts and cinema in the ante room. We have a new WAAF officer who is a bit of all right even in Orkney; and upon whom I should like to go the big grope; but as I am inexperienced in the art of throwing myself at a woman I must be content to be one of the surrounding group. I am standing the fire writing this on the mantelpiece with my eyes rather dimmer by numerous whiskeys and beers.

BIG FLASH Jack Stansfield is in bed with the flu. AND I am leaving tomorrow to report to a Flying Instructors Selection Committee in London on Tuesday along with Ross Currie, Bob Yarra, Count Barrien, Rickard and MacAuliffe. Brassed off 'nuff said. Kind regards from Smithy of Drem!!! (Hansell told me to say that). Pacy is seeing us as far as Turnhouse and is going to meet us at Inverness next Saturday in time to get us to a Sergeants' Mess Dance.

JACK OLVER—Tommy has just said that I am a shit in front of a WAAF officer. Good of him isn't it! So sad—another beer has just turned up. We are all behaving ourselves pretty well u here, all except Swift and as you can see from the above, he is right on his top form. But seriously Fergie I was damn glad to read your note to Tom and I hope you are reasonably happy amongst those lousy types who not only by (BUY—he's pissed) a bloke one beer,—hell I must be tight—two r's in beer. Well cheers for the moment Fergie and I'll drop you a line pretty soon. John Olver.

Hello Fergie I guess by the time you have read this far you have guessed that the 'boys'—self included, I hope—are on a binge. Nevertheless without reading a word that has been written before me I can say that everything that has been said is sincere. At any rate Fergie all the best from self and Don't let the poor bastards prang you. Hoping to have a beer with you soon (bought by you of course) Very sincerely, Don Andrews.

And now I must make way for Henry to stagger up to the fireplace lean on the mantelpiece and say a few lines:

My dear boy I am so sorry to have to tell you that the famous pursuit squadron that you and I knew is being subjected to the dirtiest sabotage that one can possibly conceive. Still fergie the time will come when we will all be together once more and clean up Australia home and the gum trees from the GUM (We miss you Ferg)

2350 hrs. By cripes the boys are drunk now. We've been singing all sorts of songs (WAAF Officer present—so clean!) Now everybody even Hansell is singing 'Jerusalem.' Sorry for the writing but I've gone for a shit. I've got the hiccups. Christ if I am posted. I'm going to feel as crook as you Fergie!!! There is nothing as binding to take the place of home and close friend life as the life on a squadron with a gang of OK blokes. Don't you pity the blokes who are shifted from place to place solo? S a squadron we didn't care where the hell we went, as long as we were together. In the service one learns to make friends quickly and easily, but the friends one lives and works with in all sorts of jobs are the friends that count. Here comes Hansell. He is gurgling from a chair close by.

Well you old shit, Sir Shit I mean. Now this is 12.10am. Now I reckon you're one of the very bestest little _____ one of those—Bugger there's too many plumy people talking here for me to think even if the Good Lord had gifted me with the necessary apparatus—'All right, I'll get the bloody eggs you bloody Bastards.' Stomping out said Roger. And 'If you're writing like a drinken bastard Hansell, Fergie'll appreciate it.' (SWIFT) Wish I could think of something original to say. Maybe I'm a Dull Shit

13th Dec At this moment Fergie I am more or less sober and saner. I am in Edinburgh—thought I'd have a night with Sheila—went to my dreadful interview. I made inquiries about your mail and it has been sent back to Kodak House so I was unable to do anything about it. All the best Fergie, maybe from my point of view you are more fortunate than I. I'll probably be hurried off to AFU

Yours

Tom [222]

On 20 December, a Mosquito crashed into the sea near Sumburgh and the ASR sent out could not locate it. Three Spitfires from 453 on a practice flight, including Norm Baker in 'J'[223] found it a little later, and a new ASR attempt was made, this time being directed to the wreckage. Only one body was retrieved. More pilots went on leave, more practice flying took place when allowed and some parties were held but, in the cold, windy and snowy northern islands, things were not particularly exciting.²²⁴ A scramble on 29 December found its prey to be a drifting barrage balloon.²²⁵

The first days of 1944 brought rain, snow, ice, high winds and little flying, but good news strategically. Fighter Command now had 102 operational squadrons in the UK and they were bolstered by the arrival of an increasing number of USAAF squadrons. 465 (RAAF) Squadron was planned as a Typhoon squadron, as there was now an excess of fighter pilots available. Although they could have potentially formed an 'ANZAC Wing' by equipping them with Spitfires and including one of the RNZAF Squadrons, it was not to be. 465 was eventually reclassified as a bomber squadron—but only ever on paper—and was never formed.²²⁶ 453 remained the only RAAF fighter squadron in the UK, and now represented less than one percent of the fighter force, though Australians continued to serve in small numbers throughout the RAF, in all commands. In fact, by May 1943, Australians were serving in 135 different squadrons throughout the UK.²²⁷ Despite the wishes of the Australian Government to cluster Australian squadrons together so they could from Australian Wings (as the Canadians were able to do) commanded by Australians, this just wasn't practical, since the squadrons were equipped with too many different types of aircraft and carried out too many roles. This applied not only to those RAAF squadrons based in the UK, but those in the Middle East as well.²²⁸

801 Squadron (Royal Navy Seafires) off HMS *Furious* arrived at Skeabrae for a short posting. On 13 January, the squadron received news of an impending move, and the arrival of six new pilots to replace those posted out. Tom Swift was sent home to Australia where he joined 452 (RAAF) Squadron then 80 Wing HQ (the Spitfire Wing). Swift had been one of the first pilots in the squadron when it had formed in Scotland.²²⁹ As for the move, the squadron diary recorded: 'The further south the better.'²³⁰ A few final patrols were flown in the last days at Skeabrae and Sumburgh and, after some time in transit, the squadron arrived at 125 Airfield, Detling in

Christmas parade in the Orkneys. It appears that some people were not taking it seriously!
(Courtesy of the Cowpe family)

Sgt McKinnon pictured in May 1944 at Ford in Sussex..
(Courtesy of the Cowpe family)

Kent on 19 January. Some lovely Mk IXs awaited them,[231] left behind by the airfield's previous occupants 132 and 602 Squadrons, the Spitfires taken over by 453 retaining the 'LO' code markings from 602.[232]

More pilots arrived on 21 January, and all available pilots went to 16 Armament Practice Camp (APC) Hutton Cranswick in their LO-bearing Mk IXs for firing practice, something rarely done in the inhospitable Orkneys. This was part of a scheme to get all units up to scratch in preparation for the return to France, units passing through different locations based on aircraft and weapon type.[233] Sgt McKinnon of the ground crew returned from a Merlin Engine course at Rolls Royce at the end of the month.[234]

January 1944 also saw the arrival of F/Sgt Brian William Gorman (409108), another Australian who had trained in Rhodesia. After embarking in South Africa on HMT *Oronsay* on 29 September 1942, the ship headed for the UK but was sunk about 0515 local time on 9 October. For five days Brian and others from the ship shared lifeboats and waited to be rescued but, instead, they were captured by a Vichy French coastal sloop. On 19 October they were dropped off at Dakar and transported to a prison camp at Sebikotane, where they stayed for three days. This camp was actually a converted native school, three of the classrooms being used for prisoners. Each prisoner had a metal bed frame, a mattress, two sheets, and a blanket, but nothing to protect them from the mosquitos. Two meals were served each day, weevil-infested bread and macaroni for lunch and dinner, with cold black coffee as breakfast. On the rare occasion that meat was provided it was accompanied by wriggling maggots. All clothing was confiscated and prison attire and water bottles issued. The drinking water was in short supply and what there was for washing themselves and their clothes was barely suitable for that. There was no toilet paper, nothing to clean the toilets with, and soon the prisoners had to be wary of maggots there too. The exercise yard available for all prisoners measured 40 ft x 80 ft and news of the war was deliberately kept from them. They were isolated in just about every way possible. The Vichy French officer in charge and his Senegalese guards contributed nothing to improve the lot of the prisoners and were actively hostile.

They were moved by rail to another camp at Bamako, arriving there on 25 October. In this camp 65 prisoners were crowded into three rooms with no beds for the first three weeks. This crowding made the heat even more unbearable than it already was, and the situation deteriorated as more prisoners arrived. The weevil-infested macaroni and bread continued but the meat (when provided) was better than the previous camp and there were sometimes vegetables. However, the food was cooked at a facility (if it could be called such a thing) a mile away, and so it usually arrived cold. The water was still bad, even though there was now plenty of it and, again, there was no toilet paper. Red Cross parcels arrived in early November, and it was only with a great deal of trouble that the medical supplies confiscated from the parcels by the Vichy French were eventually returned. Dysentery was common, as was malaria and, due to medical inattention by the Vichy French, one prisoner died of appendicitis. There they remained until 15 December, when they were transferred to Gambia and boarded a ship which took them back into Allied custody, as the Vichy French had surrendered in North Africa. Gorman and others remained in Africa until 12 February 1943, when they boarded a ship for the UK. Prior to this, he and nearly all prisoners, required a lengthy hospital stay to recover from their neglect at the hands of the Vichy French. Gorman spent 18 days in hospital before he could be released for the final journey to the UK.[235]

453 Squadron returned to Detling on 4 February 1944, and a lot of formation flying took place to get the newer pilots up to speed and remind everyone what having twelve planes in the air looked and felt like. RAAF Liaison Officer S/Ldr Hilton arrived at the squadron and stayed overnight to meet with as many pilots and ground crew as possible.

February also saw the squadron permanently re-equipped with Spitfire Mk IXs and a notice was sent to RAAF HQ to inform them of the upgrade—thankfully they did not object. This was part of a rationalisation program for all Allied Expeditionary Air Force (AEAF) squadrons in the lead-up to Operation Overlord.[236]

11 February saw the first operation flown from Detling by the squadron, escorting Marauders to Amiens, with the Wing being led by Don Andrews. Fred Cowpe flew as Blue 2 to Don Andrews and noted that the Don's plane was hit by flak in the gun bay of one wing.[237] On 13 February, another escort sortie was flown, though four of eleven pilots had fuel tank or R/T trouble and had to return. That night, a Luftwaffe raider dropped bombs on the airfield but no one was injured. The 14th saw Wing formation practice flying and this was put to good use on the following day when Don Andrews led the Wing twice to France. This was followed by a number of days of bad weather, including snow, and operations resumed on 20 February with an escort to Marauders in the morning and a withdrawal cover to Liberators and Flying Fortresses in the afternoon. These were the first operations of this size for Cowpe and Lyall.

21 February saw the squadron deployed from Manston, though their strength was reduced when Ken Kinross had to land immediately after take-off due to oil on his hood and, in doing so collided with Norm Baker and wrote off both planes. Norm Baker had to put up with not flying around with FU-K on the side of his plane for a little while. Everyone else managed well enough and provided the escort to Marauders. 22 February again saw the Wing provide withdrawal cover for bombers, but snow shut everything down the next day. Two more Ramrods took place on 24 February, and again on the 25th, with Fred Cowpe in 'S' losing a port wing gun panel and camera panel on the dive back home.[238] One more Ramrod took place on 28 February to finish up the squadron's operational flying for the month. Not a single enemy aircraft was engaged.[239]

Two more Ramrods were flown on 2 March, this time utilising 45 gallon drop tanks to extend the range of the Mk IXs even further. Fred Cowpe didn't make it all the way—'X' developed a fracture in a fuel pipe and he had to make a forced landing with a dead engine (wheels down, luckily) at New Romney, and he flew back to Detling after repairs were made.[240] Another was flown the next day—all these being close to or just over two hours' duration, something the squadron had rarely done up to that point. Due to the cold, the squadron received a few sets of heated flight suits and these were worn by some pilots that month, though on his first flight wearing one, Pat McDade got a blister on one foot from a short circuit then, when he turned the suit off to ease the pain, got a bit of frostbite on one thumb. The overall assessment of the suits was quite good but the gauntlets were felt to be too cumbersome.[241]

Two Escorts were flown from Manston on 4 March. That night a dance was held in the officer's mess at Detling for 184 Squadron and, since the weather didn't look favourable for the next morning, some decided to extract maximum value and kept the party going until the early hours.

The next day saw an operation run that was commonly held across airfields in the UK from time to time. Pilots were taken away from the airfield and dropped off as if they were behind enemy lines. Local authorities were notified to be on the lookout and the pilots had to make their way back to the airfield using their initiative and training. They each walked about 10 miles and had a good time of it, and some would, in fact, need to draw on that experience sooner than they wished. On 6 March, everyone lined up for their typhus inoculations. This didn't have any adverse effects and flying took place the next day for the escort sortie as planned.[242]

Two more Ramrods were held on 8 March, and news of an important visitor did the rounds. A guessing competition was held, but no bets were placed. It was in fact HRH The Duke of Gloucester who, along with three Air Vice Marshals and a Group Captain, visited on the 9th. They were met by the Airfield Commander, W/Cdr Lapsley, and escorted by Don Andrews and Russ Ewins on an inspection of the squadron and aircraft with pilots and ground crew lined up. This was followed by a cup of tea and photos. One voice, whose identity is unrecorded in the squadron record but later revealed in a private letter to be Stansfield,[243] asked: 'Don't you get fed up with this, Duke?' He replied: 'Yes, as far as having my photograph taken is concerned'.

The squadron then went to Peterhead for firing and bombing training during which time Ron Ford was posted out to 53 OTU as a flying instructor and he remained in that position until February 1945, missing out on Normandy entirely.[244] He'd been with the squadron since 14 June 1942 and scored sixes and sevens in his assessments from Don Andrews who remarked that he was 'an above average pilot and officer' and later received all sevens from his commander at the OTU. Marks of six and above were considered above average.[245] Unfortunately, while off duty on 15 June 1944, Ford slipped in the mess and suffered injuries that removed him from flying status for some time. He didn't fully recover and was later restricted to a maximum of three hours flying in a single sortie and returned to Australia on these grounds.[246] The RAF had been wrong about Ron Ford—he had done his job well.

On 18 March, during the training at Peterhead F/Sgt Brian Gorman crashed his plane, a Spitfire Mk IX (MK281), and was killed. An investigation found no mechanical fault. During the flight, the Spitfire went into a steep turn which continued through about 360 degrees before it flicked onto its back and went into a spin. This happened at a very low altitude of just 1,000 ft, an almost impossible height from which to recover from an upside-down spin. It was thought that the steep turn was unnecessary, as all Gorman had to do was to climb and return to base, having just made an attack with practice bombs. Though the bomb rack changed the flying characteristics of the Spitfire, this should not have been a major factor due to this being covered by pre-sortie lectures. While the loss of another pilot due to a flying

Aircraft, aircrew and ground crew lined up for inspection by the Duke of Gloucester on 9 March 1944. The Spitfires retain the markings of 602 Squadron, which had recently left the airfield. The LO letter code and the crest under the exhaust can be seen on the plane second from the camera; 453 had not yet re-marked them.
(Courtesy of the Cowpe family)

The Duke of Gloucester, accompanied by Group Captain Lord Willoughby de Broke, visits 453 Squadron. Don Andrews is directly behind the Duke and is not wearing an officers cap as his was a bit 'out of shape'.
(Courtesy of the Cowpe family)

accident dealt the squadron a blow, the effect went through the ranks up to the Station Commander, W/Cdr Jack Ratten. Brian Gorman was buried at Longside Cemetery in Peterhead as a Warrant Officer, his promotion had come through on 11 March, but he had not yet been informed.[247]

The pilots and planes returned to Detling on 19 March to find that 132 and 602 Squadron had arrived, replacing 184 and 118 Squadrons.[248] 453 would spend the entire Normandy campaign and (even some time beyond that) in the company of these squadrons, 602 being notable for a number of firsts and establishing a strong history for itself. On 16 October 1939, though an Auxiliary (or Reservist) Squadron, they were the first RAF squadron to fight the Luftwaffe in air to air combat over the UK, when based at dreary Drem, no less. Though the roster had changed over time, 602 had played host to pilots who had been the first to fly over Mt Everest and they were also the first Auxiliary Squadron to be equipped with Spitfires. In June 1940 they'd been the first to achieve a 'night kill' with a Spitfire and had counted in their ranks such notable names as Al Deere, Paddy Finucane and Ginger Lacy.[249] They were not inexperienced in the ways of 'Dominion' Squadrons, having flown with 452 (RAAF) and 485 (RNZAF) Squadrons in 1941 and like most fighter squadrons, had a number of Australians pass through their ranks.[250]

On 20 March, 453 squadron was given a rare full day off, and so went to town, in both senses. Three more old hands—Clemesha, Hansell and Stansfield—were posted out on the 21st and a party was held in their honour. Though attending a course, Don Andrews came back to visit the squadron for a day and delivered some stern comments about the squadron's accident rate before returning to his course.

An escort took place on the 26th, followed by some refresher classes in the days that followed: camouflage, driving, rearming and refuelling, and small arms training. They also took delivery of the squadron Auster, a high-wing monoplane used for communications, or as a small delivery plane. The weather wasn't flying-friendly for the rest of the month, operations being called off and lectures and films being the alternative. Pilots also got to have a look at the 500 lb bomb and learn about it, soon enough they'd be dropping them all over France. News of replacing the Mk IXBs with IXAs was not met with whoops of joy. The squadron thought that IXAs were for top cover and that was a 'stooge' job, they wanted to keep their IXBs and have a good chance of getting some action.[251] The Luftwaffe hadn't shown itself for a while; the squadron was eagerly awaiting their return.

Notes

1. Martyn Chorlton, *Scottish Airfields in the Second World War: Vol. 1 The Lothians*, Countryside Books, Berkshire, 2008, pp 14–16.
2. ORB–453 Sqn
3. Logbook–McCann.
4. Smith, *Hornchurch Eagles: The Life Stories of Eight of the Airfield's Distinguished WWII Fighter Pilots*, p. 185.
5. Herington, Air War Against Germany & Italy 1939–194, pp. 117, 539.
6. ORB–453 Sqn
7. Chorlton, *Scottish Airfields in the Second World War: Vol. 1 The Lothians*, p. 37.
8. Herington, *Air War Against Germany & Italy 1939–1943*, pp. 130–131.
9. Herington, *Air War Against Germany & Italy 1939–1943*, p. 337.
10. AWFA: Russell Leith
11. Leith–correspondence home 9 March 1942
12. AWFA: Russell Leith
13. Leith–correspondence home 2 August 1942
14. AWFA: Russell Leith
15. Ayris and Leith, *Duty Done*, p. 46.
16. Ayris and Leith, *Duty Done*, pp. 53, 61–62.
17. Ayris and Leith, *Duty Done*, pp. 63, 68.
18. Ayris and Leith, *Duty Done*, pp. 82, 84.
19. OAFH: 534_453: 184/23/AIR
20. Personal File–Ford.

21   Personal File–Ford.
22   Personal File–Ford.
23   Personal File–Ford
24   Personal File–Ford
25   Herington, *Air War Against Germany & Italy 1939–1943*, pp. 129–130.
26   Neil, *From the Cockpit: Spitfire*, p. 59.
27   Herington, *Air War Against Germany & Italy 1939–1943*, p. 346.
28   ORB–453 Sqn and Leith–Correspondence home 8, 16, 23 August 1942.
29   ORB–453 Sqn
30   AWFA: Nat Gould
31   AWFA: Sid Handsaker
32   Logbook–N Swift
33   Logbook–N Swift
34   Personal File–Riley
35   ORB–453 Sqn and AWFA: Russell Leith
36   Ratten–Personal File
37   ORB–453 Sqn
38   Personal File–Whiteford
39   ORB–453 Sqn
40   NLA: Trove–'Two New Australian Air Squadrons in Scotland' Brisbane *Courier-Mail* 19 August 1942.
41   NLA: Trove–'In Spitfire Squadron' *Newcastle Morning Herald and Miners' Advocate* 19 August 1942.
42   ORB–453 Sqn
43   Personal File–Steele
44   Cyril Ayris and Russell Leith, *Duty Done*, Cyril Ayris Freelance, West Perth, 2001, p. 99.
45   ORB–453 Sqn
46   Personal File–Yarra and Price, et al, *Spitfires Over the Mediterranean & North Africa*, p. 59 and Newton, *Australian Air Aces*, p. 116.
47   ORB–453 Sqn and NAA: A2217, 22/36/ORG
48   ORB–453 Sqn
49   Leith–Correspondence home 5, 11 and 31 October 1942.
50   Leith–Correspondence home 31 October 1942
51   Personal Files–Nossiter and Menzies
52   Personal File–Nossiter

53 Personal File–Nossiter
54 ORB–453 Sqn
55 Goss, et al, *Luftwaffe Fighter-Bombers Over Britain: The Tip and Run Campaign*, 1942–43, pp 15–16, 30, 90, 136, 165, 205, 206, 238 and 259.
56 File A11335 Z2–453 Crew Order Book (two files).
57 ORB–453 Sqn
58 Goss, et al, *Luftwaffe Fighter-Bombers Over Britain: The Tip and Run Campaign*, 1942–43, pp. 143–144.
59 Temora Interview–Norm Swift.
60 Logbook–N Swift
61 ORB–453 Sqn
62 Interview with Author–Handsaker
63 ORB–453 Sqn
64 OAFH: 548_453
65 OAFH: 548_453
66 OAFH: 548_453
67 Personal File–Esau.
68 Personal File–McCann
69 Wilson, Spitfire, p. 81.
70 Logbook–McCann and letter to author from his son, Fred McCann.
71 ORB–453 Sqn
72 Personal file–Blumer
73 ORB–453 and Logbook–N Swift
74 Leith–Correspondence home 29 November 1942
75 Richard C Smith, *Hornchurch Offensive*, Grub Street, London (2001), 2008, p. 73.
76 OAFH: 569_453 (identifies 122 Sqn which contradicts 453 ORB which nominates 350).
77 OAFH: 569_453
78 ORB–453 Sqn and Franks, Norman, *Royal Air Force Command Losses of the Second World War Volume 2: 1942–1943*, Midland Publishing, Leicester, 1998, p. 76.
79 OAFH: 569_453
80 File A11335 Z2–453 Crew Order Book
81 OAFH: 569_453
82 Herington, *Air War Against Germany & Italy 1939–1943*, p. 133.
83 Logbook–Andrews.
84 Personal File–Andrews

85   Personal File–Andrews.
86   Temora Interview–Don Andrews.
87   Logbook–Andrews.
88   Logbook–Andrews.
89   OAFH: 563_453
90   Leith–Southend-on-Sea Sergeants Mess Christmas dinner menu
91   Logbook–N Swift.
92   ORB –453 Sqn and Logbook–McCann.
93   Logbook–Andrews.
94   ORB –453 Sqn
95   AWM File 64 81/4/100
96   Logbook–Olver
97   Personal File–Olver
98   OAFH: 571_453.
99   Logbook–McCann.
100 OAFH: 571_453.
101 OAFH: 571_453.
102 ORB –453 Sqn
103 OAFH: 548_453
104 Christopher Shores and Chris Thomas, *2nd Tactical Air Force: Volume 1 Spartan to Normandy June 1943 to June 1944*, Classic Publications, Surrey, 2004, pp. 13–15.
105 OAFH: 548_453
106 Logbook–Andrews.
107 OAFH: 1943_MISC_453
108 Temora Interview–Colin Leith.
109 AWFA: Russell Leith
110 ORB –453 Sqn
111 OAFH: 1943_MISC_453
112 File A11335 Z2–453 Crew Order Book
113 Logbook–Andrews, Logbook–McCann and OAFH: 548_453
114 ORB–453 Sqn
115 Logbook–N Swift and Temora Interview–N Swift.
116 Herington, *Air War Against Germany & Italy 1939–1943*, pp. 124–126.
117 Email correspondence with Ruth Currie.
118 Ayris and Leith, *Duty Done*, p. 107.
119 AWFA: Edward Hannon

120 Interview with Author–Gould
121 Leith–Correspondence home 26 March 1944
122 Logbook–McCann.
123 Ayris and Leith, *Duty Done*, p. 112.
124 ORB –453 Sqn
125 OAFH: 1943_MISC_453
126 ORB–453 Sqn
127 Leith–Correspondence home 7 April 1943
128 H.L. Thompson, *New Zealanders with the Royal Air Force: Volume II European Theatre January 1943–May 1945*, War History Branch, Wellington, 1956, pp. 143–148.
129 OAFH: 1943_MISC_453
130 Logbook–Andrews and Thompson, *New Zealanders with the Royal Air Force: Volume II*, pp. 143–148.
131 Personal File–RE Yarra
132 NLA: Trove –'Wife's Nickname on Plane' *Examiner* 5 June 43 and 'Tasmanian Leads Spitfire Wing' *The Daily News* 5 June 43.
133 NLA: Trove–*Advocate* 'Tasmanian Airman Honored in London' 5 June 1943
134 OAFH: 1943_MISC_453
135 ORB –453 Sqn
136 http://contentdm.warwick.ac.uk/cdm/ref/collection/tav/id/2097
137 Personal File–Halcombe
138 OAFH: 538_453
139 Logbook–Leith
140 Logbook–Andrews.
141 AWM 64 81/4/100
142 ORB –453 Sqn
143 Personal File–McCann
144 NLA: Trove–'Tasmanian Pilot of Spitfire Fighter', *The Mercury*, Hobart, 1 September 1943
145 NAA: A11335, 60/AIR
146 Logbook–Andrews.
147 Personal File–Gray
148 OAFH: 1943_MISC_453
149 NAA: A 11335, 60/AIR
150 Logbook–Olver
151 Logbook–Leith

152 ORB –453 Sqn
153 NAA: A2217, 22/36/ORG
154 Personal File–McDade
155 OAFH: 548_453
156 OAFH: 1943_MISC_453
157 Logbook–Andrews.
158 Logbook–Andrews.
159 Personal File–Olver
160 AWM 64 81/4/100
161 OAFH: 1943_MISC_453
162 Logbook–Andrews.
163 ORB –453 Sqn
164 Logbook–Leith
165 OAFH: 548_453
166 OAFH: 1943_MISC_453
167 Logbook–Olver
168 Personal File–Baker and Logbook–Baker
169 Logbook–Andrews.
170 Personal File–Thornley
171 NAA: A 11335, 60/AIR
172 Logbook–Andrews.
173 Personal File–Daff
174 Personal File–Kinross
175 Leith–Correspondence home 22 August 1943
176 Personal File–Lyall and Logbook–Lyall
177 Personal File–Scott
178 Personal File–Cowpe
179 Temora Interview–Fred Cowpe
180 Logbook–Cowpe
181 Temora Interview–Fred Cowpe and Logbook–Cowpe
182 Logbook–Cowpe
183 ORB –453 Sqn
184 OAFH: 1943_MISC_453
185 OAFH: 1943_MISC_453
186 Christopher Shores and Chris Thomas, *2nd Tactical Air Force: Volume 1 Spartan to Normandy June 1943 to June 1944*, Classic Publications, Surrey, 2004, pp. 34–35.

187 Logbook–Andrews.
188 OAFH: 548_453 and 1943_MISC_453
189 Herington, *Air War Against Germany & Italy 1939–1943*, pp. 513–514.
190 Shores and Thomas, *2nd Tactical Air Force: Volume 1 Spartan to Normandy June 1943 to June 1944*, pp. 35–36
191 ORB –453 Sqn
192 Spitfire production website http://www.airhistory.org.uk/spitfire/
193 Personal File–Nolan
194 ORB–453 Sqn
195 Speech by Norman Baker to Melbourne Legacy, '453 Spitfire Squadron–UK and Europe–Reminiscences', 4 September 1990.
196 Speech by Norman Baker to Melbourne Legacy, '453 Spitfire Squadron–UK and Europe–Reminiscences', 4 September 1990.
197 ORB –453 Sqn
198 ORB –453 Sqn
199 AWFA: Russell Leith
200 Herington, *Air War Against Germany & Italy 1939–1943*, pp. 418–419.
201 Herington, *Air War Against Germany & Italy 1939–1943*, pp. 440–441.
202 Temora Interview–Colin Leith.
203 AWFA: Russell Leith
204 Logbook–Andrews.
205 NAA: A11335, 60/AIR
206 OAFH: 548_453
207 NLA: Trove Article–'ex-TAS boy shoots down German planes', *New England Advertiser*, 13 October 1943.
208 NLA: Trove–'Two Australians down four German planes' *Queensland Times* 11 October 43
209 OAFH: 560_453
210 Unpublished Memoir–Fred Cowpe.
211 Logbook–Handsaker.
212 OAFH: 560_453
213 McRoberts, *Lions Rampant: The Story of 602 Spitfire Squadron*, p. 177.
214 Leith–Correspondence home 19 December 1943
215 Logbook–Andrews, Logbook Olver and Logbook–Cowpe.
216 ORB–453 Sqn
217 Ayris and Leith, *Duty Done*, pp. 123–125.

218 AWFA: Russell Leith
219 Leith–Correspondence home 28 December 1943
220 OAFH: 548_453
221 Personal File–Ferguson
222 Typed copy supplied by Kim Martin, daughter of Jack Olver.
223 Logbook–Baker.
224 ORB–453 Sqn
225 Logbook–Cowpe
226 Herington, *Air War Against Germany & Italy 1939–1943*, pp. 502–503.
227 Herington, *Air War Against Germany & Italy 1939–1943*, p. 546.
228 John Herington, *Australia in the War of 1939–1945, Series Three: Air, Volume IV: Air Power Over Europe 1944–1945*, Australian War Memorial, Canberra, 1963, pp. 52, 279, 289.
229 Personal File–T Swift
230 ORB–453 Sqn
231 Logbook–Baker and Logbook–Andrews.
232 Logbook–Baker and Logbook–Cowpe.
233 Shores and Thomas, *2nd Tactical Air Force: Volume 1 Spartan to Normandy June 1943 to June 1944*, pp. 52–53.
234 ORB–453 Sqn
235 Personal File–Gorman
236 NAA: A2217, 22/36/ORG
237 Logbook–Cowpe
238 Logbook–Cowpe
239 ORB–453 Sqn
240 Logbook–Cowpe
241 OAFH: 548_453
242 ORB–453 Sqn
243 Typed letter in Baker collection
244 Ford–Personal File
245 Personal File–Lawrence–comments made regarding being given 8s.
246 Personal File–Ford.
247 Personal File–Gorman
248 Peter Jacobs, *Airfields of the D-Day Invasion Air Force: 2nd Tactical Air Force in South-East England in WWII*, Pen & Sword Aviation, Barnsley, 2009, p.112.
249 McRoberts, *Lions Rampant: The Story of 602 Spitfire Squadron*, pp. 16–17, 35, 47, 72–73, 146–147, 149, 165.

250 McRoberts, *Lions Rampant: The Story of 602 Spitfire Squadron*, pp. 148, 162, 181.
251 ORB–453 Sqn

Normandy

The planning that went into the Allies' return to Europe was monumental, to say the least, and was the product of years of work by thousands of men and women around the globe. Many books have been written about individual elements of the planning for Operation Overlord, including the weather –something over which man has no control. The evolution of the plans for the return to France did not, of course, even start in Normandy.

The Mediterranean Strategy of the Western Allies in WW2—approaching Europe via Italy rather than a cross-Channel assault in 1943—was pivotal to their eventual success over Nazi Germany. It was a strategy that arose out of circumstances that were not entirely within the control of its executioners, Britain and the United States. While alternatives and objections to *The Mediterranean Strategy* were put forward at each conference, leading to the agreement at Casablanca in January 1943 and even beyond, it was actually the only realistic option available to the Western Allies at the time. While never executed with brilliance (politically or militarily), it was successful in causing the defection of Italy, drawing in and tying up a large number of German divisions, securing the Mediterranean, and keeping Russia in the war.[1] This strategy ultimately had to be relegated to a secondary priority to ensure the success of the long-awaited and most direct assault on North

Western Europe, Operation Overlord,[2] the Allied landings in Normandy, on 6 June 1944. Much of the success in Normandy was due to the many operational lessons learned during the execution of Allied landings in the Mediterranean.[3]

Shortly after the United States entered the war in December 1941, Winston Churchill declared that the Allies had won the war, knowing that the United States was now a full participant.[4] After these world-changing events and still in the same dramatic month, Churchill travelled to Washington DC where the first of many conferences regarding the planned direction of the Second World War took place. At this conference, known as Arcadia,[5] the Western Allies agreed on a 'Germany First' policy, as Germany posed the greatest and most direct threat to the Allies, the Wehrmacht having so recently experienced great success in the invasion of Russia during Operation Barbarossa.[6] While the USSR had no genuine ties with either the United States or Great Britain, and had not lifted a finger to assist France or Britain in their time of need in 1940,[7] it served the purposes of the Western Allies for the USSR to remain in the war, wearing down the German army until such time as the Western Allies could return to fight on European soil.[8] Therefore, to keep the Russians in the war, as well as supplying direct material aid in the form of the Lend-Lease agreement,[9] the Western Allies had to devise a strategy that would draw German forces away from the Russian Front.

In the air, with the constant Rodeos, Ramrods and Circuses—almost a Battle of Britain in reverse, and certainly with faults of its own—the RAF and ever-increasing presence of the USAAF sought to keep the Luftwaffe occupied. This was almost the only way in which the Allies could take pressure off Russia by direct military action. The war in the desert was never seen by Stalin as a genuine second front,[10] nor was the later fighting in Italy for that matter. But the Allies could not be allowed to freely roam the skies over Europe, and so the Luftwaffe had to keep units available to defend against the day and night bombing raids. In this way, the Allies sought to bring the Luftwaffe into the air and bleed it dry but, in doing so, the RAF lost many of their best pilots, such as Bob Stanford Tuck and Douglas Bader.[11] Often the Luftwaffe would not put up any resistance, but it could not afford to ignore the constant raids on airfields and facilities within the range of the medium bomber force. As RAF units and pilots gained experience, staff were promoted and commanders moved out of flying posts to save them from being captured, or worse. One such promoted commander was W/Cdr Harry Broadhurst, later Air Chief Marshal Sir Harry Broadhurst.

Broadhurst had previously led the Hornchurch Wing as Wing Commander, including in operations covering the Dieppe raid. In November 1942, he arrived in the Western Desert and became Air Officer Commanding of the Desert Air Force with the rank of Air Vice Marshal, under the leadership of Air Marshal Arthur Coningham.[12] While Coningham had contributed much to the development of tactical air support in the theatre, Broadhurst brought with him valuable experiences and ideas of his own. The two RAF commanders got along well with Montgomery, and this relationship continued through Operation Overlord. For that operation, Montgomery would command 21st Army Group, Coningham would command 2TAF (2nd Tactical Air Force—the 1st was originally formed in the desert and had moved into the Mediterranean), and Broadhurst would command 83 Group.

At the time, the British and Commonwealth forces were fighting the Axis in North Africa, back and forth across the western desert.[13] At the Arcadia conference of December 1941, the American Chief of Staff, General George C. Marshall, proposed a mass assault by the most direct route to end the war as quickly as possible.[14] By this he meant an amphibious assault in North Western Europe, crossing the English Channel and heading for the industrial heartland of Germany.[15] A landing on this scale had never been attempted before. With the British unable to field enough troops to manage this feat themselves, the United States would have to recruit, equip, train and transport troops to Britain, from which the assault would be launched. A number of codenames, Operations Bolero (the build-up of US forces in Britain), Roundup (the cross-Channel assault) and Sledgehammer (an emergency assault only to be launched if Germany or Russia were about to collapse), were applied to elements of this overall strategy, the plans for which were put forth by a committee led by General Dwight Eisenhower,[16] who would eventually be appointed to command the Allied forces involved in Operation Overlord.[17]

At this time a cross–Channel assault was not practical because, regardless of logistical considerations, including the lack of landing craft and inadequate forces,[18] there was no evidence that the United States would be able to send an army (that had not yet seen combat) to defeat the most operationally successful army in existence. This operation was proposed for April 1943, less than eighteen months after the United States entered the Second World War.[19] While the Americans and British agreed in principle to the plan proposed by Eisenhower (and subsequently endorsed by Marshall and Roosevelt), the events in North Africa caused a greatly concerned Winston Churchill to request US equipment be sent there resulting in a weakening of Bolero.[20] Despite Marshall's insistence on Bolero leading to Roundup, Churchill and his Chief of the Imperial General Staff, General Alan Brooke[21] were able to convince President Franklin Roosevelt that the cross-Channel assault could not go ahead as intended. Instead, the forces left idle would be able to take some action in 1942, the intent being to defeat the Axis forces in North Africa and ease Stalin's criticism of the Western Allies' lack of action.[22] The defeat of the Axis in North Africa would achieve a number of goals. These included the improved security of shipping lanes; protection of the Middle East, including Lend-Lease routes to the USSR[23]; and the provision of a massive secured area from which operations could potentially be launched against the Axis into the Aegean, Mediterranean and Balkans.[24]

The Allied landings in North Africa on 8 November 1942,[25] codenamed Operation Torch, were, overall, not resisted with a great deal of energy by the Vichy French. This commenced the western arm of the campaign to remove the Axis powers from North Africa, the eastern arm having commenced at the second battle of El Alamein on 23 October 1942.[26] Despite successes, Allied operations did not achieve an early decisive victory and the campaign dragged out into May 1943,[27] as Hitler sent troops to Tunisia in an attempt to stave off defeat. The length of this campaign meant that there could be no Roundup in 1943.[28] Notably though, the failed Allied raid at Dieppe in August 1942 did not prevent Torch going ahead. However, the lack of a cover plan to mask Allied intentions at Dieppe would be rectified for Overlord.[29]

One of the evolutionary facets of Operation Torch was the inclusion of Servicing Commando Units (SCUs). These were not commandos in the raiding sense, their role was defined as: 'the occupation of advanced landing grounds as soon as they are captured by the army'.[30] Two such units (3201 and 3202 SCUs) were involved in the Torch landings on the first day, and they serviced Spitfires and Hurricanes on the same day. They were later relieved by the ground crew of the squadrons and the SCUs moved up to their next base of operations. Such was their success that eight SCUs were involved in the landings in Sicily, of which two landed on the first day. SCUs also accompanied the troops ashore in Italy. For Overlord, six SCUs were formed, of which four landed on D+1, with two more landing a week later.[31]

The Casablanca conference of January 1943 led to the British securing American agreement to *The Mediterranean Strategy*,[32] facets of which included opening up the Mediterranean fully to release shipping resources (by shortening travel distances), drawing in German forces and obtaining airfields for use in the strategic bombing campaign.[33] This last aspect, despite all other prior disagreements, was something that the RAF and USAAF actually agreed upon.[34] Mediterranean operations would require fewer resources than a cross-Channel attack and, therefore, more resources would be available for the Pacific.[35] The choice of the Mediterranean also played to Allied strengths, specifically air and sea power.[36] Despite all previous disagreements, even the US Joint Chiefs of Staff, who did not always side with President Roosevelt, had to admit at the Trident Conference of May 1943 that only action in the Mediterranean would provide Russia with immediate relief, and it was at this conference that the date for Operation Overlord was set as 1 May 1944.[37] Marshall himself was also forced to admit that a Channel crossing was still too great a risk while the U-boat threat remained in the Atlantic and sufficient forces were not yet based in Britain to support an extended campaign.[38]

The next step by the Allies, approved at the Casablanca conference, was to invade the island of Sicily,[39] off the boot tip of mainland Italy. The invasion of Sicily had a number of goals, the primary one being to knock Italy out of the war and thereby draw in (and contain) German divisions.[40] The subsequent landings by sea and air, the largest combined airborne and amphibious operation in the world at the time,[41] took place on 10 July 1943 under the codename Operation Husky.[42] Never ready to admit anything that might give credit to the Western Allies, Stalin still did not consider it sufficient to be declared a Second Front.[43] The invasion force could have been larger, but the Western Allies were lacking in landing craft and transport aircraft.[44] Despite Sicily's geographical proximity to Italy, its capture was regarded by the United States as the final action of the North African campaign[45], rather than the first action of the Mediterranean campaign. However, in accordance with British intentions, Sicily became the first action towards the conquest of Italy.[46] The fighting in Sicily concluded on 17 August.[47] The formal decision to invade Italy after the completion of Operation Husky was not taken until 19 August 1943,[48] though some preparations had already been made.

While the execution of air and sea operations was sometimes clumsy, hesitant or lacking in air-to-sea and air-to-ground coordination,[49] the consequences of such inadequacies in the Mediterranean theatre were less severe than what would have been experienced in a cross-Channel assault on France. Should the same operations have been launched there against only German troops—as opposed to Axis forces mainly comprising Italian troops backed by a smaller percentage of German troops—the outcome would have been disastrous.[50] The later success of Operation Overlord, to which *The Mediterranean Strategy* was eventually subordinated,[51] owed much to the operational experience gained in these early operations.[52] The famous black and white stripes which adorned Allied aircraft involved in Overlord had also been tested on other operations, but not on such a large scale. Like the term 'D-Day' they are almost universally, though erroneously, associated with operations in Normandy. After friendly fire incidents (including a number of aircraft shot down) during Operation Husky, a number of modifications to the Allied plans were made. These experiences also influenced the planning of routes flown by the transport aircraft carrying the airborne and glider troops for the Normandy operation.[53] While there were often disagreements at various levels of command throughout the Western Allied forces, generally speaking, this was due to the democratic, committee style of leadership not found in the German or Russian armies. Further, the fact that negotiation and debate was possible often led to more sound decision making than Hitler or Stalin could accomplish alone.[54] Such is the nature of Allied warfare.

The invasion of Sicily led to the downfall of Italian dictator Benito Mussolini on 24 July 1943[55], and the eventual defection of Italy to the Allies on 9 September 1943.[56] In response to the loss of Tunisia and, in anticipation of further Allied action in the Mediterranean, Hitler issued Directive 48 in July 1943, setting out how the eastern Mediterranean would be defended, with an expectation that the Allies would invade Greece.[57] This anticipation of Allied action in Greece was well founded, for Churchill pushed for action in the eastern Mediterranean in the direction of Rhodes and the Dardanelles, arguing that it would open the sea route to the USSR, but this failed to gain US support[58], and the limited action taken there by the British was not successful.[59] As US forces increased in size, so too did the ability of the United States to influence Allied policy,[60] and Churchill was unable to exert as much influence as before—and rightfully so, considering his failures in the Aegean.

Through the political and military bungling of the Italians,[61] German anticipation of the Italian defection,[62] and the risk-averse and conservative nature of Allied progress on the ground,[63] the Western Allies lost a number of opportunities to make decisive but otherwise potentially risky early landings and seek an accelerated timetable for operations in Italy.[64] This also represented the nature of western democratic warfare, in that great risk and potentially high casualty rates—the likes of which the German and Russian forces suffered regularly on the eastern front—would not be tolerated.[65] However, despite disagreements between the United States and Britain, slow progress politically and on the ground, one main goal of *The Mediterranean Strategy* was quickly achieved: the defection of Italy. It was handled poorly, but it was achieved.[66]

This in turn resulted in the Germans reinforcing Italy with divisions to hold it against anticipated invasion, as well as reinforcing the remainder of the Mediterranean with additional divisions in anticipation of action elsewhere. In this way over 40 German or German-controlled divisions were deployed and occupied in Italy, Greece and the Balkans.[67] Though they had agreed to *The Mediterranean Strategy*, the United States would not be drawn away from Italy, being ever concerned that Churchill was planning for the maintenance of the post-war British Empire,[68] igniting old British-Russian hostilities in that part of the world,[69] or simply creating a drain on already stretched resources.[70] The Allies maintained the pressure of action in Italy and the threat of other operations elsewhere in the Mediterranean, which was key to keeping the attention of German forces, who had replaced Italian units in France, Italy, the Aegean and the Balkans with units of their own.[71] The Luftwaffe also had to shift resources to the Mediterranean, including units previously based in Norway,[72] so that by 1943 20% of the Luftwaffe was based in the Mediterranean and, of all Luftwaffe aircraft lost in 1943, one third were lost in the Mediterranean.[73] The fighting in Italy also led to the capture of airfields from which the 'Second Front in the Air' was launched against German and Romanian industrial targets, such as the oil refineries at Ploesti.[74] Every one of these German units drawn away from Normandy would increase the prospect of successful landings there. These landings were by no means easy, but were certainly aided by Allied actions in the Mediterranean.

There has been criticism of the Allied Mediterranean Strategy because it did not lead to a grand breakthrough battle that decided the campaign.[75] However, the war in the Mediterranean was one of attrition, and the goal—to draw in and hold the attention of German units—was achieved, albeit at great cost to the Allies.[76] The terrain greatly favoured the defender and, overall, the Germans adapted better to the defence than the Allies did to the offence.[77] In October 1943 there were only 11 Allied divisions in Italy facing 25 German divisions, so great progress, based on numbers alone, should not have been anticipated.[78] However, some of these German units were mechanised, and the hills and mountains of Italy was far less favourable to armoured warfare than the terrain of France and Russia, so again the Germans had put themselves at a disadvantage.[79] The logical action for Hitler to have taken would have been to withdraw from Greece and Italy and defend the more rugged terrain further north.[80] This would have required fewer troops and therefore freed up units to fight in France and/or Russia. But, as on so many other occasions, including Tunisia, Hitler refused to allow his troops to retreat. So, when the Allies landed in Normandy, backed by the lessons learned in North Africa and the Mediterranean, the Germans were strung out along a circle from Norway, across the Russian front, through the Balkans and Italy, across the south of France to the Spanish border and up the western coast of Europe to Norway once again.

While the Allies were bleeding themselves and German forces dry in Italy, preparations were going ahead for Operation Overlord. A cover plan was established to deceive the Germans, and this plan was named Operation Fortitude. It had a number of elements and sub-plans, but there were three primary goals:

1. To convince the Germans the assault would take place in the Pas de Calais and therefore keep German units stationed in that area.
2. To deceive the Germans in relation to the time and date of the landings.
3. During and after the main assault, to keep German units stationed in, and focused on, the Pas de Calais and areas east, for at least 14 days.[81]

2nd Tactical Air Force (2TAF) was formed in November 1943 from RAF units, and the USAAF formed the 9th Air Force, both of these army support units coming under the command of ACM Sir Trafford Leigh-Mallory under the title of the AEAF, which also included Air Defence Great Britain, formally known as Fighter Command.[82] 2TAF at this time had three Groups (2, 83 and 84) totalling 56 squadrons, of which 83 Group had 20. They were joined by 85 Group in December 1943. By 6 June 1944 2TAF would have 100 squadrons.[83] Airfields became somewhat crowded, with multiple Wings moving into single airfields—Ford, on the south coast of England, hosting at least six squadrons at any one time in April. May 1944 saw a restructure within 2TAF with 'Airfields' becoming Wings, three squadrons to a Wing being increased to four later in the campaign. Thus, airfields became known by their location, and Wings by their allocated number.[84]

To deceive the Germans into believing that the landings would take place on the coast at some other place away from Normandy, a bombing target ratio of 1:2 was determined; for every target attacked in Normandy, two had to be attacked elsewhere. In addition, the attacks in the Pas de Calais area were twice as heavy (not just twice as frequent) as those in Normandy. As well as attacks in areas adjacent to Normandy, air raids were also conducted against German units and airfields in Norway as part of Operation Fortitude North, the goal being to alert the Germans to the possibility of an Allied landing there, and to keep Luftwaffe units tied down in Norway so they could not be transferred elsewhere.[85]

In addition to the attacks by 2TAF, heavier bombing sorties took place in Normandy and the Pas de Calais as part of what became known as the 'Transportation Plan'. This involved cutting Normandy and the Pas de Calais areas off, destroying rail links and bridges over the rivers and was so successful that by 6 June there were only two bridges left over the Seine and 75% of the rail system within 150 miles of the landing beaches was unusable. Additional sorties against bridges over the Loire cut off Normandy from the south, and any attacks that resulted in German units being forced to travel by road instead of rail, or take detours on roads due to damaged or destroyed bridges created higher fuel consumption.[86] Meanwhile, the German fuel and oil production capacity was also being attacked, putting further pressure on the German army and restricting the amount of aviation fuel available to the Luftwaffe to defend against the attacks. Oil production went down by 50%, some Luftwaffe pilot schools were shut down due to lack of fuel and in May 1944 the Luftwaffe lost approximately 50% of its fighter force and 25% of its fighter pilots—mainly due to the Mustangs escorting the daylight bombing raids. In April 1944, only 396 new German pilots arrived to replace 489 lost and, of course, they did not have as much experience. The earlier policy of sending pilots to the Eastern Front to gain experience before sending them up against the Mustangs, Thunderbolts and Spitfires of the Western Allies could not be maintained, there was simply no time to develop flying skills.[87] However, these operations came at a massive cost, as the Allies lost almost 2,000 aircraft and 12,000 aircrew from early April to 5 June 1944.[88]

Experience gained in the desert showed that the air support for the army had to be mobile and flexible, and so, before the landings took place, a number of sites for temporary airfields were selected. The sites were selected by using aerial photographs and 1:25,000 and 1:50,000 scale maps, with further advice from geologists, such as Major Shotton and Professor King of Cambridge University.[89] The first to be constructed would be the Emergency Landings Strips (ELS), followed by Refuelling and Rearming Strips (RRS) with the most permanent being Advanced Landing Grounds (ALG).[90] ELS were to have enough space for an aircraft in distress to land safely (determined to be a minimum of 1,800 ft) and that was all. RRS were to have enough length of strip (determined to be 3,600 ft for fighters and 5,000 ft for fighter/bombers) on a compacted surface for landing and take-off, with enough marshalling areas for rapid turnaround of aircraft, and enough tracking for operations in summer and autumn conditions. Rain is a common occurrence in Normandy (usually every few days) and the ability to cope with this was essential. An ALG was an RRS upgraded and used to maximum capacity by application of the 'Roulement' system, which was a method of rotating squadrons through an airfield to keep it operating at maximum capacity.[91] By basing aircraft as close to the front as possible air support would be minutes away and planes would be available for longer periods as they would not use up fuel crossing the Channel twice each time they took off. Sorties could penetrate further into the rear of the German lines, reducing their ability to deploy, redeploy and reinforce their front line units. Sorties were expected to be at a rate of 200 per day for an RRS, though only 30 of these would be for rocket-firing squadrons such as Typhoons. An ALG with three squadrons (British sector) was expected to achieve 144 sorties per day and those with four squadrons (American sector) 196 sorties per day, US squadrons also being equipped with more aircraft.[92]

There was a schedule for these landing grounds to be completed after the landing date (D):

D+3   4 Refuelling and Rearming Strips
D+10   10 Advanced Landing Grounds (5 British and 5 American)
D+14   18 Advanced Landing Grounds (10 British and 8 American)
D+24   27 Advanced Landing Grounds (15 British and 12 American)[93]

Within three weeks of the landings, 2TAF aimed to have 20 squadrons based in France for immediate battlefield support and the constant support of air cover.[94] This schedule was, of course, dictated by the progress of the land campaign which ended up falling behind schedule. By D+10, only six ALG were complete, with eleven ready by D+19. While 2TAF and 9th Air Force did their best, planes cannot take and hold ground, and their efforts were reduced by the withdrawal of seven 2TAF squadrons which were reallocated to Operation Crossbow, the attempt to counter the V-1 attacks. These seven squadrons were equipped with the fastest available Allied fighters of the time, and their removal from beachhead operations was not, in the big picture at least, detrimental to the Allied air effort.[95] The work of the SCUs, in addition to those of the Aircraft Construction Companies (who belonged to the Royal Engineers)[96] were essential to getting the RRS, ELS and ALGs up and running as fast as possible.

To this end, a great many engineering vehicles were required, in addition to the material needed to construct the sites. It was planned that, from 6 June to D+17 1.296 million square yards of square mesh track would be shipped in, in addition to just 10,000 square yards of the much heavier pierced steel plank. From D+18 to D+40, an additional 1.076 million square yards of square mesh track would arrive as well as 1.25 million square yards of prefabricated bitumen surfacing (hessian sprayed with bitumen). These figures, it should be noted, related to the British sector only. Three all-weather airstrips were required by D+90, including the German airfield at Carpiquet, the other two requiring runways of 5,000 ft made from the stronger pierced steel plank.[97]

The majority of 2TAF squadrons were day fighters: Spitfires, Typhoons and Mustangs. These were backed up at night with No.2 Group carrying out raids and No. 85 Group carrying out intruder sorties in their Mosquitos.[98] The Allies had 24-hour air superiority. To counter the massive Allied air forces involved in Operation Overlord, the Germans could offer little resistance. The USAAF 8th Air Force had waged a bombing campaign against German oil production that led to a massive decrease in aviation fuel output.[99] Not only did this reduce the capability of front line units to engage with the Allied raids, but it also meant that, during their training, Luftwaffe pilots had less time in the air before they were posted to a front line unit. Many of these new pilots, and veterans also, were shot out of the sky by the Mustangs and other fighters protecting the daylight US bombing raids, leaving few available to transfer to Normandy when the landings commenced. While Supreme Headquarters Allied Expeditionary Force estimated a possible 300 Luftwaffe fighters and 200 bombers over the beachhead during a single concentrated operation against the landing, no such sortie took place, the Luftwaffe managing only 319 sorties for the whole of 6 June, compared to 3,300 by the Allies.[100]

Proposed ELS, RRS and ALG in Normandy[101]

British Zone		American Zone	
Designation	Location	Designation	Location
B.1 (ELS)	Asnelles	ELS 1	Pouppeville
B.2	Bazenville	A.1	St Pierre-du-Mont
B.3 (RRS)	St Croix-sur-Mer	A.2	Cricqueville-en-Bessin
B.4	Beny-sur-Mer	A.3	Cardonville
B.5	Le Fresne-Camilly	A.4	Deux-Jumeaux
B.6	Coulombs	A.5	Chippelle
B.7	Martragny	A.6	Beuzeville
B.8	Sommervieu	A.7	Azeville
B.9	Lantheuil/Creully	A.8	Picauville
B.10	Plumetot	A.9	Le Molay
B.11	Longues-sur-Mer	A.10	Carentan (Catz)
B.12	Ellon	A.11	St Lambert/Neuilly
B.13	NOT USED	A.12	Lignerolles
B.14	Amblie	A.13	Tour-en-Bessin
B.15	Ryes	A.14	Cretteville
B.16	Villons les Buissons	A.15	Maupertus
B.17	Carpiquet	A.16	Brucheville
B.18	Cristot	A.17	Meautis
B.19	Lingèvres	A.18	St Jean de Daye
B.20	NOT USED	A.19	La Vieille
B.21	Sainte-Honorine-de-Ducy	A.20	Lessay
		A.21 (prev E 1)	Saint-Laurent-sur-Mer
		A.22	Colleville
		A.23	Querqueville
		A.24	Biniville
		A.25	Bolleville
		A.26	Gorges
		A.27	NOT USED
		A.28	Pontorson
		A.29	St James

Notes

1. Michael Howard, *The Mediterranean Strategy in the Second World War*, Greenhill Books, London, 1993, p. 36.
2. Howard, *The Mediterranean Strategy*, p. 38.
3. Carlo D'Este, *Fatal Decision: Anzio and the Battle for Rome*, Aurum Press, London, 1991, (2007), p. 29.
4. Williamson Murray and Allan R. Millett, *A War to be Won: Fighting the Second World War*, Belknap, Cambridge, 2000, (2001), p. 262.
5. D'Este, Fatal Decision, p.12.
6. Andrew Roberts, *Masters and Commanders: How Roosevelt, Churchill, Marshall and Alanbrooke Won the war in the West*, Allen Lane, London, 2008, p.86.
7. Keith Sainsbury, *The North African Landings 1942*, London, 1976, p. 103.
8. Richard Overy, *Why The Allies Won*, Pimlico, London, 1995, (2006), p.307.
9. Overy, *Why The Allies Won*, p.309.
10. Antony Beevor, The World At War, 1942, keynote address at the Australian War Memorial for 'Kokoda Beyond the Legend', 6 September 2012.
11. Smith, *Hornchurch Eagles: The Life Stories of Eight of the Airfield's Distinguished WWII Fighter Pilots*, p. 119.
12. Smith, *Hornchurch Eagles: The Life Stories of Eight of the Airfield's Distinguished WWII Fighter Pilots*, pp. 126–127.
13. John Delaney, *Fighting the Desert Fox: Rommel's Campaigns in North Africa April 1941 to August 1942*, Cassell & Co, London, 1998, (1999), p. 7.
14. Sainsbury, *The North African Landings 1942*, p.81.

15 Sainsbury, *The North African Landings 1942*, p.81.
16 Howard, *The Mediterranean Strategy*, p.26
17 W.H.F. Jackson, *Overlord: Normandy 1944*, London, 1978, p.112.
18 Sainsbury, *The North African Landings 1942*, p.92.
19 Howard, *The Mediterranean Strategy*, p.26.
20 Sainsbury, *The North African Landings 1942*, p.111.
21 Evan Mawdsley, *World War II: A New History*, Cambridge University Press, Cambridge, 2009, p. 220.
22 Mawdsley, *World War II*, pp. 299–304; Dominick Graham & Shelford Bidwell, *Tug of War: The Battle for Italy 1943–45*, Pen & Sword Books, Yorkshire, 1986, (2004), p. 20.
23 Douglas Porch, *Hitler's Mediterranean Gamble: The North African and The Mediterranean Campaigns in World War Two*, Weidenfeld & Nicholson, London, 2004, p.663.
24 Sainsbury, *The North African Landings 1942*, p. 83 and Mark A. Stoler, *Allies in War: Britain and America against the Axis Powers 1940–1945*, Hodder Arnold, London, 2005, (2007), p.86.
25 Antony Beevor, *The Second World War*, Weidenfeld & Nicholson, London, 2012, p. 383.
26 Beevor, *The Second World War*, p. 376.
27 D'Este, *Fatal Decision*, pp. 15–17.
28 D'Este, *Fatal Decision*, p.18 and Stoler, *Allies in War*, p.86.
29 Mary Kathryn Barbier, *D–Day Deception: Operation Fortitude and the Normandy Invasion*, Stackpole, Mechanicsburg, (2007), 2009, p. 2.
30 J. Davies and J.P. Kellett, *A History of the RAF Servicing Commandos*, Airlife, Shrewsbury, 1989, p. 2.
31 Davies and Kellett, *A History of the RAF Servicing Commandos*, pp. 9, 11–13, 29, 55, 82.
32 Howard, *The Mediterranean Strategy*, p.35.
33 Howard, *The Mediterranean Strategy*, p.35.
34 Graham & Bidwell, *Tug of War*, p. 22.
35 Stoler, *Allies in War*, p. 87.
36 Porch, *Hitler's Mediterranean Gamble*, p.667.
37 Mark Stoler, *The Politics of the Second Front*, Westport, 1977, p. 93 and Max Hastings, *Overlord: D-Day and The Battle for Normandy*, Vintage Books, New York, 2006, p. 21.
38 Porch, *Hitler's Mediterranean Gamble*, p.415.
39 Stoler, *Allies in War*, pp. 86–87.
40 Graham & Bidwell, *Tug of War*, p. 25.
41 Samuel W. Mitcham, Jr and Friedrich von Stauffenberg, *The Battle for Sicily: How the*

      Allies Lost Their Chance for Total Victory, Stackpole, 1991, (2007), p.63.
42   D'Este, *Fatal Decision*, p.24.
43   Stoler, *The Politics of the Second Front*, p.86.
44   Mitcham and Stauffenberg, *The Battle for Sicily*, pp. 65–66.
45   Graham & Bidwell, *Tug of War*, p. 20.
46   Stoler, *The Politics of the Second Front*, p. 80.
47   Mitcham and Stauffenberg, *The Battle for Sicily,* p.303.
48   Stoler, *Allies in War*, p.125.
49   D'Este, *Fatal Decision*, p. 24.
50   Porch, *Hitler's Mediterranean Gamble*, p.670.
51   Morris Matloff and Edwin M. Snell, *Strategic Planning for Coalition Warfare 1943–1944 vol. 2*, Washington, 1953, p. 245.
52   Porch, *Hitler's Mediterranean Gamble,* pp. 669–672 and D'Este, Fatal Decision, p.29
53   Antony Beevor, *D-Day: The Battle for Normandy*, Viking, London, 2009, p.27.
54   Porch, *Hitler's Mediterranean Gamble*, p. 676.
55   Howard, *The Mediterranean Strategy*, p.41.
56   Richard Lamb, *War in Italy 1943–1945: A Brutal Story*, Penguin, London, 1993, p.19.
57   Hugh Trevor-Roper (ed), *Hitler's War Directives 1939 –1945*, Pan, London, 1964, (1966), pp.209–214.
58   Matloff and Snell, *Strategic Planning for Coalition Warfare 1943–1944 vol. 2*, p. 254.
59   Mawdsley, *World War II*, pp. 313–314.
60   Jackson, *Overlord*, p.108.
61   Lamb, *War in Italy 1943–1945*, pp. 2, 13–19, 127.
62   Howard, *The Mediterranean Strategy*, pp. 41–42; Matloff and Snell, *Strategic Planning for Coalition Warfare 1943–1944 vol. 2*, p. 247.
63   D'Este, *Fatal Decision*, p. 28.
64   Graham & Bidwell, T*ug of War*, p. 25.
65   Antony Beevor, 'In Conversation' with Robin Prior, at the Australian War Memorial, 5 September 2012.
66   Mitcham and Stauffenberg, *The Battle for Sicily*, p.233–235.
67   Porch, *Hitler's Mediterranean Gamble*, p.663.
68   Stoler, *The Politics of the Second Front*, p. 81
69   Stoler, *The Politics of the Second Front*, p. 81
70   Matloff and Snell, Strategic Planning for Coalition Warfare 1943–1944 vol. 2, p. 257.
71   Porch, *Hitler's Mediterranean Gamble*, pp.663–664.
72   Porch, *Hitler's Mediterranean Gamble*, p.663.
73   Porch, *Hitler's Mediterranean Gamble*, p.668.

74. Graham & Bidwell, Tug of War, p. 23; Matloff and Snell, Strategic Planning for Coalition Warfare 1943–1944 vol. 2, p.248; Mawdsley, World War II, p. 314.
75. Porch, *Hitler's Mediterranean Gamble*, p. 661.
76. Porch, *Hitler's Mediterranean Gamble*, p. 680.
77. Porch, *Hitler's Mediterranean Gamble*, p. 681.
78. Jackson, *Overlord*, p.107.
79. D'Este, *Fatal Decision*, pp. 444–448.
80. Howard, *The Mediterranean Strategy*, p.44.
81. Barbier, *D-Day Deception*, p. 13.
82. Jacobs, *Airfields of the D-Day Invasion Air Force*, pp. 1,4 and 6.
83. Jacobs, *Airfields of the D-Day Invasion Air Force*, pp. 8, 11 and 17.
84. Thomas, Andrew, *Osprey Aircraft of the Aces: Volume 122, Spitfire Aces of Northwest Europe 1944–45*, Osprey, Oxford, 2014, p. 18
85. Barbier, *D-Day Deception*, pp. 72, 144, 49–50.
86. Barbier, *D-Day Deception*, pp. 178–179, 191.
87. Williamson Murray, *Luftwaffe: Strategy for Defeat 1933–45*, Grafton Books, London, (1985), 1988. pp. 361, 365, 367, 370–371.
88. Murray, *Luftwaffe: Strategy for Defeat 1933–45*, p. 357.
89. IWM File WO 205/525 and Major-General Sir J. D. Inglis K.B.E., C.B., M.C. (1946) The Work of the Royal Engineers in North-West Europe, 1944–45, Royal United Services Institution. Journal,91:562, 176–195, p. 178.
90. Jacobs, *Airfields of the D-Day Invasion Air Force*, pp. 22–23.
91. IWM File WO 205/525
92. IWM File WO 205/525
93. Jacobs, *Airfields of the D-Day Invasion Air Force*, p. 25.
94. Herington, *Air Power Over Europe 1944–1945*, p. 15.
95. Herington, *Air Power Over Europe 1944–1945*, p. 160.
96. Davies and Kellett, *A History of the RAF Servicing Commandos*, p. 83.
97. IWM File WO 205/525
98. Jacobs, *Airfields of the D-Day Invasion Air Force*, p. 21.
99. Hastings, *Overlord: D-Day and The Battle for Normandy*, pp. 42–43, 266.
100. Hastings, *Overlord: D-Day and The Battle for Normandy*, pp. 43–44 and Jacobs, *Airfields of the D-Day Invasion Air Force*, p. 18.
101. Francois Robinard, Philippe Trombetta and Jacques Clementine, *50 aerodromes pour une victoire Juin-Septembre 1944*, Heimdal, Bayeux, 2012, pp 30–331.

April 1944

For 453 Squadron, like so many others allocated to 2TAF, April 1944 saw a steady increase in operations in preparation for the Normandy landings. The landings were still two months away, but the scattered nature of the targets required a longer build-up. The Allied air plan was to attack targets all over France so as not to give the landing area away so, for every target attacked in Normandy, targets elsewhere also had to be attacked.

The start of the month saw the squadron (along with 132 and 602) participating in a 5-day exercise codenamed 'Jim Cook', which was designed to test ground control and Wing organisation. The Wing Commander led the first day's flying and, at night, the squadron held a dance, reviewed as one of the best parties they'd had for a long time![1] Weather prevented flying on 2 April, but ground strafing was practised on the 3rd and divebombing on the 4th. Some attacks were flown on the last day of the exercise, but the bad weather meant that overall, the pilots felt the operation was a bit disappointing. That night a send-off was held for Russ Ewins, who was posted to No. 1 Delivery Flight at Croydon for a rest. He'd been one of the first posted to the reformed 453 in Scotland.[2] His written assessment by Don Andrews upon leaving the squadron was that he was 'most conscientious and absolutely reliable'. W/Cdr Lapsley added the comment that Ewins would make a good squadron commander.[3]

6 April saw the squadron take on 602 Squadron in a game of football (soccer) which they lost but, in a subsequent game of rugby, the Australians were victorious. Both that day and the next were plagued by poor weather so, after a lecture on tactics on the morning of the 7th, the rest of the day was free for the squadron to do as they pleased, which involved, among other things, golf and trips to town (Maidstone), just four miles away.[4] Despite a third day of bad weather, practice bombing was carried out on 8 April.[5]

On 9 April, four aircraft were sent on a weather recce sortie and no enemy aircraft were seen. This would be a common theme for their operations. The Luftwaffe was spread thin, fighting in Russia, the Mediterranean and at night over Germany against thousand-bomber RAF raids. Those not fighting at night had to fight during the day, defending against the USAAF 8th Air Force, often over the same targets visited by the RAF the night before. RAF Bomber Command sorties were not escorted by fighters at night, but the 8th Air Force brought with them their 'little friends' in the form of P-51 Mustangs, P-47 Thunderbolts and P-38 Lightnings. Luftwaffe pilots not engaged in defending against these raids still had to maintain patrols from Norway to Spain and the south of France.

An officer from Public Relations arrived and planned to stay a few days, hoping to get a story out of the members of the squadron, who were feeling out of sorts with the lack of publicity for what was the last remaining RAAF Spitfire squadron in the UK (452 and 457 having been withdrawn from operations in March and May of 1942 before returning to Australia).[6]

On 10 April, the squadron practised formation flying to get the newer pilots up to speed. This was followed by an early evening sortie from 1840 for two hours, providing twelve Spitfires for close escort to 25 Douglas Bostons attacking a power station at Monceau-sur-Sambre[7] near Charleroi, about 25 miles south of Brussels. The escort comprised of other Spitfires from the Wing and the formation was led by Don Andrews flying 'D'. The bombing was assessed as good and, again, no enemy aircraft were seen, though Allan

Harris in 'U' was hit by flak, damaging the hood and tailplane.⁸ The squadron returned to base at 2040 which, in Australia, would have meant darkness. However, in the lengthening days approaching the European summer, plenty of light remained for safe landings. The length of the days in June, at the height of the European summer, is well illustrated by the squadron record which shows aircraft returning from sorties after 2300 hours. Regardless of the time of year, it's well and truly dark 'back home' in Australia by then.

On 11 April the squadron escorted Douglas Marauders, a variant of the Boston, to Charleroi, with Chievres airfield as a secondary target and good results were observed all round, the Luftwaffe failing to show once again. With the afternoon and evening free, the squadron, including the Medical Officer and Adjutant, met up at the County Hotel in Ashford for a dinner. The 'evening' ended about 2am, with members heading back to base, as the diary notes: 'after taking Aspros as a precautionary measure'! The next night was rather more subdued, staff going to a local cinema and having an apparently rare early night.⁹

The Ashford County Hotel in 2015. (Author)

On 13 April, after a rest day (from operations) that had surely been earned but nevertheless consisted of bombing practice, the squadron was back in the air with eleven Spitfires joining those of 132 and 602 Squadrons for an escort of 72 Marauders. The primary target was the railway marshalling yards at Namur, located about 25 miles southeast of Brussels, the disruption of transport routes for German reinforcements an essential ingredient to the Overlord plan. The Sambre River passes through both Namur and Charleroi, and taking down the road and rail bridges there was an important element of the plan to disrupt the Wehrmacht's ability to relocate forces and move reinforcements down into Normandy once the landings took place. While an assault in the Pas-de-Calais was being 'sold' to the Germans by the Allied deception plan, the bombing of these targets also pointed to Calais as a potential landing site. Unfortunately, the bomber formations, known as 'boxes', split up so the secondary target of an airfield was attacked instead, with fair results despite heavy flak. The Luftwaffe was a no-show. Norm Baker flying 'K' escorted Ken Kinross in 'E', who had engine trouble,[10] back to base, returning early at 0935. The others returned to base at 1025.

At 1215 a number of pilots flew their second sortie of the day, eight Spitfires led by Ernie Esau in 'A' and Pat McDade in 'G' escorting 132 and 602 Squadrons dive-bombing targets at Le Treport, where the Bresle River empties into the Channel, about 12 miles north of Dieppe. The weather was hazy but it was thought that good results were achieved with as much as 6/10ths cloud over the target area. There was moderate flak, but again, no Luftwaffe. One of the Spitfires from 132 Squadron could not shake their bomb loose and had to land last, lest something go wrong resulting in the airstrip being blocked and preventing others from getting down safely.[11]

Also on 13 April, F/O Lancaster (Service no. 409149) was transferred in from 611 Squadron, where he had spent most of his operational flying to date.[12] Vernon Arnold Lancaster was born on 21 September 1918 and, at the time of joining the RAAF, lived in Victoria. A tiler by trade, Lancaster

Vern Lancaster in 1944 (Courtesy of the Cowpe family)

had enlisted on 19 July 1941, and trained in Australia on the Tiger Moth. During one training flight he was told by the instructor to let go of the controls and, when he replied that he didn't have the controls, the instructor told him to prepare to bail out. He was very surprised, as he 'hadn't even flown the bloody thing, and I've got to bail out!' The instructor resolved the problem: a stick had been caught in the underside of the plane and was interfering with the controls, and the flight continued. He progressed on to the Wirraway and, in his later years, stated that, in his opinion, these should never have been built, as too many pilots lost their lives when the engine cut out. He eventually made it to the UK and was trained on Spitfires and thought they were 'Wonderful', though the training was a bit hairy, there being no two-seat trainer version and 'No-one to tell you what to do'.[13]

Lancaster may never have made it to 453 Squadron if he'd followed his early instincts. After a posting to Biggin Hill in January 1943, he spent three days wandering about the station to get to know the place, and was sent up to have a familiarisation flight around the area. While listening to the radio and radar controllers warn of an incoming raid, he looked around and saw 27 German aircraft below him, flying low to the ground. He promptly gave a warning and estimated their arrival to Biggin Hill as three and a half minutes, and the station scrambled. Feeling that he should do what he'd gone to England for, he commenced a dive and set himself up to attack the formation when he was directed to land. He was then stuck with the choice of attacking the Germans and suffering the consequences of a charge of disobeying orders or landing as directed. Being a good Sergeant Pilot he broke off the attack and landed as ordered, only to be promptly berated by the ground crew for not firing his guns![14]

April 1944 was full of instructions from various levels of higher command about preparation for Overlord, including the requirement that, prior to arrival in France: 'All Officers in 83 Group must be capable of driving vehicles up to 3 ton tenders and riding motor-cycles'. Further to this, there was a note that all officers were to have their competency assessed.[15] Movement of the equipment to France would primarily be the role of the ground crew and staff and was a lot of work, as vehicle convoys stretched for miles in their practice moves.

On 14 April the squadron was tasked with dive-bombing along with 602 Squadron, and 132 Squadron provided the fighter cover this time. The Noball (V-1 flying bomb) target was 20 miles inland from the coastal town of Berch-sur-Mer.[16] Take-off was at 1225 and the Spitfires flew past the target, lining it up so it passed along the left side of the engine cowling then appeared behind the wing root, at which time they did a half-roll to become upside down, then pulled back on the stick until they'd passed the vertical and dove down at 70 degrees[17] from 8,000 ft to 4,000 ft before dropping their bombs. There were just a few seconds between each plane, and no firing of machine guns or cannon—there was enough to do trying to keep the plane steady and on target. The Spitfires hurtled down at speeds often in excess of 550km/h, there was no looking at or checking of instruments— eyes had to stay out of the cockpit or situational awareness would be lost and a crater would be their grave.[18]

A few seconds after the dive commenced the bomb was gone and it was time to get out of the flak and away. Pulling out in a steep climb was a real effort, with their bodies crushed into their seats and goggles squeezing their faces from the G-forces created by the massive speeds achieved by the high angle of attack. Flak was heavy and Bob Yarra flying 'Y' (MK324) as Red 3, was hit by flak just after dropping his bomb. His aircraft exploded and the starboard wing separated from the fuselage. He didn't have any opportunity to bail out, and was posted as missing, believed killed, immediately upon the squadron's return. He had been with 453 nearly a year and it was recorded in the squadron log that he was 'a very good type'.[19] However, he didn't survive and was buried by the Germans on 17 April.[20] Yarra is now in the Commonwealth War Graves Commission Cemetery in Abbeville, France.[21] In a letter to Yarra's family, Don Andrews described him as 'a pilot of undoubted ability and courage',[22] much like his brother had been. The Wing Commander in charge of 125 Airfield at Ford, W/Cdr Lapsley, also wrote to the family and said:

He and the other lads in 453 have been with me since January. They are a splendid and as gallant crowd of lads as one could wish for and your boy was an outstanding member of the squadron both in the air and on the ground and he is a great loss to us all.[23]

The workload for 15 April was much lighter due to poor weather, with just three aircraft taking off at 1210 for a Ranger sortie to the Brussels-Antwerp area but the Luftwaffe was not seen. Fred Cowpe, flying 'V' was unable to lower his landing gear upon return and had to make a belly landing, doing so safely and without injury.[24]

The squadron then had three days off operations, during which they relocated to Ford—on the south coast of England and directly across the Channel from Normandy—with 132 and 602 Squadrons. Most of 132 arrived on the 17th, but some were not able to get through the fog.[25] Due to the fact that only skeleton staff remained at Detling, many staff ate at local establishments, until the weather cleared on the 18th, and the squadron flew the short trip down to Ford with 602 and the remainder of 132.

453 Squadron returned to action on 19 April. Twelve Spitfires armed with 500 lb bombs took off at 1050 for a Noball target, led by Don Andrews in his favourite, '?'.[26] Flak was heavy during the dive, and increased at lower levels with other positions adding to the crossfire and making the pull-out very dangerous, the aircraft having to be held perfectly straight during the dive to get a hit. Despite this heavy flak, all bombs but two were seen to hit the target and all aircraft returned safely at 1210.[27] Safely sure, but the flak was close enough to scratch the wings of Baker, being described as 'accurate and frightening'.[28] One element to making it safely out of a dive or strafing run was 'skidding'.[29] On the climb out and away from the target, instead of pulling quickly up in a straight follow-through, which would be more likely to induce a blackout, pilots could induce some lateral movement by skidding to the left or right by use of the rudder,[30] which was better than just making a regular turn as the banking wings would obviously tell the AA gunners where the plane was headed. There were no G-suits at the time, pilots flew in uniform, and their vision dimmed in the steep climb upwards and for a few seconds the plane continued on its course until blood circulation began to return to normal, their vision started to return and they were able to take complete control again.[31]

The squadron was settling in at Ford, though they were still primarily in tents and sleep was somewhat hard to come by—not due to partying this time, but the volume of sorties flown by Spitfires and Mustangs during the day, and Mosquitos at night.[32] After a rest on 21 April, during which the senior officers of 453 met with the Mosquito squadron on base, fellow Australians of 456 Squadron, two sorties were flown on the following day. The first involved eleven Spitfires taking off at 1050 to contribute to the fighter cover for Marauders and B-25 Mitchells over the Pas de Calais. The gun positions there had been hit by a similar raid escorted by 132 Squadron two days earlier.³³ Once again, flak was heavy, but directed at the bombers, and the fighters were unmolested by the Luftwaffe. This sortie returned at 1235. Upon their return, the aircraft were bombed up for a Noball sortie, and twelve took off at 1845 for a dive-bombing sortie. Bombing was fair and a number of bombs overshot, except that of Froggy Lyall, whose bomb didn't seem to want to let go and 'hung up' on the pylon until he was able to get rid of it on the way back near the coast.³⁴ An unidentified aircraft with grey markings was seen at zero feet headed east as the squadron travelled south from Cayeaux (Cayeaux-sur-Mer). Could this have been the only Luftwaffe aircraft the squadron had seen in three weeks?

The first sortie on 23 April comprised eleven aircraft up at 1050 led by Don Andrews in '?', flying escort for two formations of 54 Marauders. Bombing was assessed as poor, despite good visibility and there being no flak and no Luftwaffe interference. 132 Squadron also participated and two sections of them went down and strafed an E-boat in the Seine on the way home.³⁵ A petrol store was seen at Port Jerome, and noted for later attention. Norm Baker had to return early on this sortie due to a 'misunderstanding re pitch'.³⁶ Pitch relates to the angle at which the propeller blades cut through the air, and this can dramatically influence fuel consumption and aircraft handling. 'Fine pitch' is for high revs and is generally used for take-off and combat to give maximum performance, and 'coarse pitch' is generally for lower revs while cruising or landing, though, if necessary, it could also be used to reduce speed during a dive to give greater control.³⁷ The second sortie of the day was dive-bombing, with eleven Spitfires taking off with 500 lb bombs³⁸ at 1755 and hitting a Noball target at Beauvoir. 132 Squadron hit the target 15 minutes before 453, so the location was well and truly given a good going-over.³⁹ All bombs landed in the target area and heavy flak of both heavy and light calibres was noted. Ernie Esau, flying 'A', was hit by flak on the way in to bomb, a fist-sized hole in his starboard wing just missed the main strut, and all aircraft returned at 1910.[40] Ralph Dutneall nearly ripped the wings off his plane pulling out sharply after his dive-bombing run, but he made it back safely.[41] By Foggy Lyall's estimate, the damage to the planes was 'About half the squadron with various size holes'.[42]

24 April was a designated training day with bombing and strafing practice held at Goodwin Sands near Dover. Two sorties were flown on the 25th, Anzac Day. Twelve took off at 1025, with Ernie Esau flying 'H' while 'A' was repaired. The squadron escorted Marauders attacking the gun battery at what records refer to as Grisberg (though most likely it was Crisbecq). The bombing concentration was good, but flak was heavy. Most batteries had their own AA capability, but the Germans were concentrating on the bombers and the Spitfires were left alone. The Luftwaffe was a no-show. The early evening sortie was led by the Wing Commander, but the weather over the Channel and target were poor and the Noball target received little to no damage, bombing being assessed as poor.

On 26 April, the first sortie was aborted when the Marauder bombers were recalled. At 1310, eight aircraft took off on a low-level Ranger, looking for trouble and the Luftwaffe. Pat McDade led one flight in 'S' and Ernie Esau led the other in 'H'. Four flew to Rouen in the north of Normandy, and the others did a circuit of St Valery, Fleury, Nantreuil, St Just and Forges before returning to base. The Luftwaffe failed to challenge the Australians and all aircraft were back by 1450. Fred Cowpe described his part as a 'Very nice trip on the deck'.[43] The final sortie of the day was flown at 1905 by ten aircraft, though Don Andrews had to return at 1910, as '?' had engine trouble. Rather than pull out of the sortie, he jumped into 'N' and by 1915 was back in the air and caught up with the rest of the squadron before the target area was reached. 453 Squadron, along with 132, acted as escorts to twenty four B-25 Mitchells bombing marshalling yards at St Ghislain just a few miles west of Mons in Belgium. Flak was heavy but inaccurate and the Luftwaffe didn't show.

27 April was just as busy, with three sorties being flown. The first was of twelve aircraft, led by Don Andrews in '?' taking off at 1200 for the Cherbourg peninsula. Bombs were dropped at 4,000 ft after the dive, but no hits were claimed. No flak disturbed the men of 453, nor did the Luftwaffe. It was noted that there was heavy flooding along the east coast of the peninsula between Carentan and St Sauver (Saint-Sauveur-le-Vicomte). This was part of the German plan to disrupt any landing by gliders or parachutes in the fields of Normandy, which was, and still is, a very rural area. Come the night of the 5-6 June, many American paratroopers would find themselves weighed down by equipment, and they struggled in vain to get out of their 'chutes before they drowned. A huge and suspicious barn was seen at Tresville and reported by the squadron upon their return.[44] This reference was most likely Fresville, the probable location of the 'barn' being the old WW1 airship hangar at Montebourg-Ecausseville.

The airship hangar at Montebourg-Ecausseville, (2017). At 150 metres long, 31m high and 40 m wide at the base, 453 Squadron was right to be suspicious about it, but nothing came of it. To truly get an idea of scale it should be noted that the door (black rectangle in this photo) on the large green panel on the front of the hangar is a standard-sized door found on any house. (Author)

The second sortie of the day was by eleven aircraft, bombed up for a railway-canal bridge at Baupte.[45] Of all the bombs dropped, the squadron only claimed one near miss. They were met by light flak of medium intensity but no enemy aircraft were seen. Here too it was noticed that the river and canal area was flooded, in the boomerang-shaped Etienville-Baupte-Carentan area, where US paratroops would land on the night of 5–6 June. The last sortie of the day was for twelve Spitfires, dive-bombing again, this time to a bridge at Pont de la Rocque near Coutances, located about 14 miles west of Saint-Lo. With all the practice they'd had in recent days it was surely time for success to come their way. On this flight, all twelve bombs were classed as on-target, and the bridge was severed at the northern end. The southern approach to the bridge and buildings there were also severely damaged, and the bridge was deemed destroyed. Froggy Lyall recorded in his logbook: 'Wizard bombing'.[46] There was intense light flak over the target, but it was ineffective, as was the Luftwaffe. The railway line 200 yards east of the target was also severed, and one section of four planes, piloted by Esau 'H', Lawrence 'G', Baker 'K', and Harris 'N', got down low and strafed an army lorry which was left smoking on the beach as they crossed the French coast heading home. The squadron diary recorded the comment: 'it seems a long time since the boys have fired their guns.'[47]

With so many sorties flown in a few days, operations eased off on 28 April, and only one sortie was flown, and escort to bombers targeting the railway marshalling yards at Mantes-Gassicourt, 30 miles west-northwest of Paris but the weather caused the operation to be aborted, as was another escort on the following day. On the afternoon of the 29th, twelve aircraft took off for another escort. Instead of throttling back or flying an S-pattern to keep pace with the bombers, the Spitfires were now the slowest of the formation, and they could not keep up with the Mosquitos they were sent to assist. They only managed to meet up with them as they were leaving the target area.⁴⁸ For all its great qualities, the Spitfire was not a match for the 'wooden wonder'. The Luftwaffe was a no-show and flak was focused on the Mosquitos. The squadron diary entry for the sortie states that 'No important information was obtained from these operations'.⁴⁹ Clearly, the pilots were on the lookout for anything that might assist the ongoing planning and modification of the landings, especially such things as the flooding of rivers and canals as mentioned on the 27th.

The first sortie flown on the last day of April was by ten aircraft, led by Don Andrews in '?'. Two embankments were targeted with 11-second delay action bombs, allowing the Spitfires to get down low and drop them, rather than make a high-angle dive-bombing attack. The first target was at Ferrieres-en-Bray and the other north of Gournay-en-Bray, which are 30 miles east of Rouen. On the first target, one direct hit was claimed and the railway line severed. But, despite two bombs seen to explode in the second target area, no claims were made. One ship and two barges were reported in Dieppe harbour on the return leg. The second sortie of the day was launched at 1730, twelve Spitfires being fitted with 500 lb bombs for a Noball target at Marquenneville, about eight miles south of Abbeville. Dive-bombing results were judged as excellent, though the last two sections had to break away from their attacks as a low-flying P-47 disturbed the attack runs. The Spitfires recovered and came around for another pass, but not all bombs landed in the target area. All planes returned safely at 1845.

Orders were received for Don Andrews to be posted to 91 Group as Tactics Officer⁵⁰ and for Ernie Esau to Air Defence Great Britain (ADGB), the renamed Fighter Command, both in over-strength positions—that is, as additional staff not filling any vacancy. Don Andrews called his time on fighters a 'glorious two and a half years'.⁵¹ The sorties flown this day were the last for Don Andrews as CO of the squadron. The return for April 1944 showed that they had dropped 112 five hundred pound bombs that month.⁵²

Ground crew working on FU-S. Without the perpetual hard work of the 'erks', the pilots would have achieved nothing. (Courtesy of the Cowpe family)

Notes

1. ORB–453 Sqn
2. ORB–453 Sqn
3. Personal file–Ewins
4. ORB–132 Sqn
5. ORB–453 Sqn
6. ORB–453 Sqn and Thomas, *Spitfire Aces of Burma and the Pacific*, p. 7.
7. ORB–132 Sqn
8. Logbook–Harris.
9. ORB–453 Sqn
10. Logbook–Baker.
11. ORB–132 Sqn
12. ORB–453 Sqn and Personal File–Lancaster.
13. Personal File–Lancaster and Temora Interview–Vern Lancaster.
14. Temora Interview–Vern Lancaster.
15. NAA: A11335, 1061/ORG.
16. ORB–132 Sqn
17. Interview with Author–Handsaker and 'Versus The V's' in *Victory Roll, The Royal Australian Air Force in its sixth year of war*, RAAF Directorate of Public Relations, Halstead Press, Sydney, 1945, p. 119.
18. Author interview by email with Lindsay Richards–2016
19. ORB–453 Sqn
20. Personal File–RE Yarra.

21 CWGC Website
22 Personal File–RE Yarra.
23 Personal File–RE Yarra.
24 ORB–453 Sqn and Logbook–Cowpe
25 ORB–132 Sqn
26 Logbook–Andrews.
27 ORB–453 Sqn
28 Logbook–Baker and Logbook–Andrews.
29 Temora Interview–Fred Cowpe.
30 Interview with Author–Handsaker (Phone) 20/3/15.
31 AWFA: Russell Leith
32 ORB–453 Sqn
33 ORB–132 Sqn
34 Logbook–Lyall.
35 ORB–132 Sqn and Logbook–Cowpe.
36 Logbook–Baker.
37 Interview with Author–Roberts (Phone) 11/11/15.
38 Logbook–Andrews.
39 ORB–132 Sqn
40 ORB–453 Sqn and ORB–132 Sqn
41 Logbook–Andrews.
42 Logbook–Lyall
43 Logbook–Cowpe
44 ORB–453 Sqn
45 Herington, *Air Power Over Europe 1944–1945*, p. 32.
46 Logbook–Lyall
47 Logbook–Baker and Logbook–Harris.
48 Logbook–Andrews.
49 ORB–453 Sqn
50 Logbook–Andrews.
51 Logbook–Andrews.
52 ORB–453 Sqn

May 1944

Like April, May began with an exercise, this one carried out over three days involving patrols out over the Solent for just over an hour, at which point they were relieved by two replacement aircraft. While this was going on, the rest of the squadron was on 60 minutes readiness. This replicated what became the cab-rank system, whereby aircraft would be patrolling, waiting for forward air controllers with the ground forces to allocate a target for attack, with aircraft bombed up and ready to take off as soon as a target was allocated to the patrolling aircraft. This system aimed to maintain an ongoing supply of ground attack aircraft for deployment as the ground forces required.

On 2 May, eleven aircraft, led by Pat McDade in 'S', took off at 1525 and joined other squadrons in a short one-hour sortie led by the Wing Commander to bomb the viaduct at Le Havre, east of the landings beaches, on the coast of Normandy. Bombs were dropped after diving down to 3,000 ft and good hits were reported by other squadrons, but the accuracy of 453 was poor.[1] There was intense light flak but everyone returned safely. Don Andrews did not participate in the sortie, he was busy handing over command of 453 to S/Ldr Donald Hamilton Smith, and a send-off was held that night for Andrews and Esau. Both were presented with silver mugs:

a full pint for the Squadron Leader and a half pint for the Flight Lieutenant. The party broke up at midnight. The departure of Andrews was the subject of a Queensland-based newspaper article back in Australia. On 14 June the *South Coast Bulletin* published 'Squadron-Leader D. G. Andrews' and named him as Squadron Leader of 'the Britain based Australian Spitfire fighter-bomber squadron' and mentioned his 320 operational flying hours.[2] This was significant: pilots were supposed to be rested (posted away from the squadron to an instructing role or other non-operational duties) after 200 hours.[3] He had well and truly earned his rest.

Squadron send off for Don Andrews and Ernie Esau. The inscription on Don's mug read:
'S/LDR D.G. ANDREWS D.F.C. FROM THE BOYS OF
No 453 SQUADRON R.A.A.F.'
(Courtesy of the Cowpe family)

Thirty sorties were flown on low convoy escort sorties on 3 May, and the three-day exercise was complete. Thundery showers prevented flying on the 5th and most of the squadron went down to Brighton for the day. In response to the squadron's hopes for more publicity, four war correspondents arrived: F/Lt Andrews from Overseas Headquarters

(OHQ) and Messrs Williams, Folkard and Smith, all civilians. An article titled 'Australian Spitfire Squadron Command' was published in the *Morning Bulletin* of Rockhampton, Queensland on 4 May, which gave thirteen lines of a narrow column to the handover from Don Andrews to Don Smith, and sang Smith's praises for his recent award of a Russian Medal for Valour, and previous 'outstanding service at Malta.'[4]

Donald Smith (Service no. 407256) worked as a farmer and grazier in South Australia before joining the RAAF on 18 August 1940. After training at 3 EFTS Essendon and 2 SFTS Wagga Wagga he was posted to the UK and completed his flying training at 60 OTU before being posted to 452 (RAAF) Squadron.[5] In July 1942 he flew a Spitfire off an aircraft carrier on a one-way flight to Malta, one of the most bombed places in the world. While there, he served with 126 Squadron and was credited with shooting down two Ju-88s, a Me-109 and an Italian Cant 1007 bomber.[6] However, on 14 July 1942 he was severely wounded in a dogfight. His was one of just four Spitfires that took off to engage a raid of more than 20 bombers with a fighter escort. Climbing above the bombers, Smith dove through the fighter cover, shot down a bomber and was chased by the Me-109 cover he had passed. He was attacked—severing an artery in his ankle—and his R/T was damaged, so he could not communicate with the other Spitfires or ground control. With the Spitfire hard to control due to the damage inflicted by his pursuers, Smith attempted to engage them, but his guns would not fire—the air lines to the control column had been damaged. He dodged repeated attacks by two of the fighters, the other two going off to check on the downed bomber, and was harassed all the way back to Malta, where he landed with his badly damaged plane, falling unconscious as attempted to climb out of the cockpit.[7] He was sent back to the UK to recover.[8] After hospital he served for a short time with 41 Squadron and came highly recommended by them, scoring 8 out of a maximum of 9 for all his proficiencies, the score accompanied by the comment: 'This officer has proved himself to be definitely above the average in every respect in the performance of his duties as Flight Commander.'[9] While recovering in hospital from his wounds, he was looked after by nurse Margaret Price, an English girl from Kent. They married in October 1943.[10]

On 6 May, the squadron received word that the squadron crest was nearing completion and it was hoped that it would be presented very shortly. They trained in low-level flying for the day, no doubt 'beating up' a few farms in the process. The following day saw the formation of what was known as No. 6453 Echelon, comprising some Australian ground crews. The idea was to have RAAF ground crews servicing RAAF aircraft, slightly relieving the burden on RAF ground crews who had been servicing not only their own aircraft, but those of the Free French, Belgian, Dutch, Polish and other displaced air forces since 1940.[11] This day also saw the first operational sortie led by Don Smith, flying '?' as Andrews had done. Take-off for the Ramrod was at 0930, providing close escort to Bostons bombing Cambrai railway marshalling yards. Despite there being no flak, the bombing was assessed as poor, perhaps due to the 5/10ths cloud and haze. Nine enemy aircraft were seen on an aerodrome at Lille-Vandeville but no-one went down for a closer look.[12]

On 8 May, a second, unrelated, Smith arrived, F/Lt Henry Lacy Smith (Service no. 411539) from 132 Squadron, who was noted to be an experienced Flight Commander. His farewell from 132 Squadron was held at The Black Rabbit near Arundel.[13] Henry Lacy Smith was born on 24 February 1917 and, at the time of joining the RAAF on 24 May 1941, was enlisted in the 2/4th Pioneers. In some records the name Lacy is enclosed in inverted commas, as if to indicate it was a nickname or some abbreviation, but it was actually his father's middle name, Richard Lacy Smith. Smith Jnr. had done some dual flying at the Kingsford Smith Flying School, and had this edge over many other RAAF applicants. He passed his EFTS at Narrandera and, in October 1941, was shipped to Ontario (Camp Borden),

Canada via San Francisco. There he passed his SFTS before being shipped to the UK. His first operational posting was with 66 Squadron on Spitfires from September 1942 to January 1943, at the end of which he was assessed as: 'Always keen to take part in operations against the enemy'. In April 1943 he commenced duties at 132 Squadron and remained there until his posting to 453 Squadron.[14]

The morning sortie was an escort for Marauders and the second sortie for the day included the new Smith flying 'G' in his first sortie with 453, for dive-bombing where 50% hits were seen, the aim of the pilots undisturbed by flak or the Luftwaffe. Allan Harris in 'R' claimed a direct hit.[15] Everyone was back for dinner at 1850. On the following day, Pat McDade went on a period of well-earned leave, returning on the 17th.

While the boys were away in Europe, their mothers met up in Australia. From left to right are the mothers of: Lyall, Kinross, Roberts, Daff, Stansfield, Aldred and Olver. (Courtesy of the Olver family)

On 10 May Lionel Hansell was posted to No 1 Delivery Flight, Croydon, where it was hoped he'd meet up again with Russ Ewins who had been posted there the previous month. The morning sortie of twelve aircraft was led by Don Smith flying 'Q' this time, taking off at 1000 for a Noball target east of Abbeville, to which all three squadrons from the Wing gave their attention.[16] It was estimated that about 50% of bombs dropped in the target area, and one building was seen to take a direct hit. There was moderate light flak in response to the presence of the Spitfires, but no contest in the air, and the planes returned at 1115. The afternoon sortie targeted another Noball site which was hit by about 60% of the bombs dropped. A send-off was held for Lionel Hansell at a local pub that evening.

Two sorties were flown on 10 May, the first taking off at 0940 with twelve Spitfires for a Ramrod as close escort to Marauders bombing the Creil railway yards, about 28 miles north of Paris. Bombing by the Marauders was excellent and no enemy aircraft were seen by 453, though 602 Squadron was bounced by ten FW-190s and each formation lost one aircraft.[17] The afternoon sortie took off at 1525, with 10 aircraft to dive-bomb a Noball target SE of Abbeville.[18] Despite no flak, good weather and only 2/10ths cloud cover results were only rated as fair. Two FW-190s and some lorries were sighted at Abbeville but not engaged.

On 11 May, two more sorties were flown, the squadron keeping up its high rate of operations. The first took off at 1055, Don Smith in '?' leading ten other dive-bombing Spitfires on a Ramrod, the planes releasing much lower than normal, 1,500 ft this time. Bombing was accurate and opposed by intense light flak which failed to bring any of them down. The second sortie of twelve aircraft took off at 1835, with only the two Smiths flying the same aircraft they'd used in the morning. It was yet another Ramrod, against a grid reference, thought to be the location of a V-1 ramp, but this time the bombs were dropped from 2,000 ft. The flak was light and the Luftwaffe failed to interrupt the sortie, all pilots returning at 1945.[19]

The following day saw yet another exercise being held at the airfield, though the squadron was released at 1700 and most went into town as quickly as they could manage after the two daily ops. The first was a short Ramrod

Henry Lacy Smith (right) with friend John Caulton of New Zealand with a Mk IX Spitfire (FF-G) during their time on 132 Squadron. Smith's dog is 'Butcher'.
(Courtesy of the Caulton family)

across the Channel against a bridge, with several near misses noted, the bridge disintegrating from the concussion and all planes returning at 0910. The second sortie of the day was of twelve Spitfires up at 1515 on another Ramrod to bomb a road and rail crossing at Hardelot, about eight miles south of Boulogne. Bombs were dropped from 2,000 ft with three near misses noted and a number of German minesweepers spotted off the coast on the return flight. This sortie was back at 1640, just in time for the dismissal at 1700.[20]

On 13 May, two sorties were flown, the first being Ramrod 891, dive-bombing road and rail targets with good results, the planes releasing at 1,500 ft for better accuracy. There was another sortie at 1450 against a Noball target. A good concentration was achieved despite very hazy weather and moderate, small calibre flak. 'K' hadn't been used on the 12th, but was flown twice on the 13th, by Clarence Rice in the morning and Norm Baker in the afternoon. There was just something about flying a plane against the Germans with FU-K on the side that some pilots could not resist. The time for the landings was fast approaching and everyone would need to be as fresh and rested as possible for the campaign ahead. Most from the squadron were now being allocated leave at the rate of two or three staff at a time.

Poor weather on 14 May gave the squadron a break and flying resumed the next day, with aircraft sent to Manston airfield for a large escort sortie. Somewhere along the line there was a mix-up, and only seven aircraft took off with the 90 gallon drop tanks required for the escort of Mitchell bombers. Two of these were 10 minutes late, taking off at 0845, those being Clarence Rice in 'E' and David Murray in 'J'. The original target was bypassed, and some railway marshalling yards were attacked instead. There was no flak or enemy aircraft encountered, but heavy cloud at 10,000 ft obscured the target. Fred Cowpe described the day as a 'Glorious cock-up'.[21] While a comfort for the bombers, the Australians remained disappointed by the lack of dog-fighting action. At 1900, George Roberts, flying 'P', led three other Spitfires on a Ranger over to Normandy. They crossed the coast at Cabourg, east of the Caen canal at Ouistreham, then swept through Lisieux, St Sylvain and Caen quickly due to a lack of cloud cover. South of Colombelles, they found and attacked a train on the line running east from Caen, leaving the engine and tender in a cloud of steam. No enemy aircraft were seen and the flak directed at them from St Aubin, on the return leg, was ineffective. All aircraft returned at 2015.[22]

On 16 May, weather restricted the squadron to practising low-level flying and F/O Low was posted to 132 Squadron as Adjutant, commencing duty there on the 21st.[23] His replacement was F/Lt Keith Giles (Service no. 263012).[24] Giles was an RAAF officer who had enlisted in August 1941 and had served at a number of different postings, including Iraq, before arriving at 453 and accompanying them to Normandy. Prior to enlisting, he worked as a solicitor in Sydney.[25] Norm Baker took off alone on the 16th, as his No 2 had trouble with their plane, and Baker conducted a solo weather recce at 20,000 ft from Caen to Beauvais and Rouen.[26]

After a few more days of poor weather, operational flying resumed on 19 May, with four aircraft, led by Pat McDade in 'S', flying across the Channel and deep into Normandy on a Ranger over the Falaise area. The Spitfires stayed down low and crossing the coast east of Cabourg. No enemy aircraft were seen, but much activity was noted in the Caen and Lisieux marshalling yards. Allan Harris recorded 'No Joy' in his logbook.[27] The second sortie was a dive-bombing Ramrod. Eleven Spitfires led by Don Smith in '?' took off at 1915, equipped with delayed-action 500 lb bombs for better ground penetration. All three squadrons from the Wing—453, 132 and 602—contributed to a massive dive-bombing sortie against a Noball target at Bonnieres, located near a loop in the Seine, about 60 km west northwest of Paris. In the attack, each plane deliberately flew past the target, half-rolled then pulled back on the stick, diving down to drop their bombs from 3000 ft, now heading west back to England and not requiring any great deviation from their course so as to take as much advantage from the speed they'd built up. The target was obscured by cloud and the results were rated as unsatisfactory. Flak over the target was intense but no enemy aircraft were encountered.[28]

A practice parade for the Airlift Party of pilots and ground crew was held on 20 May in anticipation of the landings. The first sortie of the day was by eleven aircraft on a dive-bombing sortie, followed by another in the afternoon. The first sortie took off from Ford at 1005 on Ramrod 898, and they dropped bombs from 2,000 ft, the planes diving through a hole in the cloud, which limited their accuracy. Of all the bombs dropped, only six fell in the southern part of the target area. The Spitfire of Joshua Scott, who was flying 'R', was hit by flak in the fuselage but he was able to keep pace with the others and all landed safely at 1135.[29]

Olsson (left) and Kinross (right). Kinross still has his gloves on—they went almost to the elbow. (Courtesy of the Cowpe family)

The second sortie of the day was Ramrod 904, the number indicating the frequency of such sorties made by 2TAF, the morning effort having been numbered 898. The target was a road and rail junction at Hornoy[30] about 30 miles west of Amiens, but no direct hits were scored, partially due to the hazy weather.[31]

21 May saw the squadron return to the role the Spitfire was designed for: air-to-air combat. The pilots were glad to have a break from dive-bombing and two sorties were flown, the first by four Spitfires at 0925 led by Pat McDade in 'S' for a Ranger south along the Seine, also looking out for trains and motorised enemy transport (MET). The Luftwaffe was nowhere to be seen. The first sortie returned at 1105. This sortie was overlapped by another, led by Don Smith in 'G', and they took off from Ford at 1035. Near Conches-en-Ouche, with the flight flying at 25 ft, 'L' (MK566),[32] flown by Jack Olsson, was hit by flak in the radiator, causing him to lose all his glycol. He was unable to gain height, and had to make a forced landing 3-4 miles east of Bernay.[33] He was seen to land safely and reported over the radio that he was 'O.K.'. The remaining three aircraft shot up a truck south of

Louvieres-en-Auge, in the Falaise area, where the squadron would see much action towards the end of the Normandy campaign.[34] Upon returning to Ford, the remainder of the flight reported the incident and Olsson was reported missing. In fact he was captured almost immediately. Letters from Pat McDade and W/Cdr Lapsley, were sent to Olsson's family, with the briefest of details about him being shot down and the hope that he could possibly evade capture and make it back to the UK. In June, the squadron received official notification that he was indeed a prisoner of war, and this was passed on to his family.[35] A photograph of Olsson and a few lines in The Mercury newspaper of Hobart on 13 June publicly reported him as missing.[36] Olsson later wrote to the squadron, asking for underpants, and to: 'Give my best to the boys and wish 'em luck'. By September, he was in Stalag Luft III but only received his first Red Cross parcel in October. In January 1945 he was moved to Stalag IIIA, which he described as 'very crowded—conditions bad'. He was liberated on 21 April, 1945.[37]

A third sortie was launched at 1130, three aircraft led by George Roberts in 'P'. They also swept through the area south of the Seine and attacked road and rail targets in the vicinity of Bernay. A train in motion was attacked, as were some carriages in sidings west of Bernay. A staff car was also strafed and a heavy road vehicle was also attacked five miles east of Lisieux. There was intense light calibre flak in and around Bernay and Caudebec, but all aircraft returned safely at 1250.[38] Froggy Lyall flew 'T' on this sortie and recorded: 'One big railway engine and several road vehicles destroyed. Great fun!'[39] Rusty Leith wrote home on 21 May:

> You remember me mentioning a lad from Victoria named Jack Olver (he used to share a room with me at Hornchurch and we stayed on the Berkshire farm together) well the other day he had an accident taking off and broke his back. He is hospital recovering but apparently was miraculously lucky.[40]

Jack had crashed a Mk II Spitfire on take-off on 25 April while at RAF Central Gunnery School Catfoss and was off operations for a number of weeks. He had fractured two vertebrae[41] and could well have been struck off flying duties altogether, but he wasn't the type to give in and settle for a non-flying job. He recorded: 'A/C wiped off, I damn near was too!'[42]

The squadron was given a rest day from operations on 22 May, but improving weather on the 23rd was seen as a good sign. On 24 May, after the morning sortie of twelve Spitfires returned from successfully dive-bombing a Noball target at Febvin-Palfart 26 miles northwest of Arras, the squadron was addressed by Air Marshal Conningham, Air Officer Commanding (AOC) 2nd Tactical Air Force. He shook each pilot's hand and spoke with them individually, no doubt providing words of encouragement for the big operations to come. With members of the Australian press present, some good photos and coverage was expected.

Further instructions arrived in preparation for the eventual move to France, including instructions for waterproofing of vehicles, and that each vehicle was to carry, in addition to any other goods and regardless of the type of vehicle, 1,000 rounds of .303 ammunition,[43] which was a bit less than a combat load for a single Spitfire, but every little bit of gear they could carry with them would be valuable. Each vehicle was issued with traffic forms and instructions, including how to act in the event of a motor vehicle collision. The documents instructed troops to 'not admit liability by word or deed, or even discuss the question of blame ...'[44]

Furthermore:

Should a Police Officer appear on the scene and require a statement from you or any service personnel, this may be given to him but only to him and out of the hearing of any other person, always providing there is time to do this under your Movement Schedule.[45]

Even the part of the form by which the drivers were to exchange details had the disclaimer: 'This slip is handed to you for your convenience and is not to be taken as an admission of liability.'[46] With so many thousands of vehicles on the roads headed for the coast pre and post landings, the military didn't

June 1944: Norm Baker after a flight to France. The pilots loved to fly (of course) but that didn't mean it wasn't stressful. (AWM UK1342)

Of interest in the photograph of Fred Cowpe is the thick armoured glass of the windscreen which can be seen projecting into the cockpit running from the rear vision mirror down to the cowling. Earlier model Spitfires had this plating on the outside of the canopy. The bombs painted on the fuselage denote dive-bombing sorties. Carleen and May were the girlfriends of Fred Cowpe and Froggy Lyall. Fred later named his daughter Carleen.
(AWM UK1329)

want to be handing out money for every single motor vehicle collision and was very careful to discourage blame-taking by military personnel. Orders also stated that should any military vehicles be damaged, where possible, they should be towed to their destination.[47]

25 May was a rest day, for the pilots at least; the ground crews always had some maintenance and minor repairs to do. The next day provided the pilots with a free day in the morning, but the afternoon was taken up with parachute dinghy drill at Brighton, yet more practice for events likely to occur in the coming weeks. Despite the drab weather it was warm, so perhaps the experience was not as bad as the pilots expected of England, though it certainly could not compare to the experience of Australian beaches.

Don Smith visited RAAF Overseas HQ to discuss arrangements for a pool of Australian pilots to be posted to 83 Group Support Unit. These were to be made available to fill up any gaps (a euphemism for casualties) that may be 'caused by the anticipated intensive operations overseas' as the squadron Summary of Events records it.[48] No doubt this was to keep the Australian squadron as Australian as possible. For every aircrew member in an Australian squadron, there were at least three others serving on non-RAAF squadrons. Evidence of this can be seen with the postings of Lancaster from 602 and Smith from 132 in April and May respectively. Warrant Officer (W/O) Richard Arthur John York, who had previously served with 453 for just under three months in 1943, was one such pilot in 83 Group Support Unit and was transferred back to the squadron on 28 July 1944 after a number of pilots were lost in quick succession.[49] Another was Bruce Fuller who had also previously served with 453, 277 and 116 Squadrons and was rotated back through 83 GSU, returning to 453 Squadron in July 1944.[50]

On 27 May, the squadron took advantage of improved weather and launched a single sortie. Don Smith in '?' led eleven aircraft, taking off at 1730 and with 132 Squadron they bombed Douai, 14 miles northeast of Arras. Bombing was carried out from 5,000 ft, the aircraft having dived down

Don Smith suited up and ready to go Don Andrews' old Spitfire. This is clearly FU-?, as it retains the Gremlin. (AWM UK1333)

from 12,000 ft. The crossroads and railway sidings were targeted and bomb bursts were noted in the target area. There was no flak in the target area, but plenty at Gravelines where they crossed the coast, halfway between Calais and Dunkirk. All aircraft returned safely at 1850. Allan Harris thought that a railway target such as this was too big to be dealt with by Spitfires and commented in his logbook: 'Bombing seemed ineffective. Target too large.'[51]

Two Ramrod sorties were launched on the 28th and Bruce Fuller was admitted to hospital with acute appendicitis. He'd miss out on participating in what would become known as The Longest Day. The first sortie was Ramrod 933, the target being a railway junction and sidings at Hanebroekweg (just four miles NW of Ypres), the second was Ramrod 938 against a Noball target at Campagne-les-Hesdin, about 21 miles north of Abbeville.

29 May had the squadron at readiness from dawn till dusk, which was a very long time with the lengthening days of the European summer. A Ramrod sortie was flown at 1150 from Lympne, the squadron flying there early and refuelling to get the most out of the short range of the Spitfire. Before take-off, some of the pilots swam in the pool at the home of the late Sir Phillip Sassoon.[52] The formation of eleven aircraft led by Don Smith in 'G' flew to a Noball target at Behen, five miles southwest of Abbeville. The squadron dropped eleven 500 lb delayed-action bombs and returned at 1315. Froggy Lyall described it as 'Three squadrons one after the other. Aircraft everywhere.'[53] No doubt the image of so many Spitfires dive-bombing one after the other was a frightening sight to behold for those on the receiving end. The day was not yet over and at 1550 Clarence Seeney in 'B' and Joe Boulton in 'N' were scrambled to intercept a U-boat which unfortunately wasn't located. They returned at 1645 but, meanwhile, Pat McDade in 'M' and Froggy Lyall in 'U' had been scrambled at 1625 for a dinghy search (for a downed pilot) which was located and turned out to be a buoy, though it was painted yellow and was therefore easily mistaken for a downed pilot's dinghy.[54] The third scramble was at 1800 by Clarence Rice and Ralph Dutneall in 'L' and 'K' respectively. They were vectored for suspected enemy aircraft but none were seen and they returned at 1905.

While 453 participated in just the one Ramrod, on 29 May there was, in fact, a massive operation by sixty-six squadrons from 2TAF in the Pas de Calais area. While attacking certain targets was a definite goal, the day's operations also sought to convince the Germans that the Allies would operate out of bases normally not used to attack the north-west of

France and, therefore, stretch their range more than usual. However, the rate of operations required of 2TAF in Normandy prevented this from happening again.[55]

Two new pilots arrived, F/Sgt Allan William Dowding (Service no. 425139) and F/Sgt Douglas Graham Saunders (Service no. 417422), both Australians.[56] Allan Dowding, a station hand from Goondiwindi, was born on 19 August 1921 and signed up for the RAAF at Brisbane on 31 January 1942, his previous application having been refused (like many) due to his educational standard. He completed his basic flying in Australia and left for the UK in March 1943 to complete his training before being posted to 453 Squadron.[57] Douglas Saunders was born on 28 March 1923 and was working as a wool clerk, having trained as a wool classer, when he signed up for 'the duration of the war and up to 12 months thereafter', as the form stipulated, on ANZAC Day, 25 April 1942. His basic flight training was conducted in Australia and he also left for the UK in March 1943. 453 Squadron was also his first operational posting.[58]

The two new pilots were spared from operations on 30 May. Morning and afternoon sorties kept the squadron busy. The morning effort was by eleven Spitfires which took off at 1005, and with 132 Squadron, bombed Cap D'Antifer, on the coast 13 miles north of Le Havre. Bombing from 1,000 ft yielded good results, including a direct hit on the coastal Wuerzburg (radar) installation. The radar and associated buildings were also strafed and, in response, the light flak was intense and accurate, but not enough to bring anyone down. Weather over the target was hazy, but it appeared that good results were achieved. The afternoon sortie at 1530 consisted of ten aircraft led by Don Smith in 'G' bombing the radar station at what is recorded in the squadron diary as 'Arramanenes' but which was probably Arromanches, where a Mulberry harbour would be established during the return to France. A radar station was located just east of Arromanches, on the headland overlooking the town.[59] Despite the hazy weather, the attack went ahead, and bombing took place from 10,000 ft down to 2,500 ft from the southwest to the northeast, with a direct hit claimed on the radar station. The bombing concentration was assessed as good and strafing runs were also made, with additional hits claimed on the huts and radar station. All aircraft returned safely at 1630.[60] The landings were now less than a week away.

After early morning readiness on the last day of May, the squadron was stood down and everyone was able to catch up on some sleep. 237 five hundred pound bombs were dropped in May.

Notes

1. Logbook–Lyall
2. NLA: Trove–'Squadron Leader D. G. Andrews' *South Coast Bulletin*, 14 June 1944.
3. Cundy, A Gremlin on my shoulder, p. 99.
4. NLA: Trove–'Australian Spitfire Squadron Command' *Morning Bulletin*, 4 May 1944.
5. Personal File–Donald Smith
6. NLA: Trove–'Spitfire Commander transferred' *Townsville Daily Bulletin* 15 June 1944.
7. Herington, *Air War Against Germany & Italy 1939–1943*, p. 251.
8. Newton, *Australian Air Aces*, p. 109.
9. Personal File–Donald Smith
10. NLA: Trove–'He married his nurse' *The Telegraph* (Brisbane) 19 October 1943
11. Alan Brown, *Flying for Freedom: The Allied Air Forces in the RAF 1939–45*, The History Press, Gloucestershire, 2000, (2011), p. 161.
12. ORB–453 Sqn
13. ORB–132 Sqn
14. Personal File–Henry Lacy Smith
15. Logbook–Harris.
16. ORB–132 Sqn
17. Logbook–Baker and Logbook–Harris.
18. ORB–132 Sqn
19. ORB–453 Sqn
20. ORB–453 Sqn

21 Logbook–Cowpe
22 ORB–453 Sqn and Logbook–Harris.
23 ORB–132
24 OAFH: 1945_Misc
25 Personal File–Giles
26 Logbook–Baker.
27 Logbook–Harris.
28 ORB–453 Sqn
29 ORB–453 Sqn
30 ORB–132 Sqn
31 ORB–453 Sqn
32 Norman Franks, *Royal Air Force Command Losses of the Second World War Volume 3: 1944–1945*, Midland Publishing, Leicester, 2000, p. 37.
33 Logbook–Baker.
34 ORB–453 Sqn
35 Personal Files–Olsson.
36 NLA: Trove–'Spitfire Pilot' *The Mercury* 13 June 1944
37 Personal Files–Olsson.
38 ORB–453 Sqn
39 Logbook–Lyall
40 Leith–Correspondence home 21 May 1944
41 Olver file–medical letter dated 5 July 1944
42 Logbook–Olver
43 NAA: A11335, 1061/ORG
44 NAA: A11335, 1061/ORG
45 NAA: A11335, 1061/ORG
46 NAA: A11335, 1061/ORG
47 NAA: A11335, 1061/ORG
48 ORB–453 Sqn
49 Personal File–York.
50 Personal File–Fuller
51 Logbook–Harris.
52 Logbook–Lyall
53 Logbook–Lyall
54 Logbook–Lyall
55 Barbier, *D-Day Deception*, pp. 102–103, 145.

56 ORB–453
57 Personal File–Dowding
58 Personal File–Saunders
59 Tim Saunders, *Battleground Europe: Normandy: Gold Beach–Jig*, Leo Cooper, Barnsley, 2002, pp. 121–127.
60 ORB–453 Sqn

June 1944

June 1 saw an 'early' rise for a briefing at 0815, which would be considered luxury for any infantry unit! Due to poor weather, the plans for the day could not be carried out, but all members of the squadron were around when another new pilot, F/Sgt Brian Inglis (Service no. 418230), reported for duty.

Brian Scott Inglis was born in Adelaide on 3 January 1924 and when he signed up on 25 April 1942 was enrolled as a student at Melbourne University. He was posted to 1 ITS at Somers in Victoria where he recalled that it rained a lot,[1] and completed his EFTS and SFTS in Australia. He deemed Temora, in country New South Wales, where he first flew Tiger Moths, a 'very good flying area' with 'excellent instructors', despite the last words of his instructor as he left the ground for his first solo: 'See if you can get around in one piece'! Inglis progressed to the unpopular Wirraway, which he described as 'skittish' and more difficult to fly.[2] In March 1943 he sailed for the UK and completed his training there. In January 1944, while at 57 OTU (Eshott, on the east coast of the UK, north of Newcastle) his Pilot Air Firing Record graded him as 'Steady and consistently good'.[3] He would later admit that he tried to get a good score by coming in much slower and lower than normal, but actually ended up damaging the propeller on anti-invasion fencing. He found taxiing in the ice during winter difficult with the pneumatic brakes on a Spitfire: they were either on or off. 453 Squadron was his first operational posting and he 'had been waiting a number of months' to get to one.⁴

June 1944: Flight Sergeant Brian Inglis. (AWM UK1423)

Also on 1 June, Bruce Fuller was checked on in hospital and was reported to be making satisfactory progress, but he'd miss the 'big show' coming up. That night, 456 (RAAF) Squadron hosted a dance and invited the men of 453. A good time was had by all.

On 2 June, there were no morning ops, but there was a dive-bombing effort in the afternoon, with twelve aircraft taking off at 1630 with Ralph Dutneall flying 'K' and Joe Boulton flying 'N'. This was the first operational flight with 453 for Doug Saunders, who piloted 'M'. The target was a Wuerzburg (radar) site at Cap-Gris-Nez that 602 Squadron had bombed earlier in the day.⁵ Twelve 500 lb bombs were dropped on the run from north to south, with only a short dive of 4,000 ft to 3,000 ft. Two near misses were claimed, nothing more, with the intense and accurate light calibre flak no doubt contributing to the result.

The morning of 3 June was also free, but Ramrod 962 was flown in the afternoon, with planes taking off at 1345, ten minutes after 132 Squadron.[6] Once they had formed up the squadrons headed across the Channel and together spent an hour in the area Domfront, Flers and Caen strafing targets of opportunity. Seven to eight long trucks, perhaps tank transporters, were sighted and strafed on the road between Domfront-Flers and Flers-Tinchebray by 453, and 132 strafed a train.[7] Three aircraft described as 'radial engine, square wing tipped' and presumed to be FW-190s were seen at 100 ft flying north in the same area but were not engaged. The flak encountered was inaccurate. Upon the return of the rest of the pilots, Don Smith decided they should carry out a dive-bombing exercise, no doubt taking advantage of the long European summer days.

5 June was supposed to have been the day of the landings in Normandy but, due to poor weather, the operation was postponed. However this wasn't nearly as simple an exercise as it sounds. The original date of 5 June had been confirmed to the forecaster, W/Cdr J.M. Stagg, back on 22 May,[8] and plans had been focused with that date in mind. Even moving the whole operation by just one day was a massive undertaking. General Eisenhower needed a forecast from D-4 to D+2/+3 to know if the operation should go ahead or not. Four days' warning had to be given to enable all the troops to get to their final locations because they were spread out all over the UK.[9] Both the British and Americans had their own forecasting teams, and a consensus had to be reached before any predictions could be presented to Eisenhower. On 3 June Stagg had been told by General Morgan:

> Good luck Stagg; may all your depressions be nice little ones: but remember, we'll string you up from the nearest lamp post if you don't read the omens right.[10]

It was not just about getting the naval forces across the Channel; Eisenhower was aware that, as far as ground forces went, the Allies would not have an overwhelming strength—they would need all the help air

Jack Olver in civilian clothes. This type of photo was similar to those used in forged documents if shot down. (Courtesy of Olver family)

support could give them. The landings were thus delayed by a day.[11] On the 4th, it was determined that the landings would go ahead on 6 June, and this decision was confirmed at 0415 on 5 June.[12] It was on.

Pilots had new identification photos taken for use 'overseas' and the squadron was visited by F/Lt Andrews, the Australian Public Relations Officer. He showed the photos that had been taken on the recent visit by war correspondents, and many orders were placed for copies to send home.

4 June was also the day that the famous 'invasion stripes' were painted on the aircraft, three white bands alternating with two black bands around each wing and the fuselage between the cockpit and tail. While black and white markings had been applied to Typhoons for the Dieppe raid and, when fighting off the hit-and-run raids against the southeast of England, they had not been used on such a scale before. The decision to apply the markings to all aircraft (except 4-engined aircraft such as heavy bombers which should not have been able to be confused with Luftwaffe aircraft as the Germans had nothing of equivalent size) was a direct result of confusion regarding the identification of aircraft in earlier Allied amphibious operations, especially the invasion of Sicily on 20 July 1943. These markings retain their recognition for their special purpose to this very day and are commonly known as 'D-Day' or 'invasion' stripes.

A fine example of markings used on D-Day, also commonly known as 'invasion stripes'.
(Author)

At 1655, six aircraft, led by Don Smith flying 'J' joined Spitfires from 132 and 602 Squadrons for Ramrod 970, to dive-bomb a radar target at the peninsula lighthouse at Le Havre.[13] 500 lb bombs were dropped after a north-to-south dive from 10,000 ft to 4,000 ft and a good concentration in the target area was reported. On the return flight, a large coast-watching vessel was also strafed, and all aircraft landed at 1755.

Tension and excitement filled the air on 5 June: the landings were just a day away. The day was spent at lectures and briefings, the ground crew doing touch-ups on the markings. Don Smith didn't fly on this day, he was attending a conference at Tangmere with the other Squadron Leaders and the Wing Commander.[14] Of all the meetings and conferences to attend during his time as Squadron Leader, this was the one he did not want to miss. The next day the war would change direction, and he, and the men of 453, were going to be part of it. Upon his return to Ford, he was ordered to open his sealed 'Top Secret' envelope which contained the plan for Operation Overlord as it concerned 125 Wing.[15]

At Ford, two sorties were flown, the first by just two aircraft, Ken Kinross in 'E' and Clarence Seeney in 'S' for a quick low-level hour-long flight from 1025 to 1125 over a convoy travelling south of St Catherine's Point, which was uneventful. Another patrol took off at 1720, with twelve aircraft on a short coastal patrol, all returning at 1845. This was the first operational sortie with 453 for Allan Dowding and he was allocated 'R'.

That evening, the Wing was briefed for the following day's operations. Firstly they were addressed by W/Cdr Lapsley who laid out the air plan and the role to be played by 125 Wing. Next was Group Captain (G/Cpt) Rankin who spoke words of encouragement to the assembled pilots and ground crew and wished them all luck. They were then briefed on the outline of the Overlord plan and the sectors into which Normandy had been divided. Next followed the tactical orders: who would be where, when, and for how long.[16] The biggest combined operation in history was about to take place, everyone had to know their role. The Luftwaffe had been hard to come by for a long time now, but if ever they were going to put in a maximum effort, the Allies' return to France would be the trigger and 453 would be ready for them.

The last sortie of the day was launched at 2115, with Allan Dowding, piloting 'M', and the first with 453 for Brian Inglis, in 'Y'. They patrolled at 3,500-4,000 ft over a southbound convoy, and returned at 2235.[17] Brian Inglis would retain a strong memory of that day, with visions of the fleet stretched out before him: 'The numbers of ships was astonishing' and even though it was late (relatively speaking) in England, 'visibility is good, even nine o'clock at night'.[18] Froggy Lyall described it as a 'Marvellous sight'.[19]

That night, as the pilots slept as best they could, given their level of excitement, 24,000[20] British and American paratroopers and glider-borne infantry flew across the Channel to lead the way back to France. Their role was to seize causeways, bridges and towns behind the landing beaches and act as a buffer for any German forces trying to reinforce the Normandy defences. Any bridges left standing would also force the Germans into a bottleneck which would result in bunching up and delays and, therefore, potentially fewer targets geographically speaking, but certainly bigger targets for 2TAF.[21] Many of these paratroopers and glider-borne forces would land scattered across fields miles from their objectives, but they banded together in groups, regardless of parent unit, and caused chaos wherever they could. Of the two US Airborne Divisions (101st and 82nd) dropped, only some men of the 82nd had seen combat before. It would be their D-Day in more ways than one. Likewise, not all of the British 6th Airborne Division had seen combat before. Radio messages were broadcast via the BBC to resistance groups, coded messages announcing the coming of the Allies. One particular message quoted a poem by famous French poet Paul Verlain:

Les sanglots long des violons de l'Automne
Blessent mon Coeur d'une langeur monotone

(The long sobs of the violins of Autumn
Wounds my Heart of a monotonous languor)[22]

Field Marshal Erwin Rommel would later call 6 June 'The Longest Day', a name which stuck for both sides, gave its name to a widely popular book and an all-star movie, and encompasses the enormity of that one particular day in just three words. For the Western Allies, they are powerful words that have retained their meaning for generations since. Even the term 'D-Day', though a generic military term for the commencement of an operation (operations start on D-Day at H-Hour), has been almost exclusively claimed for Normandy.

On 6 June, all the pilots of 453, and many other squadrons of 2TAF, were up at 0400 for dawn readiness. The squadron diary recorded: 'We are glad we are not Germans'.[23] The first sortie after a breakfast of beans and fried bread[24] was flown at 0800, ten aircraft led by Don Smith in 'J' patrolling at low level (2,000–3,000 ft)[25] in the Utah Beach (American zone) area where they saw thousands of ships of every description. The landings were observed and the aircraft returned at 1015. The second sortie was flown over the same area but the third was sent to the Gold Beach (British zone) area. This returned at 1920 and was replaced by the last of the day, with eleven aircraft led by a partially-rested Don Smith back in '?'. This sortie took place from 2130 to 2315 and, as with the others, was uneventful.[26] At his OTU, near Newcastle, Rusty Leith wanted to be back with his squadron and in on the action, and was 'cheesed off' at being left out.[27]

Pilots had been briefed to expect torpedo or glide-bomb attacks against the Allied fleet from German anti-shipping aircraft, as had occurred during the landings at Salerno and Anzio. But, in the end, such attacks didn't occur.[28] Had such a raid taken place, it would have met impressive resistance. For D-Day, the Allies had amassed 171 squadrons of day fighters. There were an additional ten squadrons of Mosquitos for night defence, plus more for intruder night operations. Coastal Command blocked the Channel at both ends with Sunderlands and Beaufighters. 36 squadrons of Spitfires were allocated to low cover tasks, enough to have six squadrons over the landing area at all times. These were backed up by rotations of three squadrons of P-47 Thunderbolts operating as high cover over the beachhead and rotations of four squadrons of P-38 Lightnings in the mid-Channel area, these being the most distinctive of all Allied fighters and therefore—in theory—the least likely to be shot down by the fleet. Fleet gunnery was directed by Royal Navy Seafires against shore batteries, the bombing of the night 5–6 June had not been effective due to the weather conditions and Bomber Command had warned that 'night attacks against coastal batteries were extremely unreliable and almost wholly futile'. The Seafire sorties went ahead and the aircrews carried out their allocated spotting tasks despite variable weather.[29]

Despite almost no contact with the Luftwaffe for a number of weeks, Fred Cowpe expected a massive air battle to accompany the landings, but it was a one-sided affair. At one point during the morning he thought he saw some Me-109s and went after them with his section but they turned out to be Mustangs, the American silver (perhaps dulled by the cloud) being confused with the grey camouflage common to 109s and both having a squarish wing profile. Along sections of the coast there was a muddy area that spread a few hundred yards out to sea where the cliffs had been blown away by bombing or shelling. For aircraft, the biggest risk was collisions, there being so many planes and so much cloud about. On the last sortie of the day, Cowpe was back in his Spitfire and thought the engine sounded terrible. He did an engine test with four ground crew sitting on the tail and ran it up to +10 lb of boost and it was a bit better and he decided he'd take off last so that if he had to return he wouldn't get in anyone's way. As he was doing this, another Spitfire stopped nearby, and in the seat was Sgt McKinnon, one of the ground crew. They swapped planes and Fred went off after the squadron.[30]

During the morning, the destroyer USS *Corry*[31] was seen by the pilots of 453 to be sinking off Isles St Marcouf. While the Allies lost many landing craft across the Normandy coast that morning, very few vessels of the larger classes were lost. There is debate about how this ship came to be sunk, but it may have been caused by gunfire from the fortified position at Crisbecq, one of many large gun batteries overlooking the coastline. Construction of the battery began in 1941 and, with a 28 m elevation, it had a panoramic view of the coastline. It was originally intended to have three main bunkers with 210 mm guns, but only two had been completed by 6 June 1944, though all three guns were in place. Each gun could fire one 135 kg shell per minute out to a range of 27 km, and the position was self-contained, with its own anti-aircraft and anti-tank defences. There was also a dummy position in the field behind the gun position to draw fire and aerial bombing away from the real positions.³² As was the case all along the coast, the bombing of the battery was inaccurate on the night before the landings and the operations of the battery were not adversely affected. On 6 June, the battery was engaged by a number of battleships of the invasion fleet, including USS *Texas, Arkansas, Tuscaloosa, Quincy* and *Nevada*. While the large guns were all put out of action, this battery was in communication with another at Azeville and the two fired their smaller artillery pieces in support of each other for a number of days against assaults by US forces. Finally, on 9 June, the Azeville battery fell and, on 12 June, the Crisbecq battery was taken, the majority of German troops having withdrawn from the position.³³ The site was levelled in the 1970s and trees were planted over the top. It was rediscovered in 2004.³⁴

A view towards the coast from an open emplacement within the perimeter of the 'Marcouf' battery at Crisbecq. (Author)

On D-Day, 453 Squadron put 19 different pilots into the air, in 43 sorties across the Channel to Normandy to protect the landings. The Allies flew over 3,300 sorties that day, of which about 1,500 were made by fighters and, during daylight hours, there were usually 100 fighters over the beachhead at any given time.³⁵ Expecting strong resistance, Don Smith stuck to his most experienced pilots, some of whom flew three sorties—some consecutive and others broken up across the day. The newest arrival and least experienced pilot, Brian Inglis, was left out altogether and Allan Dowding and Doug Saunders, who had been with the squadron less than ten days flew only one sortie each. While they may have been upset or disappointed at missing out on the biggest all-arms operation of all time, Don Smith was not going to risk their lives in what was expected to be a hard-fought battle. That it was not as hard-fought in the air as it was on land came as a big surprise for many pilots.

Flying Officer George Roberts in FU-P at Ford on 6 June 1944. This photo is likely to have been taken after the second sortie where he flew 'P' and returned at 1515. Roberts flew 'P' again on the fourth sortie of the day but, since the planes returned at 2315, it probably would have been too dark for this photo. Note the Kangaroo above 'Ann'.
(AWM UK1428)

Jack Olver, who had spent time in hospital after a crash in April, called the CO on the 6th. He wanted to come back to the squadron and claimed to be fit and ready to go.[36] Two flights in a Spitfire at 83 GSU proved his fitness, and Olver was accepted back.[37] While the pilots flew sorties across the Channel, the remaining squadron staff prepared the unit for movement when they were not refuelling or servicing Spitfires. Allan Harris recorded comments in his logbook for the first sortie on 6 June: 'Beginning of 'Second

Front'. Much bombardment of coastline by navy. No flak. No German a/c. Landing according to plan'. Then for his second sortie: 'Bombarding continuing fires all over beachhead. No enemy a/c. Allied tanks seen moving inland'.[38] The Allies were back in France, their Normandy landings achieving a strong foothold and a front 60 miles long.[39]

At the end of the day Froggy Lyall recorded in his logbook: 'D DAY. A lot of opposition expected, but greatest danger from collision with friends'.[40]

PILOTS AND AIRCRAFT PARTICIPATING ON OPERATIONS 6 JUNE 1944

Pilot	0800-1015	1310-1515	1715-1920	2130-2315
S/Ldr Smith	J	?	-	?
F/Lt McDade	Z	-	?	-
F/O Baker	-	B	K	-
F/O Lancaster	H	H	-	B
F/O Lawrence	U	-	U	V
F/O Murray	-	F	F	F
F/O Roberts	-	P	-	P
F/O West	D	-	D	-
W/O Cowpe	V	T	T	-
W/O Daff	-	L	-	L
W/O Harris	-	-	Z	Z
W/O Kinross	-	G	-	E
W/O Lyall	N	-	N	-
W/O Rice	L	-	J	J
W/O Scott	R	-	R	M
W/O Seeney	B	-	A	-
W/O Watts	-	K	-	G
F/Sgt Dowding	-	V	-	-
F/Sgt Saunders	-	M	-	-

In Caen, 17-year-old schoolboy Pierre Verbeke was woken by the bombing near Caen on the night of the 5–6 June, and he heard more bombing again later in afternoon. Living in Caen with his parents, Pierre was aware that the Germans were on the lookout for Allied planes. He noticed that they posted lookouts on their vehicles as they drove around, and often used the smaller roads to avoid attack from the air. He'd wanted to be a pilot since he was six or seven years old, so took a great interest in what was happening above him, but was wary of the Germans; his brother had been killed by the SS in 1943. Life was difficult for the Verbeke family; there was little food but, luckily, those in the towns were supported by families from the country who sometimes shared their food with them. For Pierre, the occupation had been lived on a knife's edge: you could live or die based on how you spoke to a German. On one occasion, when he was told to carry the bags of a German soldier, he refused. The German threatened him with a grenade and so he grabbed the German and wrapped his arms around him, saying that if the German was going to use a grenade, then they would die together. For that he was lucky not to be shot.

When the landings took place, there was no news to be had, but Pierre's parents were worried enough to move the family out of Caen to the village of Tilly-sur-Seulles. Little did they know that the battle for Tilly would destroy the village as it changed hands a number of times. The family was eventually evacuated from the area by Allied troops and taken to Bayeux. From there, Pierre used to visit the American airfield at Tour-en-Bessin and the Americans let him look at a crashed B-17 there. He found them friendlier than the English, saying that the English would not allow him onto their airfield to look at the planes. In February 1945, Pierre was moved to England and volunteered to become a pilot, but only flew the Tiger Moth before training stopped when the war ended in Europe. He had no idea that any of the pilots flying above Normandy were Australian.[41] He may not have known it, but Australians were playing their part in liberating his country.

On 7 June, the squadron kept up its rate of sorties. Further packing in preparation for the big move to France took place. On the ground, the beaches had been largely secured and many coastal towns taken but many landing areas were still within range of German artillery. The British, Canadians and Americans had not yet linked beachheads to form a continuous front, while airborne troops continued to create havoc behind the front lines. The first sortie of the day was flown by eleven aircraft at 0810, led by Pat McDade in '?'. They flew low fighter cover again, covering the Utah Beach area and witnessed glider reinforcements landing in the area around Ste Mere Eglise. They saw the beach at Varreville (Saint Martin-de-Varreville) being shelled and wrecked landing craft were noted in the area. The squadron was subjected to some flak from the area between Carentan and Isigny, just a short distance inland from the beaches. The first sortie returned at 1020. The second, third and fourth sorties were spread out to cover the rest of the day, the last plane landing at 2340. On one occasion during the day, twelve aircraft—believed to have been FW-190s—were seen diving through cloud near a location nominated as 'Point de la Rase' in the squadron record. However, since Pointe-du-Raz is near Brest (about 190 miles southwest from Utah Beach) the location must have been misreported. Regardless of the true location, they were not engaged and this was the only sighting of the Luftwaffe by 453 in the first two days of the landings.[42] The frustration of the Australians was expressed in an article by *Sydney Morning Herald* war correspondent H.I. Williams in an article titled 'Spitfire Pilots Eager' in which he described the Luftwaffe as: 'not merely elusive, but invisible'.[43]

S/Ldr Hilton, a liaison officer from the Headquarters' Allied Expeditionary Air Force (AEAF), to which 2TAF belonged, visited and spoke with the pilots on 8 June. While progress on the ground was slower than expected, the Luftwaffe still had not provided any significant resistance. Once again, 453 patrolled the Utah Beach area and kept to its roster. Eleven aircraft were up at 0810 for the first sortie of the day, led by Henry Smith in 'A' and Pat McDade in 'H'. They returned at 1000 and the second sortie, led by Don Smith in '?' flew a patrol from 1310 to 1505, once again encountering no fighter opposition. The third and final sortie was flown by twelve Spitfires led by Don Smith in '?' from 1720 to 1925. During the day, the squadron saw Marauders bombing a target west of Utah and being met by heavy flak. Not a single enemy aircraft was seen, and it was noted that some coastal batteries remained in action against landing craft and destroyers—particularly in the area of Isle St Marcouf.[44]

9 June saw just a single sortie and a welcome rest day for pilots and ground crew. Two aircraft took off at 1410: Don Smith in '?' and Fred Cowpe in 'T' for a weather recce patrol to Le Havre and along the beaches to Utah then back to base. There was no flak encountered and no enemy aircraft were seen. There was heavy cloud from 1,000–2,500 ft over the beachhead. On this day, Jack Olver got his wish and returned to the squadron, but did not fly, replacing Brian Inglis who had been struck down with the chicken pox.

There was an early morning sortie on the following day, with eleven aircraft taking off at the usual time of 0810, patrolling the Utah Beach area and returning at 1000. The second sortie was led by Don Smith in '?' but Keith Daff, flying 'O', was the first of the squadron to land on newly liberated French soil when, due to engine failure, he had to land at Vierville, adjacent to Omaha Beach. This second sortie lasted from 1310 to 1450. Fortunately, Daff's problem was rectified and he returned the same day. The third and fourth sorties were uneventful and saw the last Spitfire return at 2335. The warning order for the squadron to move base was now just six hours.[45]

11 June saw final preparations for the squadron move, everything had to be ready for the actual move to take place on the following day. Eleven Spitfires, led by Don Smith in 'U', flew a morning sortie, leaving Ford at 1040 and landing at St Croix-sur-Mer at 1320, though they were not the first of the Wing to do so: 132 Squadron beat them by 45 minutes.[46] Nor was the Wing the first, the Canadians of 144 Wing beat them by a day.[47] Allan Harris recorded that the French people were very friendly and they were greeted with flowers by some people who came to the airstrip, though

he also recorded the rumour that there were some French sniping at Allied troops.[48] From this landing strip they refuelled and took off again at 1900, each pilot in the same plane, flying over Juno, Gold and Sword Beaches.

The arrival of the Australians in Normandy, though just for the one night, was reported in the *Sydney Morning Herald* by H.I. Williams in an article titled 'Australians Refuel in Normandy'. Don Smith was quoted referring to the RAF SCU and night spent at the emergency airstrip, saying:

> They are doing an excellent job. They were very good to us. They serviced us sufficiently, gave us some of their stew and biscuits and lent us blankets. They are really good fellows.[49]

It was on this second sortie that Henry Smith, commanding A Flight was shot down when his plane was hit by flak east of the Caen canal. At the time, the flight (consisting of Smith in 'B' (MJ789), Joshua Scott in 'R' and David Murray in 'D') was over the Robehomme area, south of Varaville. When flying in an easterly direction at a height of 1,500-2,000 ft Henry Smith's plane was struck just in front of the long-range tank or directly under the engine by 20 mm fire directed at the flight from a wood. The plane began to emit white fume trails, probably glycol, and lost speed. Smith performed a steep left turn to head back to the safety of Allied lines and was followed by the others. He radioed to them: 'I am going to have to put this thing down in a field'. The plane continued west, gliding towards Allied lines. The others followed Smith down, and didn't see him jettison the hood, lock it back, nor get rid of the long-range tank. Just short of Ouistreham, near Sallenelles on the eastern side of the canal, the damaged Spitfire struck the water, skidding on the surface for a short time before dipping the port wing and nosing over, slowly turning onto its back, showing its undersides above the water. For a time the flight circled above the crash in the hope of seeing Smith get out, but no movement was seen, and no-one approached the crash. Flak caused the remainder of the flight to leave, but they returned to the site shortly afterwards and found no change at the scene, and still no-one had approached to make a rescue.[50] At the time, it was not known for

A 2017 aerial photo of Ouistreham (bottom of photo) and Sallenelles (above Ouistreham in the photo, approximately where the pond-looking features are).
(Author)

sure that Smith was dead, but it was presumed. Don Smith wrote a letter to Henry's family expressing his 'deep regret.'[51] The loss of Henry Lacy Smith was the first for the squadron since the landings. Sadly, it would not be the last letter written by Don Smith in Normandy. Henry Lacy Smith's body was not recovered for more than 65 years.

After a miserable night in slit trenches dining on hard rations, the remaining pilots took off from France at 0550 and, after conducting a low cover patrol with 132 Squadron,[52] returned to England at 0755. Two of the squadron's vehicles moved off on the slow journey to the docks and to France. The second sortie of the day was of twelve Spitfires which took off at 1720 led by Don Smith in '?' for a beachhead patrol (which was uneventful) and all planes returned at 1910. This was the first operational sortie for Jack Olver on his return to 453, and he flew this and the last sortie of the day in 'X'. The last sortie of the day took off at 2130 and was led by Pat McDade in 'S' but he returned at 2230 though the remainder continued on, landing at 2340.

In the evening, F/Sgt Peters (Service no. 421000) arrived to replace Henry Smith on strength. Richard George Peters was born on 26 May 1923 in the country New South Wales town of Uralla. He signed up for service in the RAAF on 6 December 1941, having previously been employed as a clerk, and was posted to 2 ITS Lindfield. He completed his elementary flying training in Australia at 8 EFTS Narrandera where he flew solo after about 12 hours,[53] rather than the usual ten. In September 1942, Peters left for Canada to complete his SFTS at Aylmer where he flew Harvards and Yales, but apparently got so sick of writing Harvard in his logbook over and over so after a few pages he abbreviated it to 'HVD'. He arrived in the UK in March 1943. Though his last flight in a Harvard had been in February, upon arrival in the UK he spent two more weeks on Tiger Moths to get him (and all others—it was policy by this time) up to standard again before advancing to the Miles Master II, the step prior to Spitfires. He was on Masters until September, and went solo in a Spitfire, an old Mk I, on 15 September 1943, at 61 OTU. The OTU had a range of Spitfires by that time as his Flying Log Book indicates he flew Marks I, II and V while there. Peters' training continued to May 1944 and included a few hours in Hurricane IVs, though it is unclear why, as the type was well on its way out by then. The Hurricane training did include rocket projectile firing, so perhaps it was a build up to Typhoons. At the end of May 1944 he was at 83 GSU and had his first experience with a Spitfire IX.[54] 453 Squadron was his first front-line posting.[55]

Poor weather prevented a high sortie rate on 13 June, but four aircraft took off for Redhill to be exchanged for newer aircraft. Unfortunately, Doug Saunders, in serial number MH-487[56] crashed en-route and died. The squadron diary records an 'afternoon' sortie, but twelve Spitfires took off at 2130 led by Pat McDade in 'S' and patrolled seaward of Omaha Beach but the Luftwaffe did not appear. Some flak was encountered on the Cherbourg Peninsula and all planes returned safely at 2330.

On 14 June, two patrols were flown, both uneventful. F/Sgt Mervyn John Watson (Service no. 420610) arrived to replace Doug Saunders. Watson was born on 15 August 1923 in Murwillumbah and had trained as a plumber and tinsmith. When he signed up on 8 November 1941, he had

Merv Watson in Normandy. (AWM UK1524)

completed a number of the prescribed courses set for those in the RAAF Reserve. He was posted to 8 EFTS Narrandera in April 1942 and in March 1943 sailed for the UK where he completed his fighter training. Like Dick Peters, 453 Squadron was his first front-line posting.[57] He came from 83 GSU, again showing that the talks held by Don Smith on 26 May about filling 'gaps' in the squadron with Australians had been fruitful.

Funeral arrangements for Doug Saunders were made the next day by Don Smith, and eleven aircraft and crew spent the night in France once again. The morning sortie took off at 1040 and patrolled the beaches before returning to Ford and refuelling at 1240. In the afternoon, four pairs of Spitfires took off and patrolled areas along the south coast of the UK near The Needles and Portland, overlapping times so as to give continuous coverage. The pilots and planes were generating plenty of flying hours but still there was no action. The final sortie of the day was flown by eleven Spitfires from Ford, over the beaches and to an improvised airstrip, the Refuelling and Rearming Strip (R+RS) at Bazenville[58] and lasted from 2040 to 2235, again without encountering the enemy. This time, in addition to uncomfortable slit trenches and unappealing rations, they were bombed but suffered no casualties. Norm Baker recorded: 'Night hectic. Slept in ditch. Huns bombed strip. Flak terrific'.[59] Froggy Lyall also recorded his thoughts on the matter: 'landed on strip near Bayeux. Spent hectic night sleeping in ditch'.[60] Their thoughts and assessments were certainly consistent—almost word for word. Jack Olver recorded his thoughts too: 'Dusty as hell. Air raids all night'.[61]

On 16 June, after a sortie from 1230 to 1340, the pilots returned to Ford and were glad to have a bath and comfortable bed, something the infantry and many other ground troops in Normandy would not have for many weeks, at the very least. As proof of their stay in France many brought back souvenirs. Froggy Lyall recorded that he 'watched a good tank battle. Survived the dust of the airfield'.[62] That dust would be a feature of the difficulty encountered by the ground crew maintaining 2TAF aircraft in Normandy. The surfacing of the various ALGs with either the square mesh track or the bitumenised hessian did not prevent the dust being an issue, and three airfields had water piped to them to help settle the dust. However, it was found that spraying oil on the ground was a better solution. Bitumenised hessian was the best of the surfacing materials for reducing dust but there was not enough of it available.[63]

The second sortie of the day was from Ford and uneventful but the last patrol of the day finally had the type of engagement the pilots had been waiting for. Twelve Spitfires took off at 2005 and at 2045 the enemy was engaged when 12 Me-109s were sighted. The unit diary states that the Me109s were below them, about six miles southeast of Caen, but the pilots' reports all state that the location was four miles east of Caen, and that all aircraft were at the same height. The action is best described by the pilots themselves.

From the Personal Combat Report signed by David Murray in 'J' who claimed one Me-109 damaged:

During the combat I fired at 2 E/A. I observed no results from the first attack. The second E/A was doing a long slow climbing turn. I then observed two strikes on port wing tip. The enemy aircraft then rolled to the left three times and lost speed. I was forced to break away as another E/A was attacking me from behind. I did not see anymore of the E/A I attacked.[64]

From the Personal Combat Report signed by Vern Lancaster in 'H', Clarence Rice in 'G', Mick West in 'E' and Don Smith in '?', in which they claimed one Me-109 shared destroyed:

> F/Lt Lancaster states: I saw an ME109 turning in front of me with its under surfaces exposed. I closed rapidly firing from approx 200 yds until I had to break away to avoid collision. I observed strikes on the engine and under the fuselage. The e/a rolled on its back and fell away steeply towards the ground from about 2000'
>
> W/O Rice states: I watched F/Lt Lancaster's attack and breakaway and then attacked and followed the e/a down to 1000' firing at the same time.
>
> F/O West states: I watched this engagement and saw the e/a diving steeply down, angle 70°–80° with no attempt being made to control it. I watched it until it was below'—still falling—then I was forced to pull out. I consider it absolutely inevitable that the e/a diving at that angle below 500' must have hit the ground.
>
> S/Ldr Smith states: Immediately after the engagement here described I saw two e/a burning on the ground in the area where the engagement took place. Only 453 Sqn was concerned in this fight. Only two e/a are claimed destroyed.[65]

From the Personal Combat Report signed by Pat McDade in 'S' who claimed one Me-109 damaged:

> When the enemy formation climbed towards cloud I had my section to top of cloud layer and waited for them to appear. 2 enemy aircraft came up almost under my section, one immediately went back into cloud. I then noticed the other enemy aircraft to climb by turning away from him. When he

was about 1000 feet above cloud I turned quickly and attacked. I fired a short burst from 500 yards range and saw strikes on the cockpit and engine.[66]

From the Personal Combat Report signed by Ken Lawrence in 'F' and Clarence Seeney in 'B' in which they claimed one Me-109 shared destroyed:

> F/O Lawrence states: Following the initial attack of our A/C, I came out of the cloud base and found 1 M.E.109 slightly beneath me. I throttled back and skidded to one side and attacked the ME from astern from 200 yards range. I observed strikes on the fuselage. This e/a rolled on its back and went down in a steep dive towards the ground.
>
> W/O Seeney states: I was following F/O Lawrence in his attack and observed strikes from his fire. When F/O Lawrence broke off his attack I followed the e/a down firing all the way from 300 yards range. The engine of the e/a stopped and glycol streamed out of it (1000'). Finally the e/a crashed into the ground.[67]

From the Personal Combat Report signed by Don Smith in '?' and Jack Steward in 'N' in which Don Smith claimed one Me-109 damaged:

> S/Ldr D.H. Smith (Aus) states: I attacked an M.E. 109 which was climbing towards cloud base. I was using a Gyro sight and fired just as the E/A entered cloud. I kept on firing aiming at his line of flight and almost immediately the E/A re-appeared below cloud. The E/A was losing speed and trying unsuccessfully to regain cloud cover. It then stalled and fell steeply away out of control. I was then compelled to turn violently by the E/A behind me and I lost sight of the one I attacked when it was still falling vertically at 2,000 feet.
>
> W/O Steward states: I saw S/L Smith attack a M.E. 109 and observed it fall away out of control. I fired a short burst at it from long range but did not see effects. I was forced to turn away before the E/A hit the ground but I last saw it still falling vertically away below 1,500 feet.[68]

The pilots returned satisfied and relieved. They had finally encountered the enemy (in significant numbers) and survived the engagement, returning victorious to Ford, with two Me-109s claimed destroyed and three claimed damaged. Don Smith remarked at the debrief:

> That was a good show chaps, I knew you buggers could look after yourselves. I climbed up on top and looked over the side, who was that clown turning left and suddenly turned right?[69]

Ford was one of many busy airfields in the south and southeast of England during the first weeks of the landings. To Fred Cowpe, the 'Tower Controller was outstanding', he would have sections of four aircraft stacked up at intervals of 500 ft and as soon as one section had landed, that section would be directed off runway and they would make a ninety degree turn to taxi to dispersal and everyone would then step down 500 ft and the next lot would come in. If someone messed up, they'd be sent to the back of the queue, and with little fuel left no pilot wanted to have that done to them—things were tight enough. To make things a little easier, the planes had their navigation lights on, but the worry of a Luftwaffe intruder, like the ones who would stalk bombers back from their night time raids, was always present.[70]

Doug Saunders' funeral was held on 16 June and was attended by Allan Dowding to represent the squadron. He was buried at Brookwood Military Cemetery in Surrey.[71]

Once again, the variable Normandy weather closed in on 17 June and the Noball sortie launched at 2115 was aborted due to 10/10th cloud cover over the target. Landing with bombs was dangerous, so the squadron had to find a clear piece of Channel to drop their bombs in, which was now a bit easier ten days after the landing.[72]

On 18 June it was announced that the scheduled departure for France was the following day, so final packing and preparations took place (but the move was later postponed). While the ground staff were on the now-it's-on/now-it-isn't rollercoaster, the pilots flew three sorties. Jack Olver in 'X' and Herb Watts in 'J' took off at 1800 for a sortie over the Channel. An ASR launch operating in the Channel had sighted an apparently pilotless aircraft flying out to sea from land which was seen to fall into the sea and then explode.[73] No doubt it was one of the first V-1s launched at England. Nothing was found and the pilots returned at 1850.

While Olver and Watts were up searching the Channel, twelve Spitfires took off at 1820 for an escort to Bostons and Mitchells on Ramrod 1017. They joined Spitfires of 132 and 602 Squadrons to provide strong cover for the bombers. The bombing took place in the Foret de Bourse[74] near Falaise, but was not observed by the squadron as it was through cloud. The sortie was uneventful and all returned at 2010. The final sortie was flown at 2100 and led by Don Smith in '?'. The sortie was a shipping and low level patrol, taking the squadron over the battlefield in the area of Caen and Tilly (probably Tilly-sur-Seulles between Bayeux and Caen, and not Tilly-la-Campagne which is south of Caen). Flak was encountered south of Caen, near Saint Vaast la Hougue at the far western end of the landing area past Utah Beach and Grainville southwest of Caen. Artillery was observed firing to the southeast from north of Tilly during one of the many battles for the village. Joshua Scott in 'R' and Froggy Lyall in 'V' returned at 2140 and 2150 respectively though the rest of the squadron remained on patrol, finally returning at 2310. There was no Luftwaffe to be seen.

The first sortie on 19 June was Froggy Lyall in 'Y' and Jack Steward in 'J', taking off at 0635 for an escort of Wellingtons on an ASR in the Channel[75] which was entirely uneventful and saw them returning at 0855. At 1535 eleven Spitfires took off to escort Mitchells, which was, again, entirely uneventful. Most returned at 1655, though two returned earlier, including Allan Harris in 'Z', recording that his plane was: 'Very shaky and useless.'[76] Fred Cowpe wrote the whole sortie off as a 'cock up. Climbed through 18,000' of cloud'. He credited himself with an hour's worth of cloud flying in his logbook.[77]

On the morning of 20 June, the squadron put up twelve aircraft at 0800 and they flew a coastal patrol across the beaches, returning unchallenged at 1020 except for some flak. Another similar patrol was flown in the early evening. That night, the CO took the Adjutant and Mick West to visit the OCs of RAF Stations at Tangmere and Marston, where they spent time with G/Cpt 'Sailor' Malan, W/Cdr Charles, W/Cdr Walker and W/Cdr Checketts (RNZAF Ace Johnny Checketts). During this time, Keith Daff in 'C' and Herb Watts in 'L' were put on shipping cover patrol from 2100 to 2225, but it was uneventful and no enemy aircraft were seen. The V-1's, known as 'Divers' by the pilots, were starting to make a regular appearance and the pilots of the Wing were looking forward to the chance of shooting one down,[78] but it wasn't to be. Others were tasked with that, including some of the secret jet boys flying Gloster Meteors.

Only one operational sortie took place on 21 June, this being an escort to Halifax bombers, with 132 and 602 Squadrons also participating.[79] Take-off was at 1910 with Pat McDade in 'S' and Vern Lancaster in 'H' commanding the formation of twelve Spitfires. This was Ramrod 1030 and the target for the Halifax was a Noball target in the Neufchatel-en-Bray area, about 25 miles northeast of Rouen. The coastline was crossed at Le Treport on the inward leg and Dieppe on the outward leg,[80] since going over the same place twice on a sortie only gave the flak gunners a better chance of shooting someone down the second time round. Bombing appeared to be good and a fire was noted. There was much flak, and everyone was back by 2045. During the sortie, the squadron bounced some bogies (unidentified aircraft, which then became bandits when identified as hostile) but they turned out to be Thunderbolts, and they weren't engaged.[81] The Americans would not be so careful later on when the roles were reversed. The great storm which damaged the Mulberry harbours took place on 19-21 June,[82] but the fact that this did not affect the volume of flying undertaken illustrates the constant effort made by Allied pilots to support the landings, despite the poor and habitually variable Normandy weather.

Patrols continued on 22 June, but there was no update on the scheduled move. The first sortie for the day was launched at 0920 with eleven aircraft for a patrol over the western beaches (Utah and Omaha) and was noted as 'entirely uneventful' in the squadron diary.[83] The afternoon sortie was the same, but only ten aircraft took part, the flight lasting from 1618 to 1825. There was an early scramble of four aircraft at 0850 on the following day, but nothing eventuated and they returned at 0920. Meanwhile the 'A' Echelon of ground crew arrived in France and were promptly sent to the wrong airfield, ending up at B.9 instead of B.11.[84] The second sortie took off at 1620 and did a low cover/shipping patrol with the most interesting thing happening being the sighting of a barrage balloon seen drifting north of Le Havre. The diary also recorded that:

> F/S Boulton's doubts/hesitancy were resolved and he took his courage and everything else in both hands and offered himself lock stock and barrel to L.A.C.W. Palmer who is in the Signal Section at Station Ford.[85]

The first sortie of 24 June was led by Don Smith in '?' and they took off at 0620 with all twelve aircraft landing at ALG B.9 Lantheuil/Creully[86] at 0810, just after 602 Squadron, so as to maximise their time in the operational area. Just ten minutes after they arrived, the airfield was attacked by nine Me-109s and 453 was lucky to escape with no casualties, though the airfield's AA defences shot down one Me-109 and local defence Spitfires got two more.[87] 453 Squadron refuelled and carried out an armed recce in the area of Caen, with a quick turnaround enabling them to be airborne at 0940. This ALG had only been open for a few days and already the dust was a problem.[88] The squadron claimed one truck destroyed, four damaged and an armoured car damaged. Some rolling stock was also worked over by the guns of 453, and all aircraft returned safely to B.9 at 1100. There they refuelled and returned to Ford in the evening.

On 25 June, the squadron finally received orders to move as a whole unit to France. Ten Dakotas arrived to transport men and their belongings to ALG B.11 at Longues-sur-Mer. The Spitfire pilots took their small bags with them, while the remainder were transported in the Dakotas. These took off from Ford at 1500 and arrived at Longues-sur-Mer at 1620, escorted by

Spitfires, though not of their own squadrons. Upon landing, the planes were met by ambulances, ready to load wounded for flights back to hospitals in the UK.[89] Construction was still taking place at B.11.[90] The ALG at Longues-sur-Mer was constructed with a base of square mesh track, to a length of 3,600 ft, sections of which can be found today in the fences of residents of the towns near where the various ALG were located. Pierced steel plank was very heavy and thus could not be shipped as easily as square mesh track, so was used mainly for hard-standings for stationary aircraft,[91] but it too can be found today in the fences of many French farms in Normandy.

While the remainder of the squadron moved, the Spitfires continued to operate from B.9 though four[92] aircraft came to grief. Clarence Seeney hit a soft patch of ground on landing and his aircraft (ML 134)[93] flipped onto its back, but he escaped with minor injuries. The dust swirled up by the aircraft also obscured the vision of other pilots, and this resulted in David Murray's Spitfire tipping over onto its nose after landing, though these two aircraft were being brought over from England and were not involved in the numerous sorties of the day. The first operational sortie was at 1015 with twelve bombed-up Spitfires led by Don Smith in '?' to some woods south of Caen where they dive-bombed a target. While the bombs were seen to explode in the woods, nothing else—such as a fire or secondary explosion—provided evidence of any particular success. This was a very short sortie and all aircraft landed at 1055. The second and third sorties of the day were flown over the eastern end of the landing beaches and shipping.

Construction of the gun battery had started in September 1943 and four 152 mm German naval guns were installed in the casemates. Each gun weighed approximately 20 tons and could fire six shells per minute, each of these weighing 45kg, with a range of 20 kilometres and a firing arc of 120 degrees.[94] This allowed the guns to cover the area from Omaha to Gold beaches. Each position was 15 metres long, ten metres wide and six metres high and mounted on a stable platform so that the position would not lean or collapse if one side was severely damaged or undermined by enemy fire.⁹⁵ The plateau where the battery (and later the airfield) was located is 65 metres above sea level. Fortunately for the Allies, the battery was manned by poor quality troops who had little gunnery training.⁹⁶ As part of his tour of the Atlantic Wall Field Marshal Erwin Rommel visited the battery on 9 May 1944. He favoured a forward defence and believed that the Allies would have to be defeated on the beaches. They could not be allowed to get a foothold from which to develop their return to Western Europe. Field Marshal Gerd von Rundstedt, on the other hand, favoured holding certain panzer units back from the front so that an armoured counterattack could be made at the landing area, wherever that may be.⁹⁷

In the two weeks before the landings, the battery was bombed twice with a total of approximately 1,500 tons of bombs dropped. While the guns were not put out of action, much of the communications had been cut and, as they were buried beneath the ground, were hard to repair. Communications with the observation bunker at the clifftop were cut. On the night before the landings, a bombing raid targeting the battery missed and most of the 600 tons dropped hit the village behind. At 0537 on 6 June, the battery was

One of the four gun emplacements at Longues-sur-Mer. (Author)

An aerial view towards the east along the coast, from a point just west of the gun battery at Longues-sur-Mer. The four gun casemates can be seen at the bottom of the photo and directly east (above) are the fields where B.11 was established. The indentation in the top third of the photo is Arromanches and remnants of the mulberry harbour can be seen off the coast to the north (left). (Author)

targeted by the French cruiser *Georges Leygues* and then the battleship USS *Arkansas*. At 0605 another French cruiser, the *Montcalm* engaged the battery. Return fire from the battery was not effective, but some rounds targeting HMS *Bulolo* were accurate enough to force the ship to weigh anchor and move location. HMS *Ajax* responded with a 20-minute barrage from 11 km range and, at 0620, the battery ceased firing. As the landings commenced, the battery resumed fire which was returned by HMS *Ajax* and *Argonaught*, and this barrage is credited with putting three of the four guns out of action. The battery ceased fire again at 0845. In the afternoon, firing from the battery resumed. HMS *Ajax* signalled to the French cruisers to ignore the battery and that they would be responsible for putting it out of action. However the cruiser *George Leygues* fired on the battery and all firing stopped at 1900. The battery fired 170 rounds on 6 June and the remaining garrison and guns were taken by infantry assault by 2nd Battalion, the Devonshire Regiment, of the 50th (Tyne and Tees) Division on 7 June.[98]

A view from the approximate middle of the B.11 airfield back towards the gun battery 2015. Like all the airstrips, it has been returned to farmland. The gun battery is near the trees at the centre of the horizon. (Author)

Square mesh track, most likely from B.11, used to reinforce a front garden fence of a house in Longues-sur-Mer. (Author)

At the time of the landings, a young farmer, Louis Heroult, lived just a few hundred metres south of the gun battery on the family farm. He was eighteen and was not allowed within the battery position, for fear that he would report on it to the Allies. The bombing and shelling on the night 5–6 June and the following morning clearly indicated to him that something big was going on, and he and his family left the farm and went south to the countryside near Lingèvres, where they thought it would be safer. After about a week, and with great difficulty crossing the front lines—risking being fired upon by both sides, they returned to the farm and were greeted with destruction and dead animals. There was a lot of work to be done: dead animals to bury, live ones to milk, and a lot of cleaning up to do. Over the following weeks and months, Louis had some interactions with Allied troops who would trade (presumably food and fuel) for farm goods. Seventy years later, he still lived within walking distance of the battery.[99]

In the north-east of Normandy, Eliane LeBoucher was a young girl living with her family on their farm near the village of Duclair, at a bend in the Seine. For them there was little activity when the Allies landed, they'd had enough over the years of occupation, including a visit from the Gestapo when her father had been accused of keeping a shotgun on the farm, something that was forbidden. German soldiers lived on the farm, in the best rooms, and neither played with the children nor spoke French to the family. The family constantly feared that anything they said to the Germans might be misunderstood or misinterpreted and result in punishment of some sort. This part of France would not be liberated for a number of weeks but, unlike those in the immediate coastal area, the family did not move from the farm. When the Canadians eventually passed through, the soldiers gave one of the girls a bar of soap. The girls had anticipated receiving food so started to eat it and had to be quickly corrected on the proper use of soap![100]

In Bayeux, a much smaller town then than it is now, Jean Bansard was an 11 year-old boy living with his brothers, sisters and parents. His father fixed sewing machines and his mother sold wool. Travel was strictly regulated in the coastal areas and a pass was required for anyone within 10 kilometres of the coastline. Obviously such things as damaging signs erected by the Germans was prohibited (many things could be categorised as sabotage), but it was also forbidden to be seen to be acting defiantly—such as carrying the French flag when walking down the street. Punishments varied, but the most severe was deportation (to a camp) or firing squad. There were many shortages; shoes that had worn soles were reinforced by pieces of wood, and bicycle tyres were especially difficult to replace. Sometimes pieces of car tyre would be bound to the bicycle rims by wire—a very uncomfortable way to travel. Curfew was from 10.00pm to 6.00am and the Germans carried out patrols to ensure compliance. Farmers ate better than those who lived in the towns or cities, so the youngest children were usually sent to collect what they could from friendly farmers—the youngest children were less likely to be searched by the Germans. Without refrigeration it was difficult to store food for long periods of time—ice boxes were easily spotted, so food was sometimes concealed in sandstone jars and preserved with salt. On 6 June, with the bombardments all along the coastline and from the air, many members of the Bansard family hid in the cellar, but Jean and his father stayed upstairs and in bed, not wanting to be buried in the cellar if the house was damaged. The first troops to arrive did not stay but moved quickly through to secure the area. The trucks and tanks that followed the infantry let the people know they were secure and had been liberated.

In addition to sweets for children, many soldiers gave out cigarettes, and soon children were asking for cigarettes 'pour papa'. Within a short time, Jean was a regular smoker. While relations were certainly very warm between the liberators and the civilians, Jean soon found discarded condoms in the laneways and his future wife (herself just a young girl at the time) reported an attempt by American troops to exchange oranges for the services of a family's maid. Another occurrence within the first few days of liberation was the purge of collaborators, with people accused of assisting the Germans being paraded through the streets. One such man was walked down the main street with a funeral wreath around his neck. In later years, participating at memorial ceremonies for the anniversary of the landings was mandatory for school children, but Jean now prefers the more personal experiences of memorialisation rather than grand ceremonies with bands and heads of state.[101]

The arrival of the Australians was reported in *The Argus* of Melbourne on 29 June: 'A week ago the site of this airfield was still a prosperous farm ... the farmer and his labourers continue to gather the crops in patches of the farm that this airfield has left him'. The farmer reportedly also sold his cider to the troops at the airfield for five francs per water bottle. The article downplayed claims by other correspondents of female French snipers, and focused on the positives, such as the French appreciation of the presence of Australians. It also pointed out that, while the British were in quite a good mood due to finally being able to return to Europe to kick the Germans out of France, a little more appreciation and understanding of the French

June 1944: Flying Control at work on an RAF airstrip established shortly after the initial landings in Normandy. This scene would have been typical for the ALGs.
(AWM SUK12444)

position should be shown, with one British soldier quoted as complaining that the Normandy locals: 'don't speak our lingo, you know'.[102]

While the pilots and Spitfires of 453 Squadron had been operating over, and sometimes from, Normandy since the landings, the ground crew had spent many hours keeping the aircraft ready for action, all the while standing by for the order to move to their port of embarkation and the short trip across the Channel. The SCUs would, generally, not be used at the airstrips constructed in the rear areas (a relative term), so 453 Squadron, alongside 132 and 602 (and many other squadrons besides) would need their own ground crew. Many were flown over by Dakota to an established airstrip and then moved in convoy to their new location. No doubt some of their relatives had been in France during the First World War, and now the Australians had returned—pilots and ground crew alike, to play their part in the liberation of France.

Leading Aircraftman (LAC) Lawrence Dominic Murphy (Service no. 26181) was born on 2 February 1922 and was a workshop attendant awaiting a motor mechanics apprenticeship when he enlisted on 1 April 1940. When he learned that no apprenticeship would be offered with the firm he was working for, he joined the RAAF. After trade training, he embarked for the UK in July 1940, arriving in September and served with RAAF EATS squadrons—456 and 460—before arriving to service the Spitfires of 453 in May 1944.

Corporal Frederick George Russell Webb (Service no. 11080) was born on 25 April 1917 and was working as a gas labourer when he enlisted in June 1940. To ensure that he was of good character, inquiries were made with the state (Victorian) Police, as was done for all applicants at the time. The Victorian Police replied that he was not on their files and his fingerprints had not been recorded. They also confirmed that he was not a 'member of, or connected with the Communistic Organisation'. After trade training in Australia, Webb was classed as a Fitter IIE and posted to the UK, arriving

Australian ground crew attached to 453 Squadron, June 1944, Normandy. Back row: E. Spicer, F Rowe, L Murphy, F Keelty, D Hood, S Parker. Sitting: B. Hill, F. Webb. (AWM UK1520)

there in September 1941. He had previously served with 453 Squadron for eight months, and had also served with 455 and 460 Squadrons. His time with 455 Squadron also saw him spend a short time in Russia while the squadron was deployed there in the Allied attempt to protect the supply convoys bound for Murmansk.[103] He'd been posted back to 453 in preparation for the return to Europe.[104]

Sergeant Seth Cyril Parker (Service no. 8230)was born on 11 August 1912 and had been a plumber for 10 years when he enlisted on 23 January 1940. After training he was classified as a Fitter IIE and, at his request, was posted overseas, arriving in the UK in August 1941 and serving with a number of UK and RAAF squadrons before arriving at Ford to join 453 in June 1944. He had previously served with them alongside Fred Webb from February to October 1943. His wife caused a bit of a stir in September 1943 when she wrote a letter of complaint to the RAAF, stating that:

> On leaving Australia he was demoted to LAC (and) shortly after arriving in England was promoted again to Corporal.

That was over two years ago. Can you please enlighten me as to why he is still a corporal?

His demotion was presumably not disciplinary, but on posting, his temporary rank of Corporal would have been reallocated to another member of ground crew who would remain behind—the rank belonged to the position, not the person. The letter from Parker's wife went on to complain that other men he had served with and who had 'never got any farther than Melbourne and Sydney have been promoted again and again ... I can see that, to get any consideration, fighting men must not leave Australia'. The RAAF replied that Mrs Parker's concerns would be forwarded to the RAF, who were responsible for such things. They in turn replied that Parker was currently listed sixteenth on the roster, and that he had not been recommended for promotion on the last two occasions assessments had been carried out.[105] With the thousands of ground crew in the UK and, considering that they were less likely than aircrew to become a casualty—and therefore less likely to have someone above them wounded or killed to create a vacancy—promotions were not nearly as common as in some other areas of service.

Two members of the Royal Engineers (responsible for constructing the airstrip at B.11 Longues-sur-Mer,), From left to right: Sergeant E. Davey and Lieutenant H. Truscott with Mick West and Joe Boulton. (AWM UK 1521)

These ground crew were essential for keeping the squadrons operational and in the air. They would not have all the so-called luxuries of being based in the UK, it was just a matter of working on the aircraft and sleeping in tents. Communication between pilots and ground crew was essential—was a brake grabbing on landings? That might cause the plane to veer or swerve to one side. Was the landing gear taking too long to come up? That would mean the hydraulics would have to be looked at—and for that to happen the whole plane would have to be raised off the ground on jacks.[106]

26 June saw the squadron ground crew getting the area finalised for operations while the pilots continued to fly operations. Wing Headquarters set themselves up in a nearby farm and it was so dusty that many people were wearing goggles.[107] Artillery could be heard in the distance, but no fire was directed at Longues-sur-Mer or the airstrip located just northeast of the village. Herb Watts came down with the chicken pox and was taken off operations. As he was expected to be gone for more than seven days, he required a replacement, and one was requested from 83 GSU.

After the slower tempo of the previous week, operations stepped up again as the squadron was so close to the front line. The first sortie of the day was by eleven Spitfires led by Don Smith in '?'. They were up at 0540 patrolling the landing area from end to end but nothing was encountered. There was some flak but no damage was sustained. Ten aircraft returned at 0715, with Hector Aldred in 'D' returning early at 0600. The second sortie was up at 1505, rain having delayed operations, but at least temporarily settled the dust,[108] and consisted of twelve Spitfires led by Pat McDade in his regular 'S' carrying out the same patrol and covering the same area as the first and returning at 1640, with no enemy aircraft encountered. After a quick refuelling, the third sortie of eleven Spitfires took off at 1720, though Fred Cowpe is noted to have left early at 1705 in 'T' accompanied by Jack Olver in '?' and Ralph Dutneall in 'K'. Patrols were made across the entire landing area, and no enemy aircraft were seen or encountered. Again, there was some flak, but no aircraft were damaged. The last sortie of the day, of eleven Spitfires, took off at 2205 to cover the landing area, and all returned safely at 2230, with the exception of Allan Harris in 'Z' who landed early at 2215 with his R/T unserviceable.[109]

Australian Spitfires in Normandy. (Courtesy of the Olver family)

Operations continued the following day and the morning sortie of eleven Spitfires took off at 0600 on a patrol. Keith Daff flying 'O' was hit in the radiator by flak east of Caen and had to land at B.10 located at Plumetot. During the patrol, an estimated 150 Sherman tanks were seen facing east in the vicinity of Fontenay. A German battery was noted at 'Vense' (perhaps Vendes) and fires were seen in a wood at 'Aranville' (perhaps Granville-sur-Odon). The return of aircraft was staggered, the last in at 0735. Eight aircraft took off for the second sortie of the day at 1015 and one section led by Pat McDade in 'S' located an appealing target of German transport, but the dust from the airstrips had fouled the cannon and machine guns (a problem not unique to 453 Squadron by any means)[110] so they could not exploit the opportunity and they returned with other dust-related troubles at 1045.

When west of Martinville, the four remaining Spitfires led by Vern Lancaster in 'H' bounced a formation of eight FW-190s. The FW-190 was vastly superior to the Me-109 by this stage of the war, and the Spitfire Mk IX had been developed specifically to counter it. At 1050 the Spitfires were at 10,000 ft and the FW-190s were sighted below at 8,000 ft.

From the signed Personal Combat Report submitted by Jack Olver who flew 'R' on that sortie in which he claimed one FW-190 damaged:

> Yellow Section 4 A/C chased and bounced 8 F.W.190's. I was flying Y.4. The 190's were flying line abreast. I chose the extreme port F.W.190 and opened fire at 200 yds. Starboard cannon and MG's only fired and then after a few rounds that cannon stopped. I saw strikes on FW's port wing. In the ensuing dog fight I fired at several other 190's with MG's but claim nothing.[111]

By this stage of the war virtually all combat aircraft had armour plating, especially around the cockpit so the value of machine guns was much less than it had been during the early years of the war.[112] Firing with only one cannon would also have thrown Olver's aim off, the uneven recoil interfering with the smooth control of the aircraft.

From the signed Personal Combat Report submitted by Dick Peters who flew 'K' as Yellow 2 on that sortie, in which he claimed one FW-190 damaged:

> Yellow section four aircraft, I was flying Yellow 2. Kenway reported 2 bogies flying West and were sighted by Yellow 3. We dived down sun and overtook the aircraft which turned out to be 8 FW 190's. The 190's broke as we opened fire and a general dog fight developed after breaking hard starboard to avoid a 190 I fired at one aircraft from fairly long range. I saw no hits. Then I dived on a 190 from about 1,000 ft. above and saw strikes on starboard wing. I saw Yellow 1 fire at a 190 and as the 190 dived away I saw it trailing smoke.[113]

From the signed Personal Combat Report submitted by Dick Peters and Vern Lancaster, in which Vern claimed one FW-190 probably destroyed and one FW-190 damaged:

> Yellow section with self as No. 1, were informed of two bogies to the west so we went to investigate. The aircraft were seen by Yellow 3 and turned out to be 8 FW 190's. We attacked from astern and up sun. I fired from about 300 yards just as the e/a broke. I observed strikes on the port wing which were seen by yellow 2. I then broke and a general dog fight developed. I fired at another 190 from about 250 yards and observed strikes. I then had to break, but yellow 2 saw it go down with smoke pouring from it. In view of yellow 2's evidence I claim 1 probably destroyed and 1 damaged.
>
> F/Sgt Peters states: I saw my No.1. F/Lt. Lancaster fire a burst at a FW 190. After we broke off I saw the e/a. go into a dive, seemingly out of control, with black smoke pouring from it. In my opinion this e/a. would probably have been destroyed.[114]

From the signed Personal Combat Report submitted by Clarence Rice who flew 'G' on that sortie, in which he claimed one FW-190 damaged:

> I was flying Yellow 3 and sighted the bogies as reported by 'Kenway' some distance away. We caught up and attacked them out of sun. I opened at 250 yards closing to 150 yards (one cannon only firing) and saw strikes on enemy aircraft. In the dogfight that followed I attacked another at an extreme deflection shot but saw no strikes[115]

All aircraft returned safely to Longues at 1115, and had it not been for the dust fouling their armament, the encounter may have gone even further in the favour of 453 Squadron, as pilots without effective armament aren't going to be as aggressive, nor successful. The squadron diary specifically notes 'Engagement broken off owing to failure of cannon.'[116] While Spitfires had to make do with their standard air filter system (which worked well), Typhoons had a filter fitted to the air intake under the propeller, which had hinged doors fitted to the later versions so they would flex open if there was a backfire, this didn't help the machine guns and cannon, however.[117]

The evening patrols took off at 2030 with a total of nine Spitfires. Six formed one section to patrol south of Bayeux, and the other three patrolled west of Caen. The first six had an uneventful patrol while the three remaining

Joshua Scott having a shave in Normandy. The facilities were less than what they were used to in England, but still far superior to that of the PBI (Poor Bloody Infantry).
(AWM UK1519)

aircraft were reduced to two when one returned with engine trouble. This section of two aircraft encountered heavy flak southwest of Caen. Vern Lancaster in 'H' and Ralph Dutneall in 'Z' were attacked by six FW-190s, who snuck up from 9,500 ft while the two Spitfires were at 10,000 ft. The engagement took place at 2100, 15 miles west of Caen, in the vicinity of Lingèvres, where the squadron would later be based.

From the signed Personal Combat Report submitted by Vern Lancaster in which he claimed one FW-190 destroyed:

> Yellow Section patrolling line West of Caen. Yellow 2 and self as Yellow 1. Were patrolling and about to turn East from

western end of patrol, when we were bounced from below and out of cloud by approx: six FW 190's. I just saw them in time and warned my number two to break, but was hit myself in the Perspex by a canon shell from a 190 it exploded in the cockpit and dazed me. I kept on turning however, and after a couple of turns a FW 190 came in front of me and did a complete slow roll. I chased it and attacked from 20° to line astern, closing from 300 to 200 yds firing all the time. I observed strikes all over the aircraft, and then a flash under the cockpit followed by a streak of flame. The aircraft carried on its vertical dive in flames straight through cloud I then had to return home as I had been hit, and did not know how badly. Cine Camera was U/S through failure of ground crew to remove camera patch. I claim one F.W. 190 destroyed.[118]

The perspex of Lancaster's hood was wrecked and he received minor wounds from shrapnel and perspex but he fought back and the remaining FW-190s retreated. The Australians returned to B.11. Two FW-190s destroyed in a day, not bad at all.

Five Spitfires took off at 0640 for an early bombing sortie on 28 June to support the Canadian attack at Authie, four miles northwest of Caen. The signal for the bombing to commence was red smoke, but the Canadians failed to place the smoke as planned and the sortie was aborted, the planes returning at 0720. The pilots were rested until 2135, at which time ten took off on an armed recce. The aircraft patrolled the Domfront-Argentan-Mezidon area to the south of Caen, each Spitfire carrying a 500 lb bomb. All were dropped on targets but results were poor, the closest anyone got was 50 yards,[119] and strafing gave much better results. Targets were found north and west of Flers, which is located about 30 miles south-southwest of Caen. The squadron claimed four trucks and a motorcycle as destroyed with five trucks and one tank damaged. They also strafed a barn which exploded, leading the pilots to believe that it was a fuel dump. Don Smith in '?' was shaken up when flak exploded underneath one wing and there was intense heavy flak encountered near Villers-Bocage which was still in the hands of the Germans, but all planes

Spitfires in Normandy: It is likely that these belong to 453 Squadron. A figure very closely resembling the 'Gremlin' on FU-? can be seen on the furthest Spitfire above the port cannon. (AWM O45229)

returned to Longues at 2235. During the day, three pilots returned to Ford Airfield in England in an Avro Anson to pick up three new Spitfires.

Three armed recce sorties were flown on 29 June, one each in the morning, afternoon and evening. The first took off at 1045, nine Spitfires again headed for the area around Flers where three trucks were claimed damaged by strafing. Some flak was encountered near St Louvre and the weather got worse as the day progressed, with heavy rain encountered in some areas. All planes returned at 1200. The second armed recce sortie took off at 1525, though two planes returned almost immediately. The remaining ten Spitfires went looking for trouble, patrolling the Thury-Harcourt, Flers, Argentan and Mezidon area, and found some trucks on the road. Seven parked trucks were claimed destroyed near Conde and two others (one destroyed, one damaged) on other roads in the circuit flown. Heavy flak was encountered near Aunay, just a few miles south of Villers-Bocage. One plane returned at 1600 with the remainder landing at 1640.

F/Sgt Lynch (Service no. 423776) arrived in the afternoon from 83GSU to replace Herb Watts, who was still out with chicken pox. James Holburn Lynch was born on 25 May 1917 and was a station hand in the town of Orange in country New South Wales when he signed up for the RAAF in July 1942. By December he was at 5 EFTS Narromine and in March 1943 he was on a ship to Canada where he continued his training. In December 1943, Lynch was on the high seas again and went to the UK to complete his training. 453 was his first posting to an operational squadron.[120]

The airfield was subjected to a thunderstorm in the evening, which tested the waterproofing of tents to the limit. Many staff needed little encouragement to dig additional drainage trenches for their accommodation. The evening sortie also encountered this bad weather on its armed recce from 2100 to 2210 during which one more truck was claimed destroyed and another damaged. Trucks were seen moving northeast out of Villers-Bocage and heavy flak was again encountered in the area, but all aircraft returned safely.

On the last day of June, the squadron launched four sorties. The first was a section of four aircraft led by Norm Baker in 'H' on a morning patrol from 0915 to 1010, which was uneventful. The second was of nine Spitfires for a general patrol over the front line from 1135 to 1245. Some FW190s were sighted over the Falaise area, but they were not engaged. The third sortie took off at 1425, with twelve Spitfires led by Don Smith in '?' patrolling a circuit of Conde, Falaise and Thury-Harcourt. Two trucks were claimed destroyed and another two were claimed as damaged, but the squadron was subjected to much flak, especially west of Thury.

Dick Peters in 'J' was flying as No.2 to Don Smith. He went down for his attack on the convoy which included some flak trucks and, just at the bottom of his strafing run, he was hit from behind by flak, which made a loud noise and blew out the perspex in his hood, giving him a serious head injury, though he didn't remember it hurting. At the bottom of his run he'd been at about 100 ft and the next thing he knew he was at 5,000 ft. Despite his serious injury and being only new to operations, he kept his cool and returned to B.11, escorted by Fred Cowpe in 'T', who talked him through the trip. Peters passed out twice on the way back,[121] but he eventually made a safe landing. The airfield had been warned that a wounded pilot was coming in and, as the ground crew rushed out to his plane, they found him unconscious in the seat, still strapped in, having just managed to switch the engine off. He was evacuated to 52 MFH and was highly regarded for the way in which he dealt with the situation. Peters was recommended for a medal by Don Smith, but it was declined, though the incident was mentioned in his later award of a DFC for his cumulative effort on operations.[122] It is interesting to note that instructions issued in August 1944 stated that, for even a Mention in Dispatches (a written form of recognition, but not a medal): 'Units are requested in the submission of Mentions in Dispatches to submit recommendations on the assumption that one in 175 persons will be eligible.'[123] Not showing quite the same level of respect for his efforts, the other pilots said that the Germans would be 'having themselves on if they thought they could harm [Peters] by hitting him in the head.'[124] Dick Peters later recorded a very short entry in this logbook regarding that last flight. 'Hit by Flak, Wounded. Shot up trucks.' He was out of action and wouldn't sit in a Spitfire for more than two months. Though he was declined a medal for bringing his plane back in (relatively) good order despite such a severe wound, an endorsement in his logbook was authorised, but no other entry was ever made.[125] Vern Lancaster also made a trip to the hospital with an eye irritation which turned out to be perspex splinters from his earlier engagement, and he was quickly dealt with by the medical staff there.

The final sortie of the day saw twelve Spitfires taking off at 2035 on an armed recce in the area Caen-Vire-Domfront. Four more motorised enemy transport (MET) were claimed as damaged and it was observed that Villers-Bocage was now a pile of rubble after an attack by 200 heavy bombers earlier in the evening. The weather was worsening and all planes returned at 2130.

So ended June 1944 for 453 Squadron and the others of 2TAF. During the month, 453 Squadron had dropped forty 500 lb bombs, and had flown 687 sorties since 6 June (compared to 656 for 602 Squadron and 682 for 132 Squadron).[126] The Allies had returned to France, met by bottles of calvados, boxes of camembert and a German military not willing to give up without a fight, though the Luftwaffe was often conspicuous by its absence. Luftflotte 3, responsible for France, lost 362 aircraft in Normandy during the first week of the landings. In the second week, they lost another 232. Reinforcements could not plug the gaps even though 200 fighters had been transferred to the Normandy front by 7 June, and another 100 more by 10 June. In addition, 45 torpedo bombers were sent to the south of France (from where they could attack across the Cherbourg peninsula), and 90 bombers were sent to Belgium.[127] By 30 June, the Allies had flown approximately 130,000 sorties in support of Operation Overlord. To defend Normandy, the Germans had managed just 13,829 in return.[128] A saying steeped with black humour had circulated among German troops, along the lines of: 'If the plane is silver it's American, if it's camouflaged it's British, and if it's not there at all, it's the Luftwaffe.' The German army could be forgiven for feeling that they'd been let down, but the fight was not over yet.

Notes

1. Temora Interview–Sir Brian Inglis.
2. Temora Interview–Sir Brian Inglis.
3. Personal File–Inglis
4. Temora Interview–Sir Brian Inglis.
5. ORB–125 Wing Summary June 1944
6. ORB–132 Sqn ORB Events June 1944.
7. ORB–132 Sqn ORB Events June 1944
8. J.M. Stagg, *Forecast for Overlord*, Ian Allan, Shepperton, 1971.
9. Stagg, *Forecast for Overlord*, p. 18.
10. Stagg, *Forecast for Overlord*, p. 91.
11. Stagg, *Forecast for Overlord*, pp. 102–103.
12. Stagg, *Forecast for Overlord*, pp. 114–115, 118.
13. ORB–602 Sqn and ORB 132 Sqn
14. ORB–125 Wing
15. ORB–125 Wing
16. ORB–132 Sqn and ORB–125 Wing
17. ORB–453 Sqn
18. Temora Interview–Sir Brian Inglis.
19. Logbook–Lyall
20. Hastings, *Overlord: D-Day and The Battle for Normandy*, p.74.
21. Herington, *Air Power Over Europe 1944–1945*, p. 130.
22. Barrett Tillman, *Brassey's D-Day Encyclopaedia*, Potomac Books, Washington, 2004, pp. 52, 93.

23 ORB–453 Sqn
24 Cowpe, F, 'Anti-Climax–I Think Not', in *Spitfire News: Journal of the Spitfire Association*, No. 58, March 1993
25 Fred Cowpe, 'Anti-Climax–I Think Not', in *Spitfire News: Journal of the Spitfire Association*, No. 58, March 1993
26 ORB–453 Sqn
27 AWFA: Russell Leith
28 Herington, *Air Power Over Europe 1944–1945*, p. 124.
29 Herington, *Air Power Over Europe 1944–1945*, pp. 14, 123–125.
30 Cowpe, F, 'Anti-Climax–I Think Not', in *Spitfire News: Journal of the Spitfire Association*, No. 58, March 1993
31 Uncredited: *Batterie de Crisbecq Marine-Kusten Batterie 'Marcouf'*, Editions Aubert'Graphic (undated), p. 14.
32 *Batterie de Crisbecq Marine-Kusten Batterie 'Marcouf'*, pp. 4–8.
33 *Batterie de Crisbecq Marine-Kusten Batterie 'Marcouf'*, pp. 14–16.
34 *Batterie de Crisbecq Marine-Kusten Batterie 'Marcouf'*, pp. 19, 22.
35 Jacobs, *Airfields of the D-Day Invasion Air Force*, p. 18.
36 ORB–453 Sqn
37 Logbook–Olver
38 Logbook–Harris.
39 Hastings, *Overlord: D-Day and The Battle for Normandy*, p. 121.
40 Logbook–Lyall
41 Interview with Pierre Verbeke 10 September 2015
42 ORB–453 Sqn
43 NLA: Trove–'Spitfire Pilots Eager' *Sydney Morning Herald* 9 June 1944.
44 ORB–453 Sqn
45 ORB–453 Sqn
46 132 ORB Events June 1944 and Herington, *Air Power Over Europe 1944–1945*, p. 138.
47 441 ORB Summary
48 Logbook–Harris and Logbook–Cowpe
49 NLA: Trove–'Australians Refuel in Normandy' *Sydney Morning Herald* 13 June 1944.
50 Personal File–Smith
51 Personal File–Smith
52 ORB–125 Wing
53 Logbook–Peters

54 Logbook–Peters
55 Personal File –Peters and Logbook–Peters
56 Spitfire Aircraft Production http://www.airhistory.org.uk/spitfire/
57 Personal File–Watson
58 Logbook–Baker, Logbook–Olver and Shores and Thomas, *2nd Tactical Air Force: Volume 1 Spartan to Normandy June 1943 to June 1944*, p. 144.
59 Logbook–Baker.
60 Logbook–Lyall.
61 Logbook–Olver
62 Logbook–Lyall.
63 Uncredited: *The Administrative History of The Operations of 21 Army Group on the Continent of Europe 6 June 1944–8 May 1945*, Germany, 1945, p. 13, 42.
64 NAA: 11335 Z1
65 NAA: 11335 Z1
66 NAA: 11335 Z1
67 NAA: 11335 Z1
68 NAA: 11335 Z1
69 Cowpe–*Sequel to D Day* p.1.
70 Cowpe–*Sequel to D Day* p.1.
71 CWGC website
72 ORB–125 Wing
73 ORB–453 Sqn
74 ORB–132 Sqn
75 Logbook–Lyall.
76 Logbook–Harris.
77 Logbook–Cowpe
78 ORB–125 Wing
79 ORB–132 Sqn and ORB–602 Sqn.
80 ORB–132 Sqn
81 Logbook–Lyall.
82 Hastings, *Overlord: D-Day and The Battle for Normandy*, p. 138.
83 ORB–453 Sqn
84 ORB–125 Wing
85 ORB–453 Sqn
86 Robinard, et al, *50 aerodromes pour une victorie Juin-Septembre 1944*, pp. 300–301, Logbook–Baker says Creully.

87   Logbook–Baker.
88   ORB–602 Sqn
89   ORB–132 Sqn
90   ORB–125 Wing
91   Shores and Thomas, *2nd Tactical Air Force: Volume 1 Spartan to Normandy June 1943 to June 1944*, pp. 141–142, 144.
92   ORB–453 Sqn says two, Logbook–Harris says four.
93   Personal File–Seeney
94   Stephane Reigner, *The German Battery at Longues-sur-Mer*, (transl. John Lee) Editions Memorial, Caen, 2002, pp. 10–12.
95   Reigner, *The German Battery at Longues-sur-Mer*, pp. 10–12.
96   Reigner, *The German Battery at Longues-sur-Mer*, pp. 15, 22–24.
97   Reigner, *The German Battery at Longues-sur-Mer*, pp. 7, 25.
98   Reigner, *The German Battery at Longues-sur-Mer*, pp. 26–29.
99   Interview with Louis Heroult, translated by Frederique Verbeke 10 Sept 2015.
100 Interview with Eliane LeBoucher by Frederique Verbeke with questions by Author, 2015.
101 Interview with Jean Bansard by Frederique Verbeke with questions by Author, 2015
102 NLA: Trove–'RAAF Planes at New Base in Normandy' *The Argus* 29 June 1944.
103 Personal File –Webb and AWM https://www.awm.gov.au/unit/U59440/
104 Personal File–Webb
105 Personal File–Parker
106 AWFA: Harry Mason
107 ORB–125 Wing
108 ORB–132 Sqn
109 Logbook–Harris.
110 ORB–125 Wing
111 NAA: 11335 Z1
112 Price, *Osprey Aircraft of the Aces: Volume 5, Late Mark Spitfire Aces 1942–45*, p. 72.
113 NAA: A11335, Z1
114 NAA: A11335, Z1
115 NAA: A11335, Z1
116 ORB–453 Sqn
117 Shores and Thomas, *2nd Tactical Air Force: Volume 1 Spartan to Normandy June 1943 to June 1944*, p. 176 and Shores, Christopher and Thomas, Chris, *2nd Tactical Air Force: Volume 4 Squadrons, Camouflage and Markings, Weapons and tactics 1943–1945*, Midland Publishing, Surrey, 2008, p. 602.

118 NAA: A11335 Z1
119 Logbook–Baker.
120 Personal File–Lynch
121 Cowpe–Sequel to D Day p. 2.
122 Personal File–Cowpe
123 NAA: A11335 168/P1
124 Temora Interview–Dick Peters.
125 Logbook–Peters
126 ORB–125 Wing
127 Herington, *Air Power Over Europe 1944–1945*, p. 136.
128 Murray, *Luftwaffe: Strategy for Defeat 1933–45*, pp. 375–376, 378.

July 1944

Although the weather on 1 July worsened as the day progressed, two patrols were flown over the front lines but the Luftwaffe was not to be seen. There was a six-plane scramble at 1600 towards Caen where two FW-190s were seen, and Allan Harris in 'Z' took a shot at one but didn't allow enough deflection and they got away.[1] One truck was shot up on the way back and the planes returned at 1710, though one did not last the sortie and had to return early at 1620.

Poor weather continued on the following day. The first sortie saw twelve Spitfires up at 1350 to bomb Mezidon. The pilots dove from 9,000-4,000 ft travelling east to west, and all bombs landed in the target area, although it had already been given a good going-over before 453 arrived. A number of vehicular tracks were broken up (anything to slow down the Germans or hinder their mobility was useful) and some vehicles were claimed destroyed. There was some heavy calibre flak, but it was sporadic and ineffective. All planes returned by 1435. The next sortie was up at 1640 with six aircraft led by Don Smith in 'U'. A front line patrol was conducted and it was noticed that there were lots of individual vehicles travelling in the Thury-Harcourt area, no doubt trying to avoid presenting a worthy target by bunching together. A large tank was seen, and although it appeared to be a Tiger, it was not attacked. Some flak emplacements were spotted and noted for future reference, and all planes returned safely by 1805, with only one having to return early this time.

F/O Rusty Leith returned to the squadron in the afternoon to take the place of Dick Peters. He had previously served with 453 from June 1942 to December 1943 so was known to many of the old hands. He had been posted from 57 OTU to 83 GSU on 13 June, so had missed out on D-Day, and was eagerly awaiting a return to the squadron.[2] He was allocated a tent with Vern Lancaster and Mick West, which covered a small dugout to protect them from shrapnel—both Allied and German.[3] The first thing he did after arriving was take a ride on a horse the Germans had left behind and which had been bought off the French by a squadron doctor.[4] The squadron doctor drove over to 52 MFH to visit Herb Watts and Dick Peters, and reported that both were doing well.

The next sortie took off at 1735 for a frontline patrol, five Spitfires making a circuit from Caen to Falaise then Conde and back to Caen again. One truck was damaged by strafing, but otherwise the trip was uneventful. This was the first sortie flown by Jim Lynch, and he recorded in his logbook: 'Ran into heavy flak over Caen on first ops trip. Frightened hell out of me.'[5] The last sortie took off at 2040, six Spitfires being led by Pat McDade in 'U'. It was another front line patrol but they encountered five FW-190s near Argentan. At 2100 the Spitfires were at 6,000 ft when they sighted the FW-190s, who were at the same height, but the Germans went into a dive down to the deck in an effort to get away. The Spitfires gave chase and got within firing range near Chartres, after about 100km.

From the Personal Combat Report signed by Pat McDade 'U', Jack Olver 'W' and Allan Dowding 'R' in which they each claimed one third FW-190 destroyed:

> F/Lt McDade states: Five Enemy A/C dived away South of our six A/C gave chase at high speed at deck level. Closed

to 600 yds but could get no closer fired a burst and observed one strike on port wing root. Green Sect (F/O Olver and F/S Dowding) who were slightly closer also fired and destroyed the enemy.

F/O Olver states: Fired several bursts at 800 yds, observed some strikes port wing, eventually FW 190 commenced to smoke and crashed into a field burned fiercely.

F/Sgt Dowding states: Flying Green 2. Fired at same time as Green 1 (F/O Olver) observed strikes on E/A then saw it crash in field burning.[6]

From the Personal Combat Report signed by Jack Olver and George Roberts in which they each claimed one half FW-190 destroyed:

F/O Olver states: Flying Green 1. After first FW 190 had crashed the other four E/A turned back towards our three A/C. I climbed to 1000 ft and observed 1 FW 190 below and behind me and another 200 yds behind. I began hard starboard taking a short burst 30° head on at 190 (no claim) after 360° turn I was 150 yds behind the lower FW 190 which was firing at Green 2 (F/S Dowding) and at 30° to E/A. With 1 1/4 rings deflection fired 1 sec burst observed strikes all over cockpit and wing roots. After another 1 sec burst at 100 yds astern E/A burned, rolled on to back and crashed into the woods west of Chartres.

F/Sgt Roberts states: Two E/A turned towards me and I broke starboard firing at full deflection about 150 yds. Later fired again observing strikes on cockpit. F/O Olver set it on fire and it crashed.[7]

3 July saw continued poor weather and the pilots engaged in what is boldly described in the squadron diary as 'discussing matrimonial problems and endeavoured to find a common plan for the proper instruction and control of modern wives!'[8] Perhaps emboldened by this conversation, the pilots flew an evening front-line sortie. Eleven took off at 2155 led by Don Smith in 'W' and they encountered some serious flak near La Foret de Cinglais near Bretteville-sur-Laize. They spotted numerous trucks and other enemy vehicles, including some in the vicinity of Villers-Bocage, but

none were engaged. All planes returned safely at 2255 though, once again, some returned early. With the frequency of sorties, dust and sub-standard facilities compared to those back in England, the ability of the ground crews to keep aircraft serviceability up to the usual standards was hampered but they worked hard to keep as many flying as possible.

In the first week of July, Rusty Leith wrote home to his family:

> I had quite a nice trip around the district the other day and one evening went on the scrounge for eggs etc. with some success. My French is improving too. I find that I can understand the French more easily than I can speak to them. The food we get is really quite good even though it is all out of tins. However, we are able to get a little fresh stuff such as milk, rhubarb, onions and greens from the locals. I suppose really we can consider ourselves lucky that we haven't got the eternal bully beef although stew runs it a good second. Bread is very scarce and beer hasn't been seen as yet but I believe we will be getting both soon. Although there are quite a lot of new faces in the squadron there were many that I knew.[9]

Strafing on 4 July achieved more success and Don Smith flew back to England for a press conference. One of the articles which resulted was 'Spitfire Still World's Best says Australian' in the *Army News*, which quoted Don Smith stating how the Spitfire remained superior to the German fighters, and that the Germans were hard to come by in the air.[10] Another quoted him saying that the Luftwaffe 'haven't carried out a single patrol. We wish they would.'[11]

The first sortie was twelve Spitfires on an armed recce, taking off at a relatively early 0725, though it was already in full daylight in the European summer. They flew a circuit from Caen to Thury-Harcourt, then Falaise, Mezidon and back to Caen. Some flak was encountered at Thury-Harcourt and the pilots observed Allied artillery firing on Carpiquet airport where three hangars on the eastern side of the airfield were burning. The Canadians were having a rough time of it trying to take the airfield from the SS. At 2025 the day's final patrol took off: twelve Spitfires on an armed recce led by Vern Lancaster in 'K' and Pat McDade in 'S', on a circuit Beny to Vire then Flers, Domfront and Thury-Harcourt. Very few German vehicles were seen, but anything out and about was pounced on, resulting in claims of two destroyed and one damaged. Accurate flak was encountered at Thury-Harcourt and Villers-Bocage but everyone returned safely, the last arriving at 2140.

The Germans struck very early in the morning of 5 July, machine-gunning and bombing the airstrip but they only sent a single aircraft and there were no casualties and no damage to stores or aircraft.[12] The first sortie took off at 0540, much earlier than in recent days for an armed recce on a circuit from Caen to Domfront then Alençon, back to Domfront and Falaise. They saw very few vehicles on the roads, and the heavy cloud cover down to 2,000 ft hampered the ability of pilots to pick out targets at long range. They spotted two ambulances and, while the pilots may have questioned the authenticity of the red crosses on German vehicles, they didn't attack, and returned to Longues at 0700. The squadron noted that, while the Germans' ability to ditch their vehicles and run was improving, they wondered how much time the enemy was losing by having convoys broken up. No doubt the Germans had to wait for them to be reassembled before their journeys could be resumed.[13] Every delay that 2TAF could force on the Germans would help the Allied progress.

At 1220, twelve Spitfires took off for another armed recce on a circuit from Falaise to Flers then Vire, Beny and Villers-Bocage. One truck was damaged by strafing and a staff car was destroyed, but little else was seen apart from a concentration of German vehicles southeast of Argentan which was not attacked. Five of the twelve aircraft had to land at other strips because they were short on fuel, but all returned the same day. The Medical Officer visited 52 MFH again and reported that Dick Peters had been evacuated to England.

The day's last sortie took off at 1840 for another armed recce, twelve Spitfires led by Pat McDade in 'S' flying on a circuit Thury-Harcourt to Conde then Flers, Vire, Beny then Villers-Bocage. Four enemy vehicles were claimed as destroyed and one claimed as damaged. There was a lot of flak about, especially around Falaise but everyone returned safely at 1950. It wasn't entirely safe for the Normandy locals though, as Baker recorded: 'Wong hit a cow—the cad. (Got in his line of fire).'[14] 'Wong' was the nickname of David Murray, who was, perhaps, not the best shot in the squadron.

On 6 July, two armed recces were carried out. The first returned with no claims, but the evening sortie was better. The circuit flown this time was from Caen to Argentan, then Sees, Alençon, Mortagne-au-Perche, Bernay and Lisieux. A number of claims were made by the pilots during the sortie, including three vehicles destroyed—one of which was identified as a petrol bowser. One truck was claimed damaged, as was a staff car and two other vehicles at another location. Most of the flak encountered was near Argentan and Falaise, and it was the flak which claimed a victim.

Norman Baker in 'F' (MK260) dove down from 4,000 ft to just 15 ft[15] to attack a truck and waited until the last possible moment to let rip with his cannon and machine guns. It was good shooting alright and, as he passed over the exploding truck, he felt and heard the Spitfire being hit by AA fire which he at first thought was debris from the exploding truck. He managed to climb out of immediate danger up to 4,000 ft again but, with black smoke pouring out of the engine,[16] his gauges indicated that he wasn't going to make it all the way home.[17] He decided he was going to make a wheels-up landing, which reduced the chance of the aircraft tipping over (often caused by the radiator fairings acting as big scoops)[18] and would wreck the aircraft sufficiently that the Germans would not end up with a Spitfire of their own. Trailing black smoke behind him and with oil in his windscreen[19], Baker skimmed the roofs of some farms, just missed the top of an apple orchard and then down he went into a field, skidding through the earth and wrecking the plane as he went. Unlike some, he hadn't locked open the hood, and it came away easily enough. He unstrapped his harness and unplugged his helmet from the R/T and oxygen, and was out and away from the plane—he wasn't going to wait for an explosion.[20] His No. 2, Jim Lynch in 'O', saw him get out of the plane well enough and indicate that he was safe. Jim roared low over the field, waggled his wings and left, there was nothing more to do. Lynch described Baker's landing as a 'perfect forced landing', he then 'Came home on my own flat out'.[21]

In the evening W/Cdr Lapsley notified Don Smith that Sir Charles Portal (Chief of Air Staff) and Sir Archibald Sinclair (Secretary of State for Air)[22] would pay them a visit the next day. The diary records that 'A very good tidying up was immediately commenced'.[23] The Allies had now been in Normandy for a month. HQ AEAF ordered that the black and white stripes above the wings be removed,[24] something that would have serious consequences for 453 Squadron.

Behind German lines, near Mont de Cerisy, a local resident, Marcel Hellouin, ran to the crash site and saw Baker return to the plane to set off the charge to destroy the IFF (Identification Friend or Foe), the radio system used to differentiate friendly from enemy aircraft to the plotters in the control rooms whose job it was to manage the war in the air. He called out to Baker, who ran over to him as a truck full of Germans climbed the hill. With an Australian unable to speak much French, and a Frenchman unable to speak much English, they communicated with gestures and, after sprinting to temporary safety, Baker was left with a plain coat while Marcel went for advice. In the distance, the Germans fired randomly into the fields and called for the pilot to surrender. Back in the village, the Germans arrived and questioned the locals, including Marcel. Despite the Germans' bluffs and allegations of claiming to know who had hidden the pilot, no one admitted anything, and they left a short while afterwards, leaving a solitary guard with the wrecked Spitfire. Baker moved from his concealed position into a field and found a herd of cows. Being used to farm animals, he herded them before him and found a piece of high ground where he could observe anyone approaching, and still retain the cover of the animals.[25]

After assessing the situation, Baker continued moving, crossing fields and a railway line and avoiding some Germans in a Volkswagen. He eventually saw a Frenchman in the road and, as the two walked towards each other, he decided to be bold and tried his limited French. He said he was the pilot who had crashed and the Frenchman smiled knowingly—the Australian accent can be hard to conceal. He took Baker to a thicket near a woodworking factory and said: 'Je suis Russe'. Thinking the man had introduced himself, he replied, 'I am Baker, from Melbourne'. The 'Frenchman' corrected the misunderstanding, telling Baker that he was a Russian, from Leningrad, which lightened the mood a little. Baker was eventually escorted to the house of Arthur Lebailly, and after gaining access through a window to conceal him from as many villagers and refugees as possible, he was, for the moment, safe. After a meal Baker was given Arthur's bed and soon fell asleep in the company of Russian and German deserters.[26] Stress can do that to you.[27]

The next morning, Baker and Arthur cycled to Athis where Arthur gave Fred Brisset, the next person in the escape chain, a rundown of the situation. As the network of those willing and able to assist pilots had been disrupted by the fighting, Baker was sent to Ste Honorine-la-Guillame, where he could be hidden at Fred's parents' house. There he stayed for two weeks, his accent and very limited French covered by a story, for anyone who didn't need to know the truth, that he was a refugee from Conde who was so badly shellshocked that he was rendered deaf and dumb. In this way, Baker could go outside and help with work in and around the house, rather than have to hide for his entire time behind German lines. 14 July—Bastille Day—was also Fred's mother's birthday. After playing 'Mademoiselle from Armentieres' on the violin, Fred's father nearly got them all into trouble by playing the Marseillaise on his horn. Alcohol can do that to you.[28]

Baker was moved on 20 July after reports of a Gestapo search party reached his protectors. He was taken to the village of Berjou, where he was looked after by two school teachers, the Ricordeau family. This was much safer, as staying in a building near a German rest camp was much more preferable than being hunted by the Gestapo. He slept in a bedroom next to that of a German Colonel and played the role of the shellshocked labourer well, defeating all attempts made by the German soldiers to talk to him. Boldly playing his role to the utmost, and, with the organising skills of Miseur Bourg, assistant to the Ricordeaus, Baker even had his hair cut by an SS soldier who used to be a barber, and who claimed to have cut the hair of Field Marshal Rommel.

On 3 August it was decided to try and get Baker and two others—an RAF Sergeant and a Colonel of the Free French Forces—across to the Allied lines. Despite assistance from Rene Lechevallier and a Mademoiselle France, they were unable to make it through the lines after a number of attempts, and returned to Berjou. The town had by now been evacuated, however, so the group moved on to Bas-Hamel. Baker was put up in the chateau and kept in a room where he stayed most of the time, reading and listening to music—but only in the presence of people who could actually 'hear' so as not to give the game away. One day a German soldier came to complain about the music, the General wanted it turned down. However, occasionally Baker forgot that he was a supposed to be a deaf mute and, when a German asked him for a dish to wash himself (using sign language—perhaps the German remembered Baker was a deaf mute), Baker went inside the house and asked Madame Ricordeau: 'Le Boche, une assiette pour laver?' She replied, 'Monsieur! Monsieur! Votre accent! Vous parlez Francais comme une vache Espagnol!' (You speak French like a Spanish cow).[29] Being a deaf mute, shellshocked or, in the language of the day, 'an idiot', was a common tactic successfully employed by a number of airmen in avoiding Germans, including some Australians, two of whom were

P/O Martin of 609 Squadron, and P/O Jubb of 76 Squadron when they found themselves in similar trouble.[30]

Not long after this incident it nearly all fell apart for Baker. The supposedly deaf and dumb farmhand heard a knock on the door of his room and then said, 'Entrez'. Having spent so long hiding in plain sight, sometimes it was just too hard to keep up the charade. Unfortunately, it was a German who wanted to speak with one of the schoolteachers. Baker took the German for a walk, hoping that they'd find who he was looking for, because he certainly didn't know. At the bottom of a staircase they met Annie, the youngest of the family's children. As Annie was only five years old, Baker didn't know what would happen next: the whole act could fall apart instantly depending on the little girl's reaction. Trying French, Baker asked where the lady was and the girl (thankfully) led the German away. Baker would really have to be on his guard: one more slip like that and he and the whole family—children included—could end up against a wall.

Staying in a village with a German headquarters unit wasn't going to improve his chances of escape so, after a few aborted attempts, Baker was given over to two students of Caen University and it was up to them to get him back to Allied lines. They tried for La Bertiniere, where he had spent his first two weeks in hiding but found his potential hiding place in ruins. They'd actually been lucky to make it that far after a run-in with German military police but, in the darkness, his papers passed scrutiny and they moved on. With about thirty other refugees they spent the night in a barn, well aware that the front lines were not far away. The next morning, 17 August, the Germans arrived and prepared defensive positions in and around the town, kicking the civilians out. That night they sheltered in a wood overlooking the village—the same wood occupied by a German mortar unit who attracted Allied artillery fire—and Baker later admitted that it was a 'warm night'.

In the morning, one of the civilians brought some milk back from the village (farming habits die hard), and said there were British troops in a nearby field. Baker set off at a run, through the fields and hedges, arriving to see British infantry and armour. He approached them without being shot by sentries and told them his story. In typical British fashion, he was offered a cup of tea. He was free. He was passed up through brigade headquarters then to the HQ of the 11th Armoured Division and then to Bayeux. He managed to stop by 453 Squadron before being returned to England. From then on, he was known as 'Baker the Escaper'. His gratitude to the French people who risked their lives for him would last the rest of his life, and he would champion their bravery in speeches and letters—from local speaking engagements all the way to Paul Keating, the Prime Minister of Australia at the 50th Anniversary of the D-Day Landings. To Baker, it was not an invasion—you don't invade a friendly country—it was the start of the liberation of Western Europe from the Nazis.[31] In a visit to France and his saviours many years later, Baker was presented with the airspeed indicator and turn and bank indicator from his wrecked Spitfire. They're proudly on display with his family in Australia, a memory of the war but also, and perhaps more importantly, of charity and survival.

Successful negotiations with 83 Group HQ on 7 July enabled Herb Watts, recently returned from hospital, to remain at the squadron following the loss of Baker. The morning consisted of more polishing and tidying in preparation for the VIP visit. After making their contribution, the pilots continued flying duties, with twelve Spitfires taking off on an armed recce at 1110, led by Pat McDade in 'S' and Vern Lancaster in 'H'. Four MET were claimed damaged and one staff car claimed as destroyed. One of the MET was a troop carrier and it was estimated that twelve German soldiers were killed in the strafing runs. Accurate and intense heavy calibre flak was encountered near Argentan, but all planes returned safely at 1220. Despite all the effort put in, when the VIPs arrived at 1300, Sir Charles Portal and

Sir Archibald Sinclair in a Dakota and AVM Broadhurst in his slightly eccentric Fieseler Storch[32] they only had time enough for a few words with the pilots at flying control, rendering great disappointment for the rest who had spent so much time tidying up the dispersal and accommodation areas. The artificial image of cleanliness and order would not be enjoyed by the VIPs after all.

The afternoon consisted of overlapping patrols of the beaches using flights of four Spitfires. Each patrol was to last one hour and ten minutes, and was to be overlapped by fifteen minutes, with the first taking off at 1340 and the last returning at 1840. The patrols were flown as high cover—perhaps a welcome break from low-level flying. Though a report was received of enemy aircraft over Longues, nothing was seen and the patrols were uneventful. While the pilots enjoyed more strafing success on the following day, the ground crew and airfield staff prepared to defend against a rumoured German counter-landing which was expected to occur from midget-submarines in the British bridgehead. The rumour had come from Wing Headquarters and led to many staff carrying rifles and adopting a warlike posture for the day, but nothing eventuated and life quickly returned to normal.[33]

For the pilots, 8 July was another early start, eleven Spitfires, led by Don Smith in '?', taking off at 0545 for another armed recce of the battlefield. A number of MET were encountered across the circuit flown, as were some tanks. One tank transporter (with tank) was claimed damaged as were four tanks and three MET. A lot of flak was encountered, especially around Thury-Harcourt. There were also two camouflaged vehicles spotted defended by intense light flak. It was thought that the vehicles might be decoys to try and bait 2TAF planes into attacking them, so the surrounding flak guns could shoot the dreaded 'Jabos' down. One flight returned at 0640 and the remainder landed at 0710. The second sortie of the day was another armed recce on a circuit from Caen to

Falaise, Agentan, L'Aigle (recorded as 'Lingle' in the squadron diary), Bernay, Lisieux and back to Caen. Intense light flak was encountered at Mery-Corbon on the return between Lisieux and Caen and the squadron claimed a number of MET damaged and destroyed, including a petrol lorry. The third and final sortie of the day was led by Don Smith in 'U', eight Spitfires taking off at 1330 for an armed recce on the circuit Caen to Beny then Vire, Flers, Thury-Harcourt and back to Caen. Two MET were claimed as destroyed, one of them being yet another valuable petrol lorry and four were claimed as damaged, including a staff car. Intense flak followed them throughout the mission but all returned safely.

W/Cdr Stewart was rested from the position of Wing Leader, 125 Wing and his replacement, S/Ldr Geoffrey Page, a RAF pilot from 132 Squadron, was well known to all the pilots of the Wing. He'd been attached to a University Air Squadron before the war and, after fighter training, had participated in covering the Dunkirk evacuation and then fought in the Battle of Britain flying Hurricanes. He was shot down while attacking a bomber formation and, in addition to being wounded, his plane burned. Like many pilots of the time, he was not wearing flying gloves and, as a result, he suffered severe burns. Admitted to hospital and nominated for specialist plastic surgery under the watchful genius of Archie McIndoe, he, along with many others such as Australian Richard Hillary (who also neglected to wear flying gloves on the day he'd been shot down and burned), returned to flying. He was also a founding member of the Guinea Pig Club, made up of other hospital patients who had been operated on with these very early experiments in plastic surgery. At the time he was appointed Wing Commander, he was 24 years old.[34] Keeping the position 'in house' was a welcome move.

That night a concert was held in the Airmen's Recreation Room, with the Wing band playing and Wing members contributing their talent to the evening's entertainment.[35]

9 July was a golden day for 453. The morning weather was poor but the armed recce at 1245 was more eventful than the squadron could have hoped for. Twelve Spitfires, led by Don Smith in 'U', were to fly a circuit from Trouville to Lisieux then Falaise, Bretteville and Cabourg. At 1330, while west of Lisieux, they sighted a large number of enemy aircraft above them. It was suspected that, because of the yellow spinners on some of the Me-109s, the formation may have been led by German Ace Matoni.[36] Don Smith calmly transmitted a message to the squadron: 'Dauphin aircraft, look up above you and you'll see something very interesting'.[37] He checked with Pat McDade to find out his situation, but his section was still down on the deck 'dealing with the traffic' so to speak. So, eight against fifty it was to be. The Germans were about a mile to starboard and descending through cloud, the Australians had to act fast to gain the initiative. 'Red and Blue Sections 90 degrees port and make it snappy'. The boss was taking charge and he had a plan. They executed the crossover turn and throttled back to 120 mph and selected fully fine pitch. 'Wait for the break to starboard'. The Germans had spotted them and 'were coming down like a great waterfall'. Smith spoke again: 'Dauphin Red and Blue, full throttle open right up and stand by—we are going to break starboard ... now! Up through them and fire your guns as you go'.[38]

Responding with aggression, and knowing that the Germans had a fear of head-on attacks, Don Smith led the two sections into a powered climb. With Merlin exhausts spewing the black smoke from engine boosts engaged, 453 climbed right into the attack and a large dogfight, described in the very understated style of the time as a 'really decent mixup' in the squadron diary, ensued.[39] The Germans were split in two by the arrowhead attack and both elements of the German formations began to pull up in response to the Australian charge. Don Smith continued with encouragement and orders in case anyone was baited out of the formation: 'Keep climbing, climb like bloody hell. They'll be back'. Height wasn't everything in aerial combat, but almost. The German formations had by now reached a point at which they could make a new attack but were now approaching each other head-on instead of engaging the Spitfires. 'Okay, get stuck into the bastards'.[40] The mass of aircraft engaged in a mess of a dogfight and it was beyond anyone to follow the entire action with any degree of comprehension. Chaos followed and each pilot concentrated on their own small part of it—though, of course, too much focus could also get you killed. It was a fine balance.

From the Personal Combat Report submitted and signed by Don Smith 'U' in which he claimed one Me-109 destroyed and one FW-190 damaged:

> I was leading 453 Squadron (R.A.A.F) on an Armed Recce when we sighted 40 + mixed e/a at 10,000 ft S.W. Lisieux. Our own height was 8,000. We climbed to engage and I attacked a bunch of six e/a coming in line astern I started firing at a range of 400 yds head on. I observed many cannon strikes on the engine of one. Black smoke poured from it and several large pieces fell off. The e/a fell vertically downwards in an uncontrolled dive through the cloud. On going below cloud I saw this and two other e/a in flames on the ground.
>
> Climbing up again I saw a F.W.190 on the tail of W/O Boulton (who was flying 'H') I opened fire at 150 yds and fired a two second burst. I saw strikes on the wing root and towards the end of the fuselage. As a result the e/a fell vertically away and disappeared under my nose. I was too busy to watch him further.[41]

From the Personal Combat Report submitted and signed by Ken Kinross who flew 'L' during the dogfight, in which he claimed one Me-109 damaged:

> I chased in among a gaggle of E/A and opened up on ME 109 at 600 yds giving him a 2 second burst. E/A started to weave. I closed in and fired two long bursts from 300 yds closing in to 100 yds. I observed strikes on the engine cowling and wing. E/A broke sharply downwards, My No.2 saw a piece about 1 foot square fly off from around engine and cockpit.[42]

From the Personal Combat Report submitted and signed by Jack Steward who flew 'W' on this occasion and claimed one FW-190 destroyed:

> I found two FW 190s cruising around below cloud about 3000'. I got onto the tail of one of them and opened fire at 300 yds with one long burst. I observed strikes on his cabin and an explosion. 2 small pieces fell off. As he rolled over I caught him with another burst and his wing came off. I took no further interest in him.[43]

From the Personal Combat Report submitted and signed by Joe Boulton in 'H', in which he claimed one FW-190 destroyed:

> I chased 190 to 4000 ft and opened fire at 800 yds. closing to 300 yds. in several short bursts from dead line astern. E/a started smoking at 1,200 ft. and dived steeply down. I followed him through cloud and saw him crash in an open field and burst into flames on the ground.[44]

From the Personal Combat Report submitted and signed by Don Smith and Keith Daff, who flew 'C', in which he claimed one Me-109 destroyed:

> I got on to the tail of a 109 and opened fire at a range of 600 yds angle off 30 degrees. I closed to 2-300 yds firing in short bursts I saw strikes all along the fuselage and on the tail plane and rudder large pieces of which flew off. The e/a fell steeply away with thick black smoke (not boost) streaming from it I then had to break sharply but on S/Ldr Smith's evidence I claim this e/a destroyed.
>
> S/Ldr Smith states: I saw the e/a which W/O Daff attacked crash into a house and burn furiously.[45]

From the Personal Combat Report submitted and signed by George Roberts who flew 'P', in which he claimed one FW-190 damaged:

> I saw a FW 190 break off and go into cloud. I went in behind him and opened fire at 500 yds. but could not close. I fired a 3 sec. Burst and saw strikes on rear end of fuselage. Immediately after he went into cloud and I lost him.[46]

From the Personal Combat Report submitted and signed by Allan Dowding who flew 'V' on that sortie, in which he claimed one Me-109 damaged:

> I saw two Me 109's a line abreast with a third 10 yds behind. The leading e/a fired at me but missed. I opened fire on

the rear e/a at 400 yds with a short burst. I saw numerous strikes on his nose and top of engine. Pieces flew off from the cockpit and the hood flew off. I then had to break but claim this e/a damaged.[47]

From the Personal Combat Report submitted and signed by Clarence Seeney who flew 'D' in which he claimed two FW-190 damaged:

> I broke on to the outside aircraft of a section coming down. I followed him down and opened up with M/G and Cannon at 300 yds range closing to 250 yds. I saw strikes on his tail plane.
>
> I then broke up and came onto the tail of another FW 190. I followed him down and opened fire with M/G at 250 yards closing to 200 yards. I followed him through cloud and when I came out of the cloud I fired again in short bursts closing to 50 yards. He flicked over onto his back at 1500 and went vertically down. I last saw him still falling vertically downwards at about 1000'. I could not wait to see him crash but have no doubt in my mind that he did so. I claim this e/a damaged subject to film assessment.[48]

As can be seen, the Australians made a large number of claims following the dogfight (four destroyed and six damaged for no loss) and the Germans left with their tails between their legs. Somewhat surprisingly for an attack by such a large number of aircraft, not one Spitfire returned with significant damage. Just to rub salt into the wounds, the squadron shot up some vehicles on the way home, claiming one MET destroyed and three damaged. The evening sorties were overlapping high patrols on the line from Cabourg to Port-en-Bessin. The squadron flew in flights of four with 15 minute overlaps, with the exception of the last, which put up two flights of four, and by 2230 all aircraft had returned, the evening patrol being entirely uneventful. The success of the day was reported in the *Sydney Morning Herald* on 11 July. In the article by H.I. Williams, Don Smith came in for high praise: '[he] broke up a great attacking wave of enemy fighters by climbing into them head-on, weaving and spraying with his guns and cannon as he went'. A number of pilots were quoted and a lot of the action was recounted in detail, including the German pilot who bailed out only to land on top of his own burning plane that had crashed below him. The pilots interviewed also gave accounts of their armed recce sorties, Don Smith was quoted as saying:

> It is quite common to see a German vehicle sneak in behind a farm cart piled with some family's belongings as soon as we come over. As soon as he thinks he is safe the driver speeds up and reaches another group of refugees, where he skulks again until we are gone.

The pilots also spoke about flak traps, where guns were set up camouflaged in fields waiting for planes to come down and attack dummy trucks.[49] A shortened version of the article appeared in the *Sunshine Advocate*, a Victorian paper which singled out local Jack Steward and praised him for shooting down a German plane.[50]

Success is not rewarded with rest, and operations continued the next day, and a full squadron armed recce was sent up in the early morning. Twelve aircraft took off at 0540 for a patrol of the line Evrecy to Conde then Vire, Aunay and Villers-Bocage. This was a very successful mission, and claims were made of six flamers, three smokers and one vehicle damaged, though these were spread out through the mission and not all in the one location. Lynch recorded the success in his logbook with the words: 'First real joy'.[51] When the last of the planes returned at 0655 the weather worsened, preventing flying for the remainder of the day. This pleased the ground crew as they could spend a good amount of time on the aircraft making sure that they were kept up to standard.

Welcome news was received of the capture of Caen. Three attempts had been made to capture Caen since D-Day: by direct assault on 7-8 June, via Villers-Bocage on 13 June and during Operation Epsom on 25 June.[52] Finally, it was in Allied hands, though at the cost of many civilian casualties. The debate over it being a realistic D-Day objective, and whether Montgomery actually intended to capture it on D-Day continues.

Poor weather continued the next morning, but allowed no rest for the pilots, the first sortie returning early due to poor weather. It cleared up in the afternoon and overlapping patrols were flown during which the squadron claimed one armoured fighting vehicle and one MET as smokers. The squadron followed the 4-4-8 pattern used on 9 July, the first patrol taking off at 1825 and the last returning at 2230. Enemy aircraft were reported south of Caen and the sighting was followed up but no aircraft were seen. A cinema show was held in the Airmen's Recreation Room, including a selection of combat footage and an Errol Flynn movie, *Northern Pursuit*.[53]

On 12 July, the Wing Commander Flying, W/Cdr Page, decided that the squadron should go out in pairs and use the cloud cover to surprise what they could on the roads.[54] Twelve aircraft took off at 1455 and MET were sought out. The plan produced some results, three MET in flames, three smoking and one damaged. On one of these armed recces Allan Harris in 'Z' successfully strafed a German staff car, and while some strafing claims across 2TAF may have been exaggerated, the blood on his windscreen was enough to convince anyone that he'd definitely got one.[55] Unfortunately Froggy Lyall in 'V' was shot down by flak east of Falaise and landed behind enemy lines.

Froggy had been flying as Blue 2 to George Roberts in a formation of three when, near the village of Trun, Roberts spotted white vapour pouring out of Froggy's port radiator. He reported this over the R/T and Froggy replied that his engine temperatures were very high and after he dropped his boost and revs the formation headed north, back towards Allied lines. After a minute of trying to gain some altitude to improve chances of gliding should things get worse, the situation deteriorated when Froggy reported an engine fire. Roberts told him he couldn't see a fire, but soon Froggy was losing height and after passing over another village made a successful belly landing in a field while his squadron mates circled above.[56] While no one had seen 'V' hit by flak, Froggy later reported that the formation had been flying at 4,000 ft and there was a loud thump underneath 'V' after which the engine began to overheat. Since there was no visible flak at the time, Froggy thought it might have been a lucky rifle shot and, while this is doubtful, the end result was still the same. After crash landing, he informed the others over the radio that he was ok. He was seen to get out safely and break all sprinting records as he headed for the nearby woods.[57] While the squadron recorded his record-breaking run, his mates wrote to his family to tell them of the incident and, perhaps a little unkindly, informed them that it was the first time Froggy had ever been seen to run.

With the advice from an intel officer ringing in his ears that said crossing a front line was a piece of cake, Froggy hid until it was dark, then set off with high hopes of returning to the squadron. After a few days' walking, he swam what he thought was the River Orne, hid in a ditch and put his clothes back on while a column of 40 tanks passed by. He stood up to cross the road as the column disappeared and, as he did so, was captured by SS infantry. He was transferred to a POW camp at Alençon and, from there, escaped on 4 August with an American Boston air gunner, Sgt Harold Potter.

Froggy Lyall in what appears to be FU-N, about to take off for the last patrol on D-Day. (AWM UK1430)

For a short time they were helped by a French family, and had the idea that they would have to go to Spain and return to England by that route but American troops liberated the town he was in and rescued them on 13 August. He returned to flying with 453 in September.[58]

Meanwhile, on 12 July, all other aircraft returned by 1620 and were directed up again at 1730, Don Smith in '?' leading twelve Spitfires from 453, with another twelve from 132 Squadron also participating[59] in an escort to Mitchells who were to bomb a target in the vicinity of Chartres. The formations met up over Port-en-Bessin and, though the bombers had some difficulty locating the target,[60] the escort went to plan. When the Spitfires had separated from their bombers and were on their way back to Longues, they encountered what was estimated to be more than 15 enemy aircraft near Lisieux, east of Caen. With little fuel to spare and despite the Germans having a 2,000 ft height advantage, the men of 453, accompanied by W/Cdr Page and 132 Squadron, engaged the Luftwaffe. The engagement took place at 1915.

From the Personal Combat Report submitted and signed by W/Cdr Page and Fred Cowpe in which they shared the claim of one Me-109 probably destroyed:

> W/Cdr Page states: I was leading 'Don' section of 453 Sqn returning from a bomber escort mission and flying at 12,000', 7 miles due East of Caen when I sighted two ME 109's diving from approx 15,000' on to two Spitfires of another squadron. (Sqn identity unknown) I climbed steeply and when at 14,000' the aircraft which I was about to attack broke hard to starboard and at a range of 200 yds I hit him with my second burst observing 4 cannon strikes around the starboard wing root and the cockpit. Immediately dense greyish-brown smoke poured from the a/c—a smoke definitely NOT caused by boost increase but probably by the ignition of glycol and oil. At the same time pieces fell off the a/c and the port wheel dropped down. The a/c then dived steeply at an angle of approx 80° and following his tail I gave another burst at about 7,000' and at the range of 150 yds, observing a further 3 cannon strikes on the

fuselage. The smoke coming from the a/c increased to such an extent that I found it difficult to see the aircraft. Its dive becoming less acute, I followed him down to between 4 and 5,000' firing both cannons and machine guns and continuing with the latter when my cannon ammunition was expended. I saw at least 12 to 18 .303 flashes on the fuselage. Lack of petrol made it necessary for me to break off the engagement.

W/O Cowpe states: Whilst flying 'Don' 3 behind W/Cdr Page ('Don' 1) I saw the ME 109 which he was attacking hit by his fire and saw greyish-brown smoke and flames coming from it and the port wheel of the a/c drop fully down. I opened fire on this ME 109 at 900 yds range at a height 4-5,000' but did not see any results. He turned to starboard and I was able to close in to approx 5-600 yds and gave two bursts at which the smoke which the a/c was emitting grew more intense though the smoke made it difficult to observe any strikes. The next burst I gave was at a closer range and I saw strikes on the starboard side of the cockpit and the starboard wheel fell slightly. At 3,000' the plane rolled over on its side and turning to the right began losing height still smoking and flaming. As my petrol gauge showed that I was very short of petrol, I had to discontinue the engagement and make for base.[61]

All planes from 453 returned by 1930, though with very little fuel left (Fred Cowpe recorded in his logbook that he returned with just five gallons[62]). 132 Squadron made no claims and had two of their number shot down, but both pilots crash-landed behind Allied lines and returned to Longues that evening.[63] In the evening, Mick West returned to the squadron in a new Auster, bringing with him a very welcome load of tomatoes for the mess. Bayeux was now 'in bounds' as a liberty destination and day trips were arranged.[64]

Flying on 13 July was restricted by weather, and Don Smith took the Adjutant up in the new Auster for a tour over Bayeux and the beaches. They stopped off at B.14 at Amblie to pick up a battery-operated wireless provided by the RAAF Overseas HQ Comforts officer. An armed recce of twelve Spitfires led by Don Smith in '?' took off at 1830, this being the only operational mission of the day. Pat McDade had 'S' shot up pretty badly by heavy calibre flak over Villers-Bocage, but immediately returned to Longues at 1845, escorted by Allan Harris in 'E', and made a belly-landing without injuring himself. Claims by the sortie amounted to one tank damaged and one MET smoking and another damaged. The remainder of the squadron returned at 1955.

There was no operational flying on 14 July, but some changes in command. G/Cpt J. Rankin DSO, DFC took command of the Wing and W/Cdr Lapsley was posted out. W/Cdr Lapsley was a popular commander and it was noted that he, and other senior staff posted out, would all be missed. The Wing was reorganised into a four-squadron wing, the extra squadron being 441 RCAF, also equipped with Spitfires. They had previously flown from B.3 Ste-Croix-sur-Mer[65] as part of 144 Wing, under the leadership of the famous W/Cdr Johnnie Johnson. When the Wing was broken up, one squadron went to each of 125, 126 and 127 Wings.[66]

Unfortunately, 132 Squadron was the victim of so-called 'friendly fire' when one of their planes was shot down. The pilot (W/O Reeves—RAF) was killed by a yellow nosed P-51 Mustang, one of a flight of four. The attack came from the 4 o'clock position and a range of 100 yards, so the American could hardly miss. Neither the Spitfire nor the Mustang was flying alone, and another of 132's Spitfires was attacked by the same Mustang but without hitting it. The Mustang then took to the clouds and disappeared.[67] It wouldn't be the last time that the Wing would be involved in one of these tragic events, though it was learned that the guilty pilot was demoted from Captain to Lieutenant and sent back to the US.[68]

The Wing had its first professional entertainment since arriving in France that night, with S/Ldr Ralph Reader and his band giving a performance in the Wing Airmen's mess to a full house. The locals hung out their French flags for Bastille Day, something they'd not done since 1939.[69]

Poor weather persisted on 15 July, but a morning sortie was flown anyway. Four Spitfires led by Ken Lawrence in 'U' took off for a weather

July 1944: Pilots of 453 Squadron resting in Bayeux. From left to right: Olver, Lawrence, Smith, Lancaster, West, McDade.
(Courtesy of the Olver family)

The same location, 2015. (Courtesy of Mr Jean Bansard)

Allan 'Hairy' (because he was losing his) Harris pictured at Ford in May 1944.
(Courtesy of the Cowpe family)

recce over Caen, Lisieux, Argentan and Falaise, and returned at 1010. Vern Lancaster (who was to start a course at Millfield on the 17th) was flown over to England in the squadron Auster by Pat McDade, despite his sore neck from the previous day's crash landing. After a midday recce sortie, the squadron launched four overlapping patrols each of four aircraft. Each patrol lasted 70-80 minutes over the beach area Cabourg to Port-en-Bessin. Sixteen pilots were used so no one had to fly twice. No enemy aircraft were seen, though one barrage balloon which had come adrift was shot down. On this day, the first supply of beer arrived from England, having been arranged with RAF Station Tangmere by Mick West while he was away. Another entertainment night was held with entertainment provided by the crooning styles of Sgt Duke from 602 Squadron, and 'Mademoiselle Yvette' from a local village who sang some songs in French.[70] Luftwaffe night time raiders disturbed the squadron's sleep, as did the anti-aircraft guns, but no damage was done.

Just before 1300 on 16 July, a V-1 was spotted heading south, but despite much wishing and hoping it didn't reach German lines and score an own goal. The pilots assembled a large drying area in dispersal and hung out their washing, hoping of course that the clothing would dry out faster than the soil and thereby avoid subjecting their washing to the Norman dust.

Alan Melville, of the BBC, arrived to interview some pilots for a broadcast, including for audiences in Australia, and he spoke with a number of pilots, preparing small pieces for them to read. The squadron was not named, but was referred to as: 'a Squadron of the Royal Australian Air Force ... operating under the command of S/Ldr Donald Smith of Victor Harbour, South Australia'. Mick West was first to be interviewed and gave a summary of the incident involving Dick Peters and his return to B.11 with his head injury:

> He called up the C.O. and told him that his aircraft had been hit. He didn't say anything more. The C.O. detailed another kite to escort him home—which took about thirty-five minutes ... He'd been pretty badly wounded in the back of the head and in the shoulder and he must have lost a great deal of blood on the trip back. He made a first-class landing, and then passed out at the end of the runway ... I don't know what he thought about it: but the rest of us on the Squadron think that it was one of the outstanding bits of work that's been done since we came across here.

Jack Olver recounted shooting down two FW-190s (both shared) and Clarence Rice gave his impressions of operations on 6 June:

> It didn't look too comfortable down below there, we could see the shells bursting and the guns cracking away from some of the enemy coastal batteries which hadn't been knocked out. I remember thinking that I'd sooner be up looking down than down looking up.

Joshua Scott spoke about relations with the locals:

> We have made one very important contact—with a French farmer and his wife in the next-door village. His farmhouse has been pretty badly knocked about by the invasion, but in

spite of that he's very willing to provide us with eggs and milk. Every evening we go out on one of our important sorties—in a jeep—and ask, in our best French—for 'dix litres du lait' and 'douze oeufs' ... That farmer and his wife are a really fine old couple—and they seemed really pleased to find out that we were Australians. They remember the Aussies being over here in the last war.

Rusty Leith also spoke and gave a summary of daily life in Normandy:

> Life out here isn't so very different to what we were used to back in England. I suppose the hours of work are a bit longer: you're shaken at first light, and get out of your tent and wander over to dispersal—still feeling a bit dopey until you get to your kite. As soon as it's light, you're sent up on an armed recce—around the Caen area. You're kept at different periods of readiness all day—fifteen minutes, half-an-hour, an hour. That goes on every day if the weather's at all fit for flying ... we have to fit in our meals according to the weather and ops—much more so than we did back in England ... in between the actual flying we play football, sleep, eat, play cards, and do our washing and darning, writing letters home and reading the letters we get from home.

Jack Steward also gave some detail about the engagement a few days earlier where Don Smith had broken up the much larger Luftwaffe formation by leading the charge head-on into them:

> They'd been planning to attack us, but he broke them up within seconds. We all split up into a whole lot of separate dogfights ... I saw two of them going into some cloud. I went to intercept them and gave one of them the works from about two hundred yards. I could see the strikes on his cockpit—he broke away suddenly and half-rolled, and I caught him with another burst. His right wing came off and he tumbled down through the clouds ... It was quite a party.[71]

Broadcasts like these carried a lot of information for the people at home and they were very much a factor in the propaganda for the home front as well as being a genuine source of news. But they couldn't talk all day—there was always another sortie to go out.

Eight Spitfires in two flights of four: one led by Jack Olver in 'W' and the other by Don Smith in '?', took off at 1800 for an armed recce. In total they claimed one armoured car as smoking and eleven MET damaged. Jim Lynch described it as: 'Good fun. Fired all cannons'.[72] Jack Olver recorded after his first sortie of the day: 'Six MET damaged. Used all ammo'.[73] The success of the squadron resulted in a newspaper article on page one of the *Army News* in Darwin. The article, titled 'Spitfire's Delight' was written in a bloodthirsty tone stating that:

> An Australian Spitfire Squadron while out on patrol over Normandy saw a German military policeman directing traffic. The pilots riddled the luckless Nazi with their machine guns and then followed the direction he had so obligingly pointed out.

The article named Rice, Olver, Steward and Lynch as participating and finished with: 'The pilots were delighted with the excellent target so kindly pointed out to them'.[74] The first flight returned at 1850, the second at 1905. At 2020 one flight of four led by Jack Olver in 'W' took off to accompany some 602 Squadron Spitfires to bomb a crossroads resulting in one direct hit and two near misses.

Squadron numbers were boosted with the return of Bruce Fuller from the appendix operation that had kept him away from the squadron since 28 May.

On 17 July, ground mist prevented early operations, but this cleared during the day. Two flights of six aircraft made patrols, but these were uneventful, apart from one being jumped by American P-47 Thunderbolts, but the Spitfires saw them coming and were able to get away.[75] A twelve-plane armed recce led by Don Smith in '?' took off at 1800 during which they strafed a halftrack carrying troops. They also eyed with great suspicion a large number of trucks with red crosses travelling north and south in the area of Flers to Domfront. An estimated 20-30 ambulances of varying size and shape were spread out within a convoy of other vehicles, with one ambulance every few vehicles. The pilots felt sure that the havoc caused on the roads by 2TAF had caused the Germans to paint as many vehicles as possible with red crosses to avoid being attacked, and the pilots knew that they were not accurate enough to avoid hitting the ambulances while trying to take out single vehicles within a larger convoy, so the vehicles were not engaged. The Wehrmacht had to look after itself as the Luftwaffe was not putting up a lot of resistance on their behalf.

Rusty Leith wrote home to his family:

> We do quite well for cigarettes and sweets over here. A ration for everyone is a bar of choc, some sweets and 7 cigs a day in addition, aircrew get 3 bars of choc, some sweets and more cigs a week. I still don't use the smokes so exchange them for chocolate or give them to my ground crews. During the week our wireless arrived and it makes all the difference in the world as the AEF (Allied Expeditionary Forces) programme of the BBC is bright and breezy. Talking of titles the newest thing for mail from England is 'British Liberation Army' as the last line in the address. I tell you everyone is pretty disgusted with such a stupid address line.[76]

Jack Olver in flying gear at B.11. (Courtesy of the Olver Family)

In the afternoon Fred Cowpe, Hector Aldred, Merv Watson and Ralph Dutneall were flown to Bognor[77] in England in an Anson to pick up four new Spitfire LF IXE's which had a wing armament of two 20 mm cannon and two .50 calibre machine guns. These packed much more punch than the rifle-calibre .303s that Spitfires had been armed with since the beginning of the war. The diary noted that 'We are sure the Germans will not be pleased with the news'.[78] While the modification of Spitfires to have the two .303 machine guns in each wing replaced by a single .50 machine gun had originated in trials in November 1943, it was 84 Group who were the first to receive the Mk IXEs in significant quantities, 83 Group (to which 453 belonged) were to receive them only after 84 Group had been fully equipped. Fortunately, 125 Wing was the exception, and so it was that 453 Squadron came to fly the Mk IXE in Normandy,[79] and they loved them.

17 July was an important date in the fighting in Normandy, for this was the day that Rommel was removed from the battle by an Allied fighter or fighter-bomber. One account gives the time of attack at about 6.00pm on the N179 short of Vimoutiers and credits a Typhoon with shooting up his staff car and passengers, throwing them out onto the road.[80] For such an important event, it is natural enough that there are a number of claims made about who was responsible, much like those made about who shot down the Red Baron in the First World War. Much speculation took place in the newspapers around the globe at the time, and both sides sought to take up the case. The Germans said that he was well and still in command of troops in Normandy, and the Allies insisting that he was either wounded, badly wounded, probably dead, or actually dead. The Allies quoted resistance sources and even captured German officers.[81]

One of many claims by pilots and squadrons is that of 412 (RCAF) Squadron, which stated they had strafed Rommel's staff car.[82] The pilot alleged to have been responsible was F/Lt Charley Fox. The time of his claim is apparently a few hours earlier than that of 602 Squadron,[83] whose

Squadron Leader, JJ Le Roux, is another pilot credited with the Rommel strafing. He hadn't been with the squadron long and, on the day in question, apparently saw the staff car from a height of 100 ft and called his section down with him before strafing it. He saw it crash and someone in grey was thrown from the car. He pulled out of his shallow dive and returned to base, pleased there was one less staff car on the roads of Normandy.[84]

In 1952, the *Northern Star* newspaper of Lismore carried a story about British pilot W/Cdr Johnnie Baldwin, reporting him missing in action while serving in Korea. The article went on to say that he had been one of eight different pilots to have been credited with killing Rommel. While it was later learned that Rommel had been wounded, there were still eight pilots making a claim some years later.[85] At the time, the *Daily Express* gave credit to 'RAF Tactical Air Force pilots under W/Cdr Baldwin', and this was quoted in the *Darwin Army News* on 25 October 1944.[86] On 17 July, W/Cdr Baldwin had been flying a Typhoon with 193 Squadron.[87] That no rockets were used in the attack on Rommel does not discount the possibility that it was actually a Typhoon that made the attack.

Later in life, after seeing a newspaper article about the strafing of Rommel, Fred Cowpe thought back to that period and decided that it was a 'strong possibility' that it may have been him who 'got' Rommel. He remembered a 'large touring car with roof folded back with two figures sitting upright in the back seat (looked like a large Mercedes Benz)'. He thought to himself: 'VIPs, I'll have you'. He turned, and after firing a short burst,

> it immediately burst into flames, as (I) swept past noticed the flames were coming from the petrol tank at rear, thought what a fine looking car, though it looks odd with about 30 yards of flame pouring out behind it.[88]

Unfortunately, there is a discrepancy in dates, as in one recollection he considers it to be 13 July and states that after engine trouble he was led back to the airfield by McDade.[89] But, on that date, McDade was hit by flak and escorted back to the airfield by Harris.[90] However according to squadron records, Cowpe did not fly on 17 July[91]—his logbook has him as a passenger in an Anson from B.14 to Bognor, returning to France the next day in a newly-assigned Mk IXE.[92] It would seem, then, that there is no evidence to support any claim of 453 being the squadron responsible for strafing Rommel's staff car that day. Fred made a number of entries in his logbook for vehicles damaged in the week before and after 17 July—maybe that's what he was recalling, but Rommel it was certainly not.[93]

According to an occupant of the staff car in question, Hauptmann (Captain) Helmuth Lang, they were returning to Vimoutiers after visiting SS commander Dietrich at St Pierre-sur-Dives. As the staff car neared Livarot, they saw fighter-bombers operating over Livarot and so headed for a secondary road. Once back on the main road, one spotter in the car called a warning that they were being approached by two fighter-bombers and they accelerated to try and reach a side road and therefore be less of a target, or escape altogether. They didn't make it and the vehicle and occupants were struck by a burst of fire, almost everyone being wounded immediately. The driver could not maintain control because of his wounds, the car swerved off the road, hit a tree stump and turned over. Lang then went on to say that: 'A second aircraft flew over and tried to drop bombs on those who were lying on the ground'. One of these people was Field Marshal Rommel. Rommel was later evacuated to a hospital with severe wounds and, though he survived them, played no further part in the Normandy campaign. Even this version apparently has errors, which is natural enough for someone under the stress of being attacked by two Allied aircraft.[94]

While some have suggested that it was immediately known that Rommel was killed (which wasn't true in any case) actions later that week show the situation was not clear. On 25 July a six-man team from 2SAS and 3SAS was dropped in France to carry out Operation Gaff, the goal being to kill or capture Rommel. Their drop zone was near St Remy-les-Chevreuse between Chartres and Rambouillet, about 30 miles from Rommel's HQ at La Roche-Guyon.

Had Rommel already been 'dealt with', obviously there would have been no need to send a SAS team after him. On 28 July the team received a message that Rommel was out of action and the team were allocated a new task.[95]

The absolute truth of the matter regarding who strafed Rommel will now never be known and, though a number of authors have credited specific squadrons or pilots, others have distanced themselves from the matter entirely and merely stated that he was strafed by Allied fighters or fighter-bombers. In the end, it doesn't really matter who did it, as the fact that it happened is the most important point. Moreover, Allied air superiority over the battlefield in Normandy led to a number of similar incidents. General Marcks of LXXXIV Corps was killed in a strafing attack on 12 June, the commander of the 243rd Infantry Division, Lt-General Hellmich, was killed on 17 June and the commander of the 77th Infantry Division, Maj-General Stegmann, died following a strafing attack on 18 June.[96] On 15 August, fighter-bombers almost killed Field Marshal von Kluge, who was Commander in Chief of the Wehrmacht in Normandy at the time and, on 21 August, Colonel Guderian of 116 Panzer Division was seriously wounded by strafing aircraft.[97] While these were not targeted attacks, in that the pilots did not know who was in the vehicles, the fact was that the Allies had such overwhelming air superiority that they could take advantage of any opportunity to go after any target that presented itself—including staff cars and dispatch riders. Unlike the aerial assassination of Admiral Yamamoto by American P-38 Lightnings on 18 April 1943,[98] the attack on Rommel's staff car was not a planned event and, as such, credit for the attack may only ever be the subject of speculation. Yet the fact that it happened overshadows the question of where praise is due.

18 July saw a large offensive, Operation Goodwood, launched southeast of Caen towards Troarn. While some progress had been made to the west of Caen since 6 June, little had been made in the east, and it was here that Montgomery sought to break the German line (or not, depending on whose version of events regarding the intent of the operation is believed) with three

armoured divisions: the 7th 'Desert Rats', the 11th, and the Guards Armoured Divisions. These were supported by other divisions for the offensive, but the weight was clearly with these units. While the Allies had been continually building up forces within the bridgehead, and had the luxury of rotating some units on the front line, the Germans did not. Any unit that arrived had to be put into the line to prevent the next breakout attempt and no mobile reserve of decisive size could be formed. Thus, any offensive action by the Allies would bring in any German units nearby and keep them committed, under pressure from air, land and sea (many German units were still within range of the heavier Allied ships in the Channel).[99] Of course, the units that did arrive at the front rarely arrived in good order, units having been held up along the way by rail sabotage and continual harassment by 2TAF and the US Ninth Air Force, resulting in the few hours of summer darkness being the safest in which to travel.

The squadron flew 60 sorties (the Wing total was 225)[100] in support of this operation. All available aircraft were used, and 22 different pilots flew a minimum of two sorties each. Four 12-plane sorties were flown at 0525, 1010, 1420 and 1750 as front line patrols but no enemy aircraft were encountered and though some MET were sighted, none were engaged. The first of the sorties was tasked with patrolling a line from Trouville to Le Havre. From this area James Lynch described having seen 'Hundreds of bombers. No fighter opposition. Bombing was great sight from air'.[101] A final six-plane sortie was flown at 2055 to cap off the day, but it too was uneventful. The four pilots taken to pick up the new Spitfires returned before lunch and reported their pleasure at receiving the aircraft before being sent to participate in the day's operations. To return empty-handed from England would have been poor form and they didn't disappoint, bringing beer, bread, tinned food and tomatoes. During the day, the squadron also flew beach patrols, each of two aircraft, at 1155, 1555 and 2005 all of which were also uneventful. Pat McDade returned to the squadron, bad weather having kept him in England for a few days.[102]

PILOTS AND AIRCRAFT PARTICIPATING ON OPERATIONS

18 JULY 1944

Name	Frontline					Beachhead		
	0525-0635	1010-1125	1420-1525	1750-1915	2055-2205	1155-1305	1555-1705	2005-2105
S/Ldr Smith	?	?	-	?	-	-	-	-
F/Lt McDade	-	-	W	S	G	-	-	-
F/Lt Roberts	P	-	B	-	-	-	-	P
F/O Lawrence	U	U	-	-	-	-	-	-
F/O Leith	K	L	-	F	-	-	-	-
F/O Murray	J	J	-	J	-	-	-	-
F/O Olver	W	W	-	W	-	-	-	-
F/O West	-	A	-	H	-	-	-	-
P/O Kinross	L	-	J	-	-	-	-	M
P/O Rice	G	-	G	-	G	-	-	-
P/O Scott	R	R	-	R	-	-	-	-
W/O Aldred	-	-	H	-	-	-	L	-
W/O Boulton	V	V	-	M	-	-	-	-
W/O Cowpe	-	-	?	-	W	P	-	-
W/O Daff	-	C	-	K	-	-	-	-
W/O Seeney	-	G	-	-	-	-	G	-
W/O Steward	-	M	M	P	-	-	-	-
W/O Watson	-	-	U	-	R	M	-	-
W/O Watts	-	K	K	-	-	-	-	-
F/Sgt Dowding	M	-	R	V	V	-	-	-
F/Sgt Dutneall	-	-	A	A	-	-	-	-
F/Sgt Lynch	C	-	C	-	C	-	-	-

Note: Some pilots returned to base earlier than the nominated time.

The day was fairly quiet on 19 July, but things livened up in the evening. One sortie was flown, nine aircraft flying an armed recce at 2150 on a circuit from Falaise to Argentan then L'Aigle and Lisieux. Only one MET was claimed as damaged, and heavy flak was encountered at Mezidon but all planes returned safely at 2235. Five pilots—David Murray, Ken Wilson, Clarence Rice, Joe Boulton and Jim Lynch—went to B.14 at Amblie and, from there, took an Anson to 83 GSU in Bognor[103] where they were to collect more Spitfire LF IXEs while the rest of the squadron had a party. They were visited by sixty very welcome nurses from 9th and 29th Army Field General Hospitals who were entertained with some very carefully stashed beer, spirits and local cider. It was reported that a good time was had by all, and F/Lt Bruce Andrews (the RAAF Public Relations Officer) led the sing-alongs with the Wing Orchestra while the staff danced on the grass outside the mess.[104]

Bad weather on 20 July prevented operational flying in the morning, but the pilots who had not yet flown a Mk IXE had their turns at testing out the new machines and were quite happy with the upgrades. Jack Olver took a 45-minute flight and noted in his logbook: '.5's going strong. Very nice kite.'[105] Four-plane flights were flown in the afternoon, overlapping each other by 10-15 minutes and covering the area east of Caen near Lisieux and Bernay (recorded in the squadron diary as 'Vernay', but likely a typo). The first of these, led by Pat McDade in 'S', shot up some ground targets but made no claims, and the remainder were relatively uneventful, though during the last sortie they spotted a FW-190 who got away from them, Allan Harris recorded that the Focke-Wulf 'Went like a bomb home to his mumma.'[106] In the evening the five new aircraft arrived from England.

On 21 July, more rain turned the runways to mud, but an Anson took Don Smith, Joshua Scott and Allan Dowding to England to pick up more of the new Spitfires. Operation Goodwood was declared over at 1000 and, while no breakthrough had been achieved, the front line had been extended and German units had been drawn in to battle, preventing them from establishing a powerful mobile reserve.[107] Rain continued on 22 July and, though no flying took place, there was much digging of additional drainage trenches around the accommodation. While 453 were quite proud of their new Mk IXEs on the 22nd 602 Squadron were informed that they would soon re-equip with the newer mark of Spitfire also, only for this to be rescinded on the 29th.[108]

23 July brought relief from the rain, and there was a rumour that Winston Churchill would be addressing the squadron, so there was much rushing about and the associated cleaning and polishing of boots and brass. The AOC of 83 Group, AVM Broadhurst, brought Churchill with him in a Fiesler Storch and, while they did land at B.11 Longues, Churchill did not speak to the men of 453, but was instead driven to Arromanches by G/Cpt Rankin.[109] The diary records: 'It is unnecessary to record that we were all very disappointed'. Twice in two weeks had there been much fuss associated with an impending VIP visit, and on both occasions the preparation went unrewarded. But, sometimes, you have to take matters into your own hands, so five of the pilots (McDade, Murray, Leith, Kinross and Rice) went down into Arromanches and were in the area when Churchill went by in a jeep. 'Good Lord, it's Winnie!' exclaimed Pat McDade, receiving the friendly V for Victory hand gesture in return. The group of five quickly stood to attention and saluted him (Clarence Rice had his hat on backwards at the time). Seeing Churchill go off to a cruiser in the harbour, the adventurous pilots managed to get themselves aboard a motor launch and then somehow managed to be invited aboard the very same ship. With the assistance of RAN Lieutenant Peter Taylor, serving aboard the British ship, they were looked after very well and had a dinner of fresh meat and vegetables, the first in more than a month. Quite satisfied with the evening meal—and perhaps more than a little enlivened by a couple of drinks—upon returning to their smaller runabout to go back to shore, Leith, McDade and Murray thought it only fitting that Churchill should be saluted. They let go

an 18-shot volley into the air with their .38 revolvers before heading back to shore and making their way back to Longues. They recounted their tale to War Correspondents Folkard and White who each submitted articles to newspapers back home about the event.[110]

Disaster struck on 24 July. The weather was poor but not poor enough to prevent operations. The squadron carried out five beach patrol missions and a large armed recce. Each beach patrol consisted of a flight of four Spitfires, the first taking off at 1150 and the last landing at 2055. This first patrol included Allan Harris in a new Mk IXE 'Z' and though hit in the port radiator during the mission while strafing, he was quite happy with the shooting up of some trucks and wrote in his logbook: '.5's pretty darned good'.[111] The patrol that took off at 1345 was attacked by P-47 Thunderbolts. Rusty Leith led the flight in 'F' with Ralph Dutneall as his No. 2 in 'A', the second pair being made up of Ken Kinross in 'E' (PL206) and Hec Aldred in 'H' as No.2 to Kinross.

At 1445 the flight was headed east about seven miles southwest of Bayeux. They'd been directed there to intercept low flying aircraft approaching the area from the vicinity of St Lo. Leith spotted two aircraft approaching from behind and identified them as American P-47 Thunderbolts when they were still one mile away. How those aircraft did not identify the Spitfires can only be guessed at. Leith broadcast a warning to the rest of the flight to look out for them and, as the Thunderbolts approached to about 800 yards, he gave the order to break starboard. He and Dutneall made a steady starboard turn and climbed while Kinross and Aldred made a much tighter turn—they appeared to be the focus of the Thunderbolt's intentions. The turn should have been enough to show off the distinctive wing shape of the Spitfire, as all German aircraft that may have been encountered of that size and shape, (such as the FW-190 and Me-109) were rather more rectangular, as was the Mustang. The order to remove the black and white stripes on upper wing surfaces had come through earlier in the month, so almost three weeks later it is reasonable to expect that they had been removed in accordance with the instruction, even if it had been followed somewhat tardily. Therefore, the absence of the black and white stripes may have contributed to the misidentification.[112] Nevertheless, the Spitfire's distinctive wing shape, for whatever reason, did not identify them sufficiently. This varying degree of turn created a gap between the two sections and the Thunderbolts tucked in behind Kinross and Aldred, which, had they been German, would have allowed Leith and Dutneall to close the gap and shoot them down. Of course the Australians didn't fire as they'd correctly identified the Americans but, at about 300 yards behind Kinross and Aldred, the Americans opened fire, hitting Kinross' Spitfire in the starboard wing. The American pilot fired again, hitting the port wing, and no doubt the engine, as Kinross' Spitfire began to trail black smoke and lose altitude.

At this time, the remaining Australian pilots had to take further evasive action as the second Thunderbolt pilot began to try and set himself up for an independent attack rather than sit on his leader's wing. There was no radio message from Kinross and he crashed at the base of a clump of trees in a heavily wooded area and the plane caught fire. It was thought that Kinross had not identified he was being attacked until it was too late, and the subsequent damage to his wing during the first attack prevented him from out-turning the Thunderbolt. Not once did the Spitfires fire or even take up an attacking position to threaten the Americans. With nothing to be done for Kinross, the remaining Spitfires headed back to B.11 to immediately report the incident while the Thunderbolts circled the wreck of their victim.[113]

Upon landing, Leith complained bitterly to Don Smith and, despite briefly speaking to a Group Captain the next day, he got the impression that little or nothing would be done, and the American was never identified.[114] A report was filed though, with Don Smith making the comment that:

> The chief factor contributing to the incident appears to be that the Thunderbolt pilots concerned were either not acquainted with the appearance of Spitfire aircraft or were entirely careless in their attempt to recognise them.

However, no mention was made of the Americans being responsible in the letter sent to the Kinross family informing them of their son's death.[115] Ken Kinross' body was later recovered and he was buried at Bayeux. The Wing records note: 'This is the second such incident in 8 days and perhaps the less said about it the better'.[116] Dwelling on such incidents could be more devastating than the incident itself if it led to protests and belligerence by the pilots. The best thing to do was to get on with the job, anything else would be self-destructive. Losing Kinross to friendly fire struck the squadron a hard blow and Leith didn't sleep well that night, despite his exhaustion.[117] Rusty Leith made a record of the incident in his logbook: 'Section attacked by Thunderbolts sth Bayeux and P/O K.C. Kinross shot down—killed—our Allies (?) again.'[118]

On the sortie the squadron put up that evening, the pilots got lucky at 2000 as they were headed back to Longues, and bounced a formation of FW-190s and Me-109s.

From the Personal Combat Report submitted and signed by George Roberts who flew 'P' in which he claimed one FW-190 destroyed:

> I was flying Red 3 returning from a patrol when over Cabourg at 8,000 ft we saw approx. ten e/a. flying east at 3,000 ft. We gave chase and recognised them as Me 109's and FW 190's. 2 FW 190's pulled up in line abreast and I attacked the port one. I turned with him once and as he dived for the deck I followed him opening fire at 500 yds. range with a long burst of cannon and m/g. I saw strikes all over the fuselage and the e/a. started to pour glycol and black smoke. It did a hard turn to port and the pilot having jettisoned the hood, climbed to 3,000 ft. I followed and closed to 50 yds. firing another burst. The pilot bailed out but the parachute did not open and I saw the e/a. crash, bursting into flames, near Cambremer.[119]

From the Personal Combat Report submitted and signed by Joshua Scott who flew 'W' in which he claimed two FW-190s damaged:

> Whilst flying Red 4 in section of 4 aircraft returning from patrol we saw 10 plus mixed e/a. flying S.E. of Cabourg at 3,000 ft. We chased them and recognised them as Me 109's and FW 190's. In the dog fight which followed I had to break away from Red 3 as I was being attacked by 3 FW 190 I broke upwards to port and the e/a. continued to attack me, but after taking evasive action I got into a position to attack. I gave a 4 seconds burst at 400 yds range, height 3,000 ft and saw strikes on the wing tip of the FW 190. He rolled on his back and dived away, but the other two e/a. continued to attack me. I gave several bursts at both of them, deflection varying from 30° to 35° and saw several strikes on the wing of one of the e/a.[120]

During the mass armed recce that took off at 1625, Jim Lynch flying 'F' (MK-618) was hit by flak when attacking some German transport near Villers-Bocage. He climbed up from the attack, trying to gain as much height as possible and asked for a vector home. He was told to steer north and with a rough-running engine that was smoking badly, headed for Allied lines. He had to make a crash landing a few miles northwest of Bayeux, but before crash landing he was also shot at by what he thought were Allied, but certainly not friendly, AA guns. The field was full of anti-glider posts[121] and though the port wing struck one, breaking part of it off, he played down his injuries, stating that he came away with just a few cuts on his face. His safe landing in a small field surrounded by high trees earned him words of praise,[122] though the plane was written off.[123] His official injuries of shock, a head and neck injury, and bruised right loin earned him an admission to 50 MFH and later that night he was transferred to No 125 Wing Sick Quarters at B.11. A notice about his injury was sent to his wife, Sheila, in Orange, New South Wales.[124] The squadron encountered flak everywhere they went, and reported what appeared to be a camouflaged German artillery position near Le Bény-Bocage. The last planes on this sortie returned at 1720.

The grave of Pilot Officer Kenneth Charles Kinross, Bayeux War Cemetery 2012. He was 22 years old. (Author)

Operation Cobra was launched on 25 July[125] by the American forces pushing southwest out of the bridgehead from near St Lo. Cobra was initially planned for 20 July, during Goodwood, so that the Germans would have their attention fully drawn by Montgomery near Caen, but was postponed to the 24th until weather interrupted the air support plan and it was moved again to the 25th, by which time Goodwood was well and truly finished.[126]

However, this day was no better than the one before for 453. The first sortie took off at 0620 for an armed recce on the course Thury-Harcourt to Conde then Falaise and Bretteville. A convoy northeast of Trun was attacked. Rusty Leith, flying 'D' led his formation down on the convoy in pairs, with Clarence Seeney in 'E' coming in behind him. Leith let the convoy have a long burst from his cannon and machine guns, as did the others, and they regained height at the end of the strafing runs to form up again, making sure everyone was accounted for and to check the skies. No enemy aircraft were seen so they went down again, Seeney once again following down behind Leith. As Leith pulled out from his second strafing run, he looked behind him to see the results and saw Seeney crash into the road, his Spitfire exploding amongst the wrecks of the German vehicles.

Even such a relatively simple event can generate conflicting reports, with one account stating that Seeney hit high tension wires rather than being shot down, and another stating that he crashed in a field rather than amongst the convoy, but that is the nature of eyewitness reports. The result, however unfortunate, is the same—though not for the Germans, as Allan Harris recorded in his logbook that Seeney 'took 6 trucks with him'.[127] When attacking the same convoy, Keith Daff, flying 'C' had part of a propeller blade shot away, but managed to make it back to Longues. The claims for the sortie were three flamers, four smokers and five damaged, but it wasn't viewed by the Australians as a fair exchange. The flight led by Leith was the first to return at 0705, the others returning at 0720 and 0730. Don Smith wrote to Clarence's parents the following day, including a paragraph in the letter about Clarence's time in the squadron:

> The loss of Clarrie has deprived the Squadron of a keen and promising Pilot, whose characteristic cheerfulness, skill and courage, were an example to all the Pilots of the Squadron, who with the ground staff wish to join me in this expression of sympathy in your sad bereavement.[128]

Clarence Seeney at RAF Station Ford in May 1944. (AWM UK1350)

Losing two pilots in two days could not halt operations, however, and the flights continued. The next sortie was up at 1015 for a front line patrol. Eleven Spitfires took part, led by Pat McDade in 'S' and George Roberts in '?'. At 1115 the formation was on its way back to Longues at 12,000 ft near Falaise when a lone FW-190 was spotted. One more German shot down today would be one less they'd have to fight tomorrow, and they went after him.

The grave of Clarence Seeney in Coulonces, near Argentan. (Author)

From the Personal Combat Report submitted by George Roberts in '?' and Fred Cowpe in 'W' in which they claimed one FW-190 shared destroyed:

> F/L Roberts states: I was leading Blue section of 453 Sqdn on a Front Line Patrol and flying at 12,000 ft 12 miles E of Falaise when turning to port we saw a FW 190 flying on the deck headed west. I got permission from Red 1 to go down and diving to deck level and closing to 300yds range gave a long burst observing strikes all over the fuselage. The E/A streamed glycol and smoke and breaking to port the pilot jettisoned the hood. W/O Cowpe cut across the turn and fired at the E/A. It started climbing and at approximately 1,000 ft the pilot bailed out and I saw the E/A crash into the earth.
>
> W/O Cowpe states: On patrol with Blue Section of 453 Sqn flying 12 miles E of Falaise at 12,000 ft, I reported one E/A flying westwards at deck level. We dived down and I came up to line abreast with Blue 1, opening fire at a range of 400 yds but seeing no strikes. I looked across and saw Blue 1 firing and immediately afterwards saw glycol smoke pouring from the E/A. I followed and the hun broke to port. At 1,000 ft, 300 yds range I gave a 2 sec burst and saw five pieces fly from the E/A (3 off the starboard wing and 2 off the cockpit) The hood was jettisoned and the engine on the port side burst into flames the pilot bailed out and the E/A crashed to the ground where it burst into flames.[129]

Fred recorded in his logbook: 'Shared a FW190 destroyed with F/Lt Roberts. Blew it to bits'.[130] Two aircraft missed the combat, having returned early, but the remainder landed safely at 1145. At 1425 Don Smith in '?' led eleven others up for an armed recce in the vicinity of Elbeuf and Lisieux. Having completed the recce, the squadron was heading back to Longues when Kenway reported a number of unidentified aircraft between Lisieux and Falaise. 453 went to investigate and spotted twelve Me-109s above them. As they had done a fortnight before, the squadron climbed to the attack, confident that the new Mk IXEs were even more superior to the 109s than their Mk IXBs had been. Don Smith broadcast to the squadron after the planes had been spotted: 'OK, thanks very much Blue 3, anyone with 15 gallons stick with me, otherwise go home'.[131]

From the Personal Combat Report submitted and signed by Keith Daff who flew 'F', in which he claimed one Me-109 destroyed:

> Whilst flying Red 2 returning from an Armed Recce over the ELBEUF—LISIEUX area, Red 3 reported 12 Plus M.E. 109s flying directly above us in a S.W. direction at a height of 13,000 ft. We climbed up behind them from 10000' and at a range of approx. 800-900 yards the E/A broke to Starboard. I saw an M.E. 109 about 1000' above me at 10 o'clock and climbing towards him I gave a 2 second burst at 250 yards range and saw strikes. Liquid poured from the Wing root and the E/A broke to starboard in an endeavour to evade my fire. I followed him firing a series of 2 second bursts until he reached 4000' when I saw strikes on the cockpit and saw the hood fly off. I continued firing and when the E/A was at 3000' the pilot bailed out and the E/A dived straight into the earth and exploded.[132]

From the Personal Combat Report submitted and signed by Allan Harris who flew 'U' in which he claimed one Me-109 shared destroyed with Rusty Leith, and one Me-109 probably destroyed:

> I was Red 3 returning from an Armd Recce over the ELBEUF–LISIEUX area and was flying at 10,000' S.W. Lisieux when we saw approx 12 M.E. 109s flying directly above us at 13,000'. We climbed up behind them and they broke as we closed in. I opened fire at a M.E. 109 at 800 yards range in an endeavour to turn him, which he did an closing in to 300 yards I gave a 1 second burst and saw small pieces fly of the E/A. F/O Leith who was also attacking the same E/A came into my line of fire and I broke to Port coming round again directly behind the E/A. I gave two bursts and observed large pieces flying off the E/A from under the Wings. I gave a further burst at a range of 300 yards firing at the same time as F/O Leith. The E/A which was now at 10000' blew up and burst in flames, disintegrating as it fell to earth. I then pulled tight to look round and saw a M.E. 109 dive from cloud on to two of our Sqn, which broke up towards him. He kept firing down and I pulled over in a tight turn and followed him. Closing in to 200 yards range I gave a 1 Sec burst and almost immediately saw Glycol and belches of smoke coming

from the E/A. I took violent evasive action and followed him down. I gave a series of 1 Second bursts from 200 yards range. At 2000' the E/A started to pull out of the dive glycol and smoke still pouring from it and as I had no cannon shells left I continued firing my M/G. The E/A did a violent flick to port but as I was now very short of fuel I had to discontinue the engagement. I last saw the E/A at 400' diving at 45° with smoke pouring from it. I turned towards home and looking back a moment later saw no signs of the E/A in the air.[133]

From the Personal Combat Report submitted and signed by Jack Olver who flew 'W' in which he claimed one Me-109 probably destroyed:

I was flying as Blue 1 when on returning from an Armed Recce in the Elbeuf-Lisieux area, Red 3 reported 12 plus ME 109's directly above us at a height of 13,000 ft. I turned my section towards the direction in which the E/A was reported and after 30 secs in the dog fight which followed, I saw one ME 109 come out of cloud above and to my starboard. My No 2 and I immediately gave chase but owing to shortage of petrol I was afraid to open my engine full out and had to fire from a range of 600 yds using the gyro sight. I observed strikes on the cockpit and wing roots on two separate bursts. After the first strikes the E/A began to leave a thick trail of thick black smoke, definitely not boost smoke—as though it had caught fire. Shortage of petrol necessitated my breaking off the engagement and the last I saw of the E/A was at a height of 9,000 ft when it rolled on its back, hanging there for some seconds before it dived vertically towards the ground dense clouds of black smoke still trailing from it. Cine-Gun used. I claim 1 ME 109 Probably Destroyed.[134]

The engagement was covered by Don Smith who flew top cover to keep a lookout for any other Luftwaffe planes that may have attempted to join in. The squadron was short on fuel and, at the end of the combat, split up, with some aircraft landing to refuel at airstrips other than Longues before returning to their home strip. Jack Olver landed at B.10 and made a note of it: 'Mixed with 12-15 Me109's when very short of gas. I got one prob. dest. Landed B.10 with dead stick.'[135]

While Fred Cowpe made no claims in this engagement, he certainly made note of the events. After the message from Don Smith, Fred saw that he had exactly 15 gallons left so he decided to stay, picked a 109 and went after it. Strangely, it turned, the last thing anyone should do with a Spitfire on their tail. However tightly Fred turned though, he couldn't get inside it. He checked his instruments and everything seemed to be fine, but his problem was solved when the 109 suddenly blew up. With fuel running low he decided to get out of the action and head for an airstrip, picking B.4 at Beny-sur-Mer. He'd just crossed the front line when he ran out of fuel, still 6,000 ft above B.4. He could see Spitfires down on the airstrip about to take off but couldn't hurry them up as he didn't have the correct frequency. As he glided lower and lower he ran out of choices and luckily the Spitfires took off just as he was coming in behind them. Allan Harris also landed at B.4 and Fred asked him how he went. 'Wizard Freddie, I got two of them, one definitely destroyed and one probable. How did you go?' Fred replied, 'No good, just going to have a go when someone blew it up!' Alan had the perfect answer: 'That was me!'[136]

The confusing nature of a dogfight meant that pilots soon lost track of each other, and by the time everyone returned to Longues, they found that they were two short. Rusty Leith and Allan Dowding were both missing. Overall, the claims for the engagement were two Me-109s destroyed and two Me-109s probably destroyed.[137] During the combat, Allan Dowding flying as Red 4 in 'T' was hit by a Me-109 and later by light flak which led to the Spitfire becoming hard to handle and later uncontrollable. Unable to crash land, he was forced to bail out at just 800 feet. As he flew backwards from the Spitfire he hit the tailplane, something that could easily have killed him, but instead injured his hip and shoulder. He saw the engine of the plane on fire and watched it crash in a marsh. Due to hitting the tailplane, upon landing he was unable to walk and was captured immediately by German troops from the artillery position he had landed in. He was unable to walk for several days and when examined while a prisoner he was told that his hip was broken. This did not prevent the Germans marching him and others from his camp (Stalag-Luft VII) for 25 days to Stalag III (most likely Stalag IIIA) to avoid the ever-changing front lines. The conditions there he described as 'terrible, with louse ridden straw for bedding' and crowded blocks of 300 men or more. Food was very scarce, with two loaves of bread to be shared between 15 men 'and medical supplies were to all intents and purposes non-existent'. He was eventually released by the Russians when they captured his camp in May 1945.[138]

While the pilots may well have thought they'd had enough excitement for one day, the work was not yet done. At 1950 they and 602 Squadron each contributed eleven Spitfires to a mass fighter sweep. 602 had also suffered losses to flak and the Luftwaffe during their time in Normandy, and no doubt the Australians gave them an update on the day's events before they took off. They reported the camouflaged MET they spotted but didn't attack—they weren't tasked with that this time. Despite having 20 Spitfires (due to two early returns) to cleanse the sky with, the sweep was uneventful, the Luftwaffe was nowhere to be found, and everyone returned safely by 2115.

Allan Dowding at B.11 Longues-sur-Mer in Normandy with the regular Spitfire of Fred Cowpe and Froggy Lyall. The names 'Kathleen' and 'Mary' are just below the front of the windscreen. (AWM UK1533)

As for Rusty Leith, after attacking the Me-109 mentioned in the Personal Combat Report submitted by Allan Harris, he found himself with five gallons of fuel and 30 miles to fly back to Allied lines. It was an impossible combination. Even at 12,000 ft he could not glide back safely, though the Spitfire could usually manage about a mile of glide for every thousand feet in height,[139] and soon the engine stopped; there was no fuel left. He was aware of the danger of bailing out and striking the tailplane so, with no power to work with, he decided to stay with the plane and try for a belly landing, aware that he had to be careful to drag the tail a bit before putting the wings down, otherwise the large fairings under each wing could dig in and flip the plane on its back. The small patchwork fields of Normandy were not the ideal location for landings as many glider pilots had discovered in the early hours of 6 June, but that's all he had to work with. He locked the hood open and tightened his shoulder straps—he didn't want to knock himself out on the gunsight. He picked his spot, missed the first hedgerow, skimmed the second, then he was down and sliding across the grass. Once the plane came to a stop, he unstrapped himself, unhooked his helmet from the radio and oxygen, ditched it and got out as fast as he could in case a fire started.

With only two directions to choose from: towards or away from the front lines, he chose the best option and headed away. He ran away from the plane and crossed a few hedgerows, putting some distance between himself and the plane. After about half an hour, he found a French farmhouse and cautiously approached. Rusty applied some schoolboy French and discovered the lady of the house was friendly and he was soon provided with farmers clothes—but had to hand over his uniform in exchange; no-one could chance being discovered with an air force uniform. Explaining that they could not be caught with an Allied airman in the house, the homeowners hid Rusty in the cupboard. He didn't have much of a choice but to trust them. He heard a conversation between the lady and a male who seemed to be her son. He couldn't follow the fast French but was soon released from the cupboard and escorted to a tree, which he climbed and hid in. The man returned a little while later, warning that there were Germans nearby. Rusty's uniform was returned to him and he gladly put it back on, with the farmer's clothes over the top, which upset the Frenchman, Rusty was taking a big risk. He was given an egg, a piece of bread and a map torn from a book. To top it all off, literally, he was also given a beret. He couldn't stay at the house and endanger the occupants, so he set off on his own.

He found a stream and drank from it, then continuing on found a grassy drain next to a field and rested there. It had been a long day. He drifted off a few times but could not sleep properly, always on edge. He soon moved off again and took shelter under a tree, where he remained for most of the night despite being uncomfortable, but he wasn't going to keep moving and risk making a mistake while he was so tired. He fell asleep before dawn and was woken by a bird singing in the tree, the sun bright in the sky. Breakfast was the egg, which he had somehow managed to keep from breaking, water and some emergency ration chocolate. It wasn't great but it was all he had, and he set off again. He found the Cormielles-Lisieux road and, after carefully crossing some fields, found the road to Moyaux. This road was busier, with farmers going about their business, so he trudged along, not too fast and not too slow, just trying to blend in as a worker. He soon heard a horse and cart behind him. Checking the road was now clear except for the farmer and himself he took a risk and flashed his uniform: 'Je suis un pilote Australien'. Without hesitation the farmer offered him a seat on the cart and they moved off to Moyaux. After some time Rusty felt uncomfortable, he was too exposed, sneaking around gave him a bit of security and control over his own actions, and had to leave. The Frenchman pointed out a road on his map and with an exchange of 'Vive La France!' he was on his own again.

Once again trudging, still dressed as a farmer, he passed safely through Ouilly-du-Houley towards Firfol. Soon he had run out of water so knocked on the door of a farmhouse. A lady answered and, although she immediately saw through his disguise as a French farmer, he flashed his uniform and went through his introduction. She could not have an open conversation with an obvious evader so brought him inside the house. One of the children was sent to fetch the woman's husband and Rusty was given some cider. Not ideal on an empty stomach but it went down easily enough. Fortunately, bread and coffee followed, and the woman's husband showed great pride in finding Australia in an atlas and telling the children that Rusty was from 'Seedney'. After his short but welcome meal, Rusty was presented with a scarf and wished *bonne chance* before he was again on the road and alone. But his luck had held out, and the French had been good to him. He soon hit a main road and decided against taking it and instead wound his way through fields and orchards. He encountered large numbers of refugees from Lisieux along the way, and passed Glos before taking a road west to Les Mesnil Guillaume.

The road was much quieter, though the sound of a motor vehicle behind him brought with it the potential for discovery and he tried hard to remain casual. However, a tyre burst and Rusty turned to see Germans getting out of a car with a red cross on the bonnet to inspect their damaged vehicle. He moved on, not wanting to get involved or be engaged in conversation. Again he ran out of water and approached a farmhouse, where he was given a glass of cider, but nothing more, and he moved on. He reached the top of a hill and started down towards Pretreville. The two layers of clothes were almost too much for him but he could not afford to discard either. He again knocked at a farmhouse door and this time there was no cider, but he was given water before being sent on his way. After crossing another stream he saw yet another farm beyond another hill but he needed to rest. There always seemed to be more. More hills, more roads, more villages. When he needed rest, he found a tree and fell asleep underneath it. Waking up a few hours later, the sun was setting and he decided to approach a farm beyond a hill. He assessed the farm from his position and approached it, getting very close to the woman, children and the two men before they spotted him. He gave his now usual introduction and was greeted warmly. Cider flowed and his French was tested to the limit as they asked him question after question. He decided that the hospitality shown to him was so good that he had to stay, and asked for permission to do so. They agreed.

Once inside the house he was warned to stay out of sight; Germans were everywhere. One of the men at the house was named Georges and he had been in the resistance in Lisieux. His son was named Jean. The next morning, after breakfast Rusty began to plan his next move but the family advised him it was too dangerous. Georges presented him with an application for identification papers, just the sort of thing that the small escape photos taken at the airfields back in England were meant for. Robert Martin, a local resistance leader, arrived having been advised by Georges of their visitor. Fortunately for Rusty, he spoke good English. Two days later, Martin returned with a bicycle and rode to Fervaques carrying Rusty on the crossbar. There he was hidden in Martin's house and again handed over his RAAF uniform and other military items which may have revealed his identity. He was then taken to a local safe house—another Norman farm—owned by Jean and Renee Renoult. Though the Renoults spoke no English, Martin assured Rusty before leaving he would be well looked after. The Renoults were also harbouring two other Allied airmen at the time—Stanley Canner and Alf Sutkowski of the USAAF. Canner had been shot down flying a Mustang, and Sutkowski had been a gunner in a bomber before his plane was shot down. He was still suffering from a leg wound.

Rusty settled into the routine established by the Americans. Help on the farm, meet people from the village or resistance who wanted to meet Allied airmen (their presence was not exactly a local secret) and eat. So that he could be addressed in the presence of others, Rusty was allocated the name Andre. In return, Rusty named Renee Renoult 'Madame Nap' (Nap was short for Napoleon). Germans would sometimes visit the house looking for food, during which times Rusty and the others had to hide. But the food the Germans were after never appeared: Madame Nap told them she had none. In early August, news arrived that Robert Martin had been captured by the Gestapo. The question was, were the airmen still safe? Fortunately for the airmen, Martin gave nothing way despite being tortured. When being transported to his intended place of execution, he escaped and met the Canadians in St Pierre sur Dives.

On 19 August, the war was closing in the Renoult farm and the Germans set up a machine gun nearby to cover the road down which the Allies would have to approach. With the Germans around (and sometimes in) the house, the airmen were ushered up into the attic. There they remained for four days while the sounds of battle could be heard from time to time. About 6.00pm on Tuesday 22 August 1944, the farm and surrounding countryside were liberated and the airmen were met by a Canadian officer. They were free again. The celebration for the villages, airmen and liberating Canadian troops started with ten gallons of Calvados, and when that was gone, Jean fetched more. The next day Rusty Leith bade his French friends farewell and set out to find his squadron again.[140]

Despite being short of both pilots and planes, 453 continued operations on 26 July. On the 1230 armed recce sortie, the squadron was being led by Pat McDade in '?' (PL 220) and George Roberts in 'P'. They found a convoy target near Doudeville, about seven miles north of Yvetot. About 1330 McDade led his section in an attack on the convoy, and he was fired on by an emplaced AA battery. He was hit in a radiator and white smoke poured from his plane. He called up on the R/T that he'd been hit and the radiator temperature was rocketing up. He climbed for height and with an escort made about 10 or 15 miles back to Allied lines but it wasn't enough, and he had to put it down.[141] Fred Cowpe saw that there was a long, straight road nearby and suggested to McDade that if he landed a third of the way along it, someone would come down and pick him up. McDade crashed and got out safely, and was seen to

Pat McDade posing proudly for the camera with a Spitfire at Ford in May 1944.
(Courtesy of the Cowpe family)

run into a house. Both Fred Cowpe and Joe Boulton went down low to check out the area but there were too many wires next to the road and the nearby fields were too rough, so they couldn't get him back.[142] He was captured the same day and, in August, sent a message back to the squadron: 'Am fit and well, was slightly wounded'. He was allocated POW number 7620 and spent time at Stalag Luft III, arriving there in September 1944 with Olsson. He was freed when the camp was liberated in 1945.[143]

The sortie claimed one MET destroyed and one damaged. The remainder returned at 1400. Now deprived of his traditional '?' but, more importantly, another pilot, Don Smith led a formation of eleven Spitfires up at 1535 in 'N' on an armed recce on the circuit Falaise to Argentan then L'Aigle, Bernay and Lisieux. Scattered MET encountered during the patrol were strafed, and claims of two flamers, three smokers and one damaged were made. Flak was encountered near Mezidon and Argentan, but it caused them no trouble. Two evening patrols were carried out but were uneventful.

German flak caused more casualties on the following day. Beach patrols in flights of four was the order of the day, and the first, from 0545 to 0705 led by Jack Olver in 'W', was uneventful. The second sortie took off at 0640 with Fred Cowpe leading in 'R'. When in the vicinity of Caen, the patrol received a call from a Canadian squadron requesting assistance as they were outnumbered by FW-190s and having a bad time of it. They were on the deck southeast of Caen and in one of the areas with a high concentration of German AA guns. Not wanting to give these guns any chance of excluding them from the battle, Fred Cowpe and the others dived down from 6,000 ft on the Allied sides of the lines then ripped across the lines at 50 ft doing 430mph. They made the battle as the Germans were heading for base and Fred looked across at his fellow pilots, ensuring they were all there for the pursuit towards Lisieux. He noticed Allan Harris in 'Z' was at 150 ft, too high for Fred's liking. He warned his mate: 'Get down Alan, you are too high'. There was no response. He tried again: 'Hairy, you are too high, get down'. There was a flash in the fuel tank of Harris' plane and he went in with a streamer of flame behind him.[144]

Flak was everywhere, and so Fred dropped the plane down to 20 ft, so dangerous that he had to force himself to do it, but it was the only way to avoid the flak.[145] The section turned for base, the chase over, when Joe Boulton in 'S' called up on the R/T: 'I've been hit, covered in oil, can't see, have to crash land, think I've made the front line'. The plane was badly damaged. Fred wished him luck: 'Good on you Joe, see you later'. He did make it across Allied lines, and ended up crashing near an artillery unit.

As Fred and the rest of Blue section had dived to help the Canadians, four more Spits had been scrambled and they stayed low as they headed off on their allocated vector. When they were about 20 miles southeast of Caen, for an unknown reason, Ralph Dutneall in 'A' began to climb but was shot down by flak and crashed. Daff in 'G' called Fred over the R/T: 'Freddie will you call my No. 2, can't raise him'. Fred tried, but there was no-one alive to

The grave of Flight Sergeant Ralph Dutneall at Banneville-La-Campagne War Cemetery, Normandy (Author)

answer.[146] The high rate of fire of German flak guns of 20-37 mm (referred to in squadron records as light, in reference to the calibre) was a major threat for low-flying 2TAF aircraft, and often they were mounted in multi-barrel combinations on halftracks. The flak on this sortie was described as 'intense accurate light' and perhaps Ralph was climbing to avoid a flak gun, but that would have only made him more of a target. On landing, Fred reported the events to Don Smith, signed the duty book, then went to his tent to sleep,[147] physically and mentally exhausted by the day's events. It wasn't even 9.00am.

At 1300 all squadrons of the Wing were released from operations for 24 hours. 453 had suffered a very bad run in just a few days, losing more men than they had in a few months. The squadron Medical Officer contacted the 9th British General Hospital and, with their assistance, arranged for some nurses to come over to the squadron for a party that evening to take everyone's mind off their recent losses. Their attendance was much appreciated, though not quite as much as the return of P/O James Grady (413202) who arrived as a replacement. Grady had previously served with 453 from August to November in 1943 before being posted out to the

Air Fighting Development Unit at Wittering.[148] During the night, Joe Boulton also made it back to the squadron, and he was greeted most warmly of all.[149] To Fred, Joe returned in the night 'like an apparition'. The first thing Fred did was offer him a drink. Joe replied: 'Cowpie, I don't mind if I do'.[150]

The morning of 28 July was spent at rest. The afternoon patrol of four, which took off at 1550 got their heart rate up again when Clarence Rice in 'G' spotted a lone FW-190 between Caen and Bayeux and went after it. Although he fired a number of times and saw a few strikes, he could not bring it down and it got away by ducking in and out of the clouds. Dick York and Brian Inglis arrived as replacements from 83 GSU, and this time Inglis managed to stay for much longer than his first stint, which had lasted less than a week. The impression that he had on his return was that: 'the squadron was a bit new at the time' due to losses, but Don Smith was the man to serve under. Of him, Brian would later say: 'I always thought he was a hero in many ways. He was very mature, an excellent leader of men, and I was privileged, I thought, to serve under him'.[151] S/Ldr Hilton, the RAAF Liaison Officer at AEAF arrived in the afternoon to gain personal knowledge of the conditions in France and talk with the Australians in the units, pilots and ground crew also. The second patrol of the day returned empty-handed.

Luck was on the squadron's side on 29 July as an early morning armed recce that had taken off at 0620 came across a 35-vehicle German convoy, spotted through a convenient gap in the clouds. This was just a few miles north of Conde-sur-Noireau. Six planes attacked with bombs, diving down from 7,000 ft and led by Don Smith in a newly-allocated '?'. They tore up the convoy, blocking both ends with bombed-out trucks[152] and ripping up those in the middle with cannon and machine guns. Those without bombs went down and put in some strafing runs, no-one wanting this big convoy to make good an escape, Jack Olver called up the others on the R/T: 'Fair go Yellow, leave some for us!'.[153] In all, 18 flamers and 10 smokers were claimed.

Fred Cowpe recorded in his logbook: 'Amazing results. Sent out to prevent MET getting to American lines'.[154] Jack recorded in his: '1000 lb bombs up. 18 MET dest 10 dam. Top score in T.A.F. ever. 2nd SS Panzer Div'.[155]

Two English pilots, F/O Wilkinson and F/Sgt Sargeant, arrived to temporarily boost pilot numbers until more Australians could be found—presumably none were left in 83 GSU. Edward Sargeant was born on 1 September 1921 in the town where Reginald Mitchell went to school: Stoke-on-Trent. He enlisted in October 1941 and was promptly sent to Wales for his basic training, then it was across the Atlantic to Canada and the USA for his early flight training—much of it in Stearman PT17s and North American AT6s (Harvards). He returned to the UK (via Canada again) in March 1943 and moved on to the Miles Master (I, II and III) before taking on the Hurricane, Mustang and Spitfire. On 10 June 1944, Edward survived a crash landing in a Mustang III caused by 'U/S Summerfield (sic) Track'—that is, an improvised runway that had been damaged or was otherwise unfit for use. Whether due to the crash or not, that was his last flight in a Mustang and the rest of his time was spent on Spitfires. 453 Squadron was his first operational posting.[156]

More Australian pilots were on the way, but were still waiting at the PDRC and would not be ready for combat for some months.[157] While the constant training courses led to some frustration for pilots wanting to get to an operational squadron, in the words of Sid Handsaker, who later flew Spitfires with 451 (RAAF) Squadron: 'The quicker we [were] called on to do it [i.e. fly with a squadron], the chances are we were going to get killed'.[158]

The rest of the day was spent patrolling in four-plane flights, some of which overlapped. At 1420 Joe Boulton in 'H' accompanied Jim Grady in 'D' for an area familiarisation flight that lasted until 1515. At 1910 Don Smith in '?' (a newly marked up NH 371) led the squadron, including the newly familiarised Jim Grady in 'J' on an armed recce on the route Falaise to Argentan then Domfront, Vire and Noyers. This was Lynch's first flight since his crash landing, and he had to return immediately after take-off due to a troublesome hood.[159] A lot of MET was seen, especially west of Conde. No large convoys were found but MET scattered throughout the area were attacked with claims made of one smoker, two flamers and five damaged. All planes returned safely by 2005.

30 July saw the arrival of F/O Edward Clason Gates (Service no. 409103). Born on 4 November 1922 in Elwood Victoria, Gates spent time in army cadets whilst at school, and he was a junior sales clerk at the time he enlisted in Melbourne on 19 July 1941. He was commissioned after earning his wings and was described as a 'very zealous young officer' by his commander at 3 Air Gunnery School (AGS). 453 Squadron was his first operational posting.[160]

There was discussion about setting up an aircrew mess and everyone put their minds to the task of finding the necessary equipment while the pilots went about the business of looking for Germans. The first sortie of the day took off at 0915, with S/Ldr Smith leading in '?'. Twelve Spitfires patrolled the Thury-Harcourt and Le Bény-Bocage areas, and a total of one smoker, one flamer and four damaged MET were claimed. Two aircraft returned early with assorted troubles, but the others returned on time at 1030. The afternoon was taken up by a series of overlapping front line high cover patrols, each by a flight of four aircraft. Each patrol was planned for 70-80 minutes' duration. The third patrol took off at 1500, led by Clarence Rice in 'E'. They saw what they believed to be an Allied bomber shot down by flak near Vire. The fourth patrol was led by Fred Cowpe in 'P' at 1600 after which the squadron stopped operations for dinner. Resuming operations again at 2005, Fred Cowpe led the patrol in 'P' once again, and they were replaced by the patrol led by Keith Daff in 'C', which returned at 2220 to complete the day's operations. Some heavy calibre flak was encountered south of Tilly-sur-Seulles but it was described as 'meagre'.[161] Perhaps the gunners were concerned about attracting too much attention to themselves.

On the last day of July, Don Smith took S/Ldr Hilton to B.14 at Amblie in the Auster and, from there, S/Ldr Hilton returned to the UK. The squadron diary records that they were very happy with his visit, and were certain that he could make a good case for the Australians when decisions were made that affected them. While the boss was away, Jack Olver led a patrol of twelve Spitfires on an armed recce circuit, taking the opportunity to fly '?' for himself. They took off at 0915 and completed a circuit of Pont L'Eveque to Lisieux then L'Aigle, Argentan, Falaise and Mezidon before returning home. The claims were one smoker, one flamer and three MET damaged. The afternoon's operations consisted of front line patrols. Three overlapping flights of six Spitfires took part, and another patrol took place after dinner at 2055, but all were uneventful.

During July 1944, the squadron dropped eighteen 500 lb and twelve 250 lb bombs.

Notes

1. Logbook–Harris.
2. Ayris and Leith, *Duty Done*, pp. 127, 129.
3. Ayris and Leith, *Duty Done*, p. 132.
4. Leith–Correspondence home 3 July 1944
5. Logbook–Lynch.
6. NAA: 11335 Z1
7. NAA: 11335 Z1
8. ORB–453 Sqn
9. Leith–Correspondence home 9 July 1944
10. NLA: Trove–'Spitfire Still World's Best says Australian' *Army News* 7 July 1944.
11. NLA: Trove–'Spitfire Men Want Opposition' *The Daily News* 6 July 1944.
12. ORB–453 Sqn and ORB–125 Wing
13. ORB–453 Sqn
14. Logbook–Baker.
15. OAFH: 1944_Misc Ref I.S.9/WEA/2/181/314
16. OAFH: 1944_Misc Ref I.S.9/WEA/2/181/314
17. Jean Brisset, *The Charge of the Bull: A History of the 11th British Armoured Division in Normandy 1944*, (transl. Tom Bates), Bates Books, Norwich, 1989, pp. 295-296.
18. Neil, *From the Cockpit: Spitfire*, p. 56.
19. OAFH: 1944_Misc Ref I.S.9/WEA/2/181/314
20. Brisset, *The Charge of the Bull*, pp. 296-297.
21. Logbook–Lynch.
22. ORB–602 Sqn for titles

23 ORB–453 Sqn
24 Thomas, *Osprey Aircraft of the Aces*: Volume 122, Spitfire Aces of Northwest Europe 1944–45, p. 46.
25 Brisset, *The Charge of the Bull*, pp. 298–300.
26 OAFH: 1944_Misc Ref I.S.9/WEA/2/181/314
27 Brisset, *The Charge of the Bull*, pp. 301–302.
28 Brisset, *The Charge of the Bull*, pp. 302–303.
29 Fax to Lebailley family from N Baker.
30 Herington, *Air Power Over Europe 1944–1945*, pp. 128, 306,467.
31 Brisset, *The Charge of the Bull*, pp. 305–309.
32 ORB–125 Wing July 1944
33 ORB–453 Sqn
34 Geoffrey Page, *Shot Down in Flames*, Grub Street, London, (1999), 2011, pp. 46, 89, 126, 137, 185.
35 ORB–125 Wing July 1944
36 Uncredited: 'R.A.A.F. Spitfires in at the Kill' in RAAF Saga, RAAF Directorate of Public Relations, Australian War Memorial, Canberra, 1944, p. 23.
37 ORB–453 Sqn
38 Speech by Norman Baker to Melbourne Legacy, '453 Spitfire Squadron–UK and Europe–Reminiscences', 4 September 1990.
39 ORB–453 Sqn
40 Speech by Norman Baker to Melbourne Legacy, '453 Spitfire Squadron–UK and Europe–Reminiscences', 4 September 1990.
41 NAA: A11335, Z1
42 NAA: A11335, Z1
43 NAA: A11335, Z1
44 NAA: A11335, Z1
45 NAA: A11335, Z1
46 NAA: A11335, Z1
47 NAA: A11335, Z1
48 NAA: A11335, Z1
49 NLA: Trove–'R.A.A.F. Airmen Rout Nazi Fighters' *Sydney Morning Herald* 11 July 1944
50 NLA: Trove–'Local Spitfire Pilot' *Sunshine Advocate* 14 July 1944.
51 Logbook–Lynch.
52 Hastings, *Overlord: D-Day and The Battle for Normandy*, p. 123.

53 ORB–125 Wing
54 ORB–453 Sqn
55 Logbook–Harris.
56 Personal file–Lyall.
57 ORB–453 Sqn
58 *Exclusive Brethren: The RAAF in Rhodesia and Beyond*–Ray Jackson (ed) and Logbook–Lyall.
59 ORB–132 Sqn
60 Cowpe–*Sequel to D Day*, p. 3.
61 NAA: A11335, Z1
62 Logbook–Cowpe
63 ORB–132 Sqn
64 ORB–125 Wing
65 Robinard, et al, *50 aerodromes pour une victorie Juin-Septembre 1944*, p. 275.
66 ORB–441 Sqn
67 ORB–132 Sqn
68 ORB–125 Wing
69 ORB–602 Sqn
70 ORB–125 Wing
71 Olver files–BBC transcripts July 1944
72 Logbook–Lynch.
73 Logbook–Olver
74 NLA: Trove–'Spitfire's Delight' Darwin *Army News* Wed 19 July 1944
75 Logbook–Harris.
76 Leith–Correspondence home 17 July 1944
77 Logbook–Cowpe
78 ORB–453 Sqn
79 Shores and Thomas, *2nd Tactical Air Force: Volume 4 Squadrons, Camouflage and Markings, Weapons and Tactics 1943–1945*, p. 607.
80 Hastings, *Overlord: D-Day and The Battle for Normandy*, p. 176.
81 NLA: Trove 'Medical Miracle if Rommel Still Alive; Shot up in Normandy' *Barrier Miner* 3 Aug 1944 and 'Rommel's Wounds' *Sydney Morning Herald* 31 July 1944.
82 Robson, *The Spitfire Pocket Manual*, p.10.
83 Thomas, *Osprey Aircraft of the Aces*: Volume 122, Spitfire Aces of Northwest Europe 1944–45, p.48.
84 McRoberts, *Lions Rampant: The Story of 602 Spitfire Squadron*, pp. 203–204 and

Glancey, *Spitfire: The Biography*, p. 124 and Thomas, *Osprey Aircraft of the Aces*: Volume 122, Spitfire Aces of Northwest Europe 1944–45, p. 47.

85   NLA: Trove –'British Air Ace Missing' *Northern Star* 19 March 1952

86   NLA: Trove– 'Killed Rommel' *Army News* 25 October 1944

87   Franks, *Royal Air Force Command Losses of the Second World War Volume 3: 1944–1945*, p. 62 and Christopher Shores and Chris Thomas, *2nd Tactical Air Force: Volume 2 Breakout to Bodenplatte, July 1944 to January 1945*, Classic Publications, Surrey, 2005, p. 222.

88   Cowpe–*Sequel to D Day*, p.4. and Temora Interview–Fred Cowpe.

89   *Exclusive Brethren: The RAAF in Rhodesia and Beyond*–Ray Jackson (ed).

90   ORB–453 Sqn

91   ORB–453 Sqn

92   Logbook–Cowpe

93   Logbook–Cowpe

94   Ramsey, Winston G. (ed), 'It Happened Here: Rommel's Accident', *After The Battle*, No. 8, 1975, 42–45, pp. 42–44.

95   Roger Ford, *Fire From The Forest: The SAS Brigade in France, 1944*, Cassell, London, (2003), 2004, pp. 148–151.

96   Hastings, *Overlord: D-Day and The Battle for Normandy*, pp. 173–174 and Samuel W. Mitcham, Jr, *German Order of Battle Volume One: 1st–290th Infantry Divisions in WWII*, Stackpole, Mechanicsburg, 2007, pp. 131, 287.

97   Hastings, *Overlord: D-Day and The Battle for Normandy*, pp. 302, 307–308.

98   Beevor, *The Second World War*, p. 460.

99   Ian Daglish, *Over the Battlefield: Operation Goodwood*, Pen & Sword, Barnsley, 2005, pp. 14–19.

100   ORB–125 Wing

101   Logbook–Lynch.

102   ORB–453 Sqn'

103   Logbook–Lynch.

104   ORB–453 Sqn

105   Logbook–Olver

106   Logbook–Harris.

107   Daglish, *Over the Battlefield: Operation Goodwood*, p. 204.

108   ORB–602 Sqn

109   ORB–125 Wing

110   NLA: Trove–'When Australians gate-crashed Churchill's Ship' *The Newcastle Sun* 25

July 1944 and 'Australian Airmen meet Mr Churchill' *The Argus* 26 July 1944 and Leith-Correspondence home 25 July 1944
111 Logbook-Harris.
112 Shores, and Thomas, *2nd Tactical Air Force: Volume 4 Squadrons, Camouflage and Markings, Weapons and Tactics 1943-1945*, p. 638.
113 Personal File-Kinross
114 Ayris and Leith, *Duty Done*, pp. 135-137.
115 Personal File-Kinross
116 ORB-125 Wing.
117 AWFA: Russell Leith
118 Logbook-Leith
119 NAA: A11335, Z1
120 NAA: A11335, Z1
121 Logbook-Lynch.
122 ORB-453 Sqn and NAA File A705 166/25/178
123 Logbook-Lynch.
124 NAA File A705 166/25/178-Lynch crash
125 Hastings, *Overlord: D-Day and The Battle for Normandy*, p. 253.
126 Herington, *Air Power Over Europe 1944-1945*, pp. 228, 231.
127 453 ORB and Ayris and Leith, *Duty Done*, p. 136, Cowpe-*Sequel to D Day* p.3 and Logbook-Harris.
128 Personal File-Seeney
129 NAA: A11335, Z1
130 Logbook-Cowpe
131 Cowpe-*Sequel to D Day*, p.4. NAA File A11335 154/56/P1 quotes 20 gallons.
132 NAA: A11335, Z1
133 NAA: A11335, Z1
134 NAA: A11335, Z1
135 Logbook-Olver
136 Cowpe-*Sequel to D Day*, p.4.
137 ORB-453 Sqn and NAA: 11335 Z1.
138 Dowding Personal file and NAA: A11335, 154/56/P1.
139 AWFA: Russell Leith
140 Ayris and Leith, *Duty Done*, pp. 139-179.
141 ORB-453 Sqn and NAA Files A705 166/26/526 and NAA File A11335 154/57/P1
142 ORB-453 Sqn and Cowpe-*Sequel to D Day*, p. 5.

143　NAA: A705, 166/26/526
144　Cowpe–*Sequel to D Day*, p. 5. and Temora Interview–Fred Cowpe.
145　Temora Interview–Fred Cowpe and Unpublished Memoir–Fred Cowpe.
146　453 ORB and Cowpe–Sequel to D Day, p. 5.
147　Temora Interview–Fred Cowpe.
148　Personal File–Grady
149　Cowpe–Sequel to D Day, p. 5.
150　Temora Interview–Fred Cowpe.
151　Temora Interview–Sir Brian Inglis.
152　Cowpe–*Sequel to D Day*, p. 5.
153　Cowpe–*Sequel to D Day*, p. 5.
154　Logbook–Cowpe
155　Logbook–Olver
156　Logbook - Sargeant
157　Interview with Author–Handsaker
158　Interview with Author–Handsaker
159　Logbook–Lynch.
160　Personal File–Gates
161　ORB–453 Sqn

AUGUST 1944

August started quietly and, while the pilots were flying their sorties, the ground and admin staff spent time trying to source materials to build an Officer's and Sergeant's Mess. 132 Squadron beat 453 to it and had theirs up and running on 1 August.[1] The flight orders for the day were for high patrols. The first of four flights took off at 1525, led by Fred Cowpe in 'P'. A damaged Liberator was seen to head out over the Channel from the Orne and orbit to port, two crew successfully bailing out in the vicinity of B.4 at Beny-sur-Mer once the plane was back over land. The ultimate fate of the plane was not witnessed. This flight was overlapped by the next, and others in turn until the end of the day, with the exception of one late recce which turned back early due to bad weather.

2 August brought more bad weather (or 'Hun weather' some called it[2]), all the better for the Germans to move around in (i.e. retreat), without fear of harassment by 2TAF. The weather cleared in the afternoon and twelve Spitfires led by Don Smith in '?' took off at 1410 for an armed recce in the vicinity of Falaise and Domfront, though someone managed to drop their centreline 500 lb bomb on the runway when taking off. The pilots were glad to be taking off—they'd been on standby since 0615. The squadron was divided into three flights of four, one section being all bombed-up and the other sections having two aircraft with bombs and two without.[3] At 1500

twelve Me-109s were seen near Tinchebray flying west at 3.000-4,000 ft. Jim Ferguson was in the section that dived down on them from 7,000-8,000 ft and was the only one to make a claim, stating that he damaged one of them.

From the Personal Combat Report signed by Jim Ferguson who probably flew 'U' (though the squadron record is incomplete) in which he claimed one Me-109 damaged:

> I was flying as Red 2 at 7,000 ft on an Armed Recce when Red 1 reported 12 plus Me 109's almost directly below us at 1,000 ft. We dived to attack and the e/a who were flying line abreast dived to deck level. I attacked one e/a from line astern and when at 700 yds I gave a 3 secs burst but did not see any strikes. I then gave another long burst and this time observed strikes on the starboard wing root and saw a large object which I thought might be the hood fall off the e/a. I gave another burst of 3 secs. Again from line astern, but saw no strikes. I had to discontinue the engagement as my No. 1 broke away from the e/a. which he was chasing. I claim 1 Me 109 damaged.[4]

Another friendly fire incident took place, this time involving 602 Squadron when a section they had airborne was bounced by four Mustangs. As 453 had done in the incident with Kinross on 24 July, the Spitfires of 602 did their best to show off their distinct shape, but this did not alert any of the American pilots and they opened fire. The Spitfires of 602 headed back to B.11 as fast as they could,[5] with no losses from the incident. Strafing and bombing took place over a wide area, and claims of one MET flamer, one smoker and six damaged were made. Jack Olver did particularly well and recorded: 'Blew car off road with bombs—strafed 2 others one flamer one smoker'.[6] One 500 lb bomb and four 250 lbers were dropped on three tanks, but the best that could be claimed was a near miss. One 500 lb had to be dropped in the Channel before the sortie returned, the last planes landing at 1525.

The second sortie was carried out in the evening, an armed recce in the Lisieux, Alençon, Mayenne and Domfront areas. MET were sighted all over, but only in small numbers. A total of three flamers, eight smokers and five damaged MET were claimed. F/O Vargas of 125 Wing Intelligence Section, reported to 453 Squadron as the appointed Intelligence Officer, this new position having been created for the squadron. Any hope of administrative assistance was quickly dashed when they were informed that he was to work with the Wing, rather than look after the concerns of 453, just as he was doing shortly before arriving at the squadron.

The keen eyes of 132 Squadron discovered German midget submarines in the Orne estuary on 3 August and this set the camp into action again, reviving the excitement of the first rumoured counter-landing and everyone was on the lookout for saboteurs. The first four sorties of the day were overlapping low cover patrols, each carried out by a flight of four Spitfires. The first and second patrols witnessed some naval action—depth-charging off the mouth of the Orne River, by a MTB during the first patrol and by a corvette during the second. The third and fourth patrols were uneventful and the Luftwaffe was a no-show.

Marshal of the Royal Air Force, Lord Trenchard, talking to Squadron Leader Smith with other pilots on parade. They had just returned from an armed recce, during which they claimed 22 MET damaged. (Courtesy of the Olver family)

At 1630 Don Smith in '?' led a formation of twelve Spitfires on an armed recce around Domfront and Argentan. Jim Lynch was pretty happy, having been told that 'B' was now his plane. His R/T went out of service shortly after taking off, but he stayed with Keith Daff and had 'great fun' strafing vehicles.[7] Some MET were seen headed south from Laval and Evron, but no large convoys were sighted. That didn't mean they weren't valid targets though, and there was no point trying to bring their bombs home, so the Spitfires went down, dropping 500 lb and 250 lb bombs and strafing with cannon and machine guns, leaving wrecks scattered across their patrol area. Total claims were ten MET flamers, two smokers and seven damaged. The squadron diary records that two pilots landed safely at airfield A.10 Carentan, including Lynch, who was short of fuel.[8] All planes returned by 1800—just in time for the visit by Lord Trenchard, Marshal of the Royal Air Force, who met with some of the pilots. The visit was reported in the Newcastle Morning Herald and Miners' Advocate on 5 August, with Lord Trenchard being quoted as saying to the pilots of 453: 'I am looking forward to seeing you in Berlin.'[9]

4 August was a busy day, with 36 sorties flown in total. The pilots were able to observe some of the Allied advance in action and were happy with what they saw. The first sortie of twelve Spitfires was led by Don Smith in '?' and took off at 1115. Unfortunately, Jim Lynch was hit by flak shortly after take-off. He didn't think he would make it back to safety, but was escorted by Mick West before crash landing just on the Allies' side of the front lines at Le Bény-Bocage. Lynch was slightly injured, enough to be taken off flying and admitted to hospital. This was the second time he'd been hit by flak in less than two weeks, and the squadron diary noted: 'evidently he is an attraction for flak.'[10] He was later evacuated to an advanced dressing station for treatment.[11] Despite writing off another plane and being injured again, Lynch was more concerned that he would lose his place in the squadron because of injuries—and that's exactly what happened. He was flown to

England on 13 August and didn't fly again until 30 September, when he was posted to 83 GSU again, to await a squadron posting.[12]

The rest of the aircraft continued and patrolled the Flers, Mortain, Sille (Sille-le-Guillaume), Alençon and Falaise areas. There was not much out on the roads, but what was seen was usually headed southeast, trying to get out of Normandy. Sightings included a number of ambulances, which, despite the pilots doubting their authenticity, were not attacked. Accurate heavy-calibre flak was encountered at Thury-Harcourt. A number of horse-drawn vehicles, including some up to truck size were seen as well. Claims for the sortie totalled one MET flamer, three smokers, and one damaged. Though strikes were noted on a tank during the sortie no claim was made against it.

In the afternoon, three flights of four were sent up to patrol the area from Tilly to Cabourg. The first was led by Clarence Rice in 'G' from 1355 to 1500 with nothing of interest noted. The second took off at 1715 and was led by Fred Cowpe in 'U'. They were left one short when Merv Watson had to return early in 'F' but the three others continued, and sighted two FW-190s south of Caen, flying at about 1,000 ft. Not wanting to be the ones to let them get away, the three remaining Spitfires dove down from 10,000 ft, but the rapid descent resulted in their windscreens fogging up and they had to break off the attack. They returned very disappointed. Two more patrols were flown that day but no Germans were found, the second being cut short by poor weather.

That same day, two new pilots arrived from 83 GSU: Warrant Officers Mace (Service no. 414808) and Taylor (Service no. 413620). William Wentworth Mace was born on 17 March 1922 in the country town of Moree in New South Wales. He gave up his job as a grazier when he enlisted in Brisbane on 9 November 1941 and was sent to No 8 ITS Sandgate. He completed his EFTS in Australia and the remainder of his basic flying training in Canada. He left Halifax in March 1944 and completed his PDRC and OTU in the UK.[13] Unlike William Mace, Clifford Alan Murray Taylor completed his EFTS and SFTS in Australia, at Benalla and Uranquinty. He was born on 20 March 1921 and, at the time of enlisting on 12 September 1941, lived in Hurstville, New South Wales and worked as a bank clerk. In October 1942, Taylor left Sydney for the UK and completed his training there, after the mandatory refresher on Tiger Moths.[14] 453 Squadron was the first posting to a front-line squadron for both of them. Though the date of the entry is not known and, considering the content, it may have been made after the war, Taylor's logbook does have a very interesting comment about his gunnery school for the start of July 1944. It reads:

> Note on Hutton Cranswick:—probably the biggest bludge in the history of my service career, rather be on ops just the same.[15]

All the strafing and bombing by the squadrons of the Wing (453, 132, 602 and now 441) had resulted in total claims of over 1,000 MET flamers, smokers or damaged since D-Day. The total ticked over the 1,000 mark on 4 August thanks to the efforts of 441 (RCAF) Squadron.[16]

Weather was poor again on 5 August, with a heavy mist over the area and the squadrons had to wait for it to clear before commencing operations. However, at about 1000, a Dakota crashed onto the airfield and went up in flames,[17] the pilot perhaps unable to get his bearings, but definitely unable to judge the plane's height in the heavy mist. The location of B.11 so close to a cliff would not have helped, even if they pilot knew where he was. The weather did not clear up until 1700. The single sortie took off at 1725 with Don Smith leading in '?'. The circuit was around Falaise, Argentan and Alençon. Spotting three trucks was as juicy a target as any, and one section dived down on them from 6,000 ft while the rest remained above as cover. They gave them their full load of bombs—four 500 lb and eight 250 lb, dropped from 2,000 ft, leaving the pilots enough room to pull out and recover, while giving the rudder a kick to get that extra lateral movement on the way out of the dive to throw off any possible AA fire. All three trucks were destroyed. The squadron noted an oil fire in the main street of Mayenne and a lot of MET were seen around Conde, as were some horse-drawn MET elsewhere. Other claims for the sortie were three smokers and six damaged. The last aircraft returned at 1905.

At the conclusion of the day's flying, 602 Squadron launched 'Operation Getsumin' at their mess, named, the 'Getsumin Inn'[18] and Don Smith was invited to the opening. 453 still had not yet completed their mess, though the CO had attracted attention with his carpentry skills.

The squadron almost had a full rest day on 6 August, only putting up one sortie of twelve Spitfires at 1500. They covered Yvetot, Bernay and Lisieux but struggled with cloud and lack of MET and returned empty handed at 1630. The evening saw the arrival of F/O Adams (410204) from 83 GSU. Before joining the RAAF on 5 December 1941, Nevin Russell Adams, of Kerang, Victoria, had worked as a bank clerk and was studying accountancy by correspondence. He commenced his training at 4 ITS Victor Harbour and left for Canada in July 1942 where he continued his flying training before being shipped to the UK in April 1944. 453 Squadron was his first operational posting.[19]

Morning flying on 7 August was hampered by a sea mist, but at 1220 an armed recce of 12 planes, led by Don Smith in '?', flew the circuit Mezidon to Falaise then Argentan, Flers and Conde, returning with claims of six flamers, two smokers and ten damaged, as well as one claim of an armoured car damaged. Two Marauders were seen to crash in flames five miles southwest of Lisieux, and intense and accurate heavy calibre flak was encountered near Pont L'Eveque but the Spitfires returned unscathed.

The afternoon sortie was an armed recce in the area of Mortain, Argentan and Falaise. Twelve Spitfires took off at 1715 led by Don Smith in '?'. They patrolled the area of Argentan and Falaise and saw few targets, though Wehrmacht bicycle troops and horse-drawn transport were seen.

There was intense light and heavy flak encountered throughout the sortie, and at some stage Ed Gates in 'A' was hit, but no radio message was received from him and apparently no one saw him go down. He was in a section of four Spitfires led by Daff, who had attacked a staff car along a road about 10 miles northwest of Falaise. Two members of the section ran low on fuel and returned to base, leaving Daff and Gates together. Daff saw an AA position during an attack and called a warning to Gates not to follow him down, but there was no reply. Daff climbed to circle the area and called on the R/T a number of times, asking him if he was ok but there was no reply and, before long, Daff also had to return.[20] The sortie resulted in claims of five flamers, one smoker and three damaged. Ed Gates was not found and is commemorated on the Runnymede Memorial in Surrey, United Kingdom.[21]

Three armed recces were flown on 8 August. In fact, the whole Wing was tasked for this mission type, and the pilots were grateful to be on the hunt,[22] rather than patrolling for the Luftwaffe, which they knew would almost certainly not show. The first was at 1055, with Don Smith in '?' leading a full squadron of twelve from Alençon to Flers then Falaise and Argentan. Don Smith was credited with a tank kill using his cannon on a Panzer Mk III, which was once the mainstay of Panzer formations but was now only a light tank in relative terms, its gun and armour preventing it from making significant contributions to the large armoured clashes of 1944. A storage dump, something quite rare to be found in the German retreat, was shot up and left alight, while MET claims totalled six flamers, one smoker and seven damaged.

The second sortie was again led by Don Smith in '?' and they took off at 1520, this time on the hunt in the area of Bernay, Argentan and Falaise. Some flak was encountered and only scattered MET were seen, with claims of six flamers, two smokers and five damaged. Once again a suspected supply dump was left smoking. Jack Steward in 'P' encountered mechanical trouble towards the end of the sortie and had to land at B.6 Coulombs before returning to Longues. He was lucky to miss out on the remainder of the sortie as, at 1620 when near Falaise, the squadron was bounced by a flight of four Spitfires from 412 Squadron RCAF,[23] who were identified by their two-letter identification code painted on the aircraft—VZ. Fortunately no-one was shot down, and all were safely back at Longues by 1640, no thanks to the Canadians!

The afternoon of 8 August saw the arrival of F/O Norman John Marsh (Service no. 11362) from 83 GSU in the afternoon. His service number was different from the standard pilot's six-digit number due to the fact that his initial mustering upon enlistment was as a stores clerk. Marsh was born on 27 July 1921 and joined the RAAF on 26 July 1940, but remustered as aircrew in October 1941. He did some of his flying training in Canada, spending time at an OTU on Hurricanes, before being sent to the UK and training at a Spitfire OTU. 453 Squadron was his first operational posting.[24]

Don Smith led the last sortie of the day in '?', taking off with eleven others at 2040 for the Mezidon, Argentan, Flers and Falaise areas. Haze hindered their ability to spot targets and they returned at 2150 claiming only one MET flamer and one smoker.

G/Cpt Rankin announced the award of two immediate DFCs to Don Smith and Vern Lancaster on the morning of 9 August, and the squadron was justifiably proud. Midget submarines featured again on this day, this time allegedly accompanied by human torpedoes, in the mouth of the River Seine. Human torpedoes were used in various theatres of war and normally ridden by frogmen to their target. Six Spitfires took off at 0745 but were beaten to the punch by the navy, the pilots of 453 arriving to see two corvettes engaging two midget submarines 10-15 miles northeast of the Orne. One explosion was seen, and they witnessed three downed pilots—whom they believed to be American—get picked up by a corvette also.

Just as the pilots and ground crew were preparing for the afternoon sortie, a message arrived announcing that the Wing was released from flying duties until 1300 the next day, guaranteeing that everyone could get some rest.²⁵ This suited the men of 453 perfectly, they could afford to have a drink to celebrate the awarding of the DFCs.

On 10 August, the pilots rested and recovered, knowing they had the morning off and the one patrol in the afternoon, led by Don Smith in '?' was a fighter sweep to Dreux at 10,000 ft. Two planes landed at another ALG on the way back as they were short of fuel. After just one 'rest' day the squadron diary noted that 'It looked as though the war had passed us by'.²⁶ That evening they were reminded that it had not when a Luftwaffe raid attacked the fleet off the coast nearby and the squadron was treated to an impressive display of AA fire, the tracer rounds arcing up into the night sky from the vessels.

The squadron had now been at Longues for nearly seven weeks and, on 11 August, orders to move arrived, though unfortunately the mess was not yet complete. The morning sorties consisted of three overlapping front line patrols, each by a flight of four aircraft. The patrols were led by Clarence Rice in 'G', followed by Fred Cowpe in 'S' and then Jim Ferguson in 'H'. G/Cpt Daly RAAF visited in the afternoon and saw firsthand the conditions and situation of the Australians. The squadron staff spoke freely with him, and thought that they would be well represented when he returned to London.

The afternoon patrol took off, led by Keith Daff in 'C' on a circuit of Cabourg to Le Bény-Bocage. The weather was poor and nothing was seen. Two Spitfires had to land at B.9 Creully due to the weather. At 1625 Joshua Scott in 'R' took new arrival, Norm Marsh, in 'S' for a familiarity flight so he could get to know the area a little and they returned safely at 1750.

The sea fog made another appearance on the morning of 12 August, and did not clear until 0900. At 1140 a sortie of twelve Spitfires led by Vern Lancaster in 'D', was sent up to the River Seine, about 30 miles northwest of Paris, near Mantes-Gasicourt, to finish off what 132 Squadron had reported as barges. 132 Squadron got a head start, having taken off at 1115 to bomb and strafe the barges and were met by a high volume of flak defending the crossing points that the Germans were using to get out of Normandy.[27] They had not left much for 453, but twelve 500 lb and twenty-three 250 lb bombs were dropped on 10–12 barges in the river. An odd number of bombs were dropped because someone had a 250 lb bomb hang up under one of the wings and could not shake it loose. Two possible direct hits were claimed with the bombs, and the barges got a good going over with cannon fire as well.[28] The 250 lb bomb would have had an unbalancing effect on the plane and, of course anyone with a bomb left had to land last, because if there was an accident, then the runway could possibly be blocked or damaged and prevent the rest from landing. All went well, however, and the squadron landed safely at 1250. The new base for the squadron was to be B.19 at Lingèvres, just 12 miles away on the other side of Bayeux. While the pilots were flying, the ground staff concentrated on packing and preparing to move.

13 August was the day of the move, there would be no on-again, off-again as there had been for the moves to B.11. The pilots flew directly to B.19 and the remainder drove, leaving shortly after the planes. Everyone was on site at the new location in time for a late lunch. The landing strip was 5,000 ft long but very dusty, as were the roads around the site, and a bit of rain was wished for to settle it all down. The squadrons and facilities were also more widely dispersed than they had been at B.11,[29] making for a less crowded area, and consequently a less inviting target.

Two sorties were flown in the afternoon. The first was for twelve Spitfires led by Vern Lancaster in 'H' for an armed recce in the vicinity of Flers and Argentan. They found only scattered MET targets, but nevertheless returned at 1415 with claims of three flamers and one smoker. It was noted that the bridge at Putanges was intact and a number of Panther tanks were seen but not engaged, though the intel relating to the bridge and Panthers was passed on. The second afternoon sortie took off at 1700,

View of the land where B.19 was located. The view is from the southeast of the area occupied by the airstrip looking towards the northwest. (Author)

the formation of twelve being led by Don Smith in 'L'. Two planes returned at 1730, one escorting the other for safety and the other ten continued on the armed recce of Falaise to Conde and Flers, returning at 1820 with claims of one armoured vehicle damaged, one MET flamer and three damaged. A lot of flak positions were seen southwest of Athis[30] and the flak encountered was intense, accurate, light calibre stuff, but everyone returned safely.

Regular patrols were flown on the morning of 14 August, with eight overlapping two-plane patrols of the front line area between Cabourg and Le Bény-Bocage, each lasting 70-90 minutes. The first took off at 0950 and the last returned at 1750. All were uneventful, however Fred Cowpe had to crash-land 'S' wheels-up upon his return from the 0950 sortie. He recorded in his logbook: 'Had to land with undercarriage retracted. Very pleased as it was a lousy a/c.'[31] Things livened up in the afternoon with twelve Spitfires, led by Vern Lancaster in 'H' taking off at 1930 for dive-bombing and an armed recce. Vern had to return shortly after take-off, but the remainder continued on, dive-bombing a chateau in the Evreaux area believed to be a petrol, oil and lubricants dump by the way it exploded after a number of direct hits. The dive was not too long, from 5,000 ft down to 3,000 ft with plenty of time to pull out and, all up, the chateau was on the receiving end of eleven 500 lb bombs and twice as many 250 lb bombs. On the way back they claimed one MET smoker and another damaged, and all returned by 2045. Don Smith and Mick West left for seven days' leave in the afternoon and, therefore, missed this final show.

That evening the ALG was bombed by a single Luftwaffe aircraft at about 2230. The aircraft appeared to be in trouble, so it's not clear if B.19 was the intended target or if the pilot just needed to get rid of the bombs to lighten the plane, but they landed in the domestic area for 453 crew. There was a lot of AA fire and the sounds of the aircraft carrying out evasive manoeuvres before the familiar sound of a plane diving and then the bombs came down. One bomb landed near the CO's tent (shredding it) and the Officer's Mess, while a second landed near the Sergeant's Mess. The third landed near, but not next to, the Sergeant's living area. Not having sufficient warning to take cover, the squadron suffered a number of casualties. Merv Watson was killed, and P/O Cross suffered a penetrating wound from behind, through a buttock and up into his intestines. Joe Boulton was also seriously wounded, with a fractured right femur. Herb Watts was slightly wounded in the right shoulder, and two ground crew of 6453 Servicing Echelon were also wounded: Sgt Coates with a penetrating wound in the right thigh and shrapnel in both arms, and LAC Marchant with a shrapnel wound in the buttock. All were evacuated to 20th General Hospital.[32] The squadron was saddened by the sudden loss of Watson and deprivation of three other pilots, whose outlook was not yet certain. Cross was injured so badly he required a colostomy and his condition worsened in the first weeks after his initial surgery, requiring a swift transfer to the UK. His condition fluctuated over the following months and, at times, it was thought he might not make it. It was not until mid-December that his condition finally stabilised, but his war was over.[33]

The morning of 15 August was spent organising the funeral for Merv Watson, who was buried in the early afternoon at Hottot-les-Bagues, now a Commonwealth War Graves Commission cemetery. The funeral was led by the Wing Padre and the press were represented by F/Lt Andrews, the RAAF Public Relations Officer. In a letter to the family, Vern Lancaster, acting as Squadron Leader in the absence of Don Smith, wrote: 'The loss of Mervyn has deprived the Squadron of one of the finest types of young manhood one could wish to have in a squadron.'[34] The Luftwaffe usually sent out about 50 raiders per night,[35] hoping to score a hit on some target of value, what with Normandy being full of Allied troops and equipment, including the large Mulberry harbours. They only had around five hours of darkness to do this, and, despite having to contend with the Mosquito night fighters flying intruder sorties, on this occasion the Germans had been lucky.

The grave of Warrant Officer Mervyn John Watson at Hottot-les-Bagues. (Author)

The first sortie of 15 August took off at 0905 and was led by Jack Olver in 'U'. Eleven Spitfires headed for the Vimoutiers area, a mass of MET target having been spotted by an early patrol from 602 Squadron. 453 set off for the nominated area, but could not find the large group previously reported[36] and so attacked targets of opportunity with bombs and strafing. Two crossroads were attacked, causing cratering of the road, and some bombs were dropped near Vimoutiers also, but no results were observed. The claims for the sortie were one MET flamer and one damaged.

The next sortie was led by Vern Lancaster in 'H', twelve Spitfires bombed-up and hunting in the region of Bernay to Gace. Not a lot of moving targets were seen, but many vehicles were located hiding under trees or camouflaged, and they were on the receiving end of numerous 250 lb and 500 lb bombs. MET claims amounted to one flamer, two smokers and two damaged and armoured fighting vehicle (AFV) claims were two flamers and two smokers. The record keeper for that day must not have heard Sargeant make his report, for his logbook reads: 'Dive-bombed tank or armoured car—direct hit destroyed. Little flak.'.[37]

The last sortie of the day was an armed recce around the Bernay area, which was led by Jack Olver in '?'. Twelve Spitfires took off at 1810 and pickings were slim. At 1915 all had returned with a total claim of one armoured truck flamer (perhaps a halftrack), one truck damaged and one dispatch rider, in the words of the squadron diary, 'destroyed'.[38] Soldiers on motorcycles were hardly a match for a Spitfire—much less twelve—but they were valid targets, often carrying messages between headquarters and units in the field, or checking the way ahead for convoys. Stopping the rider stopped the message, or created disruption or confusion for a convoy.

There was a big storm in the evening, and any unpatched holes in tents soon drew the attention of their occupants.

Sorties commencing at 0650 on the morning of 16 August were uneventful. Four patrols of two planes took off at planned overlapping times, but weather issues dictated that two planes ended up at B.11 and two others at B.14 Banville. Fred Cowpe in 'T' and Ken Wilson in 'Z' were flying one of the 0750 sorties and knew they couldn't get back to B.19 (Lingèvres) and didn't have enough fuel to make it across the Channel, so they tried for B.11. Cowpe was worried about running into barrage balloons and the Royal Navy, whom he believed would shoot at anyone. Things were looking a bit doubtful, but he was in a Spitfire and, as he said in a later interview: 'It had no vices, it was perfection'. With confidence in his plane—but not his blue-water comrades-in-arms—he and Wilson got their planes down safely, using the balloon barrage at Arromanches as a navigational aid, as it was sticking up through the mist.[39] They notified B.19 that they were ok, though Cowpe left out the part about using only the second half of the runway to get his plane down.[40]

When they returned to Lingèvres there was a briefing, and he was asked to take Jim Ferguson's place in the afternoon sortie, as Ferguson was sick. They were ready to go but the weather held them back and Group had decided they would wait until it cleared up and go later rather than cancel the sortie altogether. At 1640 they were off, Cowpe in 'U' this time as Blue 1, and with Vern Lancaster in 'D' leading the way, ten Spitfires in all. Cowpe later said had a premonition that something wasn't right and admitted that 'everything felt strange'. His uneasy feeling made him feel that he shouldn't go, but he wasn't going to let his mates down.[41] They headed for the Flers-Falaise area and found scattered—but mostly stationary—MET apparently all headed in the same direction, trying to get out of Normandy.

On one attack on three trucks, Cowpe was diving down with his No. 2 only, having told 3 and 4 to stay up, when he was hit by flak on the port side. The plane immediately started to climb and he thought he would trim it down a bit but, when he reached for the controls, all he found was a hole in the side of the cockpit. He took a quick bearing off the sun and turned to head back to Lingèvres. Looking down again, he saw that his legs were shot up and bleeding, and decided he would land at the first emergency strip he found; Lingèvres could wait. He moved his legs gently, pushing the rudder bars, and found that everything seemed to be ok.[42]

In preparation for an emergency landing, he tightened his harness and made sure he was strapped in as tight as he could be, because otherwise he knew he'd be kissing the gunsight with his face when he came down. He locked the hood back, making sure that it couldn't slide forward and jam on impact, potentially trapping him in a fiery coffin. He also tested the door[43] to make sure that would open too—this didn't need to be any harder than it was already. He wasn't feeling any pain and was focused on getting back when the plane caught fire. He couldn't remember if Carpiquet was in Allied hands—he knew that there had been a lot of fighting there but the flames brought searing pain with them and he was finding it hard to concentrate. He pulled out his R/T and oxygen plugs so he wouldn't be hooked into the plane when it came time to get out—assuming that he could—he didn't want anything to slow him down. Checking himself over again, he saw that his harness on the left side was shredded, as if it had been 'chewed by rats'. His parachute was starting to burn, so there was definitely no bailing out. The flames climbed upwards and out of the open canopy as the Spitfire roared along, there was no real hope of a happy ending to the sortie, so he concentrated on getting down and pushed the joystick forward. He had to get down to safety and out of the fire.[44]

Parachuting out of a plane was dangerous business at any time and, while they carried them every flight, fighter pilots didn't actually do parachute training like the paratroopers in the army did,[45] the wings they wore were for flying, not jumping. Parachutes also had a dangerous habit of getting caught on the plane itself, and 441 (RCAF) Squadron lost two pilots when bailing out in June—one pilot's parachute catching on the tail wheel, and the others catching on the tail. The pilots became stuck and the planes took both pilots down with them. There was no recovery from accidents like those.[46] Cowpe knew he had to land and was starting to black out, slowly, as he described it: 'Like turning off a dimmer switch' and he thought: 'I'm gone, all this for nothing'[47] when the pain stopped. He was later informed that, when your nerves are burned out, there's nothing to pass the pain on. His airspeed was still fast at 240 mph and he had to try and slow down as best he could, but speed be damned and down he went, somehow managing a wheels-up crash landing at B.17 Carpiquet near the demolished hangars. All his preparations had not been in vain, however, and he managed to get out of the plane. He saw that his left flying glove was black—he'd been trying to beat out the flames with his left hand while flying with his right.[48] He didn't think the glove was of any use anymore so he pulled it off, but a lot of skin from his hand went with it, and the pain returned with a vengeance. His side was charred; he wouldn't be flying again for some time.[49] A doctor came over to him and began to talk but Fred passed out. He'd made it. When he woke up, he was in an ambulance with others on stretchers and he knew his war was over. He suffered second degree burns and was taken to 121 General Hospital. When Don Smith learned of the full circumstances of Fred's landing he recommended him for a medal, but it wasn't awarded.[50]

Claims for the sortie were one MET flamer, two smokers and four damaged and three A.M.C also damaged.

During the afternoon, three replacements arrived: F/Lt Bennett (Service no. 414189), F/O Cummins (Service no. 401368) and F/Sgt Pollock (Service no. 419337). William Bennett was born in South Africa on 11 July 1921 to Australian parents, but was educated in Brisbane and transferred to the RAF on 20 February 1940 after obtaining a transfer from his militia artillery unit. He arrived in the UK in January 1943 after his early flight training in Australia and had his first flight in a fighter on 5 March 1943, a Hurricane at 55 OTU in Annan, Scotland. He arrived at his first operational posting on 16 May 1943, 286 Squadron being equipped with Hurricanes and Boulton-Paul Defiants, both aircraft a bit behind the times in terms of fighter operations. While with 286 Squadron he, like many other fighter pilots, was sent to do commando training. Unlike many others, however, at the completion of his training he did not return to his squadron, but was selected for operations and participated in a raid on a radar station near Wissant. Far from being excited about the supposed glamour and daring often associated with the elite commandos, Bennett returned from the raid somewhat depressed about the mission, knowing that more German troops would be sent to replace the ones they had killed and another radar erected to replace the one they had destroyed. Of the experience he later said:

> My knife had killed one German soldier, my bullets had killed or wounded other members of their forces, but I felt no elation, no thrill of achievement from this thing I had done.

He had flown Spitfire Vs with 234 Squadron on 6 June, recording that he saw: 'the greatest air armada the world had yet seen'. From 6-8 June he logged 16 hours flying time and by the end of it recorded: 'my leather helmet is soggy with sweat, my eyes ache and itch from the strain of searching the sky around me, and my muscles are tortured by cramps'.[51] No doubt hundreds of other fighter pilots felt the same way, on that day and many since.

John Leslie Cummins was born on 28 August 1914 in Albury NSW and enlisted for the RAAF in Melbourne on 2 February 1941, having worked as an insurance agent up to that point. He completed his EFTS in Australia, went to Canada to complete his basic flight training and arrived in the UK in December 1941. After additional fighter training he went to the Middle East and flew with 87 Squadron and 450 (RAAF) Squadron on Kittyhawks. On his return to the UK, and prior to transferring to 453 Squadron, Cummins was a flying instructor at 1 TEU.[52]

Ronald James Pollock was born on 5 June 1917 and worked as a radio engineer when he joined the RAAF in July 1942. His ITS was at Somers and he completed his EFTS at Benalla. He completed his SFTS in Canada before serving with 186 and 130 Squadrons in the UK.[53]

Sgt Mills arrived as a replacement for Sgt McKinnon in the ground crew, who was due to be sent home to Australia under a scheme recently introduced by RAAF Overseas HQ.[54] It had been decided that the EATS was a great success but, after June 1944, no Australian pilots or wireless operators were to be sent to Canada for further training. All training was to be completed in Australia, which would naturally clog up and slow down the whole system. While this would have been disappointing to many, those

Australians who arrived in the UK after June 1944 didn't see combat in any case, as the PDRC at Brighton was almost overflowing with aircrew and there were few opportunities for them to be posted to operational squadrons. They were ready to be posted should a significant setback or unexpected massive casualties occur, but (fortunately) this did not eventuate. In the second half of 1944, a ground crew repatriation scheme was introduced. Compared to air crew, ground crew were at quite a disadvantage in the UK where they served mainly with RAAF squadrons and worked hard, but didn't enjoy the leave and promotion options open to aircrew (as Sgt Parker's wife alluded to in her letter back in September 1943). To qualify for repatriation, ground crew had to have served three years overseas with the repatriation rate set at 100 per month for UK-based ground crew and 100 every second month for those based in the Middle East. Under this scheme Senior NCOs were also given preference, providing an opportunity for those who remained behind to be promoted to take their place.[55]

William Bennett had known Vern Lancaster for some time and was picked up by him in a jeep and taken to B.19 at Lingèvres, which Bennett described as: 'a single metal matting strip in the middle of a corn field'. The aircraft were dispersed between hedges and under trees, and the accommodation consisted of tents dispersed in the same manner, with a small slit trench dug under each camp bed, a duckboard placed at the bottom of the trench to give some protection for water accumulating at the bottom. It was here that he met F/Lt Roger Bush, the officer in charge of the ground crew who serviced the squadron's aircraft. Bennet described Bush as a 'genius of improvisation, master of scroungers, wizard of engineers, manipulator of manpower and friend to all'.[56]

17 August was a day without flying; the weather was too poor in the morning and, in the afternoon, Wing released the squadrons until 1300 on the following day. The rest of the day was therefore spent tidying up and getting the squadron area in order.

18 August was described in the squadron diary as: 'a harvest of destruction'.⁵⁷ The town of Vimoutiers was just north of the main German escape route out of the Falaise pocket. The Allies had failed to close it, thus enabling many German units to escape (though at nothing like full strength). An SS Panzer Korps had succeeded in keeping the north-eastern end of it open for units to escape, but 2TAF made sure that they left much of their equipment behind. 453 added to the carnage, and the entire Wing of four squadrons spent the day flying back and forth between Vimoutiers and Lingèvres in a cycle of: take-off—attack—return—rearm—refuel. Over and over again.

The first sortie took off at 1340, eleven Spitfires led by Vern Lancaster in 'H' headed straight for Vimoutiers, the squadrons only target for the day. They saw an estimated 2,000-3,000 MET in convoys nose to tail around Orbec and Vimoutieres trying to escape the pocket, all headed east and northeast. They couldn't miss. Down they went, strafing and bombing the convoys, knowing that every vehicle or soldier they got here would be one fewer the army had to fight later on and, with the targets so bunched up, they had to make the most of it. At 1425, the last of the squadron returned to Lingèvres with claims of five flamers, 14 smokers and 31 damaged.

The next twelve took off at 1645, led again by Vern Lancaster in 'H'. David Murray in 'D' turned back pretty much right away and missed out, but the remainder continued on to just east of Vimoutiers, bombing and strafing once again. A large building with POW written on the roof was seen northeast of Orbec and studiously avoided, and they focused their attention once again on the convoys attempting to escape the Allied pincers. MET claims amounted to six flamers, seven smokers and seven damaged. They also claimed three AMCs damaged. Strikes were noted on a stationary Panther tank but no claim was made against it.⁵⁸ The Panther was one of the best tanks on the battlefield at the time, and many would say it was one of the best tanks of the war. Most Allied tanks in Normandy did not have a main armament of sufficient power to take one out, especially from the front, so cannon fire from a Spitfire certainly wasn't going to do the job. What they would need was a direct hit or near miss from a bomb to either destroy or flip the tank and put it out of action. That was a job probably best left to the Typhoons and their rockets, or the American Mustangs and Thunderbolts that carried a bigger bomb load than a Spitfire. The last planes returned from Vimoutiers at 1800, but the day wasn't over yet.

At 1830 the first of four four-plane flights took off, overlapping their flight times to give continuous coverage of the area. The first four were led by Keith Daff in 'O' at 1830 and they returned with claims of two MET smokers and one damaged. By now the roads were almost totally blocked, barely anything was moving and most of what could be seen was already destroyed. Anything that took to the fields stood out, and no German wanting to make it 'back to Berlin' would do that with the sky full of Spitfires, Typhoons, Lightnings, Thunderbolts and Mustangs. The second flight took off at 1900 and was led by Jack Olver in 'W'. They returned with claims of three smokers and three damaged. The third flight took off shortly afterwards, at 1920, and was led by Hector Aldred in 'L'. They returned with claims of only one smoker and one damaged. It was really getting hard to pick out the targets by this stage, there was so much destruction and smoke over the battlefield. The last flight of the day took off at 2010 and was led by Vern Lancaster, in 'H'. This flight gave a flak post some attention, but the results weren't observed, though the MET took a beating, with claims of four flamers, three smokers and six damaged.

The numerous sorties of the day and the collective 'bag' of enemy vehicles damaged and destroyed resulted in the army sending through a message of thanks and congratulations. The message read: 'A million congratulations to all concerned for the stupendous work undertaken today'. 453 Squadron claimed a total of 15 MET flamers, 50 smokers and 49 damaged, as well as three AMCs damaged out of the Wing's total claims of 125-106-146 for MET, 3-1-4 for AFVs and 7-6-4 for tanks. The Wing had now racked up claims against 2,000 MET since D-Day—the 2,000th going to 453 Squadron.[59] It seemed like the whole of 2TAF and the USAAF Ninth Air Force were trying to fit into a small piece of sky, all determined to smash up the retreating German columns trying to escape Normandy. Pilots recorded that it was difficult to avoid collisions in the area.[60] While such large claims may appear excessive, it should also be noted that on a number of occasions, squadrons, including 453 and 441, declined to make any claims because the battlefield was such a mess that they knew they were bombing or strafing vehicles already dealt with by other squadrons, and they documented this in their records.[61]

18 August was also notable for the return of Froggy Lyall, who had last been seen on 12 July. He simply walked in to the squadron area and announced that he was back and ready to fight once again. During his time in the POW camp, he'd seen Allan Dowding, who was injured but coping well and was able to pass this information on. Lyall said that his reception on returning to the squadron made him feel like 'I was home again'. He visited his best mate, Fred Cowpe, in hospital, and discovered that, when he'd been shot down, Fred had immediately claimed Froggy's newly tailored cap for himself![62] One pilot interviewed later in life recalled:

> You develop a strange attitude. It sounds a bit stupid I suppose now, in the cold light of day, but it's not you, it's him. You're all right. You become a little bit cold blooded about it all. Somebody's got to write to his wife or his parents and tell them, but it's not you. You don't have to do it. I wonder if he's got any clean shirts, I'm running out. That sort of thing.

While he was in the UK a pilot from this pilot's squadron was shot down over the Channel and presumed dead. He explained that:

> In those days of clothes rationing and no laundries, we all used to run out of clothes, so ... all his underclothes and socks were all pinched. Keep us going. Bloke turned up about 3 days later and he demanded all his clothes back.[63]

As a result of information provided by Froggy, Don Smith wrote to Allan Dowding's family to inform them of his updated, though still unofficial, status.[64] Herb Watts and Joe Boulton were evacuated back to the UK from the 20th General Hospital.

Flying was again busy on 19 August, but not as productive—though the main damage had been done, it was someone else's turn now. The first patrol of the day, four planes led by Joshua Scott in '?', took off at 0755. This, and two more flights of four, was tasked with a front line patrol. Scott had to return early, and the other three Spitfires continued to their patrol area near Orbec where they sighted a dogfight between Mustangs and Spitfires that resulted in one plane being shot down, though they weren't sure which type it was. Another friendly fire incident, but this time not involving 453 Squadron, they were lucky. Sargeant recorded in his logbook: 'Uneventful. Fires still burning from yesterday.'[65] They returned at 0910, overlapped by another flight of four led by Clarence Rice in 'G' then another led by Joshua Scott in '?' at 1000, making up for his earlier short flight. This final flight returned at 1125, without having to fight the Luftwaffe, the Americans, or the Canadians.

As this last flight was returning, the next was taking off. Jack Olver in 'W' led a flight of four to patrol the Bernay, Proglis (probably Broglie) and Beaumont area on an armed recce at 1110. They were replaced by nine Spitfires with Vern Lancaster leading in '?'. Jack Olver in 'W' took a final flight of six out in the early afternoon. Total claims for the armed recces were four MET flamers, four smokers and three damaged. One AMC smoker and another damaged were also added to the squadron tally. The Luftwaffe was nowhere to be seen. The squadron also contributed to low patrols over the Lisieux area, three pairs leaving at 1505, 1600 and 1755 and, finally, a larger patrol of four at 1835 led by John Cummins in '?' which was racking up the engine and airframe mileage. Some light flak was encountered near Lisieux during these patrols, but all eventually returned safely.

The day brought another surprise: Norman Baker arrived wearing army uniform, having been last seen on 6 July crash-landing his plane behind German lines. The squadron diary recorded that: 'He looked well and is keen to have another go at the Hun'.

Another new pilot arrived from 83 GSU, W/O Digby Charles Johns (Service no. 421019). Johns was born 15 February 1923 and worked as a jackeroo and station hand before enlisting on 6 December 1941. He had served with the Light Horse Militia before enlisting in the RAAF, the perfect line of work for a jackeroo, but his destiny was a steed of another kind. He was posted to 10 EFTS Temora then onto 5 SFTS Uranquinty before sailing for the UK in March 1943 where he completed his training. He flew Spitfires with 63 Squadron before being transferred to 453.[66] In the evening a number of nurses arrived from hospitals in the Bayeux area for a bit of a party. History does not record whether Baker or the nurses received the warmer welcome.

The morning of 20 August was a quiet (it's best not to fly with a hangover) but two sorties were flown in the afternoon. Vern Lancaster in '?' led the first sortie of eleven Spitfires over in the Herne-Broinne-Beaumont-Broglie area, claiming seven MET flamers, three smokers and eight damaged. Two Mk IV panzers were seen, as were two other tanks identified as Tigers but no claims were made against them. At 1750, the squadron sent up twelve Spitfires, this time led by W/Cdr Page who had not flown with the squadron for some time. He took 'C' and led them on a fighter sweep with 132 Squadron[67] over the front, but there was no fighting to be had. All planes returned safely at 1945, though a number did return early.

Also on 20 August, Froggy Lyall was officially posted to the squadron again, and was sent back to the UK on 14 days' leave. Fred Cowpe was evacuated from 121 General Hospital to the UK for treatment at more specialised facilities. On a landing craft back to the UK, he struck up a conversation with the man beside him, who turned out to be a wounded

German. Fred asked who would win the war and the German replied, 'Germany must win the war.'[68]

The weather turned again on 21 August, as is typical of Normandy. The wind and rain had people feeling a bit miserable—especially those in unpatched, holey tents, courtesy of the Luftwaffe. The dusty airstrip transformed into a sea of mud,[69] and the day was described as 'the worst flying weather since arriving at B.19'.[70] Still, it was a rest, of sorts, and a break from flying. The Luftwaffe might not have put up much of a fight in Normandy, but the flying was still dangerous, and the pilots always had to be 'on'; there was no cruising about. Constant flying, looking, listening, searching, weaving all took its toll on the pilots physically and emotionally, and the break was welcome. The Spitfire may well be one of the best aircraft ever built, and the Merlin one of the finest engines, but they too needed a break, and the ground crew needed time to work on them. Having a plane return just after take-off due to some mechanical fault was not an experience unique to 453 Squadron, nor to the fighting in Normandy, though the dust certainly didn't help.

F/Sgt Collin Royal Bundara (Service no. 419636) was posted to the unit from 83 GSU. Bundara was born on 14 July 1918 and had worked as a woodworker before joining the Army and being posted to 2nd Field Squadron (Engineers). He then signed up in the RAAF in September 1942, and started his flying training in Australia before being shipped to Canada in March 1943. In December of that year, Bundara was sent to the UK where he completed his training. He served with 165 Squadron for two months before being posted to 453.[71]

While the exact date is not recorded in squadron records, when 453 was grounded for a period during the battle of the Falaise Gap, four jeeploads of men used this time to go into the battle area looking for souvenirs, arming themselves with their .38 revolvers (carried by all pilots) and some Sten guns. There they were confronted with the results of the Allied airstrikes. Bill Bennett described the scene: 'Thousands of corpses, blackened, decaying, stinking, lay wherever we looked. God did we do this?' They had. One of the pilots accidentally trod on a body—it could be hard to tell what was what—and put their boot right through it. Many in the group threw up in response to seeing the rotting, mangled and maggot-ridden corpses, and they returned to the airfield, brought back to reality by the souvenir expedition.[72]

Only one sortie was flown on 22 August, taking off at 1840 with twelve Spitfires led by Vern Lancaster in 'H'. They performed an armed recce around Bernay, Elbeuf and Beaumont. All the good trade of the previous week had pretty much dried up, but thorough searching of fields and roads netted claims of five MET flamers, four smokers and one damaged. Jack Olver had a narrow escape in 'W' when a large piece of flak went right through his starboard wing, but he made it back to Lingèvres safely, escorted by Ron Pollock in 'J'. Don Smith and Mick West returned from leave, the CO being somewhat stunned by the condition of his tent. They brought back with them a large supply of tomatoes, which were appreciated. It was now the turn of Joshua Scott and Clarence Rice for some leave, and they went back to the UK for seven days. The squadron diary noted: 'We are now in the back areas, the allied advance being so fast'.[73]

23 August saw many morning sorties flown. Front line patrols were allocated on an overlapping schedule, six flights in all, with the first taking off at 0735 led by John Cummins in 'R'. The last sortie took off at 1235 led by Jim Ferguson in 'P', and they returned at 1355. Not one German plane was seen. That afternoon, 453 Squadron combined with 132 Squadron in a fly over of Paris in the formation of the Cross of Lorraine, paying homage to the citizens of what the BBC had led them to believe was a newly-liberated city. W/Cdr Page took off at 1530 flying 'V' of 132 Squadron, and Don Smith, in 'S', led 453 Squadron off at 1535.

Paris would not be liberated until 25 August; on the 23rd the area was still very much in German hands and, though they were engaged in street fighting with the Maquis, not all AA guns within range of the city had been silenced. The formation flew over the city at 7,000 ft[74] and attracted quite a bit of flak resulting in an unruly climb for height of twenty-two Spitfires which, fortunately, resulted in no collisions. The pilots then divided their attention between avoiding each other and getting a good view of the city from a safe height. 132 Squadron returned at 1730, and 453 returned at 1735, somewhat disappointed by their reception. So much for using the BBC radio as a source of information! Jack Olver made a note of it in his logbook: 'B.B.C. wrong again—heavy accurate flak from Paris.'[75]

The final patrols of the day were two flights of two, and a final flight of four—each patrol covering the Le Bény-Bocage to Cabourg area and overlapping by 20-30 minutes. The first patrols searched for a reported dinghy between Ouistreham and Courseulles, but only found an empty ship's raft. Taylor, who flew 'S' during the sortie from 1940–2100 apparently had no fear of the Luftwaffe, fighters being reasonably rare by this stage of the Normandy campaign and recorded some casual aerobatics in his logbook: 'Did 2 slow rolls'.[76] The last flight led by Bill Bennett in 'J' was recalled due to poor weather.

W/O John Damian Carmichael (414991) arrived from 83 GSU. Carmichael, an assistant weighbridge clerk, joined the RAAF in Brisbane on 7 December 1941 and was trained to fly in Australia at 5 EFTS Narromine and Camp Borden, Canada, before sent to the UK in January 1943. There he completed his operational training and was posted to 287 Squadron flying Hurricanes so anti-aircraft units could practise their skills—not a very exciting role for someone who wanted to be a fighter pilot. However, such skills needed to be practised and those anti-aircraft units needed aircraft to target. On 29 July 1944 he was posted to 61 OTU where he was trained on Spitfires, flying Marks IIA, VA and VB before a posting to 83 GSU where he waited for a vacancy to appear at a 2TAF operational squadron.[77] Now that the battle of Normandy was drawing to a close, it seemed that new pilots were arriving rather more frequently than they had been needed during the busiest times when the squadron suffered the most casualties.

The weather turned again on 24 August and there was no flying. The pilots had a rest day, spending time eating and sleeping. Welcome news came through that Rusty Leith was once again behind Allied lines. After a quick visit to the squadron, he was sent on 14 days' leave by the Group Captain[78] and did not return to them until well after the end of the Normandy campaign. However, returning was not simply a matter of collecting your things and returning to your unit. Each escapee had to undergo an interrogation or debriefing of sorts to establish their identity (as many discarded their dog tags or identity discs while on the run to reduce the chance of being discovered as an Allied serviceman if searched). Part of the process included trying to find out who else they had seen while behind enemy lines, information about the enemy and any methods used to evade the enemy—especially successful application of training given. Thereafter followed the signing of an official document, with a warning that disclosure of this information was an offence, and newspaper representatives were singled out as people with whom servicemen were to 'Be especially on your guard'. The form contained suggested answers about what was permitted to be said, including the line: 'I am sure you will understand that I cannot tell you anything till after the war, and I have orders not to say more than I have already told you'.[79] The squadron was genuinely happy to have Rusty back—Jack Olver even made a note of it in his logbook, just as he had for the return of Baker and Lyall earlier in the month.

On the next morning, 25 August, the squadron was visited by Air Commodore Bladen, who was attached to RAAF Overseas HQ. While it was always good to get some attention from the brass, the squadron was probably more interested in the return of Rusty Leith, the squadron's third recent successful evader. Also on the 25th, eleven bombed-up Spitfires led by Vern Lancaster in 'H' took off at 1435 to an area southwest of Rouen where the target was nominated as a concentration of tanks. When the squadron arrived, they saw that rocket-firing Typhoons had already given them the onceover, but they bombed anyway just to be sure. With all the fire and smoke the squadron decided to drop their bombs from a safer height of 5,000 ft, diving down from 11,000 ft on an easterly heading. Some of the bombs also hit a building described as a 'red bricked Chateau' which was thought to house ammunition or something else similarly explosive in nature, such as petrol, oil and lubricants, as the building disintegrated when it was hit.[80] All the bombs directed at the vehicles landed in the target area but, since there were so many fires, it was hard to tell if anything still capable of mobility was hit. No additional claims were made.

Operations up near the Seine continued in the evening, the sortie taking off at 1825 being directed to bomb barges located there and, presumably, being used to get German troops across the river and out of Normandy. Jack Olver in 'S' led the formation of twelve Spitfires up to a group of barges that had already been attacked by 132 Squadron in the afternoon. The squadron dive-bombed from 11,000 ft down to 4,000 ft, from east to west, and they recorded one large barge as damaged and five near misses, with the ferry damaged by 132 Squadron seen down at the rear and still smoking. One MET flamer and two damaged were claimed on the return journey, and excess bombs were disposed of before returning to Lingèvres, though one plane returned with a 'hung up' 250 lb bomb and had to land last.

The first sortie on 26 August took off at 0900 for an armed recce over the area of Rouen and Fleury-sur-Andelle. This was led by Don Smith in 'H', and they encountered about twenty Me-109s north of Paris. The formation of 109s was spread out between 20,000 ft and 25,000 ft and 453 had the advantage, coming in from 26,000 ft. However, very strangely, there was a Spitfire right in the middle of them and, as it left the formation, it was thought to be a 109 breaking away so it was fired on by Jack Olver, who ceased firing when he recognised it as a Spitfire. The mystery Spitfire took no evasive action and appeared to have already been 'extensively damaged and had holes along the fuselage'.[81] Its squadron letter code was read as AU, with the individual aircraft letter being either a C or G. This was a very strange situation and a chase developed with the 109s. The engagement had to be broken off due to a lack of fuel—the Spitfire's eternal weakness. The mysterious Spitfire was followed and seen to crash in a field southeast of Dieppe. The pilot, if he was even alive at this point, did not bail out. No other Spitfires were seen in the area at the time.[82]

421 (RCAF) Squadron was allocated the two letter code 'AU'. Their squadron flying records indicate that two aircraft did not return from an armed recce sortie on the morning of 26 August, the planes taking off at 0830 and the remaining aircraft returning at 1015. However, the squadron summary of events has the date listed as 25 August. What can be determined with some certainty though, is that these aircraft were Spitfire MK IX serials MK661 (F/O Libbey) and ML308 (F/O Flood) both of which are listed as shot down by FW-190s. In other records, however, the date varies by one day. The individual squadron letter code of the aircraft is not recorded. Apparently Libbey was taken prisoner, so it is possible but extremely unlikely that his plane was captured intact and flown the next day. Flood is known to have died.[83] Either way, it is a very curious incident in the history of 453 Squadron, and that of 421 as well. The most probable version of events is that the incident occurred on 26 August and the Spitfire had already been abandoned by Libbey. The pilotless plane was then perhaps gliding and being overtaken by the 109s at the time 453 arrived and engaged them in a dogfight.

From the Personal Combat Report signed by Bill Carter who flew 'G' in which he claimed one Me-109 probably destroyed:

> I was flying yellow 2 with 453 sqdn on an Armed Recce when N.E. Paris at 20,000 ft we saw approx. eight ME 109's flying at the same height as ourselves. We climbed to 25,000 ft and the Huns climbed also, but away from us. We gave chase and the starboard Me 109 broke away from the others. Yellow section followed and when we were closing in on the e/a yellow 1 and I turned port and gave chase to the remainder of the e/a. They were still heading N.E. in a gradual dive and as we closed in fairly rapidly the port e/a broke 90° to port and dived away. We closed in on the remainder and at approx. 800 yds range I gave one of the e/a a short burst but observed no strikes. The Me 109's kept flying in line abreast formation and I closed in to 300 yds range and fired a long burst and saw strikes on the e/a. 2 cannon strikes on the port radiator and other strikes on the wing roots. The e/a immediately started to pour black smoke and pieces fell from off it. I gave another burst but the smoke from the e/a was so dense that it was impossible for me to see through it. The last I saw of the e/a was when it was at a height of 3-4000 ft diving towards earth, undoubtable out of control. I claim 1 Me 109 probably destroyed.[84]

From the Personal Combat Report signed by Keith Daff who flew 'O' in which he claimed one Me-109 probably destroyed:

> I was yellow 1 of 453 sqdn. When flying N.E. Paris on an Armed Recce we saw approx. 8 Me 109's flying at a height of 20,000 ft. We climbed to 25,000 ft and the Me 109's climbed also. We gave chase and yellow 2 and I broke away from the rest of the section and getting within range of 5 Me 109's I gave 2 one second bursts at a range of 800 yards, but did not see strikes. I closed to 400 yards range and gave a series of 1 and 2 second bursts but still no strikes were observed. When at 200–300 yards range and a height of 5,000 ft I gave a further series of bursts and saw strikes on the starboard side of the fuselage, cockpit and tail plane. Glycol poured from the e/a. and it immediately dived to starboard, to all appearances out of control. I last saw it at a height of 3,000 ft still out of control. I claim 1 Me 109 probably destroyed.[85]

From the Personal Combat Report signed by Don Smith in which he claimed one Me-109 probably destroyed:

> When flying at 20,000 ft N.E. Paris in an easterly direction, we saw approx 8 Me 109's flying at the same height as ourselves. They were orbiting to the east and as we climbed to 25,000 ft they did likewise. We gave chase and the e/a which were now flying line abreast went into a shallow dive. I closed to a range of 200 yds and selecting one of the two starboard e/a which were some little distance behind the others, I chased it until I was within 100 yds range. The e/a then started climbing, turned sharp to port and pulled up almost vertically. I pulled up behind him and at approx. 100 yds range gave a 2 sec burst, 40° deflection. Due to the deflection necessary it was impossible to see strikes on the e/a. but it dived down on my port side with white smoke (similar to glycol smoke) pouring from the top front of the engine cowling and went into an inverted spin. It appeared to be completely out of control, but as there were still Huns about and shortage of petrol made it impossible for me to take the chance of another engagement, I could not stay to see the e/a crash to the ground, but last saw it when it was at a height of 4,000 ft to 3,000 ft still in an inverted spin and I feel certain that it was out of control. I claim this Me 109 probably destroyed.[86]

The dogfight resulted in claims of three probables for the squadron with no losses and all planes returned by 1020.

The middle part of the day was taken up with low patrols between Cabourg and Le Bény-Bocage. Each patrol consisted of two planes with overlapping times, the first pair, Hector Aldred in 'L' and Brian Inglis in 'E' taking off at 1130 and the last pair, Jim Grady in 'S' and Bill Mace in 'P' landing at 1810. Nothing of interest was noted by them. A flight in 'Z' as part of these patrol pairs was John Carmichael's first operational sortie with 453.[87]

On the final sortie of the day, Bill Bennett in 'J' led twelve Spitfires on an armed recce to the Rouen and Gisors area. The squadron claimed two MET flamers and two smokers, as well as one tank smoker and one armoured car damaged. This sortie was unique in that the pilots came up against what they thought was a new form of anti-aircraft fire. They believed that at least one of the shells fired at them released 'a cloud of strips of paper coloured white and yellow and small in size.'[88] It was thought that the purpose of this was to try and clog up the engine air intakes and radiators, but it had no effect. It was later revealed that this had been used against bombers before, and with the same results.[89] Quite a bit of flak was encountered and refugees were seen to be moving north and northeast away from the battle area. F/Sgt Sargeant, the last remaining RAF pilot with the squadron, was posted out to 132 Squadron, thereby achieving the squadron's return to one hundred percent Australian aircrew.

There was only one sortie on 27 August. At 1715 that afternoon, Vern Lancaster in 'H' led twelve Spitfires off on an armed recce around Paris, and the squadron returned with claims of six MET flamers, one smoker and four damaged, as well as one AFV damaged. All planes returned by 1905, with Taylor in 'R' sporting a hole in the starboard radiator from ground fire.[90] As the front line was getting further and further away from B.19, the ability of the squadron to spend productive time over the battlefield was diminishing. News came through that the squadron would soon be moving 100 miles closer to the front.

On 28 August, the squadron flew a large volume of sorties. The first took off at 0915 for an armed recce of the Rouen area with Vern Lancaster leading the way in 'H'. Though some Luftwaffe aircraft were reportedly in the area, none were seen. The squadron also sent off four patrols—each of two aircraft—to do low cover from Cabourg to Le Bény-Bocage but nothing was seen. The last of the day was led by Don Smith in '?' at 1920. The armed recce patrol covered the triangle area from Gournay to Gisors and Rouen. They returned with claims of one MET flamer, two smokers and three damaged. Carmichael recorded in his logbook: 'Attacked a couple of light tanks. A few tracers.'[91] The long distances flown claimed one Spitfire: Bruce Fuller in 'J' was unable to land at the strip on the runway and had to crash land due to lack of fuel. The plane was badly damaged but he escaped with only very minor injuries. The main danger of crash landings was the risk of the pilot splitting his head open on the gunsight as he was thrown forward by the impact of landing. To counter this risk, pilots did their straps up even tighter than normal; they wanted absolutely no give at all. All the squadron's equipment was sorted through for the upcoming move, they didn't want to have to carry any more than was essential. The Wing 'A' party was due to leave the next day.

29 August saw no flying, the weather was bad with the variable Normandy rain paying a visit[92] and the Wing 'A' party left for the new location. Late in the day, a message was received that the move was postponed, and it was rumoured that the front had moved so far ahead that even the new landing ground was not close enough to the front lines, and the squadron would have to be sent elsewhere.

Bad weather continued on the 30th and Clarence Rice and Josh Scott returned from leave. The last day of August was described in the squadron record as a 'boisterous' day with no operational flying and everyone waiting to find out where the squadron would next be based.[93]

During August the squadron had dropped eighty-one 500 lb bombs and 164 250 lb bombs—approximately 36 tons.

The battle of Normandy was over. The Allies were pushing their way through northern France and nothing as massive as Operation Overlord would ever be seen again. One pilot said that throughout the summer of 1944 he couldn't ever remember eating, though he was sure that they got three meals a day. He said they took off as soon as it was light enough, and earlier if the moon was up. They landed when the landing ground could barely be seen or were guided in by shielded lights. As soon as they were out of the plane they lit a cigarette—never was a cigarette wasted, and the non-smokers were begged or traded for theirs. Everyone received 40 packets of cigarettes a month, and they needed every one of them.[94]

The operational flying hours of 453 Squadron for the months of June, July and August 1944 numbered 1183.55, 808 and 799 respectively. They had never flown so many hours, nor would they again, and their operational hours were at least double their previous operational periods in 11 Group, their most active posting since arriving in 2TAF.[95] By the end of September 1944 the worn-out squadron would be back in England.

But that is another story entirely.

Notes

1. ORB–132 Sqn
2. ORB–125 Wing
3. ORB–125 Wing
4. NAA: A11335, Z1
5. ORB–125 Wing
6. Logbook–Olver
7. Logbook–Lynch.
8. Logbook–Lynch.
9. NLA: Trove–'Australian pilots Congratulated' *Newcastle Morning Herald and Miners' Advocate* 5 August 1944.
10. ORB–453 Sqn
11. ORB–125 Wing
12. Logbook–Lynch.
13. Personal File–Mace
14. Personal File–Taylor and Logbook–Taylor
15. Logbook–Taylor
16. ORB–125 Wing
17. ORB–132 Sqn
18. ORB–125 Wing
19. Personal File–Adams.
20. NAA: A11335, 154/60/P1 and ORB–125 Wing.
21. CWGC website
22. ORB–125 Wing

23 Identification by letter code in ORB flight ops, checked with Shores and Thomas, *2nd Tactical Air Force: Volume 4, Squadrons, Camouflage and Markings, Weapons and tactics 1943–1945*, p. 691.
24 Personal File–Marsh
25 ORB–125 Wing
26 ORB–453 Sqn
27 ORB–132 Sqn
28 ORB–453 Sqn
29 ORB–441 Sqn
30 ORB–453 Sqn, location specifics from ORB–125 Wing
31 Logbook–Cowpe
32 ORB–453 Sqn Aug 1944 and NAA File A11335 154/61/P1
33 Personal File–Cross
34 NAA: A11335, 154/61/P1
35 Hastings, *Overlord: D-Day and The Battle for Normandy*, p. 206.
36 ORB–125 Wing
37 Logbook–Sargeant
38 ORB–453 Sqn
39 Cowpe–*Sequel to D Day*, p. 6.
40 Cowpe–*Sequel to D Day*, p. 6.
41 Temora Interview–Fred Cowpe.
42 Cowpe–*Sequel to D Day*, p. 6.
43 Cowpe–*Sequel to D Day*, p. 6.
44 Cowpe–*Sequel to D Day*, p. 6.
45 Interview with Author–Handsaker and Interview with Author–Barrington
46 ORB–441 Sqn (June 1944)
47 Cowpe–*Sequel to D Day*, p. 7.
48 Cowpe–*Sequel to D Day*, p. 7.
49 Temora Interview–Fred Cowpe.
50 NAA: A11335, 168/P1.
51 AWM: MSS 1952 (Bennett)
52 Personal File–Cummins
53 Personal File–Pollock
54 ORB–453 Sqn
55 Herington, *Air Power Over Europe 1944–1945*, pp. 284–285, 291–292.
56 AWM: MSS 1952 (Bennett)

57   ORB–453 Sqn
58   ORB–453 Sqn
59   ORB–125 Wing
60   ORB–132 Sqn
61   ORB–441 Sqn on 18 Aug 1944 and ORB 453 Sqn on 25 Aug 1944
62   *Exclusive Brethren: The RAAF in Rhodesia and Beyond*–Ray Jackson (ed).
63   AWFA: Nat Gould
64   Personal File–Dowding
65   Logbook - Sargeant
66   Personal File–Johns
67   ORB–125 Wing
68   Temora Interview–Fred Cowpe.
69   ORB–125 Wing
70   ORB–441 Sqn
71   Personal File–Bundara.
72   AWM: MSS 1952 (Bennett)
73   ORB–453 Sqn and Logbook–Olver
74   ORB–125 Wing
75   Logbook–Olver
76   Logbook–Taylor
77   Personal File–Carmichael and Logbook–Carmichael
78   Leith–Casualty letter signed by GC Rankin 125 Wing
79   Leith–Warning Against Giving Information document
80   ORB–453 Sqn
81   ORB–453 Sqn
82   ORB–453 Sqn
83   Website–http://www.backtonormandy.org/the-history/air-force-operations/airplanes-allies-and-axis-lost/spitfire/4152515.html?fb_ref=Default and http://www3.sympatico.ca/angels_eight/127mems.html
84   NAA: 11335 Z1
85   NAA: 11335 Z1
86   NAA: 11335 Z1
87   Personal File–Carmichael and Logbook–Carmichael
88   ORB – 453 Sqn
89   ORB – 125 Wing
90   Logbook – Taylor

91 Logbook – Carmichael
92 ORB – 132 Sqn
93 ORB – 453 Sqn
94 Baker letter for Don Smith's medical claim
95 OAFH: 547_453.

Leaving and Returning to Normandy: A Journey

At the end of the Normandy campaign, 453 Squadron moved to Belgium and continued operations until the end of the war, spending the final months paired with sister RAAF squadron, 451, which had fought its way to Europe via North Africa and the Mediterranean. Together they operated from the UK, dive-bombing V2 sites in the Netherlands under the leadership of former 453 commander, W/Cdr Don Andrews—the youngest Wing Commander in the RAAF. At the conclusion of hostilities, the squadrons were based in Germany on occupation duties (the only Australian units to do so). Both squadrons were disbanded in 1946 and the pilots and ground crew returned to Australia, to be (once again) scattered far and wide across the country—and many of them without even a licence to drive a car!

In 1988 Russell (perhaps too old to be called 'Rusty' anymore) Leith paid a return visit to Normandy and those who had sheltered him while he was on the run during the war. While there, he went to the Peace Memorial in Caen (Memorial de Caen) which overlooks the city. Of all the flags he saw at the entrance to the museum, he noticed there was no Australian flag. This niggled at him until 1993 when he wrote the first letter in his campaign for the Australian flag to be flown there in recognition of the service of

453 Squadron, the only Australian unit to operate from Normandy during the campaign. After some time the matter was referred to the Australian Defence Attaché in Paris, whose job it became to take the issue up with the Caen Memorial. Leith was informed that the decision regarding whose flag should be flown had been a difficult one, but it had been decided that the flags should only represent the nations who were present on the Normandy beaches on 6 June 1944.

Dissatisfied, Russell started his letter-writing campaign. He received a response confirming there were no plans for Australia to be represented at the 50th Anniversary of the landings in 1994. So Russell took up his cause with the Minister for Defence, who then referred him to the Minister for Veteran's Affairs. He was later informed that the Prime Minister, Paul Keating, had received an invitation to attend the ceremonies to be held in Normandy, and that five places had been set aside for veterans to accompany him. So Russell, along with some of his ex-squadron mates—Norm Marsh, Fred Cowpe, Rod Lyall and John Steward—visited a number of the battlefield sites, including the gun battery and their old airfield at B.11: Longues-sur-Mer. In Arromanches, they spoke with Prince Charles.

After returning to Australia and recovering from a heart attack, Russell resumed his quest for the Australian flag to be flown at the Memorial de Caen. His efforts continued into 1997, and he was referred to numerous ministers; but, in June that year a promising response was received: some additional flags were proposed for the Memorial, including those of Australia and New Zealand (which had a squadron of Typhoons flying from airfields in Normandy). Finally, in June 1998, Russell received the letter he had hoped for, which confirmed that the Australian flag had been erected and flown at the memorial on 1 May, 1998. He visited the next year and saw it for himself.

After having been disbanded after the Second World War, 453 Squadron officially reformed on 16 February 2011 with a new role of Joint

Battlefield Airspace Controllers—which is air traffic control, for those not used to modern military job descriptions.

In November 2011, Henry Lacy Smith and his Spitfire, last seen crashing into the Caen Canal on 11 June 1944 were located in the mud near the shoreline. To honour their fallen comrade, whose unit had been disbanded and reformed in the years after his death, the RAAF sent a contingent to France. Almost seven decades after his death, Henry Lacy Smith was laid to rest, reinterred in a ceremony at the Commonwealth War Graves Commission cemetery at Ranville, near Pegasus Bridge in Normandy, honouring his service to France, Australia and the cause of freedom. On 8 February 2014 the Australian War Memorial in Canberra featured Henry Lacy Smith in their daily Last Post Ceremony where his service history was read to those in attendance and wreaths were placed at the Pool of Remembrance.

There are now very few Spitfires in Australia, or anywhere else for that matter. The squadron that once flew fighters has been rebuilt as one that

The grave of Henry Lacy Smith—Normandy 2017 (Author)

controls battlefield airspace, working with aircraft of all three Services, domestic and international aircraft, and those of nations participating in operations within Australian airspace. Like the 453 Squadron of the Second World War, they too are 'Ready to Strike', to be deployed across the globe at a moment's notice to apply their essential skills to humanitarian or conflict situations. They are writing a new history.

As for those who have gone before, we will remember them.

PILOTS LOST ON DUTY WITH 453 SQUADRON JUNE 1942– AUGUST 1944

Date	Name	Service Number	Circumstances
1 August 1942	C. Riley	416285	Flying accident (training)
28 August 1942	D. Steele	416291	Flying accident (training)
11 October 1942	A. Menzies	403676	Mid-air collision
11 October 1942	B. Nossiter	403278	Mid-air collision
31 October 1942	J. Furlong	401784	Engine failure (probable)
10 December 1942	M. de Cosier	405575	Flak (ship)
10 December 1942	J. Yarra	402823	Flak (ship)
15 August 1943	F. Thornley	411059	Luftwaffe Fw-190
13 September 1943	M. Nolan	414505	Flying accident (landing)
8 October 1943	H. Parker	403763	Luftwaffe Me-110
18 March 1944	B. Gorman	409108	Flying accident (training)
14 April 1944	R. Yarra	413707	Flak (ground)
11 June 1944	H. Smith	411539	Flak (ground) and crash landing
13 June 1944	D. Saunders	417422	Flying accident
24 July 1944	K. Kinross	409147	US P-47 Thunderbolt
25 July 1944	C. Seeney	414519	Flak (probable)
27 July 1944	A. Harris	412513	Flak (ground)
27 July 1944	R. Dutneall	418083	Flak (ground)
7 August 1944	E. Gates	409103	Flak (probable)
14 August 1944	M. Watson	420610	Luftwaffe—raid on airfield

Fred Cowpe Reserve in Coates Street Mount Druitt, New South Wales—just down the road from where Fred lived. (Author)

453 (RAAF) Squadron crest at St Clement Danes church in London (Author)

Epilogue:
A matter of pride

The formation of squadrons early in the Second World War and the training of aircrew and ground crew took up all the resources available. Everyone was too busy learning to do the job required of them for all the seemingly little things to be followed up. One of these seemingly little things was the matter of the squadron crest.

On 30 December 1942, S/Ldr Andrews wrote to the Royal College of Heralds asking if the first incarnation of 453 Squadron had a crest, and if not, 'what the procedure is for getting one authorised'.[1] He was duly informed that the Australian Air Board had decided that no action would be taken regarding crests until the war was over (perhaps because they would be disbanded anyway), but that EATS squadrons may use the 'general' RAAF badge. Attached to the reply was an appendix setting out the instructions to be followed, including the cost of such a procedure: 10 pounds, 10 shillings. This of course could not come from public funds and, presumably, would have to be raised within the squadron. Furthermore, the badge design and motto were to be accompanied by an explanation of why they were selected, and any such design or motto must not reveal the nature of the squadron's operations. Further, if the squadron changed its function, the badge would remain the same and no changes would be permitted. Correspondence would then go back and forth until a design had been approved.

On 22 September 1943, the squadron was informed that RAAF Headquarters, Melbourne had approved the adoption of unit badges by RAAF Squadrons serving overseas. They were also advised that there would be a long time delay between submission of the design and its approval by His Majesty.

It wasn't until 13 February 1944 that S/Ldr Andrews submitted the squadron design of a leaping kangaroo which was popular within the squadron, perhaps in the style of the Australian airline company QANTAS, and three proposed mottos:

- We yield the sky to none
- On Wings we ardently pursue
- Our way is to the stars

A response was received shortly afterwards rejecting the kangaroo on the basis that another squadron had already submitted it for a crest of their own. It was also suggested that the motto be shortened, perhaps to 'Never Yield'. 453 however, wanted to keep the kangaroo, but accepted that, if the matter could not proceed, then they would accept a sketch of a hawk or falcon to review. They found 'Never Yield' to be acceptable.

A crest with an Australian Little Falcon, a bird known for hunting live prey was considered very suitable by the Chester Herald 'especially in view of the aircraft with which you are now equipped'.[2] 'Never Yield' was submitted to the squadron for approval by the Chester Herald in charge of such matters. The squadron didn't approve of the design and two further suggestions were made. As with the kangaroo, the designs were unmistakably Australian. The first was of an Aboriginal standing poised to throw a boomerang with the Southern Cross in the background, accompanied by the motto 'Ready to Strike'. The second design was a kookaburra with a snake dangling from its mouth, again with a Southern Cross background. No second motto was proposed to accompany the kookaburra, but the letter stated that 'an aggressive motto would be necessary'.[3] The letter with these two suggestions was dated 25 March 1944—almost 15 months of correspondence for a squadron crest to be designed and approved, and the war continued on.

Six days after submitting these suggestions, 453 received a reply informing them that 1 Squadron (RAAF) had already used a kookaburra with a snake in its mouth, but suggesting that they could use one without the snake. The letter also suggested omitting the Southern Cross, as it complicated the design. In support of the kookaburra angle, it was suggested that the Aboriginal be dropped as it was similar to the crest of a New Zealand squadron that had a Maori warrior striking with a spear. (This was 485 Squadron (RNZAF), which, like 453, was a squadron that had been born from EATS and was flying Spitfires.[4]) As well, it was noted that yet another crest with a human figure would not be suitable as human figures generally did not fit well in crest designs. Enclosed with the letter was a sketch of a kookaburra to be judged by the squadron.

On 11 April, the squadron replied that the kookaburra had met with general approval and that 'Ready to Strike' was the preferred motto. On 14 April they were advised that the design and motto would be put forward, but that the people responsible were really very busy at the moment! It goes without saying that the artists were somewhat busy at this time, too.

It is surely a point of pride that the correspondence about the squadron quest went on for so long and was not cast aside as a triviality amongst the masses of correspondence produced within the RAF during the war.

Notes

1 NAA: A11335 169P1.
2 NAA: A11335 169P1
3 NAA: A11335 169P1
4 Errol W. Martyn, *Swift to the Sky: New Zealand's Military Aviation History*, Penguin, Rosedale, 2010, p. 123.

Glossary

ADGB	Air Defence Great Britain
AEAF	Allied Expeditionary Air Force
AFU	Advanced Flying Unit
AFV	Armoured Fighting Vehicle
AGS	Air Gunnery School
ALG	Advanced Landing Ground
AMC	Armed (or) Armoured Motor Car (e.g. an armoured car/light reconnaissance vehicle)
AOC	Air Officer Commanding
APC	Armament Practice Camp
ASR	Air Sea Rescue
AVM	Air Vice-Marshal
BAGS	Bombing and Gunnery School
Bogies	Unidentified aircraft
CO	Commanding Officer
EATS	Empire Air Training Scheme
E/A	Enemy Aircraft
ED	Embarkation Depot
EFTS	Elementary Flying Training School
ELS	Emergency Landing Strips
ENSA	Entertainments National Service Association
FAA	Fleet Air Arm
F/Lt	Flight Lieutenant
F/O	Flying Officer
F/Sgt	Flight Sergeant

GCC	Ground Control Centre
G/Cpt	Group Captain
GSU	Group Support Unit
ITS	Initial Training School
LAC	Leading Aircraftman
Mae West	Inflatable vest worn by aircrew
MET	Motorised Enemy Transport (e.g. a truck)
MFH	Military Field Hospital
MGB	Motor Gun Boat (like a MTB but with guns only)
MTB	Motor torpedo boat
NCO	Non-Commissioned Officer
OC	Officer Commanding
OHQ	Overseas Headquarters
OTU	Operational Training Unit
PDRC	Personnel Dispatch and Reception Centre
(P)AFU	(Pilot) Advanced Flying Unit
P/O	Pilot Officer
PRC	Personnel Reception Centre
PR	Photographic Reconnaissance
PRU	Photographic Reconnaissance Unit
RAAF	Royal Australian Air Force
RAF	Royal Air Force
RCAF	Royal Canadian Air Force
RP	Rocket projectile
RRS	Refuelling and Rearming Strips
R/T	Radio/telephone
SCU	Servicing Commando Unit
SE	Servicing Echelon (Ground crew)
SFTS	Service Flying Training School
Sortie	One operational flight by one aircraft
S/Ldr	Squadron Leader
TAF	Tactical Air Force
USAAF	United States Army Air Force
Vic	Formation of three (normally) aircraft in the shape of the letter 'V'
W/Cdr	Wing Commander
W/O	Warrant Officer
W/T	Wireless/Telephone (radio)

Bibliography

UK National Archives

AIR/27 series squadron records

Office of Air Force History (Royal Australian Air Force)

Squadron and Headquarters records and press releases

Australian War Memorial Files

AWM64 series squadron records
AWM online photographic collection
AWM: MSS 1952 (Bennett)

Australian National Archives

A705 series Casualty Records
A1196 series Squadron Records
A2217 series RAAF WW2 records
A2676 series War Cabinet Minutes
A5954 series assorted documents relating to the defence of Australia
A9186 series Unit Histories
A9300 series Personal Records
A9301 series Personal Records
A11335 series Squadron Records

Interviews with the author

Sid Handsaker (21 November 2014 and 10 December 2014)
Lysle Roberts (30 June 2015)
Joe Barrington (23 July 2015 and 28 July 2015)
Nat Gould (3 February 2015)
Louis Heroult—September 2015 (translation by Frederique Verbeke)
Pierre Verbeke—September 2015 (translation by Frederique Verbeke)

Interviews held at the Temora Aviation Museum

Don Andrews
Fred Cowpe
Sir Brian Inglis
Vern Lancaster
Colin Leith
Richard (Dick) Peters
Norm Swift

Researcher Allan Hillman

Wing records—125 Wing
Squadron records—453, 602, 132 and 441 Squadrons

Books and Academic Journals

Ayris, Cyril and Leith, Russell, *Duty Done*, Cyril Ayris Freelance, West Perth, 2001.

Barbier, Mary Kathryn, *D-Day Deception: Operation Fortitude and the Normandy Invasion*, Stackpole, Mechanicsburg, (2007), 2009.

Beevor, Antony, *The Second World War*, Weidenfeld & Nicholson, London, 2012.

Beevor, Antony, *D-Day: The Battle for Normandy*, Viking, London, 2009.

Breffort, Dominique, *German Fighters Volume II: Bf 110—Me 210—Me 410—Fw 190—Me 262—Me 163—He 162*, Histoire & Collections, Paris, 2014.

Bridge, Carl, 'Appeasement and After: Towards a Re-assessment of the Lyons and Menzies Governments' Defence and Foreign Policies, 1931-1941', *Australian Journal of Politics and History*, Vol. 51, No. 3, 2005, 372-379.

Brisset, Jean, *The Charge of the Bull: A History of the 11th British Armoured Division in Normandy 1944*, (transl. Tom Bates), Bates Books, Norwich, 1989.

Brown, Alan, *Flying for Freedom: The Allied Air Forces in the RAF 1939-45*, The History Press, Gloucestershire, 2000, (2011).

Chorlton, Martyn, *Scottish Airfields in the Second World War: Vol. 1 The Lothians*, Countryside Books, Berkshire, 2008.

Cundy, Ron, *A Gremlin on my shoulder*, Australian Military History Publications, Loftus, 2001, (2003).

Curnock, David, *Little Book of Spitfire*, G2 Entertainment Limited, United Kingdom, 2011.

D'Este, Carlo, *Fatal Decision: Anzio and the Battle for Rome*, Aurum Press, London, 1991, (2007).

Daglish, Ian, *Over the Battlefield: Operation Goodwood*, Pen & Sword, Barnsley, 2005.

Davies, J. and Kellett, J.P., *A History of the RAF Servicing Commandos*, Airlife, Shrewsbury, 1989.

Delaney, John, *Fighting the Desert Fox: Rommel's Campaigns in North Africa April 1941 to August 1942*, Cassell & Co, London, 1998, (1999).

Dennis, Peter, Grey, Jeffrey, Morris, Ewan, Prior, Robin, and Bou, Jean, *The Oxford Companion to Australian Military History*, 2nd edn, Oxford University Press, South Melbourne, 2008.

Ford, Roger, *Fire From The Forest: The SAS Brigade in France, 1944*, Cassell, London, (2003), 2004.

Freudenberg, Graham, *Churchill and Australia*, Pan Macmillan, Sydney, 2008.

Franks, Norman, *Royal Air Force Command Losses of the Second World War Volume 2: 1942-1943*, Midland Publishing, Leicester, 1998.

Franks, Norman, *Royal Air Force Command Losses of the Second World War Volume 3: 1944-1945*, Midland Publishing, Leicester, 2000.

Gillison, Douglas, *Australia in the War of 1939-1945, Series Three: Air Volume I: Royal Australian Air Force 1939-1942*, Australian War Memorial, Canberra, 1962.

Glancey, Jonathan, *Spitfire: The Biography*, Atlantic Books, London, 2007.

Goldrick, James, 'Australian naval policy 1939-45', in *The Royal Australian Navy in World War II*, David Stevens (ed), Allen & Unwin, St Leonards, 1996, pp. 1-17.

Goss, Chris with Cornwell, Peter and Rauchbach, Bernd, *Luftwaffe Fighter-Bombers Over Britain: The Tip and Run Campaign, 1942-43,* Stackpole Books, Mechanicsburg, 2010.

Graham, Dominick, & Bidwell, Shelford, *Tug of War: The Battle for Italy 1943-45*, Pen & Sword Books, Yorkshire, 1986, (2004).

Grey, Jeffrey, *A Military History of Australia*, Cambridge University Press, Melbourne, 1990, (2008).

Hastings, Max, *Overlord: D-Day and The Battle for Normandy*, Vintage Books, New York, 2006.

Herington, John, *Australia in the War of 1939-1945, Series Three: Air, Volume III: Air War Against Germany & Italy 1939-1943*, Australian War Memorial, Canberra, 1954.

Herington, John, *Australia in the War of 1939-1945, Series Three: Air, Volume IV: Air Power Over Europe 1944-1945*, Australian War Memorial, Canberra, 1963.

Horner, David, *High Command, Australia and Allied Strategy 1939—1945*, Australian War Memorial, Canberra, 1983.

Howard, Michael, *The Mediterranean Strategy in the Second World War*, Greenhill Books, London, 1993.

Inglis, Major-General Sir J. D., K.B.E., C.B., M.C. (1946) The Work of the Royal Engineers in North-West Europe, 1944–45, *Royal United Services Institution Journal*,91:562, 176-195.

Jackson, W.H.F., *Overlord: Normandy 1944*, London, 1978.

Jacobs, Peter, *Airfields of the D-Day Invasion Air Force: 2nd Tactical Air Force in South-East England in WWII*, Pen & Sword Aviation, Barnsley, 2009.

Laird, Malcolm and Mackenzie, Steve, *Spitfire—The ANZACS*, Ventura Publications, Wellington, 1997.

Lamb, Richard, *War in Italy 1943-1945 A Brutal Story*, Penguin, London, 1993.

Long, Gavin, *The Six Years War, Australia in the 1939—45 War*, Australian War Memorial, Canberra, 1973.

Macintyre, Stuart, *A Concise History of Australia*, 3rd edn, Cambridge University Press, Melbourne, 2009.

Martyn, Errol W., *Swift to the Sky: New Zealand's Military Aviation History*, Penguin, Rosedale, 2010.

Matloff, Morris and Snell, Edwin M., *Strategic Planning for Coalition Warfare 1943-1944 vol. 2*, Washington, 1953.

Mawdsley,Evan, *World War II: A New History*, Cambridge University Press, Cambridge, 2009.

McRoberts, Douglas, *Lions Rampant: The Story of 602 Spitfire Squadron*, William Kimber, London, 1985.

Mitcham, Jr, Samuel W., *German Order of Battle Volume One: 1st—290th Infantry Divisions in WWII*, Stackpole, Mechanicsburg, 2007.

Mitcham, Jr, Samuel W. and von Stauffenberg, Friedrich, *The Battle for Sicily: How the Allies Lost Their Chance for Total Victory*, Stackpole, 1991, (2007).

Mitchell, Gordon, *R.J. Mitchell: Schooldays to Spitfire*, The History Press, Stroud, (1986), 2009.

Murray, Williamson, *Luftwaffe: Strategy for Defeat 1933-45*, Grafton Books, London, (1985), 1988.

Murray, Williamson, and Millett, Allan R. *A War to be Won: Fighting the Second World War*, Belknap, Cambridge, 2000, (2001).

Neil, Wg Cdr T.F., *From the Cockpit: Spitfire*, Ian Allan Ltd, Shepperton, 1980.

Newton, Dennis, *Australian Air Aces*, Aerospace Publications, Fyshwick, 1996.

Overy, Richard, *Why The Allies Won*, Pimlico, London, 1995, (2006).

Page, Geoffrey, *Shot Down in Flames*, Grub Street, London, (1999), 2011.

Porch, Douglas, *Hitler's Mediterranean Gamble: The North African and The Mediterranean Campaigns in World War Two*, Weidenfeld & Nicholson, London, 2004.

Price, Dr Alfred, *Aircraft of the Aces: Men & Legends, Volume 1: The Legendary Spitfire Mk I/II 1939-1941*, Del Prado, Madrid, (1996), 1999.

Price, Dr Alfred, Drecki, Tomasz, Gretzyngier, Robert and Matusiak,Wojtek, *Aircraft of the Aces: Men & Legends, Volume 13:Spitfires Over the Mediterranean & North Africa*, Del Prado, Madrid, 2000.

Price, Dr Alfred, and Holmes, Tony, *Aircraft of the Aces: Men & Legends, Volume 17: RAF Aces of the Battle of Britain*, Del Prado, Madrid, (1995), 2000.

Price, Dr Alfred, *Osprey Aircraft of the Aces: Volume 5, Late Mark Spitfire Aces 1942—45*, Cadmus Communications, USA, (1995), 2010.

Ramsey, Winston G. (ed), 'It Happened Here: Rommel's Accident', *After The Battle*, No. 8, 1975, 42-45.

Reigner, Stephane, *The German Battery at Longues-sur-Mer*, (transl. John Lee) Editions Memorial, Caen, 2002.

Roberts, Andrew, *Masters and Commanders: How Roosevelt, Churchill, Marshall and Alanbrooke Won the war in the West*, Allen Lane, London, 2008.

Robinard, Francois, Trombetta, Philippe and Clementine, Jacques, *50 aerodromes pour une victorie Juin-Septembre 1944*, Heimdal, Bayeux, 2012

Robson, Martin, *The Spitfire Pocket Manual*, Conway, London, 2010.

Sainsbury, Keith, *The North African Landings 1942*, London, 1976.

Saunders, Tim, *Battleground Europe: Normandy: Gold Beach—Jig*, Leo Cooper, Barnsley, 2002.

Shores, Christopher and Thomas, Chris, *2nd Tactical Air Force: Volume 1 Spartan to Normandy June 1943 to June 1944*, Classic Publications, Surrey, 2004.

Shores, Christopher and Thomas, Chris, *2nd Tactical Air Force: Volume 2 Breakout to Bodenplatte, July 1944 to January 1945,* Classic Publications, Surrey, 2005.

Shores, Christopher and Thomas, Chris, *2nd Tactical Air Force: Volume 4 Squadrons, Camouflage and Markings, Weapons and Tactics 1943—1945,* Midland Publishing, Surrey, 2008.

Smith, Richard C., *Hornchurch Eagles: The Life Stories of Eight of the Airfield's Distinguished WWII Fighter Pilots*, Grub Street, London, 2002.

Smith, Richard C., *Hornchurch Offensive*, Grub Street, London (2001), 2008.

Stagg, J.M., *Forecast for Overlord*, Ian Allan, Shepperton, 1971.

Stanley, Peter, 'He's (not) Coming South' The Invasion that wasn't, in Steven Bullard and Tamura Keiko (eds.) *From a hostile shore: Australia and Japan at war in New Guinea,* viewed 1 May 2014 <http://ajrp.awm.gov.au/ajrp/ajrp2.nsf/Web1/Chapters/$file/Chapter2.pdf?OpenElement>

Stockings, Craig, 'Others People's Wars', in *Anzac's Dirty Dozen*, Craig Stockings (ed), Newsouth, Sydney, 2012, pp. 73-99.

Stoler, Mark A., *Allies in War: Britain and America against the Axis Powers 1940—1945*, Hodder Arnold, London, 2005, (2007).

Stoler, Mark, *The Politics of the Second Front*, Wesport, 1977.

Thomas, Andrew, *Osprey Aircraft of the Aces: Volume 87, Spitfire Aces of Burma and the Pacific*, Osprey, Oxford, 2009.

Thomas, Andrew, *Osprey Aircraft of the Aces: Volume 122, Spitfire Aces of Northwest Europe 1944-45*, Osprey, Oxford, 2014.

Thompson, H. L., *New Zealanders with the Royal Air Force: Volume II European Theatre January 1943—May 1945*, War History Branch, Wellington, 1956.

Barrett Tillman, *Brassey's D-Day Encyclopaedia*, Potomac Books, Washington, 2004.

Trevor-Roper, Hugh, (ed), *Hitler's War Directives 1939-1945*, Pan, London, 1964, (1966).

Wilson, Stewart, *Spitfire*, Aerospace Publications, Fyshwick, 1999.

Uncredited: 'Versus The V's' in *Victory Roll, The Royal Australian Air Force in its sixth year of war*, RAAF Directorate of Public Relations, Halstead Press, Sydney, 1945.

Uncredited: 'R.A.A.F. Spitfires in at the Kill' in *RAAF Saga*, RAAF Directorate of Public Relations, Australian War Memorial, Canberra, 1944.

Uncredited: *Batterie de Crisbecq Marine-Kusten Batterie 'Marcouf'*, Editions Aubert'Graphic (undated).

Journals and Magazines

Cowpe, F, 'Anti-Climax—I Think Not', in *Spitfire News: Journal of the Spitfire Association*, No. 58, March 1993.

Unpublished Sources and Correspondence with the Author

Beevor, Antony, '*In Conversation*' with Robin Prior, at the Australian War Memorial, 5 September 2012.

Beevor, Antony, *The World At War, 1942*, keynote address at the Australian War Memorial for 'Kokoda Beyond the Legend', 6 September 2012.

Pilot's Flying Logbooks

Don Andrews
Norman Baker
Joe Barrington
John Carmichael
Fred Cowpe
Sidney Handsaker

Allan Harris
James Lynch
Fred McCann
Jack Olver
Norm Swift
Clifford Taylor

Speech by Norman Baker to Melbourne Legacy, '*453 Spitfire Squadron—UK and Europe—Reminiscences*', 4 September 1990.

Unpublished Memoir—Fred Cowpe (undated).

'*Sequel to D-Day*'—Fred Cowpe (undated).

Exclusive Brethren: The RAAF in Rhodesia and Beyond—Ray Jackson (ed).

Numerous emails with the families and pilots from 453 and 451 Squadrons.

Websites

Australian War Memorial https://www.awm.gov.au/

Australians at War Film Archive (AWFA) http://australiansatwarfilmarchive.unsw.edu.au/

Commonwealth War Graves Commission (CWGC) http://www.cwgc.org/

Department of Defence Ministers—http://www.minister.defence.gov.au/2011/02/16/parliamentary-secretary-for-defence-senator-feeney-celebrates-the-reformation-of-number-452-and-453-squadrons-at-raaf-base-williamtown/

National Library of Australia (NLA) http://www.trove.nla.gov.au

Old Spitalfields Market (London) http://www.oldspitalfieldsmarket.com/the-market/the-history-of-the-market

Spitfire Aircraft Production http://www.airhistory.org.uk/spitfire/

Museum of Australian Democracy http://static.moadoph.gov.au/ophgovau/media/images/apmc/docs/08-Bruce-Web.pdf

Acknowledgements

My wife Heather, who believed in my ability to complete this project from the first moment I mentioned it.

Sidney Handsaker, Spitfire pilot with 451 (RAAF) Squadron.

Joe Barrington (and family), Spitfire pilot with 451 (RAAF) Squadron.

Nat Gould, Spitfire pilot with 457 (RAAF) Squadron.

Lysle Roberts, Spitfire pilot with 457 (RAAF) Squadron.

Lindsay Richards, (and family) Spitfire pilot with 451 (RAAF) Squadron

The Spitfire Association (Australia).

The families of the pilots of 453 (RAAF) Squadron, across Australia and as far away as the United Kingdom, who have been so generous with their support and enthusiasm for the project.

Allan Hillman and other members of the Whitebeam Battlefield Research Forum.

The men and women of 453 Squadron in all its forms from 1941 to today.

Staff at the National Archives of Australia, Canberra.

Staff at the Australian War Memorial, Canberra.

Staff at the National Archives, UK.

Staff at the Temora Aviation Museum.

Staff at the Point Cook RAAF Museum.

Staff at the Armidale Folk Museum.

John Fox and Brian King of the RAF Airfield Construction Officers' Association.

Steve McGregor, ex-President of the Spitfire Association (Australia).

Keith Webb.

Frederique Verbeke and her father, the late Pierre Verbeke.

Jean Bansard, Louis Theroult and Eliane Boucher, residents of Normandy.

Pilots Cédric Renouard and Nicolas Bobeaux.

And a special note of gratitude to a certain hiking group in France, whose enthusiastic response to my impromptu talk on what I (mistakenly) thought was a battlefield tour inspired this work.

www.ingramcontent.com/pod-product-compliance
Lightning Source LLC
Chambersburg PA
CBHW060028180426
43195CB00051B/2206